United States Stamps:
A History

Volume I:
Colonial Days to the Columbians

William Frangipane

Outskirts Press, Inc.
Denver, Colorado

United States Stamps: A History
Volume I: Colonial Days to the Columbians

Outskirts Press
http://www.outskirtspress.com

ISBN-10: 1-59800-387-9
ISBN-13: 978-1-59800-387-1

Library of Congress Control Number: 2006923007

Outskirts Press and the "OP" logo are trademarks belonging to
Outskirts Press, Inc.

Printed in the United States of America

To Ann,
My wife, my love, my hero.
You are the reason that I do
Everything that I do.

Foreword

Like many collectors, I came back to stamps after a long absence. It was a childhood pursuit, shared with my dad, Leo, Sr. After he passed away in 1998, I inherited his collection and it brought back fond memories. So I started stamp collecting again, this time sharing the passion with my children, Laura and Matt. We collected United States postage stamps, building on my dad's old collection.

When we went to learn more about United States stamps, we found a lot of information. There were catalogs such as Scott's yearly one, publications such as Linn's Stamp Magazine, and many books. The books though covered a specific topic or time frame of United States stamps. But there was no complete book or general reading on United States stamps. So that started the idea of researching and writing such a book for beginning and intermediate stamp collectors.

This first book covers United States stamps from colonial times, through the postmaster provisional issues and first general issues all the way down to the first United States commemorative issues, the Columbian stamps. It is the first in a series of books that hopes to cover the complete landscape of United States stamps.

The author welcomes comments, corrections, and suggestions as we journey together down the road of United States stamps!

Table of Contents

United States Stamps:
A History

Volume I:
Colonial Days to the Columbians

1 Early History of the Postal System and the Postmaster's Provisionals

Beginnings of American Postal Service

The human need to communicate led to the formation of postal systems in the ancient times. Some were very sophisticated such as the ancient Persian and Roman. With the founding of the English American colonies came simple postal systems. For example, in 1639, the Massachusetts Bay Colony arranged for the mail to and from England to be left at Richard Fairbanks's Tavern in Boston. This inn was the nation's first post office. Formal postal systems were started in Boston in 1676 and in Philadelphia in 1683. Postal routes began connecting the larger cities of the American colonies in the late 1600's. A central postal organization for the British colonies was established in 1691. In 1755, the King of England appointed Benjamin Franklin and William Hunter as the Deputy Postmaster Generals for the North American Colonies. Franklin served in this role until 1774. He was fired, then, for his part in the American Revolution. On July 26, 1775, the Continental Congress appointed Franklin its Postmaster General. Benjamin Franklin, therefore, is honored as the first American Postmaster General. In 1789, Samuel Osgood of Massachusetts became the first Postmaster General under the United States Constitution. The Postmaster General of the Unites States remained part of the presidential cabinet until the1970's.

The early postal service was not reliable and rates were high. Few Americans could afford this luxury. When Washington was elected our first president, there were only 75 post offices and less than 2,000 miles of post roads in the entire country.

However, the postal service became part of the nation's growth. It was the means by which business and personal communications were delivered over a large and growing country. Foot, post rider, wagons and stagecoaches, and later, steamboats and railroads all delivered this mail.

Time Line of Events of the Early United States Post Office	
1639	First American "post office" in Boston
1691	Central postal organization for the English colonies established
1753	Franklin and Hunter appointed postmaster generals of the colonies
1775	Franklin appointed postmaster general by the Continental Congress
1789	Samuel Osgood first postmaster general under the Constitution
1799	First simplification of United States postal rates
1816	Postal rates established which lasted until 1845
1837	Rowland Hill urges postal reform in England
1840	World's first postage stamp, England's penny black
1842	New York Post private carrier service with stamps established
1845	Postal reform in the United States and first U. S. provisional stamps

Early Postal Service

Before 1845, postage rates were based on distance the letter was mailed and number of sheets of paper in the letter. Envelopes were considered another sheet of paper. So most letters were just folded and addressed on a blank outside portion of the sheet of paper. Only when a letter weighed more than an ounce was weight considered. Letters with four or more sheets of paper or weighing more than one ounce were charged four times the single rate. Above one ounce, there was an additional charged for each extra quarter ounce. Up until 1798, there were multiple, complex, mileage zones for postage, each having higher rates. In 1799, postage rates was simplified somewhat, to just six zones. Single letter postage rates, at that time, ranged from 6 cents for letters sent under 40 miles to 25 cents for letters sent over 500 miles. During the War of 1812, there was a 50 percent increase in postal rates to help pay for the war.

Starting May 1, 1816, new rates were introduced. These are summarized in the table outlined below. These rates were in effect until they were lowered and simplified in 1845.

Mail was usually sent with the postage unpaid. The recipient would pay it when the letter arrived. Before July 1, 1851, the postage rate was the same whether it was prepaid or not. So there was little incentive to prepay. In fact, people of the time considered receiving a prepaid letter an insult to their financial ability to pay the collect postage. He or she did not have to accept the mail. Instead, after inspecting it unopened, one could simply reject it. A large amount of mail went unclaimed after being inspected and wound up at the dead letter office. And the post office had to pay for transporting and storing all of this mail without any reimbursement! Local delivery was unusual. Mail usually was dropped off and picked up at the post office.

Drop Letters

Drop letters were mail that was "dropped" at a post office for the addressee to pick up. It was local mail, not transported between post offices. For a hundred and fifty years, the drop letter rate was cheaper than mail that had to be transported between post offices. The earliest rate was that of 1794, which set the postage on such letters at 1 cent per letter. Until February 1861, drop letters could be prepaid or sent collect. Since drop letters didn't travel to other post offices, postal clerks treated them less formally. So they have minimal postmarks.

Early Postal History

One large branch of stamp collecting is postal history. This side of the hobby studies how mail moves through a postal system. Postal history emphasizes covers. It studies them to learn about postal rates, transportation of mail, extra services, operation, local post offices, and other postal information, as they evolved over time.

A *cover* is an envelope or a folded letter that has gone the mail. Folded letters are covers with the address and other information on the outside of the folded sheet of the letter. They were popular until the middle of the 19th century, when postage was charged by the number of sheets of paper rather than weight. If a stamp attached to a cover to pay the postage, it is referred to as being *on cover*.

There are covers without stamps from this era before postage stamps, called *stampless covers*. Though there were not true stamps at

3

this time, these covers had various handwritten notes and handstamps on them. These stampless covers reveal much about the United States postal history in the era before adhesive stamps.

The *franking* of a cover is the postage applied to it to pay for its delivery through the postal system. The franking may be a postage stamp, postage meter strip or added printing. At this time, of course, there were no printed stamps. So postmasters marked the folded letters with pen and ink to indicate either paid or due. Until the 1850's, letters usually were considered unpaid, except those with a paid marking and the correct rate. If the letter was due payment by the recipient, instead of being marked "due," usually it was marked with a number indicating the amount that was to be collected at delivery. These handwritten markings were used placed by the postal worker

Figure 1-1. An Example of a Stampless Cover. This letter represents a cover from the era before postage stamps. It was sent from Baltimore to Philadelphia. Note the postal marking showing the origin at the Baltimore post office. The "5" represents five-cents of postage due to paid by the recipient.

A *postmark* is any official marking placed on a cover. Postal markings are placed on a letter to show the mailing place, date, rate, route, accounting and so on. Postmarks can be collected on stamps that are off cover, also, if the marking happens to land on the used stamp. Postmarks can be handwritten, handstamps, or printed. Most postmarks at this time were handwritten with pen and ink. When the increase in mail volume forced some local postmasters to obtain handstamps to save from writer's cramp, the first standardized postmarking handstamps were distributed by the Post Office

Department in 1799. These handstamps printed the various postal markings and often the name of the post office on the cover. These handstamps usually were circular with a wide variety of styles. These handstamp impressions on the letter cover are described as the first stamps, and are collected today.

A *cancellation* is a postmark placed on a stamp to prevent its future use. Cancellations are added by handstamp, machine, or pen. All cancellations are postmarks, though all postmarks are not cancellations. A cancellation may be a pen mark, handstamp pattern, or printed design. Many fancy handstamp cancellations were placed from the mid to late 1800's and are sought after by today's collectors.

Figure 1-2. Amos Kendall. He was Postmaster General, under President Andrew Jackson and the first to have the vision of postal reform in the United States.

Advertised Letters

An advertised letter was one listed in the local newspaper by the Post Office Department. This was done as early as the 1790's, in its efforts to deliver mail to the proper addressee. The letters for which no one had called for at the local post office were a cost for the system because the recipient paid the postage. Letters that had not been called for were to be listed alphabetically in the local newspaper. Letters picked up as a result of being advertised had the additional fee to pay for the advertisement.

Need for Reform

Americans, by the middle of the 1830's were unhappy with the high cost and poor service of the postal system. As a result, many letters were carried outside of the United States Post Office, by travelers, stagecoach drivers, post riders, and railroad workers.

In 1835, President Andrew Jackson appointed Amos Kendall, his Postmaster General. He was the first who placed improved delivery of the mail first over profit. In 1840, Kendall learned of the English postal reform act. Kendall sent George Plitt to England to report on the English reforms. The Plitt report was the first step toward reforming the American postal system.

Postal reform in England was the work of Rowland Hill. Hill researched the postal system of England, and in January 1837 he published a pamphlet calling for reforms, called "Post-Office Reform: Its Importance and Practicality." The English postal rates, like those in America, were high, complex, based on distance, and usually paid by the receiver. Hill called for a fixed postage rate that was prepaid. He thought distance was a minor factor in costs. In arguing for a prepaid fee, Hill cited all the effort involved in collecting fees. He suggested the use of stamps for pre-paying postage. Through his lobbying, Hill's proposals became effective, in England, on January 10, 1840.

Figure 1-3. Roland Hill. This commemorative stamp from St. Helena honors Sir Roland Hill, who started postal reform in England and is the father of the postage stamp.

The new rates were one English penny for letters of up to one-half ounce, two pence for up to one ounce. This world's first stamps had a portrait of then Queen Victoria. The one-penny stamps were printed with black ink on white paper. They were and still are called "penny blacks." For the two pence stamps, deep blue ink was used with the same design. The stamps did not have the country's name on them. Today, Great Britain remains the only country not to carry its name on its stamps, in honor of it being the home of the world's first postage stamp.

Figure 1-4. Penny Black. This is the world's first postage stamp. First printed in England in 1840, it features a portrait of then Queen Victoria.

Plitt returned to Washington with the Hill pamphlet and his own report, urging the United States to follow the new British system. But by now there was a new Postmaster General, Charles Wickliffe, part of the cabinet of the President Tyler. He reviewed the Plitt Report, and in 1841, he rejected it for financial reasons. If Wickliffe were to adopt a plan like England's, with its postage stamps and fixed lower rate, it would triple the postal deficit. This was in spite of its support in Congress by the powerful and influential Senator Daniel Webster. Putting money ahead of service, American postal reform had to wait a little longer.

Private Carrier Companies and the First American Adhesive Stamp

Because of poor governmental postal service, the early 1840's saw the rapid growth of the private mail companies. These businesses offered either local delivery in one city or between city deliveries. They were able to deliver mail in less time and for less cost. Letters were picked up by company carriers and delivered to the door of destination. Often these private companies used hand stamps in their processing. These private carrier hand stamps are collected today.

One private carrier service, the New York Post, had an important role in the development of the first United States adhesive stamp. Henry Thomas Windsor, a British merchant, realized that the United States had an overpriced, underserviced postal system. He saw a business opportunity using the British mail system with a local private post company. He joined with a New York stockbroker, Greig, to buy one such company, the New York Post. They renamed it, the City Despatch Post.

The City Despatch Post set a rate for the delivery of mail for within New York City of three cents. It followed the British postal system with prepayment of postage. With that came the first American postage stamp. The 1842 City Despatch Postal Stamp was engraved and printed on sheets of forty stamps. They were made without perforations, printed with gray-black ink on grayish-white paper. The stamp design had a portrait of George Washington within an oval frame. Above the portrait are the words, CITY DESPATCH POST, below, THREE CENTS.

Figure 1-5. City Dispatch Stamp. This is considered by many, the first United States postage stamp. The private New York City Dispatch Post issued it in 1842.

The service was a success, taking over most of the local postal market in New York City. City Despatch Post caught the attention of Postmaster General Charles Wickliffe. He, through the postmaster of New York, John Lorimer Graham, bought the company for the United States government. The United States City Despatch Post became part of the Post Office Department on August 16,1842 and remained so until November 28, 1846. The United States City Despatch Post printed its own stamps for the next four years. During these years, the United States Postal Office operated a private postal service in New York City that issued adhesive postage stamps, while at the same time the federal postal system did not issue any stamps!

Finally Postal Reform

In 1845, Cave Johnson, the incoming postmaster general to President-elect Polk, favored lower postal rates and postal reform. This led to on March 3, 1845, the day before Polk was inaugurated, Congress passing the postal reform act of 1845. The law became effective on July 1st of that year.

Postal letter rates were simplified. There were just two distance charges, one for distances less than 300 miles and the other for distances over that. The rate was five cents per half-ounce for up to 300 miles, and ten cents for over 300 miles. There was a two-cent charge for drop letters, mail dropped at the same post office where the recipient picked it up and therefore not requiring transportation.

Circulars, printed notices for mass distribution, were the junk mail of the 19th century. Up until 1845, they did not receive any special or discount rates, and were charged full letter rates. The 1845 postal act provided for the first discount circular rate. Up to the present day, similar mail receives a postal rate discount. All circulars, handbills, and advertisements were charged postage of two cents a sheet, regardless of distance sent. But he act didn't require that circulars be prepaid, so of course, the recipient refused most of them.

There, still, were no postage stamps. Prepayment of postage was optional. Though postal revenues dropped, the philosophy was good postal service at a low rate came first.

The 1845 Reform Act Postage Rates

Rates based on sheets of paper for the letter.
Rates same for prepaid or collect.
Rates were effective July 1, 1845 through July 1, 1851.

- Drop letters .... 2 cents
- Circular rate, regardless of distance .... 2 cents
- Pamphlet rate, regardless of distance ...... 2½ cents
- Single sheet under 300 miles .... 5 cents
- Single sheet over 300 miles .... 10 cents

Postmaster Provisional Stamps

The postal reform act of 1845 led to the postmaster provisional stamps. These stamps are the first non-private prepayment of United States postage. The local postmasters made them in eleven offices between 1845 and 1847. They thought by issuing stamps, this would lead to more letters being prepaid. Both large cities and small towns issued these stamps. The local postmaster's salary was based on the cash he brought in to his office. So many postmasters from towns and cities of all sizes viewed stamps as a way of increasing their income. Many of the provisional stamps feature the postmaster's signature. This was a carryover from the stampless era when the signature was proof of prepayment by the mailer.

PRINTING TECHNIQUES

There is a wide variety of printing techniques and provisional designs seen. There are four basic printing processes used to make stamps and these will now be reviewed. All were used, at one time, to print United States stamps. These are intaglio, gravure, lithography, and typography.

Intaglio

Intaglio is an Italian word for incised or engraved. It is printing where the image for the stamp is made by the part of the printing plate below the surface. First, the image is engraved into a master die. Then, it is transferred to the printing plate by an intermediate transfer roll.Ink is applied to the engraved plate, and then wiped clean, leaving ink just in the recessed areas. Then, the stamp paper is pressed against the printing plate under pressure, forcing the ink from the recessed areas on to the paper. Intaglio printing was used for most stamps, from their introduction up until the present day.

Originally, intaglio printing was done on a press that used a flat plate. This made one sheet of stamps at a time. In the early twentieth century, printing plates were curved into cylinders on a rotary press. Then, printing could be done on a continuous roll of paper rather than individual sheets. The stamp design from the rotary press is slightly longer than that from the flat press, everything else being equal. This is because of the curvature of the plate lengthens the stamp design in that direction.

Until the 1950's, intaglio printing requiring the paper be wet so the ink would adhere to the stamp during printing. With the advent of stamp presses that create more pressure, printing could be done on dry paper.

Intaglio printing leaves the ink raised above the surface of the stamp paper. The ink texture is felt with one's fingertip or fingernail. The raised effect of the ink is seen, easily, with a magnifying glass. The printing on the stamps is sharp and clear. The back of the stamp often has an impression of the design because of the great pressure applied to it during printing. These characteristics are more pronounced on dry compared with wet-paper printings.

Gravure

Gravure is another form of recess printing. It uses printing cylinders that have the design below the surface. Originally, these were prepared by photographic and chemical means, called photogravure. The stamp design is photographed through an extremely fine screen to create a pattern of dots. Next, a chemical or electrical process etches the dot design into the printing plate. The dots are all of the same size but of varying depth based on the intensity of the ink at that spot.

Gravure is used for multicolored stamps, using primary colors (red, yellow and blue) and black. By varying the number and density of these colors, virtually any color can be created.

A computer that directs a diamond stylus etches the cells that will hold the ink on modern cylinders.

For the actual printing of the stamp, like intaglio, the press forces the paper into the recesses of printing cylinder, to create the impression.

The dots of gravure printing are seen under magnification. The pattern consists of dots of the same size but of varying intensities, based on the depth of the recesses on the printing plate.

Lithography

Lithography uses the basic chemistry principle that water and oil do not mix. The design area is a flexible metal plate. The area not to be printed stays wet, repelling the oil based ink. With offset lithography, the printing base places an impression on a rubber cylinder that, in turn, rolls over the surface of the paper, transferring the ink.

Lithographed stamps are usually multicolored. Stamps are completely flat, in contrast to other printing methods, because the surface of the printing plate is flat. The designs of lithographed stamps though intricate have lines that are not sharp. The edges of printed areas appear as irregular string of beads because the ink consists of tiny droplets; flatten by the printing rollers as they are transferred. Thus there is a dull appearance to the lithograph compared with other forms of printing.

Typography

Letterpress (printer's term) or typography (the stamp collecting term) is relief printing. This is the opposite of intaglio. Instead of the ink being held in a recessed area of the plate, the raised area is inked. This is how a rubber handstamp or old-fashioned typewriter operates. The plate may be wood, ivory, rubber, stone, brass, or metal.

The United States used this form of printing on only a few stamps, mostly overprinting.

Letterpress stamps usually are printed in a single color. It can cause raised areas in the back of the stamp as the plate press is forced down into the paper. This contrasts with a depressed area on the back seen with intaglio.

An excess of color around the edges of lines of the design is seen. This is the result of ink squeezed outward with the pressure of the plate. This halo effect is best seen under magnification.

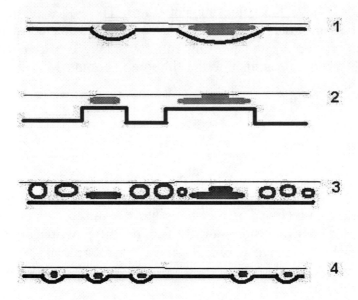

Figure 1-6. Summary of Stamp Printing Techniques. This diagram summarizes the four major stamp printing methods. (1) Intaglio. The ink on the paper comes from the part of the printing plate BELOW the surface. (2) Typography. The ink on the paper comes from the part of the plate ABOVE the surface. (3) Lithography. The ink on the paper comes from the plate ON the surface, separated by water droplets. (4) Gravure. The ink on the paper comes from POCKETS BELOW the surface of the plate.

TABLE DESCRIPTION

Before getting to the first United States stamps, the postmaster provisional stamps, in detail, there will be a description of the summary table used throughout this book. The summary is in three parts spanning the life of the stamp. First comes information about the stamp's design phase and production. Second is information about the stamp itself, including size, color, varieties, perforations, and uses. Finally listed is information for the collector today, including relative value, surviving multiples and covers. Note not all the information is given for every issue.

Stamp Production

Printer: This is the name of the bank note company or if the Bureau of Engraving and Printing made the stamp.

Designer: This is the name of the person or persons responsible for the stamp's layout, features, and vignette.

Engraver: This is the person or persons who did the actual engraving of the master die. Often, different workers did different parts of the die.

Format: There describes the sheet on which the stamps are printed. The sheet is the paper that comes off the printing press. It is the same size as the plate used to print the stamps. The number of stamps on a sheet is given and how the sheet is divided into panes. Panes are parts of a sheet that are sold by the post office.

Plate Numbers: This is a list of the different numbers of the plates used to print the stamps. Printers assigned a unique number to each plate. The plate number usually is located in the selvage.

Date of Issue: The official date of release of the stamp. For some stamps, only the month or year is known.

Earliest Known Use: This is the date of the earliest documented use of the stamp.

Use: This lists typical postal rates paid by the stamp at the time of issue.

Quantity Printed: This gives the total number of stamps printed. More stamps may have been issued than actually sold. For many stamps, unsold stamps were destroyed.

Quantity Issued: This is the total number of stamps actually sold by the Post Office Department.

Stamp Features

Size: The dimensions of the stamp are given both in metric and English units.

Watermark: This gives information about any watermark made in the manufacture of the stamp paper.

Perforation: Stamps need a method of separation from one another. There are three such methods for United States stamps.

The earliest stamps were imperforate. They had to be cut apart with scissors.

The most common method is a series are rows of round holes, perforations, punched between stamps. The user tears down the row of perforations to separate the stamps. The teeth are the tips of paper that protrude along the tear line after stamps have been separated. While joined, the paper between the holes is known as bridges.

Perforations are classified by how many holes (or teeth when separated) there are in 2 centimeters. For example, 10-½ perforation means there are 10-½ perforations for each 2-cm. length of stamp.

Rouletting is the third method of stamp separation. A knife cuts between two stamps so they can be separated. Often the roulette cutting is in a wavy line to simulate perforations.

Colors: There often are minor ink variations for a stamp. Especially early United States stamps had a great variety in inks. This reflects the non-uniformity of ink manufacture at the time. Major ink differences, such as an actual change in the color of the ink, rate a separate listing.

Varieties: This lists non-color varieties of the stamp. It includes plate varieties (plate cracks, double transfers, etc.), printing varieties (double impressions, printed on both sides of the paper, etc.), and paper varieties (different paper used for the same stamp)

Errors: Stamp manufacturing errors include missing perforations, missing colors (on multicolor stamps), and inversion errors (on multicolor stamps where one color is upside down relative to another).

Collectable Stamp Today

Collectable Cancellation Colors: This is a list of the various collectable colors of ink used to cancel the stamp.

Collectable Cancellation Varieties: This is a list of the various collectable cancellations used on the stamp.

Value Unused: Value Used: A dollar system guides the relative value of the stamp, both unused and used. Such a system should remain relatively unchanged over time, not varying month to month, like the present day value of the stamp. Each sign ($) represents an order of magnitude (tenfold) value difference. Therefore, one star represents a value of up to $1, two stars, up to $10, three stars, up to $100, and so on.

Surviving Covers: For the postal history and cover collector, there is an estimate given of the number of covers with the stamp that are in existence, today.

Largest Known Multiples: For each stamp, the largest known intact multiple, both in the unused and used state is given.

THE PROVISIONAL STAMPS ONE BY ONE

New York City Provisionals

New York City Provisional

Stamp Production

Printer:	Rawdon, Wright, Hatch & Edson
Format:	Sheets of 40 stamps, 5x8
Date of Issue:	July 14, 1845
Earliest Known Use:	July 15, 1845
Use:	Single-rate domestic letter under 300 miles from New York for prepayment of postage
Quantity Issued:	143,600

Stamp Features

Size:	20.5 x 28 mm (0.8 x 1.1 inches)
Watermark:	None
Perforation:	Imperforate
Colors:	Black
Varieties:	Bluish wove paper
	Signed ACM (for Alonzo Castle Monson), connected
	Signed ACM, AC only connected
	Signed A.C.M.
	Signed MMJr (for Marcena Morris)
	Signed RHM
	Without signature
	Blue wove paper
	Signed ACM, connected
	Signed RHM
	Signed ACM, AC only connected

Without signature
Gray wove paper
Signed ACM, connected
Signed RHM
Without signature

The Collectable Stamp Today
Collectable Cancellation Varieties:

blue pen, black pen, magenta pen, red square grid (New York), red round grid (Boston), blue numeral (Philadelphia), carrier, Paid, date stamp

Price Unused: $$$$$
Price Used: $$$$

The first and most widely used provisional stamp was issued in New York City on July 14, 1845. This was just two weeks after the Postal Act of 1845 went into effect. The postmaster of New York, Robert H. Morris contracted with Rawdon, Wright, Hatch, and Edson, a bank note engraving company, to print these stamps. The stamps were all five-cent denomination. Between July 1845 and January 1847, the printer made 18 deliveries of sheets to the New York post office, for a total of 3,590 sheets of 40 (arranged 5 by 8 stamps), or 143,600 total stamps. Eventually, the New York provisional stamps were distributed and used in post offices other than New York City's. These cities included Albany, Boston, Philadelphia, and Washington. This was an experiment by Postmaster General Cave Johnson, testing the general use of postage stamps.

The New York provisional stamp was printed with black ink on thin white paper. It has a portrait of George Washington inside an oval frame. Above the portrait are the words, POST OFFICE, below, FIVE CENTS. To prevent counterfeiting, Morris or one of his assistants signed his initials over the portrait of every stamp. The Scott Catalogue listing of the New York Provisionals reflects the different stamp papers and the different signed initials. Today, about 5,500 New York City provisional stamps survive, with 500 unused.

The stamps usually were canceled with handstamp, containing the word, PAID, in red ink. Others were stamped with a circle, with the works, NEW YORK, inside, and with the date.

Alexandria Provisionals

Alexandria Provisional Issue

Stamp Production
Format: Typeset printing
Date of Issue: 1846
Earliest Known Use: August 25, 1846
Use: Prepayment of basic postal rate from Alexandria, Virginia

Stamp Features
Watermark: None
Perforation: Each stamp cut to shape
Colors: Black on buff paper
Black on blue paper
Varieties: Type I: 40 asterisks in the circle
Type II: 39 asterisks in the circle

The Collectable Stamp Today
Collectable Cancellation Varieties:
Red circular town, Paid, blackhandwritten number used for accounting
Price Unused: $$$$$$
Price Used: $$$$$$

Postmaster Daniel Bryan issued the Alexandria, Virginia provisional stamp. It was printed by the simple typeset method. It features a simple circular design of 39 or 40 asterisks. Inside are the words, ALEXANDRIA POST OFFICE, forming another inner circle. Inside this circle, at the center of the stamp are the words, PAID 5.

Almost all of the Alexandria provisional stamps were printed on buff paper. A unique stamp is the postmaster's provisional five-cent black on blue paper. It is nicknamed, "Blue Boy," due to its beautiful color. The nickname is from the famous painting of that name by Thomas Gainsborough of Thomas Buttall, a young man wearing a suit of blue clothing.

Annapolis Provisionals

Annapolis Provisional Issue

Stamp Production
Format:	Envelope
Date of Issue:	1846
Use:	Prepayment of basic postal rate from Annapolis, Maryland

Stamp Features
Size:	18.5 mm diameter (0.7 inches)
Watermark:	None
Colors:	Carmine red on white envelopes
Varieties:	Two envelope sizes

The Collectable Stamp Today
Price Used:	$$$$$$

Martin E. Revell, the postmaster of Annapolis, Maryland, sold envelopes with a design in the upper right corner, for prepayment of postage. It consists of a circle, with the words, POST OFFICE ANNAPOLIS, on the perimeter. The center design is an eagle. The circle then was stamped with the numeral 5 and PAID. The envelopes were white and came in two sizes.

Baltimore Provisionals

Baltimore Provisional Stamp

Stamp Production
Format:	Plate of 12 stamps (2 x 6), with positions 1,2,3,4,5,6,8,10, and 12 being 5-cent stamps and positions 7, 9, 11 being 10-cent stamps

Date of Issue:	1845
Use:	Prepayment of postage from Baltimore, Maryland

Stamp Features

Size:	53-54 x 16-17 mm (2.1 x 0.6 inches)
Watermark:	None
Perforation:	Imperforate
Colors:	5 cent, Black on white paper
	10 cent, Black on white paper
	5 cent, Black on bluish paper
	10 cent, Black on bluish paper
Varieties:	None

The Collectable Stamp Today
Collectable Cancellation Varieties:

	blue circular town, blue straight line, Paid, blue 5 or 10 in oval, black ink
Price Unused:	$$$$$$
Price Used:	$$$$$

Baltimore Provisional Envelop

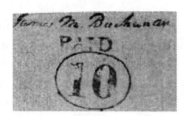

Stamp Production

Format:	Envelop
Date of Issue:	1845
Use:	Prepayment of postage from Baltimore, Maryland

Stamp Features

Watermark:	None
Colors:	5 cent, Blue
	5 cent, Red
	10 cent, Blue
	10 cent, Red
Varieties:	Signature colors in black, blue or red ink. Various colored papers were used for the envelopes

blue circular town, blue 5 in an oval

$$$$$$

James Madison Buchanan, the postmaster of Baltimore issued both stamps and envelopes for the prepayment of postage in 1845. The simple stamps consisted of the postmaster's signature with either 5 Cents or 10 Cents, printed below.

The envelopes had three separate handstamps. At the top was Buchanan's signature, in black, blue, or red ink. The next handstamp was the word, PAID, in blue or red ink. Then the numeral 5 or 10, within a circle, that was in blue or red ink. The PAID and numeral ink were the same color.

Boscawen, New Hampshire Provisionals

Boscawen, New Hampshire Provisional Issue

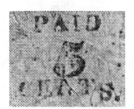

Stamp Production
Format: Typeset printing
Date of Issue: 1846 (not certain)
Use: Prepayment of postage from Boscawen, NH

Stamp Features
Watermark: None
Perforation: Imperforate
Colors: Dull blue on yellowish paper
Varieties: None

The postmaster of the tiny town of Boscawen, New Hampshire, Worcester Webster, issued simple, typeset, 5-cent stamps. In an interesting side note, Worcester was a relative of the famous statesman and supporter of postal reform, Daniel Webster. The stamp just has the wording, PAID 5 CENTS. Only one copy of the stamp survives, today.

Brattleboro Provisionals

Brattleboro Provisional Issue

Stamp Production

Printer:	Thomas Chubbuck of Brattleboro
Format:	Sheets of 10 stamps, 2 by 5
Date of Issue:	1845
Earliest Known Use:	Aug. 28, 1847
Use:	Single-rate domestic letter under 300 miles from Brattleboro, Vt. for prepayment of postage

Stamp Features

Size:	21 x 14 mm (0.8 x 0.6 inches)
Watermark:	None
Perforation:	Imperforate
Colors:	Black on buff paper
Varieties:	None

The Collectable Stamp Today
Collectable Cancellation Varieties:

	Paid, red pen, blue numeral 5
Price Used:	$$$$$

The Brattleboro, Vermont provisionals were released the summer of 1846. The postmaster, Frederick N. Palmer, went to great expense to produce his stamp for such a tiny post office. The stamp is small and rectangular in shape. The central design element is Palmer's autograph initials, F.N.P. At top is the town name, at sides the letters, P.O., and at bottom the denomination, 5 Cents. It was printed in black on a thick buff paper. The soft, porous quality of this paper makes it extremely susceptible to thinning, and almost every Brattleboro copy known shows some surface scuffs or thins. The stamps were printed from a plate of ten subjects, arranged in two horizontal rows of five. Directly below the center stamp of the bottom row is an imprint, Eng'd. by Thos. Chubbuck, Bratto.

Lockport, New York Provisionals

Lockport, New York Provisional Issue

Stamp Production

Format:	Handstamp
Date of Issue:	1846
Use:	Single-rate domestic letter under 300 miles from Lockport, New York for prepayment of postage

Stamp Features

Size:	34 x 25 mm (1.3 x 1.0 inches)
Watermark:	None
Perforation:	Imperforate
Colors:	Red and black on buff paper
Varieties:	None

The Collectable Stamp Today
Collectable Cancellation Varieties:

	Black ink X
Price Used:	$$$$$$$

Hezekiah W. Scovell, the postmaster of the small New York town, authorized this postmaster provisional. It is a simple handstamp design. The stamp consists of two parts. The handstamp is an oval with the words, LOCKPORT N.Y. and PAID. Written, by hand in black ink is the numeral, 5, representing the postage paid. The paper is a buff color. Only a single complete stamp exists, and it is found on a cover. Other partially complete stamps exist.

Millbury, Massachusetts Provisionals

Millbury, Massachusetts Provisional Issue

Stamp Production

Format:	Singles from a woodcut hand press
Date of Issue:	1846
Earliest Known Use:	Aug. 21, 1846
Use:	Single-rate domestic letter under 300 miles from Millbury, Massachusetts, for prepayment of postage

Stamp Features

Size:	22 mm diameter (0.9 inches)
Watermark:	None
Perforation:	Imperforate
Colors:	Black on blue paper
Varieties:	None

The Collectable Stamp Today
Collectable Cancellation Varieties:

	Paid, red circular town with date in the center
Price Unused:	$$$$$$$
Price Used:	$$$$$

This stamp, authorized by the local postmaster, Asa H. Waters, was printed from a simple hand press woodcut, one at a time. It features a primitive likeness of George Washington, surrounded by the words, POST OFFICE, PAID 5 CTS, in a circular design. The ink is black, the paper, bluish.

New Haven Provisionals

New Haven Provisional Issue

Stamp Production
Format:	Handstamp
Date of Issue:	1845
Use:	Single-rate domestic letter under 300 miles from New Haven, Conn. for prepayment of postage

Stamp Features
Size:	31 x 26 mm (1.2 x1.0 inches)
Watermark:	None
Perforation:	Handstamp on covers
Colors:	Red with blue or magenta signature
	Red with black signature on blue paper
	Dull blue with blue or black signature on blue paper
	Dull blue with blue signature
Varieties:	None

The Collectable Stamp Today
Price Used:	$$$$$$

Some provisionals were just handstamps on envelopes. One example was that of New Haven, Connecticut, in 1845. Postmaster Edward A. Mitchell devised a system whereby customers brought in their own envelopes to the office and he would handstamp them for five cents of postage per handstamp. He used a brass handstamp in the upper right corner of the cover. The envelopes were stamped by hand in red or blue ink and the postmaster signed his name in blue, black, or magenta.

The New Haven provisionals were reprinted several times over the years as souvenirs. The original postmaster Edward A. Mitchell made 20 reprints with dull blue ink, signed by him with lilac rose ink on white paper, in 1871. There were additional unsigned reprints made in 1872. Thirty more reprints were made in 1874, with carmine ink, with a dark blue or ink signature on hard white paper. These were given to Cyrus B. Peets, Mitchell's chief clerk. In 1923, Edward A. Mitchell's grandson made reprints with lilac ink on soft white wove paper, with the date 1923 in the place of the signature. In 1932, the New Haven Philatelic Society bought the handstamp. They printed 260 stamps, half in red and half in dull blue on hard white woven paper. A facsimile of the Mitchell's original signature was added. Then, the original brass handstamp was processed so no further handstamps could be made from it.

Providence Provisionals

Providence Provisional Issue

Stamp Production

Format:	Cooper plate of 12 stamps, 3x4 (Position 3 is the only
10 cent	stamp)
Date of Issue:	Aug.24, 1845
Earliest Known Use:	Aug. 25, 1845
Use:	For postage prepayment from Providence, Rhode I sland

Stamp Features

Size:	38 x 33 mm (1.5 x 1.3 inches)
Watermark:	None
Perforation:	Imperforate
Colors:	Gray black (5 cents, 10 cents)
Varieties:	Each plate position different

The Collectable Stamp Today

Collectable Cancellation Varieties:	Black pen, red circular town, Paid, red numeral 5.
Price Unused:	$$$$$
Price Used:	$$$$$
Largest Known Multiple:	Complete panes of 12 stamps

Welcome B. Sayles, postmaster of Providence, Rhode Island, authorized one of the more widespread used provisional stamps. The stamps came in two denominations, five and ten cents. Both stamps were printed on a single primitive cooper plate. This plate had 12 positions, arranged in four rows of three positions, each. Only the top right position, number three, was a ten-cent stamp. The rest were five-cent stamps. Since the engraving was done directly on the plate, without the use of a master die, each position, and therefore, each stamp made from that position, differs from the rest. Complete sheets of the stamps still are in existence.

The stamps were printed with gray black ink on yellowish paper. The simple design consists of a rectangle with an oval within. Within the oval are the words, POST OFFICE, PROV. R. I., FIVE (or TEN, depending on the denomination) CENTS. The stamp was reprinted in 1898, from the original plate. The reprints usually have one the letters, B, O, G, E, R, T, D, U, R, B, I, or N on the back of the stamps.

St. Louis Provisionals

St. Louis Provisional Issue

Stamp Production
Engraver: J. M. Kershaw
Format: Cooper plate of 6 stamps, 2x3 (3 plates used)
Date of Issue: Nov. 1845
Use: Multiple uses, depending on denomination, for prepayment from St. Louis, Missouri

Stamp Features
Size: 18 x 22 mm (0.7 x 0.9 inches)
Watermark: None
Perforation: Imperforate

Colors:	Black on greenish paper (5 cents, 10 cents, 20 cents)
	Black on gray lilac paper (5 cents, 10 cents, 20 cents)
	Black on bluish paper (5 cents, 10 cents)
Varieties:	Several depending on the position on the plate

The Collectable Stamp Today
Collectable Cancellation Varieties:

	black pen, initials of the postmaster, red circular town, Paid, red grid.
Price Unused:	$$$$$
Price Used:	$$$$$

The St. Louis, Missouri, postmaster, John M. Wimer, issued provisional postage stamps in November 1845. They featured the Missouri coat of arms with a bear on each side. Therefore, these provisional stamps are nicknamed the "St. Louis Bears." They were issued in three denominations: five, ten, and twenty cents, all of the same design. They were printed from a cooper plate, which each had six stamps, arranged in two rows of three stamps each. The paper used was a colored pelure, which varied depending on when the stamps were printed. The first stamps were on greenish paper. The second printing was on gray lilac paper. The last printings were on bluish paper.

Essays

There is an essay, that is, proposed postmasters' provisional stamps from Albany, New York, even though no actual stamps were issued from there. Gavit and Company made them between 1847 and 1851 and they feature Benjamin Franklin. Because he is dressed in an animal skin hat, they are called the "Beaver Hat essays."

There also are essays from Rawdon, Wright, and Hatch that feature vignettes of George Washington. They were used in planning the New York City postmasters' provisional stamps.

Proofs

There are both large and small die proofs of the New York City postmaster provisional stamps. There also exist plate proofs on card of the Providence postmaster provisionals. Trial color proofs are found for these two postmaster provisionals, also. An explanation of the nature of proofs is given in the next chapter.

2 | The First United States Regular Series Stamps-The 1847 Issues

The first regular issue of United States postage stamps was created in 1847. They were authorized by the Act of Congress of March 3rd of that year and the act took effect on July 1st. From then on, stamps not authorized by the Postmaster General, the local provisional issues, were illegal. The act did not make the prepayment of postage compulsory. That did not happen until much later, April 1, 1855. Most mail still was sent without stamps with the postage paid by the recipient. So many stampless covers exist after July 1 1847. In fact, only 1.3% of letters mailed between 1847 and 1852 had postage stamps.

On July 1, 1847, the Post Office Department released a 5-cent stamp picturing Benjamin Franklin and a 10-cent stamp with George Washington. This made the United States, the fourth country, after Great Britain, Brazil and Switzerland, to issue postage stamps. The five-cent stamp paid the half-ounce domestic letter rate for a letter traveling less than 300 miles. The 10-cent Washington paid the single letter rate over 300 miles. Double weight letters were charged double rates.

No stamps were issued for the 2-cent rate for a drop letter (letter mailed for the same post office not requiring transportation). Congress, at this time, raised the circular rate to 3 cents and required the postage on circulars be prepaid and they be sent unsealed.

Summary of the Postal Act of 1847

- Regular issue postage stamps were authorized for prepayment of postage
- Stamps not authorized by the Postmaster General (the local provisional issues) are illegal
- Prepayment of postage and use of stamps not mandatory. Same postal rate for prepayment or recipient payment.
- Single letter (up to 1/2 ounce) less than 300 miles-5 cents
- Single letter (up to 1/2 ounce) over 300 miles-10 cents
- Double weight (1/2 to 1 ounce) letters charged double rates, and so on.
- Drop letter rate-2 cents
- Circular rate-3 cents

FIVE-CENT FRANKLIN

Five-Cent Franklin

Stamp Production
Printer:	Rawdon, Wright, Hatch & Edson
Designer:	James Parsons
Engraver:	Asher Brown Durant

Format:	Sheet of 200 stamps, divided into 2 panes of 100 stamps (left and right)
Plate Number:	Printed from a single plate, but no plate number or imprints in the margins.
Date of Issue:	July 1, 1847
Earliest Known Use:	July 7, 1847
Use:	Single-rate domestic letter under 300 miles
Quantity Printed	4,400,000 (delivered to Post Office)
Quantity Issued:	3,700,000

Stamp Features

Size:	18 x 23.5 mm (0.7 x 0.9 inches)
Watermark:	None
Perforation:	Imperforate
Colors:	Red brown, pale brown, brown, dark brown, grayish brown, blackish brown, orange brown, brown orange, red orange
Varieties:	6 Double transfers. Dot in S. Double impression (one copy). Cracked plate (69R). Stitch watermark.

The Collectable Stamp Today
Collectable Cancellation Colors:

	Red, orange red, blue, black, green, orange, violet, magenta, ultramarine, brown

Collectable Cancellation Varieties:

	red, blue, orange red, ultramarine, violet, and black town, Paid, Free, railroad, U. S. express mail, Way, Steamboat, Steam, Steamship, hotel, numeral, Canada, pen, Wheeling, Va. control grid.
Value Unused:	$$$$$
Value Used:	$$$$
Surviving Covers:	9,429
Largest Known Multiple:	Unused: Block of 16 (4x4)
	Used: Block of 12 stamps (6x2)

Printer

Rawdon, Wright, Hatch & Edson of New York City, a company known for bank note and stock certificate engraving, printed the 1847 series stamps. They were the printers of the New York City provisional stamps. At the time of printing, their company was located on Wall Street, close to where most of their business was needed. The company's initials (R.W.H & E) are found in small letters at the bottom of both stamps. A surviving letter indicates their contract with the United States Post Office Department was signed late May of 1847.

Design

The stamp features a portrait of Benjamin Franklin, the first American postmaster general. The Franklin portrait is based on a painting on him by Joseph S. Duplessis. Asher B. Durant was the stamp's engraver. It has his three-quarter face, looking to the left, on an oval dark background. Franklin is wearing a white neckerchief and has a fur collared coat. The portrait is surrounded with a wreath of leaves. In the upper corners, are the letters U and S, and in the lower corners, large 5's. In a curved line around the upper portion of the portrait are the words POST OFFICE, and around the lower part the words FIVE CENTS. A rectangle surrounds the outside of the stamp.

Intaglio Printing

From the first 1847 postage stamps until the end of the 20th century, nearly all United States stamps were printed by the intaglio method. Making the *master die* is the first step in creating a printing plate. This is a small, flat piece of soft steel. The typical size of one is 3 ½ inches square and one-half inch thick. The future stamp design is cut into the die as a reverse image by the engraver. Both talent and training is needed for this miniature work. Once the engraving is completed, the die is hardened. This is done by heating it in a potassium cyanide bath and then cooling it in cold oil.

The *transfer roll* is the middle step. It transfers, hence the name, the design from the die to the plate. The die is placed against a transfer roll, a cylinder of soft steel. Under great pressure, the die is pressed against the roll. This results in every line that has been cut down in the die now stands up in relief on the face of the transfer roll. The resulting impression on the transfer roll naturally is called a relief. Usually, several transfers are placed on the roll. Once completed, the transfer roll is hardened, like the die. The design on the transfer roll is a positive impression, like the completed stamp.

The *plates* used in the production of nineteenth century stamps were made of soft steel, about a quarter inch thick. Plates are rectangular. They have between 50 and 200 positions for stamp impressions. To make a plate, the transfer roll is pressed against it, entering the design. There are position dots, lightly marked on the plate, to mark where the transfer roll should go. These dots are removed after the plate is finished. This process was repeated again and again across the plate, one entry for each future stamp on a sheet. Finally, any guide lines, plate numbers, or other marginal markings are added to finish the plate.

The design on the plate is reversed, like on the die. Also like the die, the plate has crevices, not raised areas.

If the printing is done by a ***rotary press***, the finished plate is curved to fit the press cylinder. There usually are two plates per cylinder. Gripper slots are cut into the back of each plate to hold to the grippers that secures the plate to the cylinder. Because the plate is curved, this lengthens the design in the direction of the curve. Therefore, rotary press stamps are longer in one dimension, compared with the same flat plate stamps.

To print stamps from the plate, ink is worked onto it with a roller. The extra is removed from the surface with a cloth. Stamp paper is wet with water so that it can better take the ink from the plate. The paper is then placed on the inked plate. The plate with the paper is rolled under a cylinder, which forces the paper down into the lines of the plate, causing the transfer of the ink from the plate to the paper. The printed sheet is then removed from the plate, resulting in a completed sheet of stamps.

Plating

The 5-cent Franklin was printed from a printing plate that contained 2 panes of 100 stamps each. A ***sheet*** is the complete impression from a plate, while a pane is the part of the original sheet that is issued for public use. A ***pane*** may be the entire sheet, a half, quarter, or some other fraction of a pane. Panes are described by their position on a sheet. For this series, the panes are left and right. Only one printing plate printed all the 1847 five-cent stamps.

Chase did a study where he ordered when each stamp shade was printed. He concluded from this study that there were five stamp deliveries to the Post Office from Rawdon, Wright, Hatch & Edson. The first was in July 1847 and the last in December of 1850. Each run had its own ink shades and impression characteristics. In 1850, the printers cleaned the plate between the 3rd and 4th printing. This improved the printing impressions, which had become progressively worse. Just before the plate cleaning in 1850, stamps made look worn, lacking fine detail. The plate also underwent retouching at this time. Retouching is strengthening or altering of a line on a plate by re-etching it. The declining printing quality was due to the abrasive effects of components of the brown ink. There were earthen pigments in the ink: umber, ocher or sienna. Also, poor impressions resulted from primitive printing techniques.

Master Die. The die is being made in reverse of the actual stamp with the features recessed into the metal. Some of the hand tools used to make the master die are shown on the right.

Transfer Roll. The transfer roll has multiple images of the stamp in its actual form with the details of the image being raised. On the left, the master die is being pressed into the transfer roll for its manufacture. On the right, the transfer roll is pressed into the printing plate, used to actually ink the stamps.

Figure 2-1. Creating the Intaglio Plate

No.	.Delivery Date	No. Delivered	No. Sold
1st	June 3, 1874	600,000	600,000
2nd	March 13, 1848	800,000	800,000
3rd	March 20, 1849	1,000,000	1,000,000
4th	February 5, 1850	1,000,000	1,000,000
5th	December 9, 1850	1,000,000	300,000
TOTAL		4,400,000	3,700,000

Printing and Deliveries of the 1847 Five-Cent Franklin

The five-cent stamp has never been plated, that is, having described the individual characteristics of every position of the plate. Some authorities think reconstructing the original plate layout is impossible due to the lack of consistent individual positioning characteristics, the result of rapid plate wear.

The metal from which the printing plate was made was a matter of controversy for years. Stanley B. Ashbrook argued the plates were made of copper, citing so many stamps with poor impressions. Brazer and Perry argued they were steel plates, claiming that copper plates would have been too soft to have printed as many impressions as were taken. Today, it is confirmed the plates were made of steel. Two letters from Rawdon, Wright, Hatch & Edson, dated March 20 and 31, of 1847, document proposals to print the stamps from steel plates.

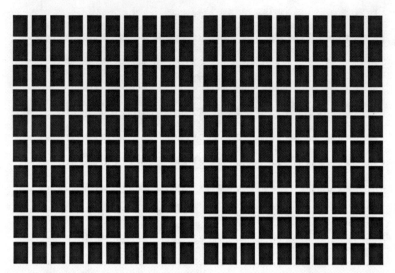

Figure 2-2. 1847 Series Plate Layout. The 1847 stamps were printed from plates of 200 stamps that were divided into 2 panes of 100 impressions, each, a left and a right. Each pane consisted of 10 rows of 10 stamps, each.

Stamp Features

The five-cent 1847 stamp was made imperforate, that is, without perforations. They are on thin bluish wove paper. There is a range of shades, thickness and texture of the stamp paper.

The gum is yellow, thin, and crackled. An apprentice engraver or printer applied it. They gummed the sheets of newly printed stamps and hung them up overnight, like laundry, to dry!

The stamp appears drab, disappointing the neophyte stamp collector. Margins are tiny, as the stamps were plated close together.

Faults are common among surviving stamps. These include corner creases, pinholes, minor defects, and repairs that have accumulated on most stamps after over a century and a half of time.

Printers made 22,000 plate impressions from the single plate, producing 4,400,000 copies. Of these, 3,700,000 were sold. The balance of the stamps, when they were made invalid was destroyed. Only 50,000 to 100,000 stamps survive, today.

Plate Varieties

Not every stamp of an issue is the same. Stamps may differ in color, paper, or design. One way stamps differ is plate varieties, subtle differences of final stamp design resulting from how the stamp was printed from the printing press plate. *Flyspecking*, looking for these tiny differences, is name stamp collectors give the study of these variations.

A *double impression* is a stamp where the paper went through the printing plate, twice. Because the two impressions do not fall on top of each other, such stamps look blurred. Strictly speaking, a double impression is a printing variety, not a plate variety. There is a surviving single stamp that has a double printing impression of the actual stamp design.

A *double transfer* is the doubling of some of the parts of the plate that then appears on the finished stamp. Most double transfers occur because of a small shifting of the relief roll on the plate. Other double transfers occur when a second new rocking is done on the incompletely removed worn or defective earlier plate impression. This process is called a *reentry*. By the same processes, *triple transfers* or *quadruple transfers* can occur.

There are 6 double transfers. There are double transfers A (top frame line) and B (top and bottom frame lines) from positions 80R and 90R, respectively. Double transfers C (bottom frame line and lower part of left frame lines), and D (top, bottom, and left frame lines and numerals) are much less common because they come from the cleaned plate. Their positions on the plate are not known. There is the type E double transfer, or Mower shift, whose characteristics include double horizontal lines at the top of the T of POST, and in the right arm of U of US, and the left numeral. Some experts feel the E double transfer is really not a double transfer, but just a series of plate scratches.

Figure 2-3. Franklin Double Transfer A. There is a doubling of the top frame line. This stamp comes from plate position 80R.

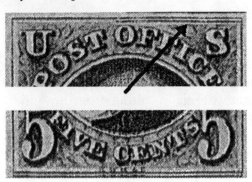

Figure 2-4. Franklin Double Transfer B. There is a pronounced doubling of both the top and bottom frame lines. This stamp comes from plate position 90R.

Figure 2-5. Franklin Double Transfer C. This has doubling of the bottom and the lower part of the left frame lines.

Figure 2-6. Franklin Double Transfer D. This has doubling of the top, bottom and left frame lines and the numerals.

Figure 2-7. Franklin Double Transfer E (Moyer Shift). This has double horizontal lines of the T of POST, the right arm of the U in US and the left numeral, 5.

Figure 2-8. Franklin Double Transfer F (Wagshal Shift). This stamp variety has doubling of both of the left frame lines, the U of US, the O of POST and of OFFICE.

Jerome S. Waghal, in 1988, found transfer F. The doubling occurs in both the left frame lines and the letters U of US, O of POST and all letters of OFFICE. This double transfer is very rare with only 8 to 10 known copies.

A *cracked plate* stamp is one printed from a portion of the plate that was cracked during manufacture. There is a cracked variety from position 69R from the before the cleaning of the plate. This variety is one printed from a portion of the plate that was cracked. It shows fine irregular, often branching lines.

Figure 2-9. Cracked Plate Variety of the 1847 Franklin. This stamp comes from the 69R position of the precleaned plate. It shows the pattern of fine, irregular, branching lines of the defect of the plate.

Sometimes foreign matter, bits of metal, gets on the plate placing *extra marks* on the stamp. The Dot in S variety was caused by a small bit of metal stuck to the transfer roll. This variety is found on all of the positions of the stamps from the 9th vertical row of the right pane. A common plate variety, it is not that valuable a stamp today.

Figure 2-10. Dot in S Variety of Five Cent 1847 Franklin. Pictured is a close of the "S" with the dot in S variety of the 1847 five-cent issue.

A *short transfer* stamp is missing part of the top or bottom of the stamp. That part of the stamp is absent on the plate. A short transfer may be accidental, the result of too vigorous polishing the plate. A short transfer may be on purpose, so the too big design will fit on too small area on the printing plate.

A ***worn plate*** stamp is one printed from an overused plate. Such a stamp lacks the usually found fine details. Many five-cent 1847 Franklin stamps were made from a worn plate.

There are other plate varieties that are not found on this issue. These will now be described for when they come up later in this book. A ***recut*** is a stamp made from a plate that was reworked, touched up, or repaired. These changes, too, make the stamp different from the original stamp. No stamps of this issue have recuts.

A ***scratched plate*** stamp shows evidence of scratching the printing plate. Scratches tend to be more linear than cracks.

If damage occurs during the transfer roll production, such as breaking away of parts of the design, that was passed on to the plate, then the finished stamp. This is called a ***broken relief***. If an intentional change is made to the relief, this change, too, is passed on. This is called an ***altered relief***.

Summary of the Plate Varieties for the 1847 Five-Cent Franklin			
Type	**Plate Position**	**Delivery**	**Rarity**
A Double Transfer	80R	All 5	1/200 copies
B Double Transfer	90R	All 5	1/200 copies
C Double Transfer	Unknown	4th and 5th	Less than 20
D Double Transfer	Unknown	4th and 5th	Less than 10
E Double Transfer	Unknown	All 5	1/200 copies
F Double Transfer	Unknown	5th	3 known
Dot in S Variety	Right Pane, 9th Row	1st through 4th	1/235 copies
Cracked Plate	69R	1st through 3rd	1/500 copies

Other Stamp Varieties

The stamp (and the ten-cent issue) is known with a stitch watermark. It is a band of parallel lines on the stamp paper. These lines are produced in the course of manufacturing of the paper by the joined ends of the cloth band on which the paper pulp is placed.

Some Franklin stamps show a preprinting paper fold. A corner of the stamp paper is folded over, and the design is then printed over the pleat.

Color

The stamp is found in several shades. Carroll Chase studied these colors. Shades include the basic red brown, pale brown, brown, dark brown, grayish brown, blackish brown, orange brown, brown orange, red and orange. The last two inks are very rare.

Use

According to stamp folklore, Congressman Harvey Shaw of New York purchased the first 1847 stamps in the office of the Postmaster General. The representative was visiting when the stamps were delivered from the printer. With fifteen cents, he purchased one each of the new five and ten-cent stamps.

Although the 5-cent Franklin's were issued on July 1, 1847, they were available then, only in New York City. Boston received the stamps on July 2, Philadelphia on July 7 and Washington July 9. The earliest known cover is dated July 7, sent from New York City to Poultney, Vermont.

The stamps were in use, officially until July 1851, when they were demonetized, that is, declared invalid for postage. They could be exchanged for cash until October of that year. The reason for the demonetization was the contract with Rawdon, Wright, Hatch & Edson. The dies and plates of the stamps remained in the hands of the printers. And the government feared the production of counterfeit stamps after the contract expired. Despite demonetization, the 1847 stamps were used illegally as late as the 1870's.

Most of the 1847 issue was used in the New England, the Mid-Atlantic States, and the Ohio and lower Mississippi valleys.

Cancellations and Covers

For postal history and used classic United States stamp collectors, the postmarks and cancellations offer many collectable varieties. Remember *postmarks* are any official marks placed on a stamp or cover while *cancellations* are types of postmarks placed on stamps to prevent their reuse. Cancellations of the first United States stamp are of many types.

Cancellations are grouped into three major types based on how they were placed: pen, handstamp, and machine. At first, the postmaster placed a simple *pen manuscript* ink mark on the stamp. Pen cancellations were common in the early years of postage stamps and at small post offices into the 1880's. Today, collectors do not like these pen-canceled stamps as much as the other types, reflected in their lower value.

From the earliest days of postage stamps up to the present day in small post office, *handstamps* are used for cancellations. Such handstamps used ink in a variety of colors. The rainbows of ink colors are collectable varieties today, especially when used on 19th century stamps. These collectable cancellation colors are listed for each stamp. *Gridiron cancellations* are the most common types of handstamp cancellations on early United States stamps. They are circles with parallel lines inside, in a large variety. From 1847 until 1900, postmasters used cancellation devises cut from wood or cork, with *fancy designs*. Such cancellations include town symbols, animals, birds, insects, Masonic symbols, flags, and *numerals*.

Machine cancellations of stamps were introduced in Boston in 1880. Each canceling machine type has its own characteristics. Collectors form collections based on type, city, or date. Today, *ink jet machine cancellations* are used.

Collectors also sort postmarks on used stamps and covers. *Town postmarks* give the name of the post office where the letter was dropped off and usually the date of the mailing. They come in a variety of styles and color ink.

Paid postmarks usually consist of the simple word, PAID. It indicates the postage was prepaid and not due upon delivery of the letter. They most commonly were used before postage stamps.

Free postal markings were used on free, no postage requiring mail, such as for governmental officials. Also, on early United States stamps, it just canceled a stamp, making it used.

Way postal markings were placed on letters received by a mail carrier on his "way" between post offices. The letters were dropped off at the first post office he reached. The receiving postmaster paid a fee to the carrier for his efforts.

Carrier postal marks have the words Carrier, City Delivery, or U.S.P.O. Dispatch. They are placed on United States Post Office carrier mail, mail carried to or from the local post office, in days before the free delivery and pick up of mail. They are similar to way postal markings.

Railroad postal markings were used to postmark mail received by route agents of the Post Office Department traveling on trains on railway mail route. The postmarks bear the name of the railroad. Actual mail sorting and distribution facilities on trains did not begin until 1864.

There are several varieties of postal marks placed on a cover or stamp while on the water. They have slightly different meaning. *Steam or Steamboat postal markings are* a form of way marking where the carrier was a boat. The inland or coastal boat carried the letter to the next post office on its route. The boat company received two cents a letter for the service

Packet postal markings were placed on mail carried by boat traveling on inland or coastal waterways. It denotes service the same as that of the railroad route agent, except the agent is traveling on a boat instead of a train.

Ship postal marks were applied to letters mailed at sea and delivered to the post office at their port of entry.

A *steamship postal mark* was used on mail from Caribbean or the Pacific ports to New Orleans or Atlantic ports carried on steamships having a United States mail contract.

There are a couple of extra service postal markings. Express mail, up until this time, meant the carriage of valuables, packages, and letters by private individuals, not the post office. However, the Post Office Department introduced express service aboard the railroad and steamboat networks in the northeast between 1842 and 1857. Mail route agents on the New York-Boston and New York-Albany train runs used *express mail postmarks* when carrying such mail.

Supplementary mail postal markings designate the special service for sending mail after the regular mail closed. For the New York City post office, starting in 1853, for a cost of double the regular postal rate, this got the mail aboard a ship after the regular mail closing but before sailing time. The service continued until 1939. Supplementary postmark types called A, D, E, F, and G were used for such service. A second supplementary service was for Chicago. For no extra fee, supplementary mail entitled a letter to catch the last eastbound train from Chicago. Supplementary postmark types B and C were used for this service.

New York City foreign mail postal markings are a group of cancellations used in the middle to late 19th century in New York City. They were placed on outgoing foreign mail. The group of handstamps features about 200 different fancy designs: stars, geometric designs, wheels, and flowers.

Precancel stamps are those with the cancellation markings placed before mailing. The purpose is to reduce the handling work by postal workers. A permit is required to use precancel stamps. Precancel postal markings first were used with the 1851 stamps. Most precancellations are overprints of the city and state names between two lines. Precancel marks are of two major types: locals and Bureaus. Locals are precancellations placed by the local post office after receiving the stamps from the Post Office Department. The Bureau precancellation marks were printed by the Bureau of Engraving and Printing, at the time of stamp printing.

Private carrier postal markings were placed by private companies. To comply with the 19th century postal monopoly law, private carrier letters had to have government postage, even though the sender did not use the postal service. The most famous are those of the Pony Express.

Intent defacing cancellations were used in the 1860's and 1870's. They were cancellations that made the re-use of the stamp impossible. They grew out of the paranoia at the time over the re-use of stamps. They are of three groups. Small pins or punches were used to pierce the stamp paper. Sharp blades were used for cutting the paper. Finally, there were canceling devices that were rotated so part of the paper is cut away.

Pen (manuscript) canceled copies are the most common found on the Unites States' first stamps. Red was the most common color used in marking these stamps, as this color most effectively canceled both the brown 5-cent and the black 10-cent stamps. About 75% were canceled in red, 15% blue, 8% black, with the remaining 2% green, orange, violet, magenta, ultramarine, and other odd shades. A pink cancel from Chicago is the most rare.

Figure 2-11. 1847 Five-Cent Franklin Cover. Here is an example of the first United States stamp paying the basic under 500 mile postage rate.

Grids (circle of parallel horizontal lines), usually with red ink, are the most common handstamp cancel. Another common marking is 13 thin bars. Numerals are common, too. Colorful fancy examples include the Binghamton New York herringbone, the blue Trenton New Jersey star, the Huntsville Alabama PAID 5 in star, the Troy & New York Steamboat in rectangle, and the green Princeton.

The five-cent 1847 Franklin stamps and covers feature a large variety of postal markings. These include the words: Paid, Free, Way, Steamboat, Steam, and Steamship. Others have hotel, railroad, or express mail markings.

One unusual postal marking, also found on the ten-cent Washington, is the Wheeling, Virginia red corner grid. This special marking is not a cancellation but a control marking, used by the local postmaster to keep track of his stamps.

Specialists have studied the on-cover uses of the stamp. In 2001, Thomas J. Alexander published a census of all known covers of the 1847 issue. There are 9,429 covers that survive showing at least one copy of the 5-cent 1847 Franklin stamp. Of these, about 250 to 275 covers were used to foreign destinations. Some domestic origin covers are quite scarce, such as from the territories, Texas, Wisconsin and California.

Special groups of 1847 covers are prized today. One is the fancy valentine. Another is a cover where the stamp is used with a private local stamp, which paid the local delivery charge. A very rare used combination is a 5 and 10-cent 1847 stamp together on a single cover.

Covers from Canada exist. At this time, one could place American postage on a letter from Canada to the United States to prepay the United States postage part of the delivery.

Cleaned stamps are common as many of the stamps were canceled with ordinary ink that is easy to remove. One can detect these by placing the stamp face down in watermark fluid. The telltale lines of the pen points then are seen.

Multiples

Figure 2-12. 1847 Five-Cent Multiple. The largest known multiple of the 1847 five-cent Franklin is a square block of 16 stamps (4 x 4), shown here. It is unused, with original gum. It was sold at the famous Ishikawa auction. Today, it is found in the Gross collection.

A square block of 16 (4x4), unused, with original gum, is the largest known unused piece of the 1847 five-cent Franklin. It was sold at the famous Ishikawa auction and today is found in the Gross collection. The largest currently known used multiple is a block of 12 stamps (6x2). A horizontal strip of 10 stamps, paying the 5 times the 10-cent rate from Washington, D.C. to Waukegan, Illinois, used in 1851, is the largest 1847 multiple on cover.

TEN-CENT WASHINGTON

1847 Ten-Cent Washington

Stamp Production
Printer:	Rawdon, Wright, Hatch & Edson
Designer:	James Parsons
Engraver:	Asher Brown Durant
Format:	2 panes of 100
Plate Number:	Printed from a single plate, but no plate number or imprints in the margins.
Date of Issue:	July 1, 1847
Earliest Known Use:	July 2, 1847
Use:	Single-rate domestic letter over 300 miles or double-rate domestic letter under 300 miles
Quantity Printed:	891,000 (delivered to Post Office)
Quantity Issued:	865,000

Stamp Features
Size:	18 x 23.5 mm (0.7 x 0.9 inches)
Watermark:	None
Perforation:	Imperforate
Colors:	Black, gray black, and greenish black
Varieties:	4 double transfers. Short transfer at top. Vertical line through second F in OFFICE (68R). Stickpin in tie (52L). Harelip (57L). Stitch watermark.

Collectable Stamp Today
Collectable Cancellation Colors:
Red, blue, orange, orange red, black, magenta, violet, green, ultramarine

Collectable Cancellation Varieties:
Paid, Free, railroad, US express mail, Way, numeral, Steam, Steamship, Steamboat, Steamer 10, Canada, Panama, Wheeling Va control grid, pen

Value Unused:	$$$$$$
Value Used:	$$$$$
Surviving Covers:	3,483
Largest Known Multiple:	Used: 14

Design, Printing, and Plating

The Washington portrait, which appears on the 10-cent 1847 stamp, is based on a Gilbert Stuart painting. The artwork is found today in the Boston Museum of Fine Arts. It was modified from a die that was already in the possession of Rawdon, Wright, Hatch and Edson. It was used on bank notes produced by the firm. It shows Washington's three-quarters face, looking to the right, sitting on a dark oval background. He is wearing a white neckerchief and black coat. There is a wreath of leaves around it. In the upper corners, are the letters U and S. In the two lower corners are Roman numerals, X, for 10. In a curved line around the upper and lower parts of the medallion are the words, POST OFFICE and TEN CENTS, respectively. A rectangle frames the outside of the stamp. The stamp is the same small size as the five-cent.

The ten-cent stamps are much sharper than the five. But like the five, ironed-out creases, pinholes, minor defects, chemically cleaned used copies passing for unused, and repairs are common. The color and impression of the stamp is fairly uniform, found only in black, gray black, and greenish black.

Only about 5,000 impressions were taken from the single printing plate. The printer delivered 1,050,000 stamps to the Post Office. About 891,000 were issued to the postmasters, 865,000 reached the public. The rest were returned and destroyed when the 1851 issue was made.

The complete plate of the 2 panes of 100 has been reconstructed. This was mostly the work of Elliott Perry. Using overlapping pairs and other multiple copies, he assigned stamps to definite plate positions. He was able to do this through study of frame lines, guidelines and, especially, position dots. In preparing the printing plate, these position dots helped the operator adjust the transfer roll to the correct position in transferring the stamp design into the plate. These tiny dots are usually located in the three-leaf ornament in the middle of the left side of the stamp.

Deliveries of the 1847 Ten-Cent Washington			
Delivery	Date	Stamps Delivered	Stamps Sold
1st	June 1, 1847	200,000	200,000
2nd	March 13, 1848	250,000	250,000
3rd	March 19, 1849	300,000	300,000
4th	February 14, 1850	300,000	115,000
TOTAL		1,050,000	865,000

Plating Varieties

There are 4 double transfers, called A, B, C and D. Double transfer A, from position 1R, shows a doubling of the X at lower right, and also in the letters U and S at the top, as well as in POST OFFICE. The double transfer B has a doubling of POST OFFICE. It is from position 31R. The double transfer C, from position 2R, shows doubling in the X at the lower right, the ENTS of CENTS and in POST and OFFICE at the top, and the U and S. The double transfer D, from position 41R, involves the left and bottom frame lines. The double transfer known as the Knapp shift from plate position 23L is a fake stamp, not a true plate variety.

Figure 2-13. Ten-Cent Double Transfer A. This variety has a apparent doubling of the lower right X. It comes from plate position 1R.

Figure 2-14. Ten-Cent Double Transfer B. This shows the doubling of POST OFFICE. This stamp comes from plate position 31R.

Figure 2-15. Ten-Cent Double Transfer C. This shows the doubling of ENTS of CENTS, POST OFFICE, US, and the right X. It comes from plate position 2R.

Figure 2-16. Ten-Cent Double Transfer D. This has double left and bottom frame lines. This stamp comes from plate position 41R

A short transfer is a faintness of the design at the top of certain examples. In this stamp's case, it was caused by overzealous cleaning up (burnishing) the plate. When removing the metal displaced by the transfer roll, some of the design also was removed.

There are stamps with a stitch watermark. Other varieties resulted from foreign material on the printing plate, including stamps with a vertical line through second F of OFFICE (position 68R), the stickpin in tie variety (52L), and the harelip variety (57L).

Figure 2-17. Ten-Cent Harelip Variety. Note the very obvious plate defect appearing on Washington's face. (Perhaps it should be called "Need a Tissue" variety?) This stamp comes from plate position 57L.

Figure 2-18. Ten-Cent Stickpin Variety. Note this plate defect on Washington's neckerchief looks like the head of a pin. This stamp comes from plate position 52L.

Figure 2-19. Ten-Cent Line Through F Variety. This stamp has a plate defect of a vertical line in the F of OFFICE. This stamp comes from plate position 68R.

Summary of 1847 Ten-Cent Washington Plate Varieties	
Plate Variety	Plate Position
Double Transfer A (Doubling of lower right "X")	1R
Double Transfer B (Doubling of "POST OFFICE")	31R
Double Transfer C (Doubling of "ENTS" of "CENTS")	2R
Double Transfer D (Doubling of left and bottom frame lines)	41R
Harelip	57R
Stick Pin	52L
Line Through Second "F" of "POST OFFICE"	68R

Use

In 1972, Harry Mark found buried in an old law book, a cover with a horizontal pair of the ten-cent 1847. The cover has a New York City postmark of July 2, and was mailed to Indianapolis. The year date, 1847 is proven by the contents of the cover. It represents the earliest known use of any 1847 stamp or United States regular issue.

Five major cities received supplies during the first 16 days of July: New York (July 1), Boston (July 2), Philadelphia (July 7), Washington (July 9), and Baltimore (July 16).

The 1847 stamps were demonetized after June 30, 1851, but several ten-cent 1847 stamps were used illegally after that date.

Cancellations & Covers

Like the five-cent 1847 stamp, pen cancellations are the most common. Of the handstamps, the New York City square grid in red is mostly seen. Grid cancels come in a variety of colors. Red, blue and black are the most common colors. Orange, violet, green, and pink are also found. Others include the St. Johnsbury, Vermont scarab and the Binghamton, New York, herringbone. Town postal markings are less common The special postal markings include Paid, Free, railroad markings, U.S. express mail marking, Way, numerals, Steam, Steamship, Steamboat, Steamer 10, Canada, and Panama.

According to Alexander, there are 3,483 ten-cent 1847 stamps still on a cover. About 200 were used to Canada. There are 5 covers sent to France and a greater number to the British Isles. There are covers used to Germany (4 known), Belgium (1), Mexico (2), Cuba and Hawaii. There are a dozen used from foreign countries, mostly from Canada and Peru.

Most of the 1847 issue covers mailed abroad were sent only partially prepaid. The sender paid domestic postage to the border. The recipient had to pay the ocean postage to the destination in cash.

Bisected uses of the 10-cent 1847 stamp on cover are popular and interesting collector items. A bisected stamp is one cut in half and used as half value of the total stamp. About 80 examples still exist. These covers resulted from lack of 5-cent stamps at some smaller post offices.

Forty-nine covers are known showing 5 and 10-cent 1847 stamps used together. Ten-cent 1847s are known used with locals and carrier stamps, but such combinations are scarce.

Multiples

In September 1927, C.H. Bandholtz discovered, in Portland, Maine, the two largest known pieces of the 10-cent 1847.

OFFICAL REPRODUCTIONS

Five-Cent Franklin Reproduction

Stamp Production
Printer:	Bureau of Engraving and Printing
Designer:	Unknown
Engraver:	Charles K. Burt (vignette), G. McCoy (lettering)
Format:	Plate of 50 subjects
Plate Number:	Single, not numbered
Date of Issue:	1875
Earliest Known Use:	Not valid for postal use
Uses:	Souvenir, not valid for postal use
Quantity Printed:	11,450
Quantity Issued:	4,779

Stamp Features
Size:	18.5 x 23.2 mm (0.7 x 0.9 inches)
Watermark:	None
Perforation:	Imperforate
Colors:	Red brown, brown, dark brown
Varieties:	None

Collectable Stamp Today
Cancellations:	Not valid for postal use, but have been found canceled.
Value Unused:	$$$$
Surviving Covers:	None known
Largest Known Multiple:	Unused: Full pane of 50 until recently

Ten-Cent Washington Reproduction

Stamp Production
Printer:	Bureau of Engraving and Printing
Designer:	Unknown
Engraver:	Charles K. Burt (vignette), G. McCoy (lettering)
Plate Number:	Single, not numbered
Format:	Plate of 50 subjects
Date of Issue:	1875
Earliest Known Use:	Not valid for postal use
Uses:	Souvenir, not valid for postal use
Quantity Printed:	10,000
Quantity Issued:	3,883

Stamp Features
Size:	18.5 x 23.2 mm (0.7 x 0.9 inches)
Watermark:	None
Perforation:	Imperforate
Colors:	Black, gray black
Varieties:	None

Collectable Stamp Today
Cancellations:	Not valid for postal use, but have been found canceled.
Value Unused:	$$$$$
Surviving Covers:	None known
Largest Known Multiple:	Unused: Full pane of 50 until recently

The reproductions of the 1847 stamps are government created issues. In 1875, a special printing program was established and continued until 1884. This program created the 1847 reproductions,

1857-60 reprints, 1861-66 and 1869 re-issues, and the Bank Note special printings of 1875 and 1880-83.

The reproductions of the 1847 stamps were made for display and sale to stamp collectors at the 1876 Centennial Exposition held in Philadelphia. In 1875, the government could not obtain the original dies or plates used to print the 1847 stamps like they could for the other later issues. So the Bureau of Engraving and Printing engraved a new die, which reproduced the designs of the 5 and 10-cent 1847 stamps. From this die, plates were made from which were printed the reproductions. Though never valid for postal use, Scott and other stamp collector catalogs have assigned these reproductions separate catalog numbers. They remain so today mostly out of stamp collecting tradition.

The reproductions were printed from plates of 50 subjects, arranged 10 across and 5 rows deep. The reproductions were issued imperforate, without gum, on wove paper that is thicker and coarser than the originals. The color of the paper is deeper than that of the original stamps. The impressions are sharper than on the original 1847's.

The size is different, too. The originals measure 18 x 23.5 mm, while the reproductions are wider and shorter (18.5 x 23.2 mm). They were not authorized for postal use, although one can find a rare canceled stamp.

Only 4,779 Franklin imitations and 3,883 Washington's were sold. The rest, the unsold remainders, were destroyed.

Differences From the Originals

Placed side by side, the differences of the original and reproductions are easily seen.

For the Franklin reproduction, to the lower left of the vignette, the white shirt frill touches the frame of the oval on a level with the top of the figure 5. A ruler placed horizontally at this point reveals just a tiny portion of the top bar of the numeral 5 above it. On the original stamp, the farthest point of the shirt's lace touches the medallion frame is at a level with the top left corner of the letter F of FIVE. A ruler placed horizontally at this point has most of the bar of the numeral 5 above it.

More noticeable is the right line of the N in CENTS. On the reproduction, this comes to a point at the bottom, while on the original, it is flattened. The initials R.W. H. & E at the bottom of the stamp are indistinct on the reproduction, instead of clear like the original. The extent of the initials is two-thirds the width in the reprints relative to the originals. The letters are 3 mm. wide on the originals and 2 mm. on reproductions

On the 10-cent Washington, the right leg of the N of CENTS is blunt at the bottom on the 1847 and pointed on the reproduction. On the upper left corner of the original, the U (of US) is round and well formed at the bottom. On the reproduction, the lower curve of the U has a flat spot near the O of POST. The facial expressions are different. The expression of the eyes on the original seems alert and the ends of the line of the mouth curve upward. The reproduction Washington has the famous sleepy look. Another difference is the coat collar appears shady, shabby or dirty. On the reproduction, there are 5 horizontal lines between the CE of CENTS and the lower line of the vignette's oval, while here are only 4 lines on the original stamp. In the 1875 issue, the serifs at the bottom of the left Roman numeral X are farther apart than those on the bottom of the right.

Figure 2-20. Differences Between the Original and Reproduction Stamps. Five-Cent Franklin.

1. **Original**-The shirt at the lower left of the oval touch the frame low on the top line of the numeral, 5. **Reproduction**-The shirt touches the frame at the level of the top of the numeral 5.
2. **Original**-The shirt touches the right of the top right corner of the F of FIVE. **Reproduction**-The shirt touches even with the top right corner with the F of the FIVE.
3. **Original**-The right line of the N of CENTS is blunt. **Reproduction**-The right line of the N comes to a point.
4. **Original**-The engravers' initials, R.W.H.& E. are 3 mm. wide and sharp. **Reproduction**- Initials are 2 mm wide and blurred.

Figure 2-21. Differences Between the Original and Reproduction Stamps. Ten-Cent Washington.

1. **Original**-The bottom right corner of the N of CENTS is blunt. **Reproduction**-The corner is pointed.
2. **Original**-The U of the US is rounded at the bottom. **Reproduction**-There is flat spot on the U, near the O of POST.
3. **Original**-The eyes appear alert. **Reproduction**-The eyes appear sleepy.
4. **Original.** The serifs of the X are the same distance apart for the left and right Roman numeral. **Reproduction**-The serifs of the X are closer together in the right X compared with the left X.

Multiples

Full panes of both values of the reproductions existed until recently. In 1976, they sold for $110,000 to Pennsylvania dealer, Irwin Weinberg, who broke them up into blocks.

TWENTIETH CENTURY REPRODUCTIONS

1947 Souvenir Sheet

In 1947, the Bureau of Engraving and Printing produced a souvenir sheet that featured reproductions of the original 1847 stamps. The souvenir sheet was made for the Centenary International Philatelic Exhibition (CIPEX) held in New York City from May 17th to 25th of that year. CIPEX celebrated the hundred-year anniversary of the first United States stamps and has been called the world's greatest stamp show.

The souvenir sheet is printed in two colors. It measures 2.67 inches high by 3.87 inches wide. The sheet features a side-by-side reproduction of the 1847 5-cent Franklin and 10-cent Washington stamps. The reproductions were made with the aid of the original 1847 die proofs. The 1947 reproductions are different colors from the original stamps. The 5-cent Franklin is blue, the 10-cent Washington, brown orange. The reproductions have the initials, B. E. & P., for the Bureau of Engraving and Printing, instead of R. W. H. & E.

Under the reproductions are the words, 100TH ANNIVERSARY UNITED STATES STAMPS. This wording and the reproductions are found inside a simple rectangle. Outside the rectangle is wording, also. At the top are the words, UNDER AUTHORITY OF ROBERT E. HANNEGAN, POSTMASTER GENERAL, below, NEW YORK, N.Y. MAY 17-25, 1947, to the left, PRINTED BY THE TREASURY DEPARTMENT. BUREAU OF ENGRAVING AND PRINTING, and to the right, IN COMPLIMENT TO THE CENTENARY INTERNATIONAL PHILATELIC EXHIBITION.

Figure 2-22. The 1947 Souvenir Sheet. The Bureau of Printing and Engraving to celebrate the 100-year anniversary of the first United States stamps printed this souvenir sheet. The sheet has reproductions of the first two regular issue stamps, but in different colors.

Stamp Collecting Stamp

A picture of the 1847 five-cent Franklin is found on an eight-cent 1972 United States commemorative stamp. The issue paid tribute to stamp collecting. It shows the first United States stamp under a magnifying glass. This stamp often is called a "stamp on a stamp."

Figure 2-23. Stamp Collecting Stamp. This "stamp on a stamp" features a picture of the first United States stamp.

1997 Souvenir Sheets

In 1997, the Bureau of Engraving and Printing issued two souvenir sheets to celebrate both the 150th anniversary of the first United States postage stamps and the Pacific '97 International Philatelic Exhibition in San Francisco.

Both sheets have the title, PACIFIC 97 SAN FRANCISCO, CA FROM MAY 29 TO JUNE 9, 1997. The sheets have reproductions of the 5-cent Franklin (on the right side of the sheet) and the 10-cent Washington (on the left side of the sheet) large die proofs. The other side of the sheet is a block of twelve perforated (4x3) stamps. The stamps are modifications of the original stamps. Even the denominations are different. The Franklin is now a 50-cent stamp while the Washington is 60.

Figure 2-24. 1997 Souvenir Sheets. In 1997, the Bureau of Engraving and Printing issued two souvenir sheets to celebrate the 150th anniversary of the first United States postage stamps. The sheets have reproductions of the 5-cent Franklin and the 10-cent Washington large die proofs. Also included with each is a block of twelve perforated (4x3) stamps, modifications of the original stamps.

ESSAYS, PROOFS & SPECIMENS

Essays

Essays are proposed designs for stamps that were never issued. Even if the design was used with only a tiny change, it is still called an essay. Essays also can show different, incomplete stages in the engraving of the master dies. These types of essays are called progressive proofs.

At this time, when the Post Office Department advertised for stamp proposals, it asked they be accompanied by essays, as examples of the stamps to be furnished. Essays can range in style from simple artist's drawings to completed stamps with gum and perforations.

Essays for the five and ten-cent Rawdon, Wright, Hatch and Edson stamps exist today. One for the 5-cent issue is a unique complete essay, consisting of an engraved vignette of Franklin with a frame that is part engraved, the rest finished in pencil, ink and gray wash. Other essays consist of just the engraved vignette or the engraved frame.

There is one complete essay of the 10-cent 1847 Washington. The vignette is engraved; while the frame is partially engraved, the rest in black ink, pencil, and gray wash. Separate engraved vignettes and engraved frames essays also exist.

Die Proofs

A proof is a copy of a stamp that is exactly like the issued stamp. Proofs taken from the master die are called die proofs. Proofs made from a plate are plate proofs. Sometimes, different color ink is used in making the proof. These are called trial color proofs.

For the 1847 series, there are large die proofs. Large die proofs were printed on paper about the size of the engraver's die block, 40 x 50 mm. They are found with red brown (5-cent) and black (10-cent) ink on a variety of papers: India, white bond, colored bond, white laid, bluish laid, yellowish wove, bluish wove, white wove, card, and glazed paper. Many show crosshatch lines surrounding the image area, engraved there to prevent slippage. The American Bank Note Company (which took over the original printing company) printed these large die proofs from 1858 to 1878. This means the dies of the 1847 designs existed then, and may exist today.

Figure 2-25. Large Die Proofs of the 1847 Series Stamps. These were printed on paper the size of the engraver's die block, 40 x 50 mm. The American Bank Note Company printed these large die proofs, between 1858 and 1878. Note the crosshatches.

For the later reproductions, there are both large and small die proofs. The large die proofs are printed with red brown (5-cent) and black (10-cent) ink.

Small die proofs of the reproductions have narrow margins. There are two types. There are 302 small die proof types that were printed for 85 albums by the Bureau of Engraving and Printing in 1903-4 on a fibrous, white wove paper. They are called the Roosevelt presentation proofs. They were made for presentation to government officials. Including in this set are the five and ten-cent reproductions of this series.

Another printing of 413 different small die proofs was made for the 1915 Panama-Pacific Exposition. A set was given to the Smithsonian Institution on March 20, 1915. These were printed on a soft, yellowish wove paper, and only three to five total sets exist. Likewise, the reproductions are found in this small proof die form.

Plate Proofs

Plate proofs are made from finished plates and show beautiful impressions, much better than the issued stamps. Plate proofs for the original 1847 stamps are printed on India paper. In 1997, the original engraver's proof book was found to contain the 5-cent and 10-cent sheet proofs of 100 stamps. They were overprinted with the word specimen, meaning they are sample stamps. These record how the stamps were originally entered on the plates and the original condition of the plate.

For the reproductions, there are plate proofs on India paper and card. Card plate proofs were made in 5 printings from 1879 to 1894.

Figure 2-26. Plate Proof of the 1847 Series Stamps. This proof shows the original state of the printing plate before it was worn down by use.

Trial Color Proofs

Trial color die proofs are large size die proofs made from the master die. For the original 1847 stamps, they are found in a variety of ink shades on India paper, bond paper, wove paper, and thin glazed card. For the reproductions, there also are large size die trial color proofs.

Plate color trial proofs are found on India paper for the issued stamp and both India paper and card for the reproduction.

The Atlanta set is another group of plate trial color proofs. The American Bank Note Company printed plate proofs of all the reproductions and reissues through the 1875 designs. They were made for the 1881 International Cotton Exhibition held in Atlanta, Georgia. They did not make them for the original 1847 stamps. However, the series reproduction Atlanta trial color plate proofs come in five colors (black, scarlet, brown, green, and blue), printed on thin cardboard.

3 | Issues of 1851

1851 Imperforate Stamps

President Millard Fillmore's Postmaster General was Fethan Hall. He lobbied hard for further American postal reform. His work led to an act of Congress, passed on March 3rd, 1851, which changed the entire United States postal rate structure. This act became effective on July 1, 1851. The act still did not make prepayment of postage compulsory, but it made it cheaper. For a single weight letter (up to a half an ounce) for a distance within the country up to 3,000 miles, the prepaid postage was 3 cents, but 5 cents if recipient paid it. For a distance over 3,000 miles, the rates were double, 6 and 10 cents. Double weight letters (more than half but less than one ounce) were charged double rates and so on. Drop letters' rate was one cent.

Circular rates were lowered. They were on a sliding scale according to distance. For a circular (under one ounce), sent under 500 miles, the charge was 1 cent, from 500 to 1,500 miles, 2 cents, 1,500 to 2,500 miles, 3 cents, 2,500 to 3,500 miles, 4 cents, and over 3,500 miles, 5 cents. These complicated circular rates resulted in many wrongly charged covers. So the following year, the postal act of August 30, 1852, simplified this circular rate structure. The one-cent rate paid for circulars of up to 3 ounces to be sent anywhere in the country.

Bound books were, for the first time, considered a separate mail class in 1851. Book postage rate was based on weight and distance sent.

Toppan, Carpenter, and Casilear

These new postage rates meant the need for new stamp denominations: one and three-cent. Included was a twelve-cent stamp, used for various odd rates. The printing contract for the 1851 stamps was given to Toppan, Carpenter, Casilear & Co., of Philadelphia. The contract originally was for 6 years but eventually was extended 4 more years, ending June 10, 1861. Because of the fear that after the contract expired, the stamp plates would be used to make counterfeit stamps, on that date they became property of the United States.

The first one, three and twelve-cent stamps were delivered on June 21,1851.

Postal Act of 1855

When Franklin Pierce became president in 1853, he appointed James Campbell as his postmaster general. Campbell, too, was a postal reformer. He lobbied Congress for what became the postal act of March 3rd, 1855. It went into effect on April 1st of that year. Prepayment of postage on all domestic letters, at last, was made compulsory. Prepayment using stamps was required on January 1st of 1856. For mail over 3,000 miles, the charge was raised to ten cents. This rate increase went to improve postal service to California. So a new ten-cent stamp was needed and added to the series.

There was an official registration of mail for the first time in 1855. The cost was five cents. This was to prevent mail theft by post office workers. The mail, at that time, contained large amounts of cash and other valuables. The registration system was not insurance, rather a tracking system. It identified the workers who handled the mail. The registry fees, at this time, usually were paid in cash, separate from the postage. However, in 1855 the Post Office Department did issued a five-cent stamp. It helped pay for foreign postage to France and the 10-cent California rate.

Postal Act of 1851:
Single weight letter (up to a half an ounce) for a distance within the United States **up to 3,000 miles**-3 cents prepaid, 5 cents, if not prepaid.
Single weight letter (up to a half an ounce) for a distance within the United States *over 3,000 miles*, 6 cents-prepaid, 10 cents, if not prepaid.
Double weight letters (more than half but less than one ounce)-double single weight rates.
Drop letters-1 cent.
Circular rates (under one ounce), under 500 miles, 1 cent: 500-1,500 miles, 2 cents: 1,500-2,500 miles, 3 cents: 2,500-3,500 miles, 4 cents, over 3,500 miles, 5 cents.
Foreign country via sea-under 2,500 miles-10 cents, over 2,500 miles-20 cents
Bound books-considered a separate mail class.

Postal Act of 1852:
Circular rate-1 cent for up to 3 ounces anywhere regardless of distance.

Postal Act of 1855:
Prepayment of postage on all domestic letters compulsory after April 1, 1855.
Prepayment, using stamps, compulsory after January 1,1856.
Single weight letter (up to a half an ounce) for a distance within the United States *up to 3,000 miles*-3 cents
Single weight letter (up to a half an ounce) for a distance within the United States *over 3,000 miles*-10 cents.
Double weight letters (more than half but less than one ounce)-double single weight rates.
Drop letters-1 cent.
Circular rate-one cent for up to 3 ounces anywhere regardless of distance.
Registration of mail-five cents.

Causes of the Various Types

There are several varieties of some of the 1851 series stamps. The types, as they are called, are based on slightly different printed designs. There are plate varieties, due to differences of the position of the plate that printed them. The changes came both from the transfer from die to the transfer roll to the plate process and from alterations made to the finished plate, itself. This is because the stamp design of the master die would not fit all the 200 positions of the printing plate. The stamps' designs are large and ornate. They had to be crowded on the plates with the minimum of margin between the individual stamps. Still, there was not enough room.

To fix the space problem, the designs on the transfer roll were short transferred. As described previously, a short transfer occurs when the transfer roll is not rocked its entire length onto the printing plate. Thus, the finished stamp does not have the complete design. Though this sometimes occurs accidentally, for these stamps, the short transfer was intended.

Also, some of the lines forming the outside parts of the design were removed from the surface of the plate by a burnishing tool. This process is called erasure.

In addition to making the finished stamp design smaller, some stamp positions on the plates had small changes made to them by recutting. This is hand engraving the plate itself to fix or add lines to the design.

Today if these varieties occurred, they would rate only minor footnote in the stamp catalogs. But in the early days of stamp collecting, a big deal was made over the slight differences including giving the types each a major catalog number. And today, stamp collectors carry on this tradition.

One looks at certain features to determine the type. These include if the design complete, if it is complete at top or bottom, if certain lines are intact or broken, if other lines were recut. The types determine the rarity and value of a given stamp. Because specific types are produced by only a certain positions on one or more plates, the quantity produced of any particular type and its value is related directly to the number of positions that type occupies on the plates.

Double reentries, double transfers, wear, and cracks and flaws in the metal, though not major types, further complicated the plate making process and result in more subtle varieties of stamps.

Margin Markings

For the first time, United States stamp panes had margin markings and plate numbers. The *margin* or *selvage* is the area outside the printed design of stamps. A block of stamps from the top, side or bottom with the attached the selvage is called a *margin block* if two rows or a strip if one row. The *imprint* is a design containing the name of the printer of the stamps that appears on the margin. A block of stamps with the sheet margin attached, bearing this imprint, is called the *imprint block*. A single row of stamps with the sheet margin attached, bearing this imprint, is called the *imprint strip*. The *plate numbers* are unique to each plate, placed on the margins of the sheet to identify the plate.

For this series, the markings, Toppan, Carpenter, Casilear & Co. BANK NOTE ENGRAVERS. Phila., New York, Boston & Cincinnati are on one line, with "No." and the plate number on the next. The imprint is centered in the side margin, reading down in the left margin, and up in the right. The imprint and plate numbers are the same color of the stamp.

End of the Series

All the stamps of the 1851 issue are imperforate. However, in 1857, they are reissued in a perforated form. Because of the Civil War, they were made invalid for postal use by January 1862. This prevented their use by the Confederacy to obtain cash for their cause.

ONE-CENT STAMPS OF 1851

Figure 3-1. One-Cent 1851 Proof. This proof of the 1851 one-cent Franklin stamp shows the complete stamp design that is typically cut away in the issued stamps.

The one-cent stamp of this series feature a profile of Benjamin Franklin. This started the long-standing tradition of having the nation's first Postmaster General on the lowest denomination stamp. The design was based on a bust made by Jean Antoine Houdon. The bust, today, resides in the Philadelphia Museum of Art. Printed above the portrait are the words, US POSTAGE and below, ONE CENT. The stamps are indigo blue. The one-cent stamps' famous student was Stanley B. Ashbrook.

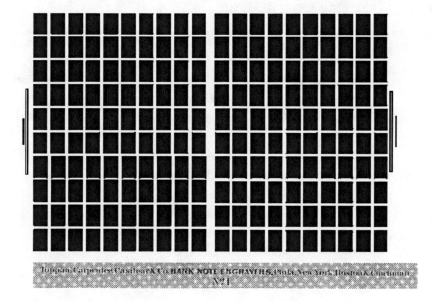

Figure 3-2. 1851 Series Stamps Plate Layout and Marginal Markings. The 1851 stamps were printed from plates of 200 stamps that were divided into 2 panes of 100 impressions, each, a left and a right. Each pane consisted of 10 rows of 10 stamps, each. For the first time there was marginal markings. The imprint marking is centered in the side margin, reading down in the left margin, and up in the right. The words, Toppan, Carpenter, Casilear & Co. BANK NOTE ENGRAVERS. Phila., New York, Boston & Cincinnati are on one line, with No. showing the plate number on the next. The imprint and plate number are the same color as the stamp.

Types of the One-Cent 1851 Stamps

Type	Definition	Imperforated Stamp Plate and Positions	Perforated Stamps Plate and Positions
I	Complete Stamp Design	7R1E	Plate 12, 99 positions
Ia	Bottom Complete, Top Ornament and Outer Line Missing	Bottom rows plate 4 except 91R4, 96R4	Bottom rows plate 4 except 91R4, 96R4
Ib	Top Complete Bottom Right or Left Plume Missing	Top row R1E (Positions 3,4,5,6,8,9)	NONE
Ic	Top Ornament and Outer Line Missing Bottom Right Plume or Ball Partially Missing	Plate 4, scattered positions (8 total)	Plate 4, scattered positions (8 total)
II	Top Line Complete Top Ornament May Be Complete Bottom Line Complete Bottom Scolls and Ornament Missing	1E (163 positions) 4R1L 2 (199 positions) 3 (entire plate) 4 (20 positions all the top rows)	4R1L 2 (199 positions) 4 (20 positions All the top rows) 11 (20 positions all the top rows) 12 (101 positions)
III	Top Line Broken Bottom Line Broken	99R2 Plate 4 (44 scattered positions)	99R2, 46L12 Plate 4 (44 scattered positions)
IIIa	Top or Bottom Line Broken But Not Both	1E (37 positions) 4 (110 positions)	4 (110 positions) 11 (180 positions) 12 (4-14 positions)
IV	Recuts	Plate 1L, all positions but 4R1L	Plate 1L, all positions but 4R1L
V	Incomplete on Sides	NONE	Plates 7, 8, 9, 10

The 1851 one-cent stamps were printed from 4 plates. Each plate had 200 positions, divided into 2 panes of 100 subjects each, and arranged 10 stamps by 10 stamps. The stamps are divided into left and right panes. After some use, plate 1's positions were reentered or recut.

Therefore, the stamps from plate 1 are subdivided into Early (E) and Late (L). A number denotes the position of each stamp on the plate. The first stamp at the left top is number 1. Continuing across, the last stamp on the right in the first row is number 10. The first stamp at the left end of the second row is number 11, and so on through number 100, the last right corner stamp of the bottom row. Next, the pane position is listed (L for left, R for right). Finally, the plate number is given.

The types of one-cent stamps, I, Ia, Ib, Ic, II, III, IIIa, and IV, are based on the completeness of the design. Plate 1 (early) produced all the type I and Ib stamps. Plate 1 (late) produced all the type IV stamps. Plate 4 produced all the type Ia and Ic. Type II stamps came from all five plates (1(E), 1(L), 2, 3, 4). Three plates, 1 early, 2 and 4, produced type IIIa. Type III stamps were produced by plates 2 (one position, 99R) and 4. Plate 1 (early) did not have a plate number. This was added when it was reentered and became plate 1 (late).

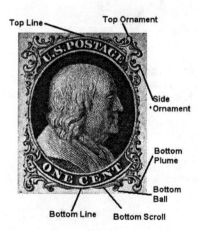

Figure 3-3. Anatomy of the 1851 Series One-Cent Franklin Stamp. This shows the named parts of the frame of the stamp. These parts and which ones are missing are important in distinguishing the different types of the stamps of the series.

Type I Imperforate 1851 One-Cent Franklin

Type I Imperforate 1851 One-Cent Franklin

Stamp Production

Printer:	Toppan, Carpenter, Casilear
Designer:	Edward Purcell
Engraver:	Joseph I. Pease or William C. Smillie (portrait), Henry Earle or John Casilear (border and lettering)
Format:	2 panes of 100
Plate Numbers:	1 Early
Date of Issue:	July 1, 1851
Earliest Known Use:	July 5,1851
Uses:	For a circular or drop letter. Three paid the 3-cent letter rate. Carriers' fee
Quantity Issued:	35,000

Stamp Features

Size:	20 x 26 mm. (0.8 x 1.0 inches)
Watermark:	None
Perforation:	Imperforate
Colors:	Blue
Varieties:	Double transfer (all stamps).

Collectable Stamp Today
Collectable Cancellation Colors:
Black, blue, red.
Collectable Cancellation Varieties:
black town, blue town, red town, Paid.
Value Unused: $$$$$$$

Value Used: $$$$$
Surviving Covers: 22
Largest Known Multiple: Unused: 1
Used: 1

This is a classic of classic United States stamps. The stamp is rare, expensive, and thoroughly studied and written about. That is because it comes from only one plate position, 7R1E (position 7 on the right pane of Plate 1 in the early state of the plate). Though it did not bear a plate number, it is referred to as Plate 1 early because in its late state, it did have that plate number. It contains the original complete design of the master die. This means that the top of the stamp shows the complete right and left ornaments as well as the complete top line. The side ornaments are complete. It has the strong double transfer, noticeable in the upper right corner and the U.S. POSTAGE.

Figure 3-4. Features of the Type I One-Cent Stamp of the 1851 Series. This stamp has the complete design of the stamp as found on the original die. This includes (1) the sides, (2) the top line and (3) ornament, and the (4) bottom line, (5) scroll, (6) plume, and (7) ornaments.

Only 90 copies exist today. Only one stamp out of every 750 one-cent stamps of this series is a Type I. This total of 90 copies includes only 3 unused stamps and 22 still on cover. Wagshal, in his 2001 book, "The Wagshal Census of 7R1E" gives a summary of all surviving stamps.

Since this stamp comes from only one position on the plate, it cannot be found as a multiple form. A type I stamp is found on the famous Newbury Cover. This cover has a strip of three 1-cent stamps, consisting of a type I, type Ib, and another Ib in a row, used on July 5, 1851, just four days after issue. The stamps have superb color and impressions, are lightly canceled with red gridirons, and on a well-preserved cover with a circular red postmark, "Richmond, Va. Jul 5." The cover is named after a famous Chicago stamp collector, Saul Newbury, who at one time owned the cover.

Type Ia Imperforate 1851 One-Cent Franklin

Type Ia Imperforate 1851 One-Cent Franklin

Stamp Production

Printer:	Toppan, Carpenter, Casilear
Designer:	Edward Purcell
Engraver:	Joseph I. Pease or William C. Smillie (portrait), Henry Earle or John Casilear (border and lettering)
Format:	2 panes of 100
Plate Numbers:	4
Date of Issue:	April 1857
Earliest Known Use:	April 19,1857
Uses:	Circular. Drop letter. Three paid the basic 3-cent letter rate. Carriers' fee
Quantity Issued:	110,000

Stamp Features
Size:	20 x 26 mm. (0.8 x 1.0 inches)
Watermark:	None
Perforation:	Imperforate
Colors:	Blue
Varieties:	Curl on shoulder (97L4), Curl in C (97R4)

Collectable Stamp Today
Collectable Cancellation Colors:
Black, blue
Collectable Cancellation Varieties:
black carrier, red carrier, pen
Value Unused: $$$$$$
Value Used: $$$$$$
Surviving Covers: 25
Largest Known Multiple: Unused: 2
Used: 3

Type Ia stamps are complete at the bottom, like type I stamps, but the top ornaments and outer line are partially missing. Type Ia stamps come from the bottom row of both panes of plate 4. They are found in 18 of the 20 bottom row positions. The other positions, 91 and 96R4, are "almost type Ia," called type Ic, described below.

The largest known unused multiple is a pair within block of 4 stamps, with the other two being type IIIa stamps. The largest known used multiple is a strip of 3 stamps.

Figure 3-5. Features of the Type Ia One-Cent Stamp of the 1851 Series. At the top of the stamp (1) the plumes and (2) outer frame line are incomplete. (3) The stamp has the complete design at the bottom.

Type Ib Imperforate 1851 One-Cent Franklin

Type Ib Imperforate 1851 One-Cent Franklin

Stamp Production
Printer:	Toppan, Carpenter, Casilear
Designer:	Edward Purcell
Engraver:	Joseph I. Pease or William C. Smillie (portrait), Henry Earle or John Casilear (border and lettering)
Format:	2 panes of 100
Plate Numbers:	1 Early
Date of Issue:	July 1, 1851
Earliest Known Use:	July 1, 1851 (Boston, first day cover)
Uses:	Circular. Drop letter. Three paid the basic 3-cent letter rate. Carriers' fee
Quantity Issued:	210,000

Stamp Features
Size:	20 x 26 mm. (0.8 x 1.0 inches)
Watermark:	None
Perforation:	Imperforate
Colors:	Blue
Varieties:	Double transfer (3R1E)

Collectable Stamp Today
Collectable Cancellation Colors:
Black, blue
Collectable Cancellation Varieties:
blue town, red town, carrier, Paid, pen

Value Unused:	$$$$$$
Value Used:	$$$$$
Surviving Covers:	75
Largest Known Multiple:	Unused:5 out of 8 irregular block
	Used:3

A type Ib is a type I at top, like a type Ia is a type I at bottom. These stamps are complete on the top as a type I. The bottom of the design is nearly complete, but either the right or left plume is incomplete.

Type Ib stamps come only from some of the top row positions of the right pane of plate 1 in its early state. Just positions 3,4,5,6,8 and 9R are type Ib. It is estimated that only 500 type Ib stamps still exist, today. Any horizontal multiples of stamps containing a type I stamp contain a type Ib stamps. Because positions 6R1E and 8R1E, the stamps flanking the type I, show the most complete design, they rate the highest type Ib prices.

The largest known unused multiple is an irregular block of 8 with 5 stamps being type Ib. The largest used multiple is a strip of 3 on a cover.

Type Ib is the only one-cent stamp not to have a perforated counterpart.

Figure 3-6. Features of the Type Ib One-Cent Stamp of the 1851 Series. The stamp has the (1) complete frame and ornaments at the top. But at the bottom of the stamp (2) the right plume is incomplete.

Type Ic Imperforate 1851 One-Cent Franklin

Type Ic Imperforate 1851 One-Cent Franklin

Stamp Production

Printer:	Toppan, Carpenter, Casilear
Designer:	Edward Purcell
Engraver:	Joseph I. Pease or William C. Smillie (portrait), Henry Earle or John Casilear (border and lettering)
Format:	2 panes of 100
Plate Numbers:	4
Date of Issue:	April 1857
Earliest Known Use:	May 20, 1857
Uses:	Circular. Drop letter. Three paid the basic 3-cent letter rate. Carriers' fee
Quantity Issued:	60,000

Stamp Features

Size:	20 x 26 mm. (0.8 x 1.0 inches)
Watermark:	None
Perforation:	Imperforate
Colors:	Blue
Varieties:	Curl in C of Cent (96R4)

Collectable Stamp Today
Collectable Cancellation Colors:
Black, blue, red.
Collectable Cancellation varieties:
black town, blue town, pen

Value Unused:	$$$$$
Value Used:	$$$$$

Surviving Covers: 15
Largest Known Multiple: Unused: 2
Used: 2

Type Ic stamp is often is mistaken for Ia. It is the same as type Ia at the top in that the ornaments and outer line are partially cut away. But unlike the type Ia that is complete at the bottom, the right plume and ball are partially complete. This type came only from plate 4 and was produced from only 8 positions of that plate. Of interest, the Scott catalogs do not recognize type Ic with a major catalog number like they do all the other types.

Since this stamp comes from scattered plate positions on plate 4, it cannot be found in multiples larger than a pair.

Figure 3-7. Features of the Type Ic One-Cent Stamp of the 1851 Series. This one-cent 1851 Series Franklin stamp is similar to a type Ia. The (1) top of the stamp is the same, with a break in the outer frame and missing parts of the top ornaments. At the bottom, instead of it being complete like for a Type Ia, (2) the right plume is partially missing.

Type II Imperforate 1851 One-Cent Franklin

Type II Imperforate 1851 One-Cent Franklin

Stamp Production
Printer: Toppan, Carpenter, Casilear
Designer: Edward Purcell
Engraver: Joseph I. Pease or William C. Smillie (portrait), Henry Earle or John Casilear (border and lettering)
Format: 2 panes of 100

Plate Numbers:	1 Early, 1 Late, 2, 3, 4.
Date of Issue:	July 1, 1851
Earliest Known Use:	July 1, 1851 (first day cover)
Uses:	Circular. Drop letter. Three paid the basic 3-cent letter rate. Carriers' fee
Quantity Issued:	12,300,000

Stamp Features

Size:	20 x 26 mm. (0.8 x 1.0 inches)
Watermark:	None
Perforation:	Imperforate
Colors:	Blue
Varieties:	Double transfers, Double transfer one inverted (71L1E), Triple transfer one inverted (91L1E), Cracked plate (2L, 12L, 13L, 23L, 33L, plate 2). Perforated 12 1/2 (unofficial), Curl in hair (3R, 4R, plate 4)

Collectable Stamp Today
Collectable Cancellation Colors:

Black, blue, red, magenta, ultramarine, green, orange

Collectable Cancellation Varieties:

Paid, Way, Steam, numeral, railroad, Steam, Steamboat, carrier, U. S. express mail, Too Late, precanceled, 1855, 1856, 1857, 1858, pen

Value Unused:	$$$$$
Value Used:	$$$$
Surviving Covers:	Several thousand
Largest Known Multiple:	Unused: 12
	Used: 10 (5x2 block)

Type II stamps come from plates 1 early (163 positions), 1 late (4R only), 2 (199 out of 200 positions), 3 (entire plate), and 4 (the 20 top-row positions). A type II one-cent stamp has its top line complete but the top ornaments may be complete or partially cut away. The bottom line is complete but the little balls of the bottom scrolls and the bottom of the lower plume ornaments are missing.

Figure 3-8. Features of the Type II One-Cent Stamp of the 1851 Series. The (1) top line of the frame is complete, but the top ornaments are partially cut away. The (2) bottom line is complete, but the bottom scroll and the bottom of the plume are missing.

Narrow spacing between stamps, especially at the top and bottom, makes fully margined copies very hard to find. Compared to other 1-cent stamps, the ink color is lighter, a powder blue. The impressions are less crisp.

Several types of double transfers have been discovered. Positions 2L, 12L, 13L, and 23L of plate 2 have what is known as the "Big Crack," a huge plate crack. There even is a triple transfer, which is similar to a double transfer, but shows a third entry or two added duplications from the transfer roll.

Toppan, Carpenter & Company experimented with a borrowed perforating machine from England in 1856. The "Chicago Perforations" are a result. They measure 12½ gauge and were used on stamps from Chicago, hence their name.

Type III Imperforate 1851 One-Cent Franklin

Type III Imperforate 1851 One-Cent Franklin

Stamp Production
Printer: Toppan, Carpenter, Casilear
Designer: Edward Purcell
Engraver: Joseph I. Pease or William C. Smillie (portrait), Henry Earle or John Casilear (border and lettering)
Format: 2 panes of 100
Plate Numbers: 2, 4
Date of Issue: Dec. 1855
Earliest Known Use: July 7, 1857
Uses: Circular. Drop letter. Three paid the basic 3-cent letter rate. Carriers' fee
Quantity Issued: Unknown

Stamp Features
Size: 20 x 26 mm. (0.8 x 1.0 inches)
Watermark: None
Perforation: Imperforate
Colors: Blue
Varieties: In a pair with a type IIIa stamp

Collectable Stamp Today
Collectable Cancellation Colors:
Black, blue, red, green
Collectable Cancellation Varieties:
red carrier, black carrier, pen, Paid
Value Unused: $$$$$
Value Used: $$$$

Surviving Covers: 60
Largest Known Multiple: Unused: 2
Used: 3 (strip)

Figure 3-9. Features of the Type III One-Cent Stamp of the 1851 Series. A Type III one-cent stamp of the 1851 series has broken (1) top and (2) bottom frame lines.

Type III stamps came from plate 2 (one position, 99R) and 4 (44 scattered positions). This type has both its top and bottom lines are broken. The amount of the break in the lines varies. Copies with wide breaks in the outer lines (more than 2 mm.) are worth more than those with smaller breaks. The sides of the stamps are complete unlike the similar type V stamps. The finest example of a type III stamp comes from 99R2. It is valued much more than the other type III stamps.

Type IIIa Imperforate 1851 One-Cent Franklin

Type IIIa Imperforate 1851 One-Cent Franklin

Stamp Production

Printer:	Toppan, Carpenter, Casilear
Designer:	Edward Purcell
Engraver:	Joseph I. Pease or William C. Smillie (portrait), Henry Earle or John Casilear (border and lettering)
Format:	2 panes of 100
Plate Numbers:	1 Early, 2, 4
Date of Issue:	July 1, 1851
Earliest Known Use:	July 3, 1851
Uses:	Circular. Drop letter. Three paid the basic 3-cent letter rate. Carriers' fee
Quantity Issued:	650,000

Stamp Features

Size:	20 x 26 mm. (0.8 x 1.0 inches)
Watermark:	None
Perforation:	Imperforate
Colors:	Blue
Varieties:	Double transfer one inverted (81L1E).

Collectable Stamp Today
Collectable Cancellation Colors:
Black, blue, red.
Collectable Cancellation Varieties:
Paid, black carrier, red carrier, pen

Value Unused:	$$$$$
Value Used:	$$$$$

Surviving Covers: Hundreds
Largest Known Multiple: Unused: 4 (2x2 block)
Used: 8 out of a block of 10

Figure 3-10. Features of the Type IIIa One-Cent Stamp of the 1851 Series. This stamp has either a (1) broken top (as in this example) or (2) bottom frame line, (intact in this example) but not both.

Type IIIa one-cent stamps come from plates 1 Early (37 scattered positions), 2, and 4 (110 scattered positions). It is similar to type III but the outer line is broken at the top or at the bottom but both lines are not broken on the same stamp. Most type IIIa stamps have the break in the top line rather than in the bottom line. Much of the top and bottom ornaments are incomplete.

Type IV Imperforate 1851 One-Cent Franklin

Type IV Imperforate 1851 One-Cent Franklin

Stamp Production
Printer: Toppan, Carpenter, Casilear
Designer: Edward Purcell
Engraver: Joseph I. Pease or William C. Smillie (portrait), Henry Earle or John Casilear (border and lettering)
Format: 2 panes of 100
Plate Numbers: 1 Late.
Date of Issue: May 1852
Earliest Known Use: June 5,1852
Uses: Circular. Drop letter. Three paid the basic 3-cent letter rate. Carriers' fee
Quantity Issued: Unknown, but most common 1-cent stamp of the 1851 series

Stamp Features
Size: 20 x 26 mm. (0.8 x 1.0 inches)
Watermark: None
Perforation: Imperforate
Colors: Blue
Varieties: Double transfer, Triple transfer one inverted (71L1L, 81L1L, and 91L1L), Cracked plate, Perforated 12½ (unofficial), Bottom frameline broken (89R1L), Printed on both sides with the reverse printing inverted

Collectable Stamp Today
Collectable Cancellation Colors:
Black, blue, red, ultramarine, brown, green, violet

Collectable Cancellation Varieties:
Paid, Way, Free, Steam, railroad, numeral, Steamboat, Steamship, red carrier, black carrier, U. S. express mail, U. S. Paid, express company cancellation, packet boat, precanceled Paid, 1853, 1855, 1856, 1857, pen
Value Unused: $$$$
Value Used: $$$$
Surviving Covers: Greater than 2,500
Largest Known Multiple: Unused: 99 out of a pane of 100
Used: 22 (irregular block)

Figure 3-11. Close-up of a Type IV One-Cent Stamp of the 1851 Series. Type IV one-cent stamp of the 1851 series is characterized by recuts to the frame. Notice how the top line (1) is sharp, the result of being recut, in contrast to the not recut bottom line (2).

Type IV stamps are similar to type II variety. That is, the top and bottom lines are complete. The top ornaments may be complete or be partially cut away, and the little balls of the bottom scrolls and the bottom of the lower plume ornaments are missing. The difference is the addition of recut lines. In May 1852, in an attempt to improve the stamps made from plate 1, 199 positions on the plate were recut, and many positions were re-entered. No two positions were identically recut although the differences are hard to detect. Therefore, all positions on plate 1 late are type IV, except 4R, which is type II. There are several varieties of recuts. The most common (found at 113 positions) is a recut once at the top and once at the bottom. Others include: just one recut at the top (40 plate positions), recut once at the top and twice at the bottom (21 positions), recut twice at the bottom (11 positions), recut once at the bottom (8 positions), recut once at the bottom and twice at the top (4 positions), and recut twice both at the top and the bottom (2 plate positions).

They are the most commonly issued one-cent stamps of the 1851 series. Type IV comes from plate 1 late.

THREE-CENT STAMPS OF 1851

Orange Brown Imperforate 1851 Three-Cent Washington

Stamp Production
Printer:	Toppan, Carpenter, Casilear
Designer:	Edward Purcell
Engraver:	Joseph Ives Pease (portrait); Henry Earle (border and lettering)
Format:	2 panes of 100
Plate Numbers:	1 Early and Intermediate, 2 Early, 5 Early and 0
Date of Issue:	July 1, 1851
Earliest Known Use:	July 1, 1851 (first day cover)
Uses:	Single-letter rate for less than 3,000 miles. Pair used for double-weight letters or for sent greater than 3,000 miles. Multiples used on foreign rates.
Quantity Issue:	20,000,000

Stamp Features
Size:	20 x 25 mm. (0.8 x 1.0 inches)
Watermark:	None
Perforation:	Imperforate
Colors:	Orange brown, deep orange brown, copper brown
Varieties:	Double transfer, Triple transfer (92L2E), Gash on shoulder, Dot in lower right diamond block (69L5E), Printed on both sides, India paper

Collectable Stamp Today
Collectable Cancellation Colors:
Black, blue, red, orange, orange-red, brown, ultramarine, green, violet

Collectable Cancellations Varieties:
> 1851, 1852, Paid, Way, Free, numeral, railroad, U. S. express mail, Steam, Steamship, Steamboat, packet boat, express company cancellation, blue carrier, black carrier, green carrier, Canada, territorial, pen, numeral

Value Unused: $$$$$
Value Used: $$$$
Surviving Covers: 2,500
Largest Known Multiple: Unused: 39
Used: 8 (2x4 block)

Red Imperforate 1851 Three-Cent Washington

Stamp Production
Printer: Toppan, Carpenter, Casilear
Designer: Edward Purcell
Engraver: Joseph Ives Pease (portrait); Henry Earle (border and lettering)
Format: 2 panes of 100
Plates: 1 Late, 2 Late, 3, 4, 5 Late, 6, 7, and 8.
Date of Issue: 1851
Earliest Known Use: October 6, 1851
Uses: Single-letter rate for less than 3,000 miles. Pair used for double letters or for greater than 3,000 miles. Multiples used on foreign rates.
Quantity Issued: 340,000,000

Stamp Features
Size: 20 x 25 mm. (0.8 x 1.0 inches)
Watermark: None
Perforation: Imperforate

Colors:	Dull red, orange red, rose red, brownish carmine, claret, deep claret, plum, orange brown
Varieties:	Double impression, Double transfer in Three Cents, Double transfer line through Three Cents and rosettes double (92L1L), Triple transfer (92L2L), Double transfer Gents instead of Cents (66R2L), Gash on shoulder, Dot in lower right diamond block (69L5L), Major cracked plate (84L, 94L, 9R, Plate 5L), Intermediate cracked plate (80L, 96L, 71R, Plate 5L), Minor cracked plate (8L, 27L, 31L, 44L, 45L, 51L, 55L, 65L, 74L, 78L, 79L, 7R, 71R, 72R, Plate 5L), Worn plate, Perforated 11 and 12 1/2 (unofficial).

Collectable Stamp Today
Collectable Cancellation Colors:

Black, blue, red, orange, orange red, brown, magenta, ultramarine, green, violet, purple, olive, yellow.

Collectable Cancellations Varieties:

1852 through 1859 year dates, Paid, Way, Free, Too Late, numeral, railroad, U. S. express mail, Steam, Ship, New York Ship, Steamboat, Steamship, packet boat, express company cancellation, red carrier, black carrier, green carrier, blue carrier, Canada, territorial, pen

Value Unused:	$$$$
Value Used:	$$$
Surviving Covers:	40,000
Largest Known Multiple:	Unused: Complete pane of 100
	Used: 24 (8x3 block)

The three-cent stamps of this series feature a profile of George Washington. This started the century long trend on the first president appearing on the United States stamp paying the basic postage rate. It is based on a portrait of Washington by Jean Antoine Houdon. The stamps have the words, US POSTAGE above and THREE CENTS below the portrait. Washington's portrait is set in a mosaic frame. There are lathe work rosettes in each of the four corners.

These stamps were made from July 1,1851 until early 1857, when the perforated varieties of it appeared.

Our knowledge database on this stamp comes from the work of Dr. Carroll Chase. He published the book, "The 3c Stamp of the United States 1851-1857 Issue," in 1929. It is still regarded as the definitive work on the subject.

Printing & Plating

Nine plates, numbered 1 through 8, and one plate having no number, named plate 0, printed this stamp. The identification of individual stamps of every stamp of every plate is made possible by all the recutting on these plates. This recutting is so varied that one can identify the position of each stamp. The most important variation used to identify a stamp position is the recut inner vertical framelines. All this tedious identification is the legacy of Chase.

The paper used for the 3-cent stamp is usually white wove. It is moderately thick, opaque, of high quality. It was machine made. The paper varies considerably stamp to stamp. Though not watermarked, stitch watermarked stamps exist.

The gum is varied but usually is pale. It was applied by hand to the panes of 100 after the sheets were cut.

Like the other stamps of this series, narrow spacing between stamps makes fully margined copies hard to find. At least half of the surviving stamps are faulty.

Stamp Color Issued	Plates	Earliest Use	Quantity
Orange Brown	1 Early 1 Intermediate 2 Early 5 Early 0	July 1, 1851	20,000,000
Red	1 Late 2 Late 3 4 5 Late 6 7 8	October 6, 1851	40,000,000

Colors

All imperforate three-cent stamps are type I. Type I stamps have an outer frame line at top and bottom as well as at the sides. The frame lines form an unbroken rectangle around each stamp.

The three-cent imperforate Washington stamps are separated and classified by color rather than by type. The two major varieties are orange brown and red. The orange-brown is valued at 7 to 9 times that of the red stamp. There are differences other than color that distinguish the two types, namely the recut lines. In fact, the only sure method of determining whether one has the more valuable orange-brown stamp is by looking at the plating differences. Also, since the orange-brown were the first stamps, coming from new plates, they have sharper features. The orange brown stamps come from plates 1 early and intermediate states, 2 early, 5 early and 0. None had plate numbers at the time of printing (plate 0 never did). Plate 1 (early) didn't even have a marginal imprint. The dull red stamps come from plates: 1 late, 2 late, 3, 4, 5 late, 6, 7 and 8.

The even subtler stamp shades can be separated by their year of use. For 1851, they are orange-brown, with rare yellowish orange-brown and even rarer bright orange-brown. For 1852, the stamp colors are brownish-carmine, and a small printing in claret and deep claret. For 1853, one sees dull red and dull rose red, and a scarce yellowish dull red. For 1854, the color was rose red. In 1855, the color was dull orange-red. The impressions generally were poor due to low quality ink. For 1856, one finds dull yellowish rose red, and brownish carmine. Finally for 1857, the colors were claret, brownish-claret, yellowish-brown and pale rose brown.

Some of the ink used for the 3 cent 1851 stamps had a small radioactive component. There is a cover that had been folded so that the stamp was held tightly against the cover for years, producing a clear second image of the stamp in reverse!

Plate Varieties

Double transfers, triple transfers, shifted transfers, recutting, and cracked plates (especially on 6 positions of plate 5L) are the major plate varieties. Two stamps are known with a true double impression, evidence that the sheet from which it came went through the printing press twice. There are stamps printed on both sides, and the unofficial perforated varieties.

Use

This stamp paid the single letter rate of three cents for any distance up to 3,000 miles. Therefore, it is found on ordinary letters mailed from one point to another throughout the country, excepting those that went between the two coasts. Until April 1, 1855, the rate for single letters traveling more than 3,000 miles was 6 cents and this produced many used pairs of the stamp. Two stamps also paid the one-half to one-ounce double-weight letter rate. The stamp is found combined with other stamps to pay the higher foreign rates.

Cancellations and Covers

Figure 3-12. Example of a Three-Cent Stamp on a Cover. Since the three-cent stamp of this series paid the basic postage rate at that time, it is found on a wide variety of covers. This cover was mailed from Philadelphia to Providence. Note the postal marking which serves both to note the source of the letter as well as cancel the stamp. This was before duplex postal markings were universal.

Because this stamp paid the most common postal rate, it is extremely common on covers. For the dull red variety, there are more than 40,000 covers, while there are more than 2,500 orange brown stamps on cover. Rarely, the stamp is found bisected on cover. Three and one third stamps were used to pay the later 10-cent rate between coasts. And a half of a three-cent was used as payment for the 1-cent postage on unsealed circulars. A cover that has a block of 12 of this stamp is the largest block known on cover. It was mailed from Texas to Denmark. Covers with this stamp and with stamps of a foreign country also can be found in rare instances.

Chase ranks the most common cancel colors as black, blue, red, green, brown, magenta, ultramarine, orange, and violet. Black and blue are the most common colors for town postmarks.

The stamps are found with a wide variety of postmarks. These include railroads, boats, steamships, steamboats, packet markings, and express companies. Some letters, franked with these stamps after they were demonetized, are struck with "OLD STAMPS NOT RECOGINZED" or "DUE 3 OLD STAMP," indicating their illegal use.

Duplex Cancellations

Up until this time, post offices used the town date to cancel stamps. This practice was inefficient, as the dates did not show up well when struck across the stamp. So when postage stamp use became widespread in 1851, the combination of town date stamp and canceling device gradually came into use. In fact, by the time of the postal regulations of 1859 required a device to cancel the stamps and posting the town name and date. This duplex stamp is what is still used today. It combines the town date with a killer mark canceling the stamp.

Multiples

While pairs and the strips of three, are not scarce, blocks of four are valued at 100 times that of a single stamp. The largest unused multiple of orange brown stamps is a block of 39, with the largest used multiple being a block of eight (2x4). For the dull red variety, the largest unused multiples are complete panes of 100. The largest used multiple is a block of 24 (8x3).

FIVE-CENT STAMP OF 1851

Imperforate 1851 Five-Cent Jefferson

Stamp Production
Printer:	Toppan, Carpenter, Casilear
Designer:	Edward Purcell
Engravers:	Joseph Ives Pease (portrait); Cyrus Durand (border): Henry Earle (lettering)
Format:	2 panes of 100
Plate Numbers:	1
Date of Issue:	January 1,1856
Earliest Known Use:	March 24, 1856
Uses:	Foreign-destination rates, usually as multiples. Registration fee. Shore to ship rate.
Quantity Issued:	150,000

Stamp Features
Size:	19.5 x 25.5 mm. (0.8 x 1.0 inches)
Watermark:	None
Perforation:	Imperforate
Colors:	Red brown, dark red brown

Varieties:	Double transfer (40R), Defective transfer (23R)

Collectable Stamp Today
Collectable Cancellation Colors:
Black, red, magenta, blue, green
Collectable Cancellation Varieties:
1856, 1857, 1858, Paid, Steamship, U. S. express mail, express company cancellation, Steamboat, railroad, numeral, pen

Value Unused:	$$$$$$
Value Used:	$$$$$
Surviving Covers:	Less than 150
Largest Known Multiple:	Unused: 4
	Used: 6 (3x2 block)

Though this stamp is considered as part of the 1851 series, it was not issued until January 1st of 1856, with the earliest known use of March 24, 1856. The stamp has a portrait of Thomas Jefferson, after a painting of him by Gilbert Stuart. It was the first United States stamp to portray someone other than Franklin or Washington. Some authorities feel this founder of the Democratic Party was chosen for the stamp because of the then Democratic President Franklin Pierce. The words, FIVE CENTS, are at the bottom, U. S. POSTAGE, at the top of the stamp. The portrait is in a rounded rectangle, filled with two rows of lathe work. The ink colors are shades of brown.

More than half of the surviving copies of this stamp are faulty. The brief period during which this stamp was made imperforate makes it a rare stamp today. Fakes are made from perforated 5-cent copies. However, these forgeries can be easily spotted as they are brown, not red brown.

Printing and Plating

All stamps were printed from a single plate, plate 1, in sheets of 200 impressions. The sheets are divided by a centerline into two panes of 100 stamps. Each pane has a vertical margin imprint on the side selvage.

The imperforate 5 cents are of a single type, type I. On the type I stamps, the projections on all sides the stamps are complete. The shades of the imperforates are red brown and dark red brown.

Plate Varieties

There are two minor plate varieties: a double transfer (40R) and a defective transfer (23R).

Use

The five-cent stamp traditionally was thought to pay for the new registration fee. Stanley B. Ashbrook, a famous student of 1851-57 stamps, believed the stamp had nothing to do with registered mail as the registration fee was paid almost always in cash, not stamps. It was, instead, needed for the inland rate (shore to ship and vice versa) on mail going overseas. The stamp, in multiples, paid foreign rates. For example, because of a French postal treaty, a strip of three 5-cent stamps or a single used with a 10-cent stamp paid the 15-cent rate to France.

The earliest known usage is a cover dated March 24. 1856 mailed from Philadelphia to Nova Scotia.

Cancellations and Covers

Less than 150 covers with this stamp survive today. It is more difficult to find a single on cover than a pair of stamps or a strip of 3. Both a block and a strip of 6 stamps exist on covers. The stamp is known on one cover originating abroad, from New Brunswick, Canada.

Multiples

A single unused block of 4 exists. The largest used block was 11 stamps, which has been broken up. Today, the largest used multiple is a block of six stamps (3x2).

TEN-CENT STAMPS OF 1851

Figure 3-13. Ten-Cent Washington Die Proof. This is a close up of the ten-cent Washington die proof showing the complete stamp design, not seen on the issued stamps.

This stamp was issued for the new ten-cent charge for letters sent over 3,000 miles (usually between the East Coast and California). Effective April 1,1855, the rate was increased from 6 cents to improve the cross-country mail service.

The stamp has Stuart's three-quarter portrait of Washington. The words, TEN CENTS, are at the bottom and US POSTAGE in an arc is at the top of the stamp. Around the upper portion of the portrait are 13 stars. The borders are scrollwork.

There was little time after the rate change was passed until it became effective to create a 10-cent stamp. It was quickly created for use in early May 1855. On close examination, one sees engraving slips and poorly executed lines, suggesting the time pressure to complete the job resulting in lesser quality work. However, the stamp is attractively designed and printed in a pretty deep green color. It is found in three shades: green, dark green and yellowish green. The spacing between stamps is a bit wider than other stamps of this series.

Types

Only one plate, plate 1, made all the ten-cent imperforates of 1851, and it also printed many of the later perforated ten-cent stamps of the 1857. As with all of the stamps of this series, it was printed in sheets of 200, cut into panes of 100.

These stamps are found in 4 types that come from different positions of this single printing plate. This plate has had all of its 200 positions identified by Mortimer Neinken, Frank S. Levi Jr., and Jerome S. Wagshal.

Like the one-cent stamp of this series, the different stamp types come from incomplete transfer from the master die to the transfer roll to the plate. The plate designs were either burnished or short transferred. A few positions had to be recut by hand, resulting in type IV, the scarcest of the four types.

Type	Definition	Imperforate Positions (Plate 1)	Perforated Plates & Positions
I	Nearly Complete	Bottom rows	Plate 1, Bottom rows
II	Incomplete Bottom	Most common 93 of 200 positions	Plate 1, 93 positions
III	Incomplete at Top and Bottom	79 of 200 positions	Plate 1, 79 positions
IV	Recuts	Least common 65L, 74L, 86L, 3R, 54L, 55L, 76L, 64L	Least common Plate 1 65L, 74L, 86L, 3R, 54L, 55L, 76L, 64L
V	Incomplete at Sides	NONE	Most common Plate 2

Figure 3-14. Anatomy of the 1851 Series Ten-Cent Washington Stamp. The completeness of this stamp determines its type. The outside parts are named in their description: (1) top line, (2) top ornament, (3) X oval line, (4) side ornaments, (5) side pearls, (6) bottom shell, and (7) bottom line.

Use

The earliest known use of a 10-cent Washington imperforate is on May 12, 1855. The stamp paid the 10-cent transcontinental rate. It was also used for foreign rates, to Europe, mostly France and Germany.

Cancellations & Covers

Cancellations include the year date, paid, steamship, territorial, express company, numerals and ink manuscript. Cancellation colors include black, blue, red brown, ultramarine, magenta and green.

Several thousand 10-cent covers still exist, today. Interesting covers include those carried by coast to coast by private carriers. To comply with the monopolistic postal law at that time, such letters had to be carried in government envelopes and have the government postage of 10 cents paid, even though the sender did not use the postal service. Western covers, illustrated with mining scenes especially are prized.

Multiples

The largest mint multiple is a horizontal strip of 8 stamps, from positions 71L-78L. The largest used multiple is a block of 21 stamps (3x7).

Type I Imperforate 1851 Ten-Cent Washington

Type I Imperforate 1851 Ten-Cent Washington

Stamp Production

Printer:	Toppan, Carpenter, Casilear
Designer:	Edward Purcell
Engravers:	Joseph Ives Pease (portrait), Henry Earle (border and lettering)
Format:	2 panes of 100 (20 positions, bottom rows of both panes)
Plate Numbers:	1
Date of Issue:	Early May 1855
Earliest Known Use:	July 11, 1855
Uses:	Greater than 3,000 mile transcontinental rate, after June 30,1851. Foreign rates to Europe, mostly France and Germany.
Quantity Issued:	500,000

Stamp Features

Size:	19 x 24.2 mm. (0.7 x 1.0 inches)

Watermark:	None
Perforation:	Imperforate
Colors:	Green, dark green, yellowish green
Varieties:	Double transfer (100R), Curl in left X (99R).

Collectable Stamp Today
Collectable Cancellation Colors:
Black, blue, red, magenta, orange
Collectable Cancellation Varieties:
1855, 1856, 1857, Paid, Steamship, U. S. express mail, Steamboat, railroad, territorial, numeral, pen

Value Unused:	$$$$$$
Value Used:	$$$$
Surviving Covers:	Several thousand of all ten-cent imperforate stamps
Largest Known Multiple:	Unused: 5 (strip)
	Used: 4 (strip on a cover)

Type I stamps are the most complete stamps. At the top, the outer lines above the X's and the U.S. POSTAGE are missing. The bottom part is nearly complete, though the left shell lacks some bottom lines. There are position dots in the lower left comers. The stamps came from the bottom row of the single printing plate. Therefore, there are 20 type I positions out of the 200-subject plate.

Figure 3-15. Features of the Type I Ten-Cent Stamp of the 1851 Series. This stamp has nearly complete design of the stamp except for (1) the missing top frame line and (2) the top lines of the X oval. The (3) side ornaments, (4) bottom shell and (5) bottom line are mostly intact/

Type II Imperforate 1851 Ten-Cent Washington

Type II Imperforate 1851 Ten-Cent Washington

Stamp Production

Printer:	Toppan, Carpenter, Casilear
Designer:	Edward Purcell
Engravers:	Joseph Ives Pease (portrait), Henry Earle (border and lettering)
Format:	2 panes of 100 (93 of the 200 plate positions)
Plate Numbers:	1
Date of Issue:	Early May1855
Earliest Known Use:	May 12, 1855
Uses:	Greater than 3,000 mile transcontinental rate after June 30,1851. Foreign rates to Europe, mostly France and Germany.
Quantity Issued:	2,325.000

Stamp Features

Size:	19 x 24.2 mm. (0.7 x 1.0 inches)
Watermark:	None
Perforation:	Imperforate
Colors:	Green, dark green, yellowish green
Varieties:	Double transfer (31L, 51L, 20R), Curl opposite left X (10R)

Collectable Stamp Today
Collectable Cancellation Colors:

Black, blue, red, brown, ultramarine, magenta, green, violet

Collectable Cancellation Varieties:

1855, 1856, 1857, 1858, Paid, Way, Free, steamship, U. S. express mail, express company, steamboat, railroad, territorial, numeral, pen

III

Value Unused:	$$$$$
Value Used:	$$$$
Surviving Covers:	Several thousand of all ten-cent imperforate stamps
Largest Known Multiple:	Unused: 5 (strip)
	Used: 9 (strip on a cover), also 10 out of a block of 21

Type II stamps have an incomplete design at bottom. Here, the outer line is broken in the middle and both shells are incomplete. The top of the design, including the outer lines, is complete. There usually is a position dot in the upper left corner of the stamp. This is the most common of the four types of 10-cent stamps, found on 93 positions out of 200, on the plate.

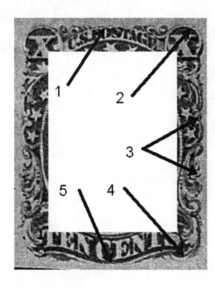

Figure 3-16. Features of the Type II Ten-Cent Stamp of the 1851 Series. This stamp has a complete design at the top of the stamp, including the (1) top line and (2) the X oval. The (3) sides are complete. The bottom, however, is missing (4) the shells and (5) bottom line.

Type III Imperforate 1851 Ten-Cent Washington

Type III Imperforate 1851 Ten-Cent Washington

Stamp Production

Printer:	Toppan, Carpenter, Casilear
Designer:	Edward Purcell
Engravers:	Joseph Ives Pease (portrait), Henry Earle (border and lettering)
Format:	2 panes of 100. (79 of the 200 plate positions)
Plate Numbers:	1
Date of Issue:	Early May 1855

Earliest Known Use: May 19, 1855
Uses: Greater than 3,000 mile transcontinental rate, after June 30,1851. Foreign rates, to Europe, mostly France and Germany.
Quantity Issued: 2.000,000

Stamp Features
Size: 19 x 24.2 mm. (0.7 x 1.0 inches)
Watermark: None
Perforation: Imperforate
Colors: Green, dark green, yellowish green
Varieties: Double transfer at top and bottom, Curl on forehead (85L), Curl to right of left X (87R)

Collectable Stamp Today
Collectable Cancellation Colors:
Black, blue, red, orange red, orange, brown, magenta, green, violet
Collectable Cancellation Varieties:
1855, 1856, 1857, 1858, Paid, steamship, U. S. express mail, express company, railroad, territorial, Canada, packet boat, numeral, pen
Value Unused: $$$$$
Value Used: $$$$
Surviving Covers: Several thousand of all ten-cent imperforate stamps
Largest Known Multiple: Unused: 5 (strip)
Used: 6 (strip) also 11 out of a block of 21

Type III stamps have incomplete designs both on the top and the bottom. At the top, the lines are missing above the top label and X's. The shells at the bottom of the stamp are incomplete, especially on the right. Most of the bottom line below TEN CENTS is missing.

Type III stamps come from 79 positions out of 200, making it the second most common variety.

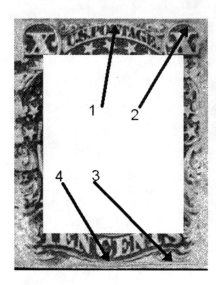

Figure 3-17. Features of the Type III Ten-Cent Stamp of the 1851 Series. This stamp is incomplete both at the top and the bottom. The top is missing both (1) the top line and (2) the lines above the X. The bottom is both (3) the complete shells, and the (4) bottom line.

Type IV Imperforate 1851 Ten-Cent Washington

Type IV Imperforate 1851 Ten-Cent Washington

Stamp Production
Printer: Toppan, Carpenter, Casilear
Designer: Edward Purcell
Engravers: Joseph Ives Pease (portrait), Henry Earle (border and lettering)
Format: 2 panes of 100 (8 of 200 plate positions)
Plate Numbers: 1
Date of Issue: Early May1855
Earliest Known Use: July 10, 1855

Uses: Greater than 3,000 mile transcontinental rate, after June 30,1851. Foreign rates to Europe, mostly France and Germany.

Quantity Issued: 200,000

Stamp Features

Size: 19 x 24.2 mm. (0.7 x 1.0 inches)

Watermark: None

Perforation: Imperforate

Colors: Green, dark green, yellowish green

Varieties: None

Collectable Stamp Today

Collectable Cancellation Colors:

                    Black, blue, red, brown

Collectable Cancellation Varieties:

                    1857, 1859, Paid, steamship, express company, territorial, numeral, pen

Value Unused: $$$$$$

Value Used: $$$$$

Surviving Covers: Several thousand of all ten-cent imperforate stamps

Largest Known Multiple: Unused: 2

                    Used: 2, also 4 out of larger blocks

Type IV issues are stamps that were reengraved after the designs had been transferred to the plate. Eight positions (54L. 55L, 64L, 65L, 74L, 76L, 86L, 3R) of the 200-subject plate are type IV, making this the most rare variety. In fact, unused, this is one of the rarest of all nineteenth century United States stamps. The recutting consisted of enhancements in the outer framelines above POSTAGE and below. Positions 65L, 74L, 86 L, and 3R are recut along the outer line at the top. Positions 54L, 55L, and 76L are recut along the outer line at the bottom. Position 64L was recut at the top and the bottom outer lines. Positions 54-55L and 64-65L form a block of four stamps all type IV, showing the three varieties of recutting.

Figure 3-18. Close-Up of the Type IV Ten-Cent Stamp of the 1851 Series. This shows the recut line at the top of the stamp.

TWELVE-CENT STAMP OF 1851

Imperforate 1851 Twelve-Cent Washington

Imperforate 1851 Twelve-Cent Washington

Stamp Production
Printer:	Toppan, Carpenter, Casilear
Designer:	Edward Purcell
Engraver:	Joseph Ives Pease (portrait), Cyrus Durand (border), Henry Earle (lettering)
Format:	2 panes of 100
Plate Numbers.	1 (no number)
Date of Issue:	July 1, 1851
Earliest Known Use:	Aug. 4, 1851
Uses:	Foreign rate in pairs to Great Britain. Bisected for domestic use. Quadruple basic rate.
Quantity issued:	2,500,000

Stamp Features
Size:	20 x 28 mm. (0.7 x 1.0 inches)
Watermark:	None
Perforation:	Imperforate
Colors:	Black, gray black, deep smudgy black, intense black.
Varieties:	Printed on both sides, Double transfer, Triple transfer (5R and 49R), Not recut in lower right corner, Recut in lower right corner, Recut in lower left corner (43L, 53L, 63L, 73L, 100L), Cracked plate (32R)

Collectable Stamp Today
Collectable Cancellation Colors:
Black, red, blue, brown, magenta, orange-red, orange, green
Collectable Cancellation Varieties:
Paid, Way, steamship, steamboat, supplementary mail type A, railroad, Honolulu, U. S. express mail, pen
Value Unused: $$$$$
Value Used: $$$$
Surviving Covers: 2,000
Largest Known Multiple: Unused: 30 (block 10x3)
Used: 16 (block 4x4).

The twelve-cent imperforate stamp is one of the three original members of the series. The stamp has a three-quarter-face portrait of George Washington, after the famous Stuart painting of him. The words, TWELVE CENTS are below and US POSTAGE, above the vignette. The portrait is surrounded in a mosaic frame, with a lathe work rosette in each corner. The stamp measures 20 mm by 25mm.

The stamp paper varies from thin to thick. It is a hard, white-woven type. The gum varies from nearly colorless to amber. The ink hues are gray black, black, deep smudgy black and intense black.

Like others of this series, these stamps were printed very close together. Many copies, therefore, lack margins, and the design is typically cut on one or more side. Faulty stamps are common.

Tracy and Ashbrook studied this stamp and their work is found in a 1926 book. Neinken also wrote a handbook about the stamp in 1964.

Printing and Plating

The 1851 twelve-cent stamps were printed from a single plate, called plate 1. While it is referred to as such, there was no number on the plate, only margin markings of the printer. The plating positions for the stamp have been reconstructed and all 200 positions are identified. There is a great deal of recutting on the plate. Nearly every position had the outer frame lines recut. This is because the original framelines were not engraved deeply enough into the master die.

Plate Varieties

Position 100L is recut in the lower left corner. Positions 43L, 53L, 63L, and 73L have recuts in both the right and left lower corners. The 89L position shows a double recut line in the upper portion of the inside right frame line. The most pronounced double transfer is 27R with the entire wording, U.S. POSTAGE and all four rosettes showing it. Position 49R has a double transfer that appears as dots in the lower right corner. There is also a double transfer at 5R.

Triple transfers come from 1R and 49R.

Another variety is stamps printed on both sides, with four known copies.

Use

The 12-cent imperforate Washington was issued on July 1, 1851, the same date as the original 1-cent Franklin and the 3-cent Washington stamp of the series. Although the 12-cent stamp of this series was issued at the same time, its earliest recorded date of use is August 4, 1851, over a month later.

This stamp was an awkward denomination. Proof is that on cover, bisects are more common than single uses! The commonly bisected stamp paid the 6-cent coast-to-coast rate, and the double letter 3-cent domestic rate. Diagonal bisects are the most common, with vertical halves very rare. One-fourth of a 12-cent stamp on cover, used for the standard postage rate, exist. It was issued for quadruple the ordinary rate, but the stamp was seldom used for this purpose. In pairs, it paid the 24-cent rate to Britain, the most common use of this stamp.

Cancellations and Covers

As mentioned above, this stamp was bisected for use. Diagonal halves and even quartered portions of the stamp have been found on cover.

The most common cancellations are black, blue, and red. Less common are brown, magenta, orange and green strikes. Postal markings found on used stamps include paid, way, steamship, steamboat, supplementary mail, railroad and pen cancels. Rare postal markings are cancellations are from Honolulu and U.S. express mail.

There are about 2,000 surviving covers with this stamp.

Carrier Stamps

Figure 3-19. Example of a Private Carrier Stamp and Cover. This is a cover with a private carrier stamp from the Honour's City Post of Charleston, South Carolina. On the right is a close of the stamp, which is 2-cents denomination, with black ink on bluish paper.

At this time, mail had to be dropped off and picked up at the local post office. Postage only paid for carrying mail from one post office to another. Since businesses could spend a lot of time picking up and dropping off the mail, they hired messengers for that purpose. Soon, private delivery services sprang up to handle this function. These private letter carriers not only carried mail to and from post offices but also between points on their routes. Their charge was usually 1 or 2 cents per letter. This was called private carrier service. ***Private carriers' stamps*** were used to pay for delivery to a post office on letters being mailed out and for delivery from the post office. And there were ***local stamps*** issued by independent mail routes and services, express companies and other private posts, used to pay for point to point delivery fees.

Figure 3-20. Example of a Local Stamp. This is the most famous of all local stamps, that of Wells, Fargo,and Company. It was used to pay the private postage for the Pony Express.

Soon a few large post offices offered home mail pickup and delivery. The postal act of Congress of March 3,1851, which became effective July 1,1851, provided for the collecting and delivery service. The charge for this carrier service was one cent in addition to the regular postage. Some post offices that offered carrier service issued their own one-cent stamps to indicate the payment of that charge. These were called *semi-official carrier stamps*. They only were valid in the city in which they were issued. They were printed under the authority of the local postmaster.

Some of these letter carriers received salaries for their work. Others were paid commissions from the fees received for the delivery and collection of letters carried by them. It wasn't until after the discontinuance of carrier fees in 1863 that all carriers were made government employees, and paid by a salary.

Figure 3-21. Example of a Semi-Official Local Stamp. This is an unused example of the Baltimore semi-official stamp, used in Baltimore to pay for local mail delivery, there. It was printed in 1851.

In 1851, the same time the new regular stamp issue of that year was printed, postmaster general Nathan Hall issued a one-cent carrier stamp for use by those post offices that offered carrier service. The new 1851 one-cent stamp could have been used, but Hall wanted a separate stamp to distinguish between postage fees between post offices and carrier fees to and from the post office.

FRANKLIN ONE-CENT CARRIER STAMP

Franklin One-Cent Carrier Stamp

Stamp Production
Printer:	Toppan, Carpenter, Casilear
Format:	2 panes of 100 each, left and right, from plate of 200
Plate Numbers:	1
Date of Issue:	Sept. 1851
Earliest Known Use:	Oct. 28,1851.
Uses:	Local carrier fee
Quantity issued:	310,000

Stamp Features
Size:	19.5 x 24.5 mm (0.7 x 1.0 inches)
Watermark:	None
Perforation:	Imperforate
Colors:	Dull blue ink on rose paper
Varieties:	Major plate crack, Corner plate cracks (91 L), Double transfer.

Collectable Stamp Today
Collectable Cancellation Colors:
red star (Philadelphia), blue town (Philadelphia), red town (New York), black town (New York), blue grid (New York), blue grid (New York), black grid (New York), black grid (New Orleans), green grid (New Orleans).
Collectable Cancellation Varieties:
None.
Value Unused: $$$$$
Value Used: $$$$$

The stamp contractor for the 1851 stamp series, Toppan, Carpenter, and Casilear, printed the one-cent carrier stamp. The one-cent carrier stamp of 1851 featured a portrait of Benjamin Franklin, similar to the one found on the one-cent postage stamp. The biggest difference was that the portrait on the carrier stamps faced left instead of right. The top of the carrier stamp was labeled with the word, CARRIERS, placed between stars enclosed in brackets. At the bottom was the word, STAMP, between similar ornaments.

Because of the short life, the Franklin carrier stamp was only used in the cities of Philadelphia, New Orleans, and Boston, and New York.

Essays of the Franklin carrier stamp, showing either the complete design or just the vignette, can be found today.

EAGLE ONE-CENT CARRIER STAMP

Eagle One-Cent Carrier Stamp

Stamp Production

Printer:	Toppan, Carpenter, Casilear
Format:	2 panes of 100 each, top and bottom, from sheet of 200
Plate Numbers:	1
Date of Issue:	Nov. 17, 1851
Earliest Known Use:	Jan. 3, 1852
Uses:	Local carrier fee
Quantity Issued:	10,225,553

Stamp Features

Size:	23.5 x19 mm (0.9 x 0.7 inches)
Watermark:	None
Perforation:	Imperforate
Colors:	Blue
Varieties:	Double transfer

Collectable Stamp Today
Collectable Cancellation Colors:

red star (Philadelphia), Cincinnati black grid, blue grid, red grid, black town, blue town, red town, Kensington, Pa. (red), blue squared target, red squared target

Collectable Cancellation Varieties:

railroad, black carrier, red carrier, carrier's initial, manuscript

Value Unused:	$$$
Value Used:	$$$

Soon after the new carrier stamp was issued, the Philadelphia assistant postmaster, John C. Montgomery, noticed the great similarity between the designs of the one-cent postage stamp and the carrier stamp. Taking this information to the printer, they together designed a new carrier stamp that would eliminate the confusion that the Franklin design caused. In what would never happen today, the printer made this eagle carrier stamp without any additional cost to the Post Office Department.

The eagle stamp, the second and last carrier stamp, came into use on November 17,1851. The Franklin carrier stamps, which had been in use for one month, were withdrawn and any remainders were destroyed. The eagle carrier stamp is a very beautiful one, prized by today's stamp collectors. The stamp features a majestic eagle surrounded by the words, U.S.P.O. DESPATCH PREPAID ONE CENT.

The use of separate stamps for carrier fees continued until 1863 when the charge for delivery of letters was absorbed into the regular postal charges.

Figure 3-22. Example of a Cover with a Carrier Stamp. This letter is franked with the one-cent Eagle carrier stamp (to pay the local carrier fee) plus the three-cent Washington, (to pay the between post offices cost).

Carrier postmarks have the words Carrier, City Delivery, or U.S.P.O. Dispatch to show the delivery of mail by U.S. Government carriers. Such postmarks, also, are found on the 1857 one-cent regular issue stamps, when they were used to the pay the carrier fee.

CARRIER REPRINTS

First Reprinting of One-Cent Franklin Carrier Stamp

Stamp Production

Printer:	Continental Bank Note Company
Format:	2 panes of 100 each, top and bottom, from sheet of 200
Plate Numbers:	Original plate
Date of Issue:	May 19, 1875
Uses:	Souvenir
Quantity issued:	10,000

Stamp Features

Size:	19.5 x 24.5 mm (0.7 x 1.0 inches)
Watermark:	None
Perforation:	Imperforate
Colors:	Blue on rose paper, indigo on rose paper.
Varieties:	Corner plate cracks (91L)

Collectable Stamp Today

Value Unused:	$$$

Second Reprinting of the One-Cent Franklin Carrier Stamp

Stamp Production
Printer: Continental Bank Note Company
Format: 2 panes of 100 each, top and bottom, from sheet of 200
Plate Numbers: Original plate
Date of Issue: Dec. 22, 1875
Uses: Souvenir
Quantity issued: 10,000

Stamp Features
Size: 19.5 x 24.5 mm (0.7 x 1.0 inches)
Watermark: None
Perforation: 12
Colors: Blue.
Varieties: None

Collectable Stamp Today
Value Unused: $$$$$$

First Reprinting of the One-Cent Eagle Carrier Stamp

Stamp Production
Printer: Continental Bank Note Company
Format: 2 panes of 100 each, top and bottom, from sheet of 200
Plate Numbers: Original plate
Date of Issue: May 19, 1875
Uses: Souvenir
Quantity issued: 10,000

Stamp Features
Size: 23.5 x19 mm (0.9 x 0.7 inches)
Watermark: None
Perforation: Imperforate
Colors: Blue.
Varieties: None

Collectable Stamp Today
Value Unused: $$$

Second Reprinting of the One-Cent Eagle Carrier Stamp

Stamp Production
Printer: Continental Bank Note Company
Format: 2 panes of 100 each, top and bottom, from sheet of 200
Plate Numbers: Original plate
Date of Issue: Dec. 12, 1875
Uses: Souvenir
Quantity issued: 10,000

Stamp Features
Size: 23.5 x19 mm (0.9 x 0.7 inches)
Watermark: None
Perforation: 12
Colors: Blue.
Varieties: None

Collectable Stamp Today
Value Unused: $$$$

Like for the general usage postage stamps, Continental Bank Note Company reprinted the official carrier stamps for souvenirs and display for the Philadelphia Centennial. There were two sets, each 10,000 copies, of reprints. The first reprinting was done on May 19, 1875, the second on December 22, 1875. The first reprinted stamps, like the issued stamps, were imperforate. The second reprinting was perforated 12.

The first reprinting of the Franklin stamp was on the original rose paper, obtained from Toppan, Carpenter, Casilear. They can be distinguished from the original stamps in that they appear muddy. The second reprinting was on thicker, paler paper, plus it has perforations.

Both of the eagle reprints were printed on the same hard, white papers used for the postage issue reprints. These reprints may be differentiated from the originals under ultraviolet light, which shows off the extra whiteness of the paper.

1857 Perforated Issues

The 1857 stamp series is just a continuation of the previous 1851 stamp series. Toppan, Carpenter and Company still printed this issue. It differs in just two respects from the earlier 1851 one. The stamps are now had perforations and there are three more stamp denominations.

Beginnings of Stamp Perforations

Separation is the word for the method used to take stamps apart from one another. Stamps up until this time were imperforate. They had to be cut with scissors or by hand, which often damaged them.

Figure 3-23. Perforation Gauge Definition. The number of holes per two centimeters is the measure used to describe a stamp's perforation. For compound perforations, such as this stamp, one states the horizontal measurements, then the vertical measurements. So this stamp's perforation is 11 by 10½.

After the postage stamp became a popular way to pay for sending mail, attention turned to improving the methods of separating the individual stamps. The use of perforations is a wonderful invention, the idea of Henry Archer, an Irish businessman working in London. The English first used Archer's product, in 1854, issuing the world's first perforated postage stamp. Perforating is punching a row of holes between stamps. It quickly became and still is the most common way to separate stamps. After the separation, there are little bridges of paper, called the teeth of a stamp. The little round holes of cut out paper, which sometimes are still loosely attached, are called chads.

The perforations on stamps are measured in a standard way.

Differing perforations on otherwise same stamp can be a deciding factor between a rare, valuable and a common junk one. One simply counts the number of holes per two centimeters. That number is a shorthand way of giving the perforation. Commercial perforation gauges are rulers that match up a stamp to possible measures for the stamp collector.

Perforations that do not measure the same on all four sides of a stamp are *compound perforations*. One notes compound perforations first by giving the horizontal (top and bottom) measurements, then the vertical (side) measurements.

United States stamps are perforated in English measurements (that is, the thousandths of an inch) rather than metric. Experts use this fact to identify faked perforations, using extremely accurate English gauges to measure both the spacing and diameter of the perforation holes.

Because of the increased usage of postage stamps in the United States, the Postmaster General asked the stamp printer, Toppan, Carpenter, to investigate the perforated stamps being made in Great Britain. The English firm of Perkins, Bacon, that printed stamps for Britain, advised Toppan, Carpenter. Perkins, Bacon now was at odds with Henry Archer. So they referred the Toppan, Carpenter firm to another manufacturer, Bemrose and Sons. In March 1856, Toppan, Carpenter received its Bemrose machine, for price of $600. Toppan had to convert it from a rouletting device to a round-hole perforator, which was not easy. The machine had perforating rollers that were rolled across the sheets, once horizontally and then vertically. The spacing between the rollers was varied to the differing lengths and widths of individual stamps. Finally in 1857, the first perforated stamps, type I, 3-cent Washington, made their appearance. For the extra work, Toppan, Carpenter received the kingly sum of an extra 2.5 cents per 1,000 stamps perforated.

The perforation of the 1857 stamps is 15½ gauge. This means there are 15½ perforations for each 2 centimeters of stamp edge.

New Denominations

In 1860, Postmaster General Joseph Holt wanted large denomination stamps for high overseas postage rates. The increased use of adhesive stamps on foreign-bound letters created this need. Three new denominations of stamps were issued: 24-cent, 30-cent, and 90-cent stamps. The 24-cent stamp paid the postage on single-weight letters to Great Britain. The 30-cent paid the postage to Germany. The 90-cent stamp was for odd high rate postage.

Foreign Postal Rates During the 1850's	
Canada	10 cents
Great Britain	24 cents
Germany and France	30 cents

Printing Contract Extended

Figure 3-24. 1857 Plate Imprint Block. Shown is an imprint block of eight three-cent 1875 stamps with the attached selvage. It shows the new marginal markings, with the name change of the printer to Toppan, Carpenter & Co.

Toppan, Carpenter, and Casilear, at first, had reservations about adding perforations and new issues. Their original contract with the government was about to expire and there was no guarantee that it would be renewed. If it were not renewed, the firm would be stuck with the costs of the perforating machine and the new plates. They asked that, if the contract were not renewed, the government would reimburse them for the cost of the perforating machine and making the new plates. The Post Office agreed. In any event, Toppan did have their contract renewed until 1861.

At this time, the company's name was shortened. Casilear retired from the firm in October 1854, but his name was included in plate imprints until 1857. John William Casilear was to become more famous in history as a great Hudson River school artist! At that time, Casilear finally was dropped from the corporate name. This is reflected in the margin markings when new plates were made. The imprint was now Toppan, Carpenter & Co., Philadelphia, with No. X (where X was the plate number). The imprints still were centered in the side margins, reading down in the left margin, and up in the right margin.

ERRORS, FREAKS, AND ODDITIES

With this issue, one sees the first errors on United States stamps. A whole branch of stamp collecting is the study of stamp mistakes. These now will be reviewed. There are three major groups of mistakes: design errors, true or major errors, and freaks and oddities (minor errors).

Design Errors

Design errors are inaccuracies of history or facts found on the stamp. They exist on all stamps of a particular design. The United States 1994 Legends of the West has the most famous design error. The souvenir sheet has a stamp of cowboy Bill Pickett with a portrait that was not him! Since they are found on all stamps of an issue, stamps with design errors are not usually valuable.

Figure 3-35. Design Error Example. Shown is the most infamous of design errors of United States stamps. It is the Bill Pickett stamp of the 1993 Legends of the West commemorative pane. The original version, shown on the left, was found by the family of the rodeo star Bill Pickett not to be him but rather his cousin, Ben. The Post Office later reissued the stamp shown on the right with the correct picture of the cowboy.

True Errors

True errors are rare and valuable flaws in stamp production. To be a true error, the stamp should have found its way to the public by being sold at a post office. Some so-called stamp errors are really just essays or proofs. Printer's waste, too, is not considered a true error. It is material, meant for destruction that found its way to collectors, usually by dishonest printing workers picking the trash.

Figure 3-36. Imperforate In Between Error. An in between perforation error occurs when the perforations are missing between two stamps, but all the other perforations present on the outer sides of the pair of stamps. Imperforate in between may be either horizontal or vertical. Here is an example of a vertical pair of stamps with an imperforate error consisting of the in between horizontal perforations missing.

Figure 3-37. Example of Stamps Imperforate Horizontally. This perforation error exists when all the rows of horizontal perforations are missing, not just those between the pair of stamps.

There are three types of true errors: stamps lacking perforations, multicolored stamps missing one or more colors, and stamps which part of the design is inverted.

To be considered an ***imperforate error***, all traces of perforations between the stamps must be missing. Even one perforation or a blind perforation between stamps disqualifies it. Blind perforations are incomplete perforations, often only tiny indentation into the paper.

Some very rare imperforate errors have no perforations completely around the stamp.

Some errors are ***imperforate in between***. The perforations are missing between two stamps, but all the other perforations present on all outer sides. Imperforate in between may be either in the horizontal or vertical direction.

Stamps may be in vertical pairs or more and ***imperforate horizontally***. All the horizontal perforations between stamps and the top and bottom are missing. Only vertical perforations exist.

Figure 3-38. Example of Stamps Imperforate Vertically. This perforation error occurs when all the rows of vertical perforations are missing, not just those between the pair of stamps.

Other stamps may be in horizontal pairs or more and ***imperforate vertically***. All the vertical perforations between stamps and left and right sides are missing. Only horizontal perforations are present.

A ***color-omitted error*** is missing all of the affected color. Even a dot of color disqualifies a stamp. They are found on multicolored stamps.

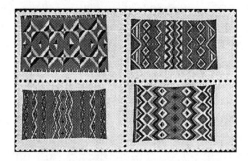

Figure 3-39. Color Missing Error. A stamp with a color omission error is missing one of the inks used to print the stamp. On this example, the block of four stamps is missing the black ink, including the wording. Obviously, color missing errors only are found on multicolor stamps.

Invert errors are the most famous and valuable of true errors. They occur on a multicolor stamp, when one part of the stamp is printed upside down in relationship to the rest of the stamp. This usually is the result of needing two or more passes of the stamp sheet through the printing press. The most famous invert error is the inverted Jenny, which occurred on the first United States airmail stamp. It has the central vignette, the airplane, flying upside down!

Figure 3-40. Invert Error. A stamp invert error occurs when one color of the stamp is printed upside down in relationship to the other color or colors of the stamp. This example is the most famous of all errors and of all stamps, the "Inverted Jenny." It is a 24-cent airmail stamp. The plane was printed first and then the frame upside down.

Freaks and Oddities

A greater variety of stamp freaks and oddities exist. They are the result of random flukes in production. These include problems of printing (misaligned color, overinking, and underinking, offsets, and albinos), paper problems (paper creases and foldovers), perforation problems (blind perforations, imperforate margins, and misaligned perforations), and problems in cutting the printed sheets (miscuts and gutter pair and snipes). Since they are fairly common, they are not nearly as desired by stamp collectors as true errors.

Color shifts happen when one plates of a multicolored printing process is out of register with the others.

With *overinking*, one sees smears and blobs on stamps, the result the excess ink on a printing plate. *Underinked* stamps, also called dry prints, are the result of too little ink on a plate during printing.

Figure 3-41. Color Shift Freak. This occurs happen when one plate of a multicolored printing process is out of register with the others.

Figure 3-43. Underinking Freak. If not enough ink is printed on a stamp then an underinking freak results. A ghost-like impression of the vignette is all that is seen.

Figure 3-42. Overinking Freak. If too much ink is placed on a stamp, an overinking freak results, with a thick layer or "blobs" of ink on it.

Offsets are stamps printed normally on one side and have an inverted impression of the stamp on the back. The offset gets on the back of the stamp when ink from the plate misses the stamp and winds up on a roller. The ink on the roller then is transferred (offset) to the back of a completed stamp.

Figure 3-44. Offset Freak. Offset stamps have an inverted impression of the stamp on the back (right) as well as a normal impression on the front (left). The offset gets on the back of the stamp when ink from the plate misses the stamp and winds up on a roller and then is transferred to the back of a normal stamp.

Albinos are blank stamps with missing ink. An albino stamp usually has an inkless stamp impression pressed on its surface. Albinos usually are found on postal stationary.

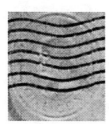

Figure 4-45. Albino Freak. Albinos are blank stamps with an inkless stamp impression pressed on its surface. They are most often found on postal stationary such as this United States one-cent envelope example.

Before printing, bunching up or folding over of paper that then gets printed results in an odd printing freak called a *paper crease.*

Figure 3-46. Paper Crease Freak. Such a stamp results when the paper is bunched up before printing, such as this three-cent stamp.

Foldovers result when a corner of sheet of stamps is accidentally folded during production. The foldover is an odd shaped stamp, with an unusual perforation and printing pattern.

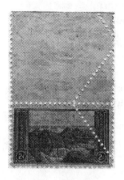

Figure 3-47. Foldover Freak. These stamps occur when a corner of sheet of stamps is accidentally folded. This results in a stamp with an unusual perforation or printing pattern. This example has very odd perforations.

Blind perforations are incomplete or partially impressed perforations that may barely indented the paper, giving a stamp the false appearance of being imperforate.

Imperforate margins are stamps with missing perforations between the edge of the stamp and the selvage. Imperforate margins do not carry the significance of true imperforate stamps.

Misperfs, short for misperforated, are odd, often bizarre perforation shifts. They happen when stamps are in misalignment with perforating equipment or when a corner of a sheet of stamps is been folded over during printing and perforations.

Figure 3-48. Blind Perforations. Blind perforations are incomplete perforations that may barely indented the paper. They may give a stamp the false appearance of being a much more valuable imperforate one.

Miscuts result from poorly aligned cutting of the printed sheet into panes.

Figure 3-49. Miscut Freak. Miscut stamps occur when the printed sheet is cut in the wrong place when divided into panes. This example is a used 8-cent Eisenhower booklet single stamp that was cut so that part of a stamp from another pane is attached to it.

The selvage between the panes on a complete stamp sheet is called a gutter. Gutter pairs and snipes result when sheets are miscut so one pane contains a portion of the adjacent pane. A *gutter pair* contains one complete stamp from each side of the gutter. It is considered a *gutter snipe* if there is less than a complete attached stamp.

Figure 3-50. Misperf Freak. Misperfs are weird perforation shift stamps. They occur when the sheet of stamps was misaligned with perforating equipment or when a corner of a sheet of stamps is been folded over during the perforation process.

Figure 3-51. Gutter Pairs and Snipes. The gutter is the selvage between the panes of a sheet of stamps that normally is cut. A gutter pair freak contains one complete stamp from each side of the gutter. For an example see the pair of Harding stamps on the left. A gutter snipe exists if there is less than a complete stamp across the gutter. For an example of a snipe, see the box of Jefferson stamps on the right.

ONE-CENT STAMPS OF 1857

Type I One-Cent Franklin Perforated Stamp of 1857

Type I One-Cent Franklin Perforated Stamp of 1857

Stamp Production

Printer:	Toppan, Carpenter & Co.
Designer:	Edward Purcell
Engravers:	Joseph I. Pease or William C. Smillie (portrait), Henry Earle or John Casilear (frame)
Format:	2 panes of 100
Plate Numbers:	12
Issue Date:	1861
Earliest Known Use:	Jan. 25,1861
Uses:	Printed circular. Drop letter. Strip of three paid 3-cent basic rate. Carriers' fee.
Quantity Issued:	Unknown

Stamp Features

Size:	20 x 26 mm. (0.8 x 1.0 inches)
Watermark:	None
Perforations:	15½
Colors:	Blue
Varieties:	Double transfer, Cracked plate (91R12)

Collectable Stamp Today
Collectable Cancellation Colors:
Black, blue, red, violet
Collectable Cancellation Varieties:
Paid, Free, black carrier, red carrier, steamboat, pen

Value Unused: $$$$$
Value Used: $$$$
Surviving Covers: 750
Largest Known Multiple: Unused: 40 stamps out of a block 78
                               Used: 3 (strip)

The same type nomenclature of the imperforate issues is used on the perforated issues of 1857, with some additions and subtractions. Like the type I imperforate one-cent stamps, the perforated stamps show the complete stamp design. The type I perforated stamps came from plate 12 that had 99 positions that produced type I stamps (other 101 plate positions made type II stamps). The largest concentrations of type I positions are found on the two bottom rows on the right pane.

All the stamps from plate 12 have a dot in the white border surrounding the medallion on the left side. This is a simple test that distinguishes a stamp is the very rare imperforate type I, from a fake made from cutting the perforations off this perforated type I stamp.

The background of these stamps often is mottled, the result of a warped printing plate. This effect is called plate wash.

There are numerous double transfers. There is a cracked plate defect, but looks more like a gash.

The earliest known use of type I was January 25, 1861. The largest mint block of this stamp is a block of 78 with 40 type I and 38 type II stamps. The largest used multiple of a perforated type I one-cent stamp is a strip of 3.

Type Ia One-Cent Franklin Perforated Stamp of 1857

Type Ia One-Cent Franklin Perforated Stamp of 1857

Stamp Production
Printer:	Toppan, Carpenter & Co.
Designer:	Edward Purcell
Engravers:	Joseph I. Pease or William C. Smillie (portrait), Henry Earle or John Casilear (frame)
Format:	2 panes of 100
Plate Numbers:	4
Issue Date:	1857
Earliest Known Use:	Aug. 1, 1857
Uses:	Printed circular. Drop letter. Strip of three paid 3-cent basic rate. Carriers' fee.
Quantity Issued:	300,000

Stamp Features
Size:	20 x 26 mm. (0.8 x 1.0 inches)
Watermark:	None
Perforations:	15½
Colors:	Blue
Varieties:	Curl on shoulder (97L4)

Collectable Stamp Today
Collectable Cancellation Colors:
Black, green
Collectable Cancellation Varieties:
red carrier, pen
Value Unused:	$$$$$$
Value Used:	$$$$$

Surviving Covers: 75
Largest Known Multiple: Unused: 10 stamps out of a pane of 100
Used: 3 (strip)

Type Ia one-cent stamps have ornaments that are complete at bottom, but the design and ornaments are incomplete on the top. This type comes only from 18 of the 20 bottom row positions on plate 4. These stamps have a deep, rich blue color.

Type Ia stamps not partially cut by the perforations are extremely rare. This is because, except for a few instances, the setting of the horizontal rows of perforations was less than the length of the stamp design.

Type Ic One-Cent Franklin Perforated Stamp of 1857

Type Ic One-Cent Franklin Perforated Stamp of 1857

Stamp Production
Printer: Toppan, Carpenter & Co.
Designer: Edward Purcell
Engravers: Joseph I. Pease or William C. Smillie (portrait), Henry Earle or John Casilear (frame)
Format: 2 panes of 100
Plate Numbers: 4
Issue Date: 1857

Earliest Known Use: July 26, 1857
Uses: Printed circular. Drop letter. Strip of three paid 3-cent basic rate. Carriers' fee.
Quantity Issued: 150,000

Stamp Features
Size: 20 x 26 mm. (0.8 x 1.0 inches)
Watermark: None
Perforations: 15½
Colors: Blue
Varieties: None

Collectable Stamp Today
Collectable Cancellation Colors:
None
Collectable Cancellation Varieties:
pen
Value Unused: $$$$$
Value Used: $$$$$
Surviving Covers: 40
Largest Known Multiple: Unused: 1
Used: 1

There are no type Ib perforated one-cent stamps, as the plate (1 early) from which they were made was not used for the perforated stamps. Like the imperforate issue, Scott does not list the perforated type Ic with a major catalog number, only a minor one. Unlike the similar type Ia stamp, which the design is complete at the bottom, type Ic stamp's bottom right plume is half complete and the right ball partially complete.

This type comes from plate 4 and from only 8 positions on it. The finest type Ic stamps are the bottom row positions 91R and 96R. The others are 47L, 49L, 31L, 82L, 83L, and 89L.

Since this type comes only from scattered positions, it cannot be found in multiples larger than a pair. However, no such pair is known, unused or used. Three scattered unused Ic stamps are found in the only known left pane of 100.

The earliest known use of this issue is July 26, 1857.

Type II One-Cent Franklin Perforated Stamp of 1857

Type II One-Cent Franklin Perforated Stamp of 1857

Stamp Production
Printer:	Toppan, Carpenter & Co.
Designer:	Edward Purcell
Engravers:	Joseph I. Pease or William C. Smillie (portrait), Henry Earle or John Casilear (frame)
Format:	2 panes of 100
Plate Numbers:	1 late, 2, 4, 11, 12
Issue Date:	1857
Earliest Known Use:	July 26,1857
Uses:	Printed circular. Drop letter. Strip of three paid 3-cent basic rate. Carriers' fee.

Stamp Features
Size:	20 x 26 mm. (0.8 x 1.0 inches)
Watermark:	None
Perforations:	15½
Colors:	Blue
Varieties:	Double transfer, Cracked plate (2L, 12L, 13L, 23L, 33L, plate 2)

Collectable Stamp Today
Collectable Cancellation Colors:
Black, blue, red, green
Collectable Cancellation Varieties:
1857, 1858, 1861, 1863, Paid, railroad, Way, steamboat, red carrier, black carrier, Free, pen
Quantity Issued: Unknown

Value Unused: $$$$$
Value Used: $$$$
Largest Known Multiple: Unused: 78 out of a pane of 100
                                     Used: 4 (2x2 block) 5 (strip)

As described for the imperforate one-cent stamps, a type II one-cent stamp is incomplete, both at the top and the bottom of the design. Though the ornaments are incomplete at top and bottom, the top and bottom outer frame lines are complete. The type II perforated stamps came from plate 1 late, 2, 11, and 12. Plate 1 late had only one position (position 4) with a type II stamp. Plate 2 made type II stamps from 199 out of its 200 positions. Plate 4 had 18 to 20 positions that were type 2, as did plate 11 (top row of both panes). It is found on 101 positions on plate 12.

The "Big Crack," a huge plate crack found on imperforate type II stamps are also found on the type II perforated stamps. This is logical as they were both were made from the same part of plate 2. Many double transfers are found on these stamps.

The earliest reported use is July 26, 1857. The largest unused multiple is a complete pane from plate 12, with 78 being type II (the remainder type I). The largest used multiple is block of 4 and strip of 5 (from top row of plate 4).

Type III One-Cent Franklin Perforated Stamp of 1857

Type III One-Cent Franklin Perforated Stamp of 1857

Stamp Production

Printer:	Toppan, Carpenter & Co.
Designer:	Edward Purcell
Engravers:	Joseph I. Pease or William C. Smillie (portrait), Henry Earle or John Casilear (frame)
Format:	2 panes of 100
Plate Numbers:	2 (99R), 4,12 (46L)
Issue Date:	1857
Earliest Known Use:	Sept. 18, 1857
Uses:	Printed circular. Drop letter. Strip of three paid 3-cent basic rate. Carriers' fee.
Quantity Issued:	Unknown

Stamp Features

Size:	20 x 26 mm. (0.8 x 1.0 inches)
Watermark:	None
Perforations:	15½
Colors:	Blue
Varieties:	None
Errors:	Horizontal pair with no vertical perforations between

Collectable Stamp Today

Collectable Cancellation Colors:
Black, blue, red, green

Collectable Cancellation Varieties:
1858, Paid, black carrier, red carrier, pen

Value Unused:	$$$$$$
Value Used:	$$$$$

Surviving Covers: 75
Largest Known Multiple: Unused: 2
                               Used: Strip of 7 in a block of 28

Type III stamps, as we have seen, are even more incomplete at the top and bottom. The top and bottom frame lines are broken. The width of breaks varies based on the positions of the plate. Stamps with wider breaks are rarer and thus more valuable. Type III stamps come from 60 scattered positions on the second through ninth rows of the plate 4, a single position of plate 12 (46L), and a single position of plate 2 (99R).

Since every stamp from plate 2, has a position dot on it, one can distinguish 99R2, the finest example, from the other lesser type III stamps, by its lack of a position dot.

This stamp is noted for a rare error. There is a horizontal pair of the stamps, with no vertical perforations between (an imperforate error).

The earliest known use of a type III perforated one cent stamp is Sept. 18, 1857, a stamp from plate 4.

Type IIIa stamps are found in combination pairs with type III stamps and these pairs are of collectors' interest.

Type IIIa One-Cent Franklin Perforated Stamp of 1857

Type IIIa One-Cent Franklin Perforated Stamp of 1857

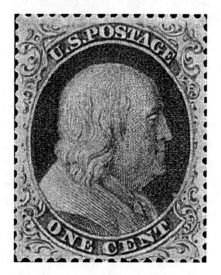

Stamp Production

Printer:	Toppan, Carpenter & Co.
Designer:	Edward Purcell
Engravers:	Joseph I. Pease or William C. Smillie (portrait), Henry Earle or John Casilear (frame)
Format:	2 panes of 100
Plates:	4,11,12
Issue Date:	1857
Earliest Known Use:	July 26, 1857
Uses:	Printed circular. Drop letter. Strip of three paid 3-cent basic rate. Carriers' fee.
Quantity Issued:	Unknown

Stamp Features

Size:	20 x 26 mm. (0.8 x 1.0 inches)
Watermark:	None
Perforations:	15½
Colors:	Blue
Varieties:	Double transfer, Triple transfer
Errors:	Horizontal pair with no vertical perforations between

Collectable Stamp Today
Collectable Cancellation Colors:
Black, blue, red, green
Collectable Cancellation Varieties:
1857,1858, 1861, 1863, Paid, black carrier, red carrier, Steamboat, pen

Perforations:	15½
Watermark:	None
Value Unused:	$$$$$
Value Used:	$$$$
Largest Known Multiple:	Unused: 50 stamps out of a pane of 100
	Used: 20 stamps out of a pane of 100

A type IIIa one-cent stamp has the outer frame lines broken at top or bottom, but not both. The stamp comes from 101 scattered positions on plate 4, 180 positions on plate 11 (all but the top rows) and 4 to 14 positions on plate 12, (depending on the wear on the plate). Bottom line breaks are much less common, coming from only a couple positions on plate 4 and one position on plate 12 (46L).

The largest unused multiple is 50 type IIIa stamps in unused pane of 100, from plate 4. The largest used multiple is 20 in block of 28 also from plate 4.

Like the type III one-cent stamp, this stamp is noted for a rare error. There is a horizontal pair of the stamps, with no vertical perforations between (an imperforate error). Only one copy of this error exists today.

Type IV One-Cent Franklin Perforated Stamp of 1857

Type IV One-Cent Franklin Perforated Stamp of 1857

Stamp Production

Printer:	Toppan, Carpenter & Co.
Designer:	Edward Purcell
Engravers:	Joseph I. Pease or William C. Smillie (portrait), Henry Earle or John Casilear (frame)
Format:	2 panes of 100
Plate Numbers:	1 late
Issue Date:	1857
Earliest Known Use:	July 25,1857
Uses:	Printed circular. Drop letter. Strip of three paid 3-cent basic rate. Carriers' fee.
Quantity Issued:	Unknown

Stamp Features

Size:	20 x 26 mm. (0.8 x 1.0 inches)

Watermark:	None
Perforations:	15½
Colors:	Blue
Varieties:	Double transfer, Triple transfer one inverted (71L, 81L, 91L), Cracked plate, Bottom line broken (89R)
Errors:	Horizontal pair with no vertical perforations between

Collectable Stamp Today
Collectable Cancellation Colors:
        Black, blue, red
Collectable Cancellation Varieties:
        1857, Paid, red carrier, black carrier, railroad, Way, Steamboat, Steam, pen

Value Unused:	$$$$$
Value Used:	$$$$
Surviving Covers:	250
Largest Known Multiple:	Unused: 3 (strip)
	Used: 6 (strip)

Recutting on top or bottom outer lines results in a type IV one-cent stamp. Sometimes, there are recuts on top and/or bottom inner lines. Numerous recut varieties exist. Type IV perforated stamps come from plate 1 late, all positions on the plate, with the exception of 4E (a type II stamp). These type IV perforated stamps came from the same plate as the type IV imperforate stamps of 1851. The perforate type IV of 1857 is much more uncommon, however. The earliest known use of the stamp was July 25,1857.

Type V One-Cent Franklin Perforated Stamp of 1857

Type V One-Cent Franklin Perforated Stamp of 1857

Stamp Production

Printer:	Toppan, Carpenter & Co.
Designer:	Edward Purcell
Engravers:	Joseph I. Pease or William C. Smillie (portrait), Henry Earle or John Casilear (frame)
Format:	2 panes of 100
Plate Numbers:	7, 8, 9, 10
Issue Date:	1857
Earliest Known Use:	Nov. 17, 1857
Uses:	Printed circular. Drop letter. Strip of three paid 3-cent basic rate. Carriers' fee.
Quantity Issued:	50,000,000

Stamp Features

Size:	20 x 26 mm. (0.8 x 1.0 inches)
Watermark:	None
Perforations:	15½
Colors:	Blue
Varieties:	Double transfer at top (8R8, 10R8), Double transfer at bottom (52R9), Curl on shoulder (57R7, 58R7, 59R7, 98R7, 99R7, 48L5), An earring below ear (10L9), Curl over C of Cent, Curl over E of Cent (41R8, 81R8), Curl in hair (23L7, 39L8, 69L8, 34R9, 74R9), Curl in O of One (62L5), Horizontal dash in hair (24L4, 36L8), Long double curl in hair (52R8, 92R8), Laid paper
Errors:	Vertical strip of stamps imperforate horizontally

Collectable Stamp Today
Collectable Cancellation Colors:
Black, blue, red, green, brown, magenta, ultramarine
Collectable Cancellation Varieties:
1857, 1858, 1859, 1860, 1861, 1863, Paid, Free, railroad, numeral, express company, steamboat, Steam, steamship, packet boat, supplementary mail type A B or C, Way, red carrier, black carrier, blue carrier, Old Stamps Not Recognized, printed precancellation of Cumberland, Maine, territorial, pen
Value Unused: $$$$
Value Used: $$$
Surviving Covers: 10,000
Largest Known Multiple: Unused: 100 (complete pane)
Used: 10 (block)

The type V stamps exist only in a perforated form. There are no imperforate type V stamps. What makes a type V is the stamp design is that it is incomplete on all four sides. To make room for perforating the stamps, the sides of the stamp design were trimmed down. The ornaments are incomplete on both sides and the outer frame line is broken at top and bottom. Thus, they are like type III stamps with the side ornaments cut away. Half of type V stamps show irregular vertical lines, side scratches, at left or right. These are not cracks, but marks caused by the burnishing work, caused when removing the design's sides.

Type V stamps were printed from plates 7, 8, 9, and 10, which made only type V stamps. Note there was never a plate 6 used for printing one-cent stamps as it was damaged during its production. Type V stamps are the most common one-cent perforated stamps by far. For several years, it was a workhouse stamp paying for local mail. Its earliest known use is Nov. 17, 1857.

A unique perforating error of this stamp exists. There is a vertical strip of 5 type V stamps, without any horizontal perforations in between any stamps.

Figure 3-52. Features of the Type V One-Cent Stamp of the 1857 Series. This stamp is similar to a Type III stamp, but with the side ornaments missing.

Type Va One-Cent Franklin Perforated Stamp of 1857

Type Va One-Cent Franklin Perforated Stamp of 1857

Stamp Production

Printer:	Toppan, Carpenter & Co.
Designer:	Edward Purcell
Engravers:	Joseph I. Pease or William C. Smillie (portrait), Henry Earle or John Casilear (frame)
Format:	2 panes of 100

Plate Numbers:	5
Issue Date:	1857
Earliest Known Use:	Dec. 2, 1857
Uses:	Printed circular. Drop letter. Strip of three paid 3-cent basic rate. Carriers' fee.
Quantity Issued:	200,000

Stamp Features

Size:	20 x 26 mm. (0.8 x 1.0 inches)
Watermark:	None
Perforations:	15½
Colors:	Blue
Varieties:	Curl in O of ONE (62L5), Curl on shoulder (48L5)

Collectable Stamp Today

Value Unused:	$$$$
Value Used:	$$$
Surviving Covers:	50-100
Largest Known Multiple:	Unused: 21 (irregular block)
	Used: 15 (irregular block)

A type Va one-cent stamp is a subtype of type V. It has not received its own major catalog number, or even a minor one. It is a transitional stamp between types III and V. Like a type V, the ornaments are incomplete on all four sides. Unique to it, the ornaments are almost complete on the right and there are no side scratches. Type Va stamps come only from plate 5. All 100 stamps on the right pane and 25 on the left pane are type Va. The earliest known use of the stamp is Dec. 2, 1857.

Figure 3-53. Features of the Type Va One-Cent Stamp of the 1857 Series. This stamp is similar to a Type V stamp in that the side ornaments are cut away. Unique to it, the ornaments are almost complete at right and there are no side scratches.

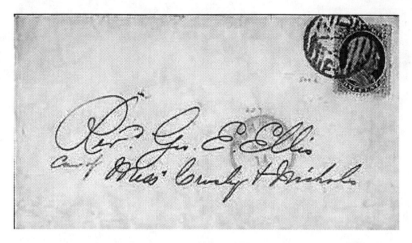

Figure 3-54. Example of a One-Cent Cover. This is an example of a cover with a one-cent perforated 1857 series stamp on it. It was used to pay the postage for a drop letter at the local post office. That is why there is no city or state address on it.

THREE-CENT STAMPS OF 1857

Type I Three-Cent Washington Perforated Stamp of 1857

Type I Three-Cent Washington Perforated Stamp of 1857

Stamp Production

Format:	2 panes of 100
Printer:	Toppan, Carpenter & Co.
Designer:	Edward Purcell
Engravers:	Joseph I. Pease (portrait), Henry Earle (frame)
Format:	2 panes of 100
Plate Numbers:	2 (late), 3, 4, 5 (late), 6, 7, 8
Issue Date:	1857
Earliest Known Use:	Feb. 28,1857
Uses:	Single letter rate under 3,000 miles
Quantity Issued:	38,750,000

Stamp Features

Size:	20 x 25 mm. (0.8 x 1.0 inches)
Watermark:	None
Perforations:	15½
Colors:	Rose, rose red, claret, dull red.
Varieties:	Gash on shoulder, Double transfer, Double transfer GENTS instead of CENTS (66R2L), Triple transfer (92L2L), Worn plate, Cracked plate (many positions), Dot in lower right diamond block (69L5L), Various recuts
Errors:	Vertical pairs imperforate horizontally in between

Collectable Stamp Today
Collectable Cancellation Colors:

Black, blue, red, orange, orange red, brown, ultramarine, green

Collectable Cancellation Varieties:

1857, 1858, 1859, Paid, Way, railroad, numeral, Steam, steamship, steamboat, packet boat, supplementary mail type A, U. S. express mail, express company cancellation, black carrier, Old Stamp Not Recognized, territorial, printed precancel of Cumberland Me, pen

Value Unused:	$$$$$
Value Used:	$$$$
Surviving Covers:	4,000
Largest Known Multiple:	Unused: 20 (4x5 block)
	Used: 9 (3x3 block)

The three-cent perforated stamp of the 1856 series comes in three types, I, II, and IIa. The type I is identical to the corresponding 1851 imperforate stamp. A type I stamp has the outer frame line on all 4 sides, including the top and bottom. If a frame line is seen at the top or bottom of the stamp, it is a type I. Of the nine plates used to make the imperforate stamps of 1851, seven plates (2 through 8) were used to print the perforated type stamps. It is more difficult to find the perforate type I stamp than the very common imperforate predecessor is. The perforate type I stamp is much more scarce unused than used. A copy that has the perforations clear of the design on all sides is very hard to find. Printing impressions usually are good.

Chase organized the colors of the type I perforated three-cent stamps by years they were printed, just like he did the imperforate issues. The same plate varieties seen in the imperforate stamps, as expected, are found in the perforate stamps.

The earliest known use on the stamp is Feb. 28,1857. There are over 4,000 surviving covers with this stamp on it, as the stamp paid the basic postage rate. Patriotic covers, reflecting the times of the Civil War, are a common collector's item.

The variety has been found with perforation errors. This stamp is found in vertical pairs, imperforate horizontally, in between.

Type	Definition	Color	Imperforate Plates	Perforate Plates
I	Complete stamp design	Orange brown	1 Early and Intermediate 2 Early 5 Early 0	
		Red	1 Late 2 Late 3, 4 5 Late 6, 7, 8	2 Late 3, 4 5 Late 6, 7, 8
II	No horizontal outer frame lines Vertical lines go beyond edge			9 (Early and Late) 12, 13, 14, 15, 16, 17, 18, 19 20, 21, 22, 23, 24, 25, 26, 27, 28
IIa	No horizontal outer frame lines Vertical lines have break			10 (Early, Intermediate, Late) 11 (Early, Intermediate, Late)

Figure 3-55. Diagram of the Type I Three-Cent Stamp of the 1857 Series. The Type I three-cent stamp has outer bottom (shown) and top (not shown) frame lines.

Type II Three-Cent Washington Perforated Stamp of 1857

Type II Three-Cent Washington Perforated Stamp of 1857

Stamp Production

Printer:	Toppan, Carpenter & Co.
Designer:	Edward Purcell
Engravers:	Joseph I. Pease (portrait), Henry Earle (frame)
Format:	2 panes of 100
Plate Numbers:	9 (early and late), 12, 13, 14, 15, 16, 17, 18, 19, 20, 21, 22, 23, 24, 25, 26, 27, 28
Issue Date:	1857
Earliest Known Use:	Sept. 14,1857
Uses:	Single letter rate under 3,000 miles
Quantity Issued:	550,000,000

Stamp Features

Size:	20 x 25 mm. (0.8 x 1.0 inches)
Watermark:	None

Perforations:	15½
Colors:	Dull red, red, rose, dark rose, brownish carmine, orange brown, claret, plum
Varieties:	Double impression, Double transfer, Double transfer with rosettes doubled and line through Postage and Three Cents (87R15), Left frame line double, Right frame line double, Triple transfer, Damaged transfer above lower left rosette, Damaged transfer above lower left rosette retouched, Damaged transfer above lower left rosette retouched with 2 lines, Cracked plate (62L18, 71L18, 72L18), Quadruple plate flaw (18L28), 1 line recut in upper left triangle, 5 lines recut in upper left triangle, Inner line recut at right, Worn plate.
Errors:	Imperforate vertically, Imperforate horizontally, Horizontal pair imperforate in between

Collectable Stamp Today
Collectable Cancellation Colors:

Black, blue, red, orange, orange red, brown, ultramarine, violet, green.

Collectable Cancellation Varieties:

1857 through 1861, Paid, Paid All, Free, Collect, numeral, Steam, steamer, steamboat, steamship, Way, railroad, U. S. express mail, express company cancellation, packet boat, supplementary mail type A B or C, black carrier, red carrier, Southn. Letter Unpaid, Old Stamps-Not Recognized, printed precancellation Cumberland, Maine, territorial, pen

Value Unused:	$$$
Value Used:	$$
Surviving Covers:	100,000
Largest Known Multiple:	Unused: 100 (complete panes)
	Used: 50

When stamps were first perforated, the three-cent issue was printed from the original plates that were used to produce the imperforate stamps (type I). It became apparent that there is not enough space at the top and bottom of the stamp, as the perforations cut into the frame lines. New plates were made with the outer frame lines removed to give more space for the perforations. Type II and IIa three-cent issues, therefore, were made only perforated. They represent stamps trimmed both at the top and bottom. Both types have no horizontal top or bottom outer frame lines. Type II frame lines go beyond the top at the top of the stamps and the bottom at the bottom of the stamps. The line appears continuous with the stamps above and below it.

Figure 3-56. Features of the Type II Three-Cent Stamp of the 1857 Series. A Type II stamp is missing the top and bottom frame lines. The outer left and right frame lines continue on for the full length of the stamp, not stopping at where the horizontal frame line was.

With so many type II stamps printed, many plate variations resulted. One is an inner line recut at right. There are seven types of recut triangles (upper left), which occur on plate 15. Several positions of type II have two or three, extra distinct frame lines. Many plate flaws exist. The most famous is the "quadruple flaw," a set of four pair of ditto marks in a vertical line near the center of the stamps.

Figure 3-57. Example of a Three-Cent Cover. This is an example of a cover with an 1857 three-cent Washington stamp. It was used to pay the under 3,000 mile basic postage rate. The letter was mailed from Boston, MA to Bath, NH.

The earliest known use of a type II stamp is Sept. 14,1857. Being used for most ordinary mail, over a half a billion of these stamps were printed. It is not surprising to find more than 75,000 surviving covers with this stamp. Civil War era patriotic covers are common. Even Confederate States patriotic covers exist! A real collector's cover is this stamp on a Pony Express envelope.

Complete panes from plates 20 through 28 still exist. And blocks of 50 stamps on cover are the largest used intact group of stamps.

The stamp is found in pairs with perforation errors, both imperforate vertically and imperforate horizontally. Both are very rare. There is even a horizontal pair that is just imperforate in between the two stamps.

Figure 3-58. Imperforate Horizontally Error of a Type II Three-Cent 1857 Series Stamp. This is a vertical pair of stamps that are imperforate horizontally. Each stamp is missing its horizontal perforations.

Type IIa Three-Cent Washington Perforated Stamp of 1857

Type IIa Three-Cent Washington Perforated Stamp of 1857

Stamp Production	
Printer:	Toppan, Carpenter & Co.
Designer:	Edward Purcell
Engravers:	Joseph I. Pease (portrait), Henry Earle (frame)
Format:	2 panes of 100
Plate Numbers:	10 (early, intermediate, late), 11 (early, intermediate, late)

Issue Date:	1857
Earliest Known Use:	July 11, 1857
Uses:	Single letter rate under 3,000 miles
Quantity Issued:	33,000,000

Stamp Features

Size:	20 x 25 mm. (0.8 x 1.0 inches)
Watermark:	None
Perforations:	15½
Colors:	Dull red, brownish carmine, rose, claret
Variations:	Double transfer, Double transfer with a line through rosettes (61R10I, 61R10L, 98R10I, 98R10L), Double transfer of rosettes and lower part of stamps (91R11L), Triple transfer, Damaged transfer above lower left rosette, Damaged transfer above lower left rosette retouched, Inner line recut at right, Inner line recut at left (79L10), Left frame line double (70R11, 80R11, 90R11, 100R11), Worn plate
Errors:	Horizontal strip of three stamps with the vertical perforations in between missing

Collectable Stamp Today
Collectable Cancellation Colors:

Black, blue, red, orange, orange red, brown, ultramarine, violet, green

Collectable Cancellation Varieties:

1857, 1858, 1859, Paid, Paid All, Free, Collect, numeral, Steam, steamer, steamboat, steamship, Way, railroad, U. S. express mail, express company cancellation, packet boat, supplementary mail type A B or C, black carrier, red carrier, territorial, pen

Value Unused:	$$$$
Value Used:	$$$
Surviving Covers:	3,400
Largest Known Multiple:	Unused: 77
	Used 9 (3x3 block)

Like the type II, the type IIa has no horizontal top or bottom outer frame lines. The difference with a type IIa stamp, the outer vertical frame lines end at the inner frame lines. Type IIa is considered by Scott to be a subtype of a type II, rating only a minor catalog number.

Figure 3-59. Features of the Type IIa Three-Cent Stamp of the 1857 Series. A Type IIa stamp, like the Type II, is missing the top and bottom frame lines. However, the outer left and right frame lines stop at where the horizontal frame lines were.

When two plates, (10 and 11, the first ones made after type I), had the frame lines re-cut to the top and bottom of each individual stamp only. Apparently the engraver found this tedious and simply drew one long continuous frame line from the top of the very top stamp on the plate to the bottom of the bottom stamp, resulting in a change from type IIa to II.

Plates 10 and 11 each was recut twice, accounting for the early, intermediate and late forms of each plate. Eighteen different positions from plates 10 and 11 had an inner line recut. All but one was recut on the right side of the stamp.

The earliest known use of a type IIa is July 26,1857.

The largest unused multiple is a block of 77. Some think a complete right pane of 100 stamps from plate 10, the intermediate state, may exist, but this has not been confirmed. The largest used multiple is a block of 9 (3x3).

The stamp exists as an error, a horizontal strip of three stamps, with the vertical perforations, in between, missing. This unique error is found on cover.

FIVE-CENT STAMPS OF 1857

The 1857 series five-cent perforated stamps come in two major types and several colors.

Type	Definition	Imperforate		Perforated	
		Color	Plates	Color	Plates
I	Complete stamp design				
		Red Brown	1	Red Brown	1
				Brick Red	1
				Indian Red	1
				Brown	1
II	Top & bottom projections cut away				
		NONE		Orange Brown	2
				Brown	2

Type I, Red Brown Five-Cent Jefferson Perforated Stamp of 1857

Type I, Red Brown Five-Cent Jefferson Perforated Stamp of 1857

Stamp Production

Printer:	Toppan, Carpenter & Co.
Designer:	Edward Purcell
Engravers:	Joseph I. Pease (portrait), Cyrus Durand (frame) and Henry Earle (lettering)
Format:	2 panes of 100
Plate Numbers:	1
Issue Date:	1857
Earliest Known Use:	Aug. 23,1857
Uses:	Foreign-destination rates, usually as multiples, especially France. Registration fee
Quantity Issued:	270,000

Stamp Features

Size:	19.5 x 25.5 mm. (0.8 x 1.0 inches)
Watermark:	None
Perforations:	15 ½
Colors:	Red brown, pale red brown, bright red brown
Varieties:	Defective transfer (23R)

Collectable Stamp Today
Collectable Cancellation Colors:
Black, blue, red
Collectable Cancellation Varieties:
1857, 1858, Paid, railroad, Short Paid, pen

Value Unused:	$$$$$
Value Used:	$$$$$
Surviving Covers:	150
Largest Known Multiple:	Unused: 6
	Used 12 (4x3 block)

The type I perforated five-cent stamps were printed from the same plate and have the same characteristics as the type I imperforate ones. The design is complete, top and bottom, including the projections. Type I stamps were printed in several colors. When the type I five-cent perforated stamps were first issued during August 1857), they were printed initially in this color.

Type I, Indian Red Five-Cent Jefferson Perforated Stamp of 1857

Type I, Indian Red Five-Cent Jefferson Perforated Stamp of 1857

Stamp Production
Printer:	Toppan, Carpenter & Co.
Designer:	Edward Purcell
Engravers:	Joseph I. Pease (portrait), Cyrus Durand (frame) and Henry Earle (lettering)
Format:	2 panes of 100
Plate Numbers:	1
Issue Date:	1858
Earliest Known Use:	March 31, 1858
Uses:	Foreign-destination rates, usually as multiples, especially France. Registration fee
Quantity Issued:	25,000 to 50,000

Stamp Features
Size:	19.5 x 25.5 mm. (0.8 x 1.0 inches)
Watermark:	None
Perforations:	15½
Colors:	Indian red
Varieties:	None

Collectable Stamp Today
Collectable Cancellation Colors:
Black, red, blue
Collectable Cancellation Varieties:
1858, 1859, pen
Value Unused: $$$$$$

Value Used:	$$$$$
Surviving Covers:	30
Largest Known Multiple:	Unused: 1
	Used 3 (strip)

The type I five-cent stamp was printed in a unique shade called the politically incorrect name, Indian red. It is scarce stamp, with a bright beautiful color. The color, once named henna brown, is an intense red brown. Expert help is recommended to verify the true Indian red when purchasing this expensive and beautiful stamp. Its earliest known use is March 31, 1858.

Type I, Brick Red Five-Cent Jefferson Perforated Stamp of 1857

Type I, Brick Red Five-Cent Jefferson Perforated Stamp of 1857

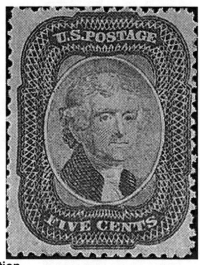

Stamp Production

Printer:	Toppan, Carpenter & Co.
Designer:	Edward Purcell
Engravers:	Joseph I. Pease (portrait), Cyrus Durand (frame) and Henry Earle (lettering)
Format:	2 panes of 100
Plate Numbers:	1
Issue Date:	1858

Earliest Known Use:	Oct. 6, 1858
Uses:	Foreign-destination rates, usually as multiples, especially France. Registration fee.
Quantity Issued:	135,000

Stamp Features

Size:	19.5 x 25.5 mm. (0.8 x 1.0 inches)
Watermark:	None
Perforations:	15½
Colors:	Brick red
Varieties:	Defective transfer (23R)

Collectable Stamp Today
Collectable Cancellation Colors:
Black, blue, red, ultramarine
Collectable Cancellation Varieties:
1859, 1860, Paid, supplementary mail type A, Steamship, pen

Value Unused:	$$$$$$
Value Used:	$$$$$
Surviving Covers:	100
Largest Known Multiple:	Unused: 4 (2x2 block)
	Used: 4 (2x2 block)

The stamp color of the brick red is more orange than other stamps of this issue. Because of the light color of this stamp, cancellations appear strong, hiding the stamps' fine detail. Also, perforations usually cut in on one or two sides of the stamp's design.

Though they are listed first in Scott's catalog, they came over a year after the perforated five-cent red brown. The date of the earliest known use is October 6, 1858. The stamp can be sometimes found on a Civil War patriotic cover.

Type I Five-Cent Brown Jefferson Perforated Stamp of 1857

Type I Five-Cent Brown Jefferson Perforated Stamp of 1857

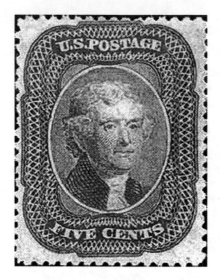

Stamp Production

Printer:	Toppan, Carpenter & Co.
Designer:	Edward Purcell
Engravers:	Joseph I. Pease (portrait), Cyrus Durand (frame) and Henry Earle (lettering)
Format:	2 panes of 100
Plate Numbers:	1
Issue Date:	1859
Earliest Known Use:	March 21, 1859
Uses:	Foreign-destination rates, usually as multiples, especially France. Registration fee
Quantity Issued:	510,000

Stamp Features

Size:	19.5 x 25.5 mm. (0.8 x 1.0 inches)
Watermark:	None
Perforations:	15½
Colors:	Brown, pale brown, deep brown, yellowish brown.
Varieties:	Defective transfer (23R)

Collectable Stamp Today
Collectable Cancellation Colors:
Black, blue, red, brown, magenta, green, ultramarine.
Collectable Cancellation Varieties:
1859, 1860, Paid, Steam, steamship, numeral, pen

Value Unused:	$$$$$
Value Used:	$$$$

Surviving Covers: 200
Largest Known Multiple: Unused: 4 (2x2 block)
                           Used: 4 (2x2 block)

This variety includes several shades of brown, including brown, pale brown deep brown, and yellowish brown. It has none of the orange shade of the brick red, or the red of other type I five-cent stamps.   Stamps with the perforations cut off are passed as the expensive imperforate of 1851. However, a true imperforate is a red brown and not a brown, a clue to such fakes. Its first known use was March 21, 1859.

Type II, Brown Five-Cent Jefferson Perforated Stamp of 1857

Type II, Brown Five-Cent Jefferson Perforated Stamp of 1857

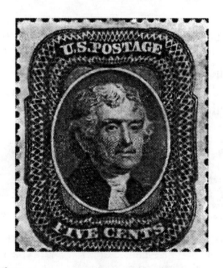

Stamp Production
Printer: Toppan, Carpenter & Co.
Designer: Edward Purcell
Engravers: Joseph I. Pease (portrait), Cyrus Durand (frame) and
                       Henry Earle (lettering)
Format: 2 panes of 100
Plate Numbers: 2
Issue Date: 1860
Earliest Known Use: May 4,1860

Uses:	Foreign-destination rates, usually as multiples, especially France. Registration fee
Quantity Issued:	825,000

Stamp Features

Size:	19.5 x 25.5 mm. (0.8 x 1.0 inches)
Watermark:	None
Perforations:	15½
Colors:	Brown, dark brown, yellowish brown
Varieties:	Printed on both sides, Cracked plate

Collectable Stamp Today
Collectable Cancellation Colors:
Black, blue, red, magenta, green.
Collectable Cancellation Varieties:
Paid, supplementary mail type A, Steamship, Steam, express company, railroad, packet boat, pen

Value Unused:	$$$$$
Value Used:	$$$$
Surviving Covers:	300
Largest Known Multiple:	Unused: 9 (3x3 block)
	Used: 4 (2x2 block)

Type II five-cent stamps differ from the type I in that the projections at the top and bottom are partially cut away, to make room for the perforations. They were printed from a new plate, number 2. This stamp first was used on May 8, 1860. The type II five-cent comes in two major color varieties, orange brown and brown.

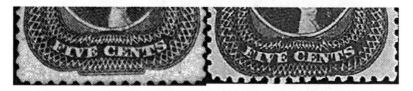

Figure 3-60. Types of Five-Cent Jefferson Stamps. It is easy to tell the difference between the two types of Jefferson five-cent stamps. The Type I, on the left, is complete and has projections off the top and bottom of the frame. The Type II, on the right, is missing most of the projection.

This type II five-cent stamp is brown, in fact it comes in several shades of it. But none have an orange tone, like last issue. Although this follows the orange brown in the Scott catalog, it was issued a year earlier.

The stamp comes in several varieties including stamps printed on both sides and stamps from a cracked plate. Over 300 covers, with this variety remain. This includes Civil War era patriotic covers. The largest unused multiple is a block of nine (3x3); the largest known used multiple, a block of four.

Type II, Orange Brown Five-Cent Jefferson Perforated Stamp of 1857

Type II, Orange Brown Five-Cent Jefferson Perforated Stamp of 1857

Stamp Production

Printer:	Toppan, Carpenter & Co
Designer:	Edward Purcell
Engravers:	Joseph I. Pease (portrait), Cyrus Durand (frame) and Henry Earle (lettering)
Format:	2 panes of 100
Plate Numbers:	2
Issue Date:	1861
Earliest Known Use:	May 8,1861
Uses:	Foreign-destination rates, usually as multiples, especially France. Registration fee
Quantity issued:	570,000

Stamp Features

Size:	19.5 x 25.5 mm. (0.8 x 1.0 inches)
Watermark:	None

Perforations:	15½
Colors:	Orange brown, deep orange brown.
Varieties:	None

Collectable Stamp Today
Collectable Cancellation Colors:
Black, blue, red, green

Collectable Cancellation Varieties:
Paid, steamship, supplementary mail type A, railroad, pen

Value Unused:	$$$$$
Value Used:	$$$$$
Surviving Covers:	40
Largest Known Multiple:	Unused: 32
	Used: 3 (strip)

Being a type II stamp, this stamp's projections at the top and bottom are partially cut away. It was not used until July 13, 1861, shortly before all of the stamps of the series were demonetized, declared invalid for postage, because of the Civil War. Because of the short period in which it was in use and the large numbers of unused stamps discovered in the South after the war, this is an unusual stamp that is more valuable used than in unused condition. That also is why only 40 covers with this stamp still remain. The stamp can be found in unused blocks, the largest being 32, but is rare used in more than singles, the largest being a strip of three.

TEN-CENT STAMPS OF 1857

The perforated ten-cent stamps were made from two plates: plate 1 that printed the imperforate stamps, and plate 2, a new plate. The perforated stamps from plate 1, therefore, are of the same types as the imperforates, type I, II, III, and IV. Type V comes from the new plate, plate 2. The four types, from plate 1, were issued on July 27, 1857. Most perforated stamps of the first four types have perforations that cut into the design.

Blocks of the perforated stamps from plate 1 are rare. Obviously, the same combination of types in blocks is possible with the perforated stamps as it with the imperforates.

There is a pen-canceled block of 10 ten-cent stamps that contains all the major varieties of perforated stamps from plate 1. The block comes from positions 54, 55, 64, 65, 74, 75, 84, 85, 94, and 95L. In this block, there are two type I, one type II, two type III, and five type IV stamps. And the type IV stamps in the block have all three types of the recuts!

Type I Ten-Cent Washington Perforated Stamp of 1857

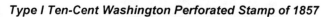

Type I Ten-Cent Washington Perforated Stamp of 1857

Stamp Production

Printer:	Toppan, Carpenter & Co.
Designer:	Edward Purcell
Engravers:	Joseph I. Pease (portrait), Henry Earle (border and lettering)
Format:	2 panes of 100
Plate Numbers:	1
Issue Date:	July 27, 1857
Earliest Known Use:	Sept. 21, 1857
Uses:	Letters up to 1/2 ounce, going more than 3,000 miles
Quantity issued:	600,000

Stamp Features

Size:	19 x 24.2 mm. (0.7 x 1.0 inches)
Watermark:	None
Perforations:	15½
Colors:	Green, dark green, bluish green, yellowish green.
Varieties:	Double transfer (100R1), Curl in left X (99R1).

Collectable Stamp Today

Collectable Cancellation Colors:	
	Black, blue, red, green
Collectable Cancellation Varieties:	
	supplementary mail type A, Steamship, Canadian, pen
Value Unused:	$$$$$$
Value Used:	$$$$$
Surviving Covers:	75
Largest Known Multiple:	Unused: 3 in a block of 6
	Used: 6 (strip)

A type I stamp is an "almost complete" stamp with tiny portions missing at the top and the bottom. Like all stamps but type V, the ornaments at sides are complete. Type I stamps come from the 20 bottom row positions of plate 1. This stamp is found on patriotic covers of the Civil War era.

Type II Ten-Cent Washington Perforated Stamp of 1857

Type II Ten-Cent Washington Perforated Stamp of 1857

Stamp Production
Printer:	Toppan, Carpenter & Co.
Designer:	Edward Purcell
Engravers:	Joseph I. Pease (portrait), Henry Earle (border and lettering)
Format:	2 panes of 100
Plate Numbers:	1
Issue Date:	July 27, 1857
Earliest Known Use:	July 27,1857
Uses:	Letters up to 1/2 ounce, going more than 3,000 miles
Quantity issued:	2,900,000

Stamp Features
Size:	19 x 24.2 mm. (0.7 x 1.0 inches)
Watermark:	None
Perforations:	15½
Colors:	Green, dark green, bluish green, yellowish green
Varieties:	Double transfer (31L1, 51L1, 20R1), Curl opposite left X (10R1)

Collectable Stamp Today
Collectable Cancellation Colors:
Black, blue, red, brown, green
Collectable Cancellation Varieties:
1857, Paid, supplementary mail type A, steamship, packet boat, railroad, express company cancellation, pen
Value Unused: $$$$$

Value Used: $$$$
Surviving Covers: 290-360
Largest Known Multiple: Unused: 3 within larger block
Used: 6 (strip)

    A type II stamp's design is complete at the top, but incomplete at bottom with the bottom frame line broken. The design comes from rows 1, 2, 4, 6 and 8 of both panes (total of 93 positions) of plate 1. This stamp, rarely, can be found on Civil War patriotic and Pony Express covers. The largest unused multiple is a strip of three stamps within a larger block. The largest used multiple is a strip of six stamps, still on a cover.

Type III Ten-Cent Washington Perforated Stamp of 1857

Type III Ten-Cent Washington Perforated Stamp of 1857

Stamp Production
Printer: Toppan, Carpenter & Co.
Designer: Edward Purcell
Engravers: Joseph I. Pease (portrait), Henry Earle (border and lettering)
Format: 2 panes of 100
Plate Numbers: 1

Issue Date: July 27, 1857
Earliest Known Use: Oct. 6, 1857
Uses: Letters up to 1/2 ounce, going more than 3,000 miles
Quantity issued: 2,400,000

Stamp Features
Size: 19 x 24.2 mm. (0.7 x 1.0 inches)
Watermark: None
Perforations: 15½
Colors: Green, dark green, bluish green, yellowish green
Varieties: Curl on forehead (85L1), Curl in left X (87R1)

Collectable Stamp Today
Collectable Cancellation Colors:
Black, blue, red, brown, ultramarine.
Collectable Cancellation Varieties:
1857, Paid, Steam, steamship, steamboat, numeral, packet boat, pen
Value Unused: $$$$$
Value Used: $$$$
Surviving Covers: 240-300
Largest Known Multiple: Unused: 6
Used: 4 (strip)

Like its imperforate counterpart, the perforate type III ten-cent stamp is incomplete at both the top and the bottom, with the top and bottom frame lines broken. It comes from 79 scattered plate 1 positions.

Figure 3-61. Example of a Ten-Cent Stamp on a Cover. This is a cross-country cover paid by an 1857 ten-cent stamp. The letter was sent from San Francisco, CA to Philadelphia, PA.

Type IV Ten-Cent Washington Perforated Stamp of 1857

Type IV Ten-Cent Washington Perforated Stamp of 1857

Stamp Production
Printer: Toppan, Carpenter & Co.
Designer: Edward Purcell
Engravers: Joseph I. Pease (portrait), Henry Earle (border and lettering)
Format: 2 panes of 100
Plate Numbers: 1
Issue Date: July 27, 1857
Earliest Known Use: Oct. 5, 1857
Uses: Letters up to 1/2 ounce, going more than 3,000 miles
Quantity Issued: 240,000

Stamp Features
Size: 19 x 24.2 mm. (0.7 x 1.0 inches)
Watermark: None
Perforations: 15½
Colors: Green, dark green, bluish green, yellowish green
Varieties: Recuts.

Collectable Stamp Today
Collectable Cancellation Colors:
Black, blue, red.
Collectable Cancellation Varieties:
steamship, packet boat, pen
Value Unused: $$$$$$
Value Used: $$$$$
Surviving Covers: 24-30
Largest Known Multiple: Unused: 2
Used: 4 (2x2 block)

The type IV stamps are the recut varieties. They are the same as those found on the imperforate stamps and come from the same positions on plate 1. They have outer line recuts at top (65L, 74L, 86L, 3R), bottom (54L, 55L, 76L), or both (64L).

Type V Ten-Cent Washington Perforated Stamp of 1857

Type V Ten-Cent Washington Perforated Stamp of 1857

Stamp Production

Printer:	Toppan, Carpenter & Co.
Designer:	Edward Purcell
	Engravers: Joseph I. Pease (portrait), Henry Earle (border and lettering)
Format:	2 panes of 100
Plate Numbers:	2
Issue Date:	1859
Earliest Known Use:	April 29, 1859
	Uses: Letters up to 1/2 ounce, going more than 3,000 miles
Quantity Issued:	10,000,000 - 12,500,000

Stamp Features

Size:	19 x 24.2 mm. (0.7 x 1.0 inches)
Watermark:	None
Perforations:	15½
Colors:	Green, dark green, yellowish green.

Varieties: Double transfer at bottom (47R2), Small curl on forehead (37L2, 78L2), Curl in E of CENTS (93L2), Curl in T of CENTS (73R2), Shell gash (98L2), Shell dash (84L2), Extra hair on forehead (7L2, 8L2, 9L2), Cracked plate.

Collectable Stamp Today
Collectable Cancellation Colors: Black, red, orange red, brown, blue, orange, magenta, green.
Collectable Cancellation Varieties: 1859, Paid, red carrier, steamship, Steam, railroad, numerals, supplementary mail type A or C, express company cancellation, Southn Letter Unpaid, territorial, pen
Value Unused: $$$$
Value Used: $$$
Surviving Covers: 1,500-2,000
Largest Known Multiple: Unused: 42 (6x7 block)
Used: 8 (block)

Type V stamps came from a newly made plate for perforated stamps, number 2. Therefore, they are found only in a perforated form. The characteristic of a type V stamp is that the sides, especially the ornaments, are incomplete. If it does not show three pearls at each side, it is a type V. The stamps vary a great deal from each other. There are two reasons for the variation. First, the transfers from the die were not exactly the same. The design was intentionally short transferred. Second, difference erasures were made between many of the stamps to provide more space for perforations.

This type stamp, by far, was the most common ten-cent perforated stamp made. The stamp can be found on patriotic covers and Pony Express covers. Because the stamps were issued near the time when they made invalid, blocks of these stamps are more valuable in a used condition than unused.

Figure 3-62. Features of the Type V Ten-Cent Stamp of the 1857 Series. This stamp is missing parts of the side ornaments. All Type V ten-cent stamps are perforated.

TWELVE-CENT STAMPS OF 1857

Plate 1 Twelve-Cent Washington Perforated Stamp of 1857

Plate 1 Twelve-Cent Washington Perforated Stamp of 1857

Stamp Production

Printer:	Toppan, Carpenter & Co.
Designer:	Edward Purcell
Engravers:	Joseph I. Pease (portrait), Henry Earle (frame and lettering)
Format:	2 panes of 100
Plate Numbers:	1
Issue Date:	1857
Earliest Known Use:	July 30, 1857
Uses:	Pairs paid foreign rate to Great Britain. Bisected for domestic use. Quadruple basic rate.
Quantity Issued:	3,000,000

Stamp Features

Size:	20 x 28 mm. (0.7 x 1.0 inches)
Watermark:	None
Perforations:	15½
Colors:	Black, gray black
Varieties:	Double transfer, Triple transfer (5R), Not recut in lower right corner, Recut in lower right corner, Recut in lower left corner (100L), Recut in lower right and left corners (43L, 53L, 63L, 73L)
Errors:	Horizontal pairs, imperforate in between.

Collectable Stamp Today
Collectable Cancellation Colors:
        Black, blue, red, brown, magenta, green
Collectable Cancellation Varieties:
        1857, Paid, supplementary mail type A, express company
        cancellation, railroad, numeral, Southn Letter Unpaid, pen
Value Unused: $$$$$
Value Used: $$$$
Surviving Covers: 400-500
Largest Known Multiple: Unused: 8
                       Used: 28 (block)

    This plate used to print the perforated twelve-cent stamps is same as the one used for the imperforate stamp. It is not numbered, but is called plate 1 to distinguish it from plate 3, which was numbered and used to produce the other variety of twelve-cent stamps. Though only two plates printed these stamps, three plates were made. No stamps ever were made from plate 2. Because the stamps come from the original imperforate plate, the frame lines are recut and of uniform strength. The plate varieties found on the imperforates also are found on the perforate stamps.

    The stamp exists with perforation errors. Used horizontal pairs, imperforate in between, can be found very rarely.

Figure 3-63. Example of an 1857 Twelve-Cent Stamp on a Cover. This is an example of a cover with a pair of twelve-cent Washington stamps. It shows the most common use of the stamp, which is, used as a pair, to pay the 24-cent postage rate to England. The letter was sent from Kanawha Court House, Virginia to London, England.

Plate 3 Twelve-Cent Washington Perforated Stamp of 1857

Plate 3 Twelve-Cent Washington Perforated Stamp of 1857

Stamp Production
Printer: Toppan, Carpenter & Co.
Designer: Edward Purcell
Engravers: Joseph I. Pease (portrait), Henry Earle (frame and lettering)
Format: 2 panes of 100
Plate Numbers: 3
Issue Date: 1859
Earliest Known Use: Dec. 3, 1859 or June 1, 1860
Uses: Pairs paid foreign rate to Great Britain. Bisected for domestic use. Quadruple basic rate.
Quantity Issued: 2,800,000

Stamp Features
Size: 20 x 28 mm. (0.7 x 1.0 inches)
Watermark: None
Perforations: 15½
Colors: Black, intense black
Varieties: Vertical line though rosette (95R), Double frame line at left, Double frame line at right

Collectable Stamp Today
Collectable Cancellation Colors:
Black, blue, red, brown, magenta, green
Collectable Cancellation Varieties:
1860,1861, Paid, supplementary mall type A, express company cancellation, railroad, numeral, Southn Letter Unpaid, pen

Value Unused: $$$$
Value Used: $$$$
Surviving Covers: 400
Largest Known Multiple: Unused: 100 (complete right pane)
Used: 20 (block)

Type	Definition	Imperforate Plates	Perforated Plates
Plate 1	Framelines Recut	1	1
Plate 3	Framelines Not Recut	None	3

For plate 3 twelve-cent stamps, the frame lines are not recut. Therefore, one sees breaks in the lines. While the faulty lines were fixed on the first plate, by recutting, this was not done on the new plate.

There is an interesting plate variety. One finds stamps with a double frame line at the left on the stamps of the fourth vertical row of the left pane and a double frame line on the right on stamps from the third vertical row. This is the result of an extra line drawn running from the top to the bottom of the entire length of the plate.

TWENTY-FOUR-CENT STAMP OF 1857

Twenty-Four-Cent Washington Stamp of 1857

Stamp Production
Printer:	Toppan, Carpenter & Co.
Designer:	Edward Purcell
Engravers:	Joseph I. Pease (portrait), Henry Earle (frame and lettering)
Format:	2 panes of 100
Plate Numbers:	1
Issue Date:	1860
Earliest Known Use:	July 7, 1860
Uses:	Foreign rate to Great Britain
Quantity Issued:	736,000

Stamp Features
Size:	19.2 x 25 mm (0.8 x 1.0 inches)
Watermark:	None
Perforations:	15½
Colors:	Lilac, gray lilac, gray
Varieties:	None

Collectable Stamp Today
Collectable Cancellation Colors:
Black, blue, red, magenta, violet, green.
Collectable Cancellation Varieties:
1860, 1861, Paid, Paid All, Free, supplementary mail type A, railroad, packet boat, red carrier, numeral, Southn. Letter Unpaid, pen
Value Unused:	$$$$$
Value Used:	$$$$

Surviving Covers: 200
Largest Known Multiple: Unused: 22 (irregular block)
                            Used: 10 (5x2 block)

The twenty-four cent and other higher denomination stamps are completely new issues for 1857. The 24, 30, and 90-cent denominations would be standard for several United States stamp series to come. The 24-cent stamp featured a portrait of George Washington after a painting of him by Stuart. It shows a three-quarter face of Washington, looking to the right, on an oval dark background. The border of the portrait oval has a rim, within is written U. S. POSTAGE, above and TWENTY FOUR CENTS, below. The entire oval is surrounded by lathe work. There is a fine outer line. The 24-cent stamp looks like the five-cent stamp of this series.

Plating and Printing

The plate for the 24-cent stamp was made in 1857, but stamps were not printed until 1860. This, also, was true for the 30 and 90-cent issues. Only a single plate, labeled 1, printed all the 24-cent stamps.

Colors

The stamp comes in lilac or gray lilac. The red lilac minor variety is a trial color proof only.

Use

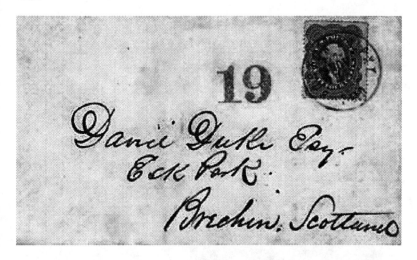

Figure 3-64. Example of an 1857 Twenty-Four-Cent Stamp on Cover. This example is a cover with an 1857 series twenty-four-cent Washington,. It shows the most common use of the stamp, to pay the 24-cent postage rate to Great Britain. This letter was mailed to Scotland.

Since these values were added in 1860, they come perforated only. And since they were in use for only a year or so, used stamps are valued about the same as unused. The stamp paid for mail to Great Britain. The United States-British mail treaty of 1848, which was in effect until revised in 1868, set the postage for a single letter between England and the United States at one-shilling. The United States equivalent was 24 cents.

Imperforate

This stamp, as well as the 30 and 90-cent issues can be found imperforate. Today, they are considered to be trial printings, not issued stamps.

Multiples

Blocks of stamps, used or unused, are very rare. The largest unused multiple is an irregular block of 22 stamps, used, a block of 10 (5x2). A plate block of 8, within a block of 12 stamps, with the marginal markings exists.

THIRTY-CENT STAMP OF 1857

Thirty-Cent Franklin Stamp of 1857

Stamp Production

Printer:	Toppan, Carpenter & Co.
Designer:	Edward Purcell
Engravers:	Joseph I. Pease (portrait), Henry Earle (frame and lettering)
Format:	2 panes of 100
Plate Numbers:	1
Issue Date:	1860
Earliest Known Use:	Aug. 8,1860
Uses:	Foreign mail to Germany and France
Quantity Issued:	356,000

Stamp Features

Size:	20 x 25 mm (0.8 x 1.0 inches)

Watermark:	None
Perforations:	15½
Colors:	Orange, yellow orange, reddish orange
Varieties:	Double transfer (89R, 99L), Complete arrowhead bottom right, Recut at bottom (52L), Cracked plate

Collectable Stamp Today
Collectable Cancellation Colors:
Black, blue, red, magenta, violet, green.
Collectable Cancellation Varieties:
1860, Paid, Free, black town, supplementary mail type A, steamship, express company cancellations, Southn Letter Unpaid, pen

Value Unused:	$$$$$
Value Used:	$$$$
Surviving Covers:	200
Largest Known Multiple:	Unused: 21 (7x3 block)
	Used: 53 (irregular block)

This stamp was printed from a single plate, numbered 1. Although part of the 1857 issue and the plate prepared then, the 30-cent stamp, like the 24 and 90-cent stamps, was not issued until 1860.

The 30-cent vignette look like a reverse image of the one-cent 1851 vignette. The stamp features a profile of Benjamin Franklin on a central oval. It has a slightly shaded border. In each corner is a shield, with a fine radiation of lines, connected with ornate, shaded scrolls. At the top are the words U. S. POSTAGE, at the sides are the words THIRTY and CENTS. The numeral, 30, is at the bottom.

Color

The orange color of the 30 cent stamp was selected after thousands of stamps were printed in black. Black was rejected because cancellations would not show against the dark background. The need to reprint stamps in a different color delayed release of the stamp. Unfortunately, with the orange color, the opposite effect occurs. When canceled, the stamp's details are largely covered.

Figure 3-65. Example of an 1857 Thirty-Cent stamp on a Cover. This is an example of a foreign cover with a 30-cent stamp of the 1857 series. It shows the most common use of the stamp, to pay the postage to France. The letter was mailed in New Orleans, Louisiana on October 28, 1860.

Varieties

There are four minor variations of the stamp, not enough to qualify as types. The stamp is found imperforate, but it is considered a trial printing, not a regular issued stamp.

Uses

The stamp paid for overseas postage. Most covers were sent to France and Germany. It can be found on Civil War era patriotic covers. Since the stamp was issued a short time before the Civil War demonetization, few used stamps and covers are found.

Figure 3-66. Unused Block of Thirty-Cent Franklin Stamps of the 1857 Series.
This is a fine example of an unused 4x3 block of thirty-cent stamps of the 1857 series.

NINETY-CENT STAMP OF 1857

Ninety-Cent Washington Stamp of 1857

Stamp Production
Printer: Toppan, Carpenter & Co.
Designer: Edward Purcell

Engravers:	Joseph I. Pease (portrait), Henry Earle (frame and lettering)
Format:	2 panes of 100
Plate Numbers:	1
Issue Date:	1860
Earliest Known Use:	Sept. 11, 1860
Uses:	Heavy, multiple rates to Europe. To the Far East, Spain, and Africa. Multiple-rate domestic uses.
Quantity Issued:	25,000

Stamp Features

Size:	19 x 24.5 mm (0.7 x 1.0 inches)
Watermark:	None
Perforations:	15½
Colors:	Blue, deep blue
Varieties:	Double transfer at bottom, Double transfer at top, Short transfer at bottom right and left (13L, 68R)

Collectable Stamp Today
Collectable Cancellation Colors:
Black, blue, red.
Collectable Cancellation Varieties:
1861, red carrier, Paid, pen, black town, NY ocean mail

Value Unused:	$$$$$
Value Used:	$$$$$
Surviving Covers:	6
Largest Known Multiple:	Unused: 21 (7x3 block)
	Used: 4 (2x2 block)

The ninety-cent stamp features a wonderful portrait of a young George Washington in his general dress uniform. It is modeled after a painting by John Trumbull, now found at Yale University. The three-quarters face is on a dark background with arched top. In this arch are the words U. S. POSTAGE. At the bottom of the portrait, are the words NINETY CENTS. There are scrollwork ornaments.

The stamp is printed in a deep shade of blue, making it one of the classic beauties of United States stamps. The irony is that the Post Office Department, at first, did not like the stamp because it felt the public would not recognize the youthful Washington.

Plating and Printing

The ninety-cent stamps were printed from a single plate, numbered 1. Like the other higher denomination stamps of this series, the plate was made in 1857, but the stamp was not printed until 1860, Sept. 11th of that year being the earliest known use.

Like the 30-cent stamp of this issue, while four different plating types exist on the plate, the differences are very minor.

Varieties

The issue exists imperforate, but like the 24-cent and 30-cent, it is a trial color proof submitted to the Postmaster General by the printer.

There are double transfers, one at the top of the stamp and one at the bottom. The double transfer at the top is the more common.

Use

Since, the stamp wasn't printed until just one year before the issue's demonization, many of the stamps were returned to the Post Office Department and destroyed. Because of the high denomination, infrequent use, and the short time of use, only five covers with the stamp remain, and genuinely used copies are scarce.

Multiples

The largest unused multiple of this stamp is a block of 21 (7x3), used, a block of four.

Official Reproductions

One-Cent Franklin 1875 Reproduction

Stamp Production
Printer:	Continental Bank Note Company
Format:	1 pane of 100
Plate Numbers:	New unnumbered plate
Issue Date:	1875
Uses:	Souvenir
Quantity Issued:	3,846

Stamp Features
Size:	20 x 26 mm. (0.8 x 1.0 inches)
Watermark:	None
Perforations:	12
Colors:	Bright blue
Varieties:	Cracked plate (91), Double transfer (94)

Collectable Stamp Today
Value Unused:	$$$$

Three-Cent Washington 1875 Reproduction

Stamp Production
Printer: Continental Bank Note Company
Format: 1 pane of 100
Plate Numbers: New unnumbered plate
Issue Date: 1875
Uses: Souvenir
Quantity Issued: 479

Stamp Features
Size: 20 x 25 mm. (0.8 x 1.0 inches)
Watermark: None
Perforations: 12
Colors: Scarlet
Varieties: None

Collectable Stamp Today
Value Unused: $$$$$

Five-Cent Jefferson 1875 Reproduction

Stamp Production

Printer:	Continental Bank Note Company
Format:	2 panes of 100
Plate Numbers:	Original 2
Issue Date:	1875
Uses:	Souvenir
Quantity Issued:	878

Stamp Features

Size:	19.5 x 25.5 mm. (0.8 x 1.0 inches)
Watermark:	None
Perforations:	12
Colors:	Orange brown
Varieties:	None

Collectable Stamp Today

Value Unused:	$$$$$

Ten-Cent Washington 1875 Reproduction

Stamp Production
Printer: Continental Bank Note Company
Format: 1 pane of 100
Plate Numbers: New unnumbered plate of 100
Issue Date: 1875
Uses: Souvenir
Quantity Issued: 516

Stamp Features
Size: 19 x 24.2 mm. (0.7 x 1.0 inches)
Watermark: None
Perforations: 12
Colors: Blue green
Varieties: None

Collectable Stamp Today
Value Unused: $$$$$

Twelve-Cent Washington 1875 Reproduction

Stamp Production
Printer:	Continental Bank Note Company
Format:	1 pane of 100
Plate Numbers:	New unnumbered plate of 100
Issue Date:	1875
Uses:	Souvenir
Quantity Issued:	489

Stamp Features
Size:	20 x 28 mm. (0.7 x 1.0 inches)
Watermark:	None
Perforations:	12
Colors:	Greenish black
Varieties:	None

Collectable Stamp Today
Value Unused:	$$$$$

Twenty-Four-Cent Washington 1875 Reproduction

Stamp Production
Printer:	Continental Bank Note Company
Plate Numbers:	Original 1
Plates:	2 panes of 100
Issue Date:	1875
Uses:	Souvenir
Quantity Issued:	479

Stamp Features
Size: 19.2 x 25 mm (0.8 x 1.0 inches)
Watermark: None
Perforations: 12
Colors: Blackish violet
Varieties: None

Collectable Stamp Today
Value Unused: $$$$$

Thirty-Cent Franklin 1875 Reproduction

Stamp Production
Printer: Continental Bank Note Company
Plate Numbers: Original 1
Plates: 2 panes of 100
Issue Date: 1875
Uses: Souvenir
Quantity Issued: 480

Stamp Features
Size: 20 x 25 mm (0.8 x 1.0 inches)
Watermark: None
Perforations: 12
Colors: Yellow orange
Varieties: None

Collectable Stamp Today
Value Unused: $$$$$

Ninety-Cent Washington 1875 Reproduction

Stamp Production
Printer: Continental Bank Note Company
Plate Numbers: Original 1
Plates: 2 panes of 100
Issue Date: 1875
Uses: Souvenir
Quantity Issued: 454

Stamp Features
Size: 19 x 24.5 mm (0.7 x 1.0 inches)
Watermark: None

Perforations:	12
Colors:	Deep blue
Varieties:	None

Collectable Stamp Today
Value Unused: $$$$$

The reason, as we have seen, that the Post Office Department issued reproductions of the 1857 stamps, as well as stamp series before and after, was to have a complete set of its stamps as part of its exhibit at the Philadelphia Centennial Exposition of 1876. Also, it received requests from stamp collectors for its obsolete issues. As the reprints of this series were perforated, they can be considered as reprints of the perforated 1857 issue, rather than the imperforate 1851 series.

The Continental Bank Note Company of New York printed the reproductions. Unlike for the reproductions of the 1847 stamps, the original plates or transfer roll were located for the 1857 series. In the summer of 1874, they were sent to Continental. The original plates of the 5, 24, 30 and 90-cent stamps were used. For the 1, 3,10, and 12-cent stamps, new plates were made from the original transfer rolls. On the new plates, the positions were set far apart, so that the sheets could be perforated further apart. This is so the perforations would not cut into the designs, as happened with the original stamps. These new reproduction plates made only a single pane of 100 stamps, unlike the double panes with a total of 200 stamps on the originals.

The one-cent stamps, made from the new plate, are type I, with the complete design. The three-cent stamps, also made from a new plate, are type I, having the outer lines at top and bottom. The five-cent stamps were made from the original plate 2, and show the same varieties as the original stamps from that plate. The ten-cent stamps, printed from the new plate, are type I, showing the complete stamp design. Likewise for the twelve-cent stamp, the design is complete, printed from a new plate. For the higher values, there was only one plate and single stamp design. Therefore, the originals and reproductions of the 24, 30 and 90-cent stamps are the same design.

The paper of the reproductions is white, crisp and hard. The stamps are gumless. The perforation gauge 12 instead of 15½, a simple test to distinguish the reproduction from the original. Scissors separated perforations are common.

The colors are much brighter than the originals. The inks are uniform, as they were made from a single printing. The 1-cent is bright blue, 3-cent scarlet, 5-cent orange-brown, 10-cent blue-green, 12-cent greenish black, 24-cent blackish violet, 30-cent yellow orange, and 90-cent deep blue.

The stamps were not valid for postage, but a rare stamp can be found used. All stamps in the series have been found, imperforate.

Essays, Proofs, and Specimens

Essays

Essays are the proposed designs for future stamps. By definition, as we have seen, they differ from actual issued stamps. Before the late 19th century, when the Bureau of Engraving and Printing took over stamp production, the various Bank Note companies competed for the stamp printing contract. They made dies that demonstrated their proposed stamps. These dies printed what survive today as essays. When the 1851 issue was proposed, several printers made and submitted essays. These essays are found on different papers, in several colors and sizes. The essays include those of Rawdon, Wright, Hatch and Edson, which printed the 1847 issue. They submitted two different 3-cent essays, one with a number 3, and the other featuring Washington. Other competing companies with essays were: Gavit & Company (two different three-cent designs, one featuring Franklin, the other, Washington), Bradbury, Wilkinson & Company of England (three-cent design featuring Washington on different papers), Draper, Welsh & Company (several similar three-cent designs featuring Washington in different colors, with different papers), Danforth, Bald & Company (similar three-cent designs with a vignette of Washington on different papers), and Bald, Cousland & Company (two different three-cent designs, one with the numeral, 3, the other, Washington).

Toppan, Carpenter, Casilear & Company, the company that did print the 1851 and 1857 stamps also made essays. These essays reflect the design phases of the future stamps to be printed. For the future one-cent issue, there are essays of just the vignette bust of Franklin. There is a completed Franklin design as a six-cent denomination, rather than one. There are several three-cent essays with the Washington vignette alone and the completed design with different frames and colors. The ten and twelve-cent essays are like the finished stamps, but differ in framing or are incomplete. There are twenty-four-cent essays, an incomplete frame and a design almost like the issued stamp. The existing thirty-cent essay has a frame that is not complete.

Figure 3-67.   Example of an 1851 Series Essay. This is an example of a proposed design from a printing company that lost the contract. It is that of Draper, Welsh & Company which created a series of similar 3-cent designs featuring Washington in different colors, using different papers.

Proofs

Die proofs are impressions taken from the original dies. Large die proofs are proofs on a large piece of paper, 50 mm or larger, usually mounted on a card. The original printing companies prepared them at the time of stamp production. Large die proofs exist for the 1 through 12-cent stamps of this original series and all the stamps of the 1875 reproductions.

Figure 3-68. Example of a Large Die Proof. This is an example of a large die proof of the twelve-cent stamp of this series.

Small die proofs are printed from the die on a small piece of paper. The Bureau of Engraving and Printing printed them later. No small die proofs exist for the original stamps. However, two sets of small die proofs exist of the 1875 reproductions.

One small die set, the Roosevelt Album, was made in 1903. They were created for presentation to government officials. There were 85 sets of proof prints that were mounted in presentation albums. The second set of small die proofs was printed in 1915 for the Panama Pacific Exposition.

Figure 3-69. 1851 Series Roosevelt Small Die Proofs. This is the complete set of 1851 series small die proofs made in 1903. They were created for presentation to government officials.

Figure 3-70. Panama-Pacific Small Die Proof Example. This is 24-cent example of a Panama-Pacific small die proof of the of the 1857 series.

Figure 3-71. Example of an 1851 Series Plate Proof. This is an example of the one-cent plate proof of the 1851 series. They differ from the issued stamps in their sharp impressions, the paper on which they are printed, and the completeness of the design.

Plate proofs, impressions taken from finished plates, differ from the issued stamps in their sharp impressions and the paper on which they are printed. Plate proofs on India paper exist for all the denominations of this series, except the one-cent. India paper is a thin, soft, opaque paper. It varies in thickness and shows particles of bamboo in it. Plate proofs on white cards can be found for the 24, 30, and 90-cent issues.

Plate proofs exist for all the denominations of the reproductions. They are found on India paper, card, and as hybrids. Hybrids are plate proofs mounted on large cards to imitate a large die proof.

Trial color proofs are proofs, either die or plate that differ from the color of the actual stamps. For this series, trial die color proofs are found for the 5, 10, 24, 30, and 90-cent denominations of the original series. Trial color plate proofs, found in several colors, exist for all the denominations of the original series and the reproductions.

The Atlanta set is another group of plate trial color proofs. The American Bank Note Company printed plate proofs of all the reproductions and reissues through the 1875 designs. They were made for the 1881 International Cotton Exhibition held in Atlanta, Georgia. They did not make them for the original stamps of any of the series. The 1851 series reproduction Atlanta trial color plate proofs come in five colors (black, scarlet, brown, green, and blue) for all the denominations from 1 through 90-cents. These were printed on thin cardboard.

Specimens

Specimens are regular stamps overprinted, in black, with the word Specimen. They exist for all values of this series, except the 90-cent. They were sample stamps for use by postal authorities.

3 Issues of 1861

1861 Ungrilled Stamps

Demonetization

When the American Civil War began in April 1861, the Post Office Department was concerned about United States postage stamps in the hands of the seceding states. They feared these stamps would be sent to the North and sold there to provide money for the Confederacy. To prevent this from happening, the Post Office Department demonetized (made invalid for use) the current issue and issued new stamps with different designs. For a short time, the new stamps could be exchanged for the old. The old stamps became invalid for postage on November 1, 1861, December 1, 1861, or January 1, 1862, depending on the part of the country. However, there were illegal uses of the 1857 series stamps after these dates. Covers, showing such use, exist today and are of stamp collector interest.

Meanwhile, the Confederacy prohibited the use of United States stamps in the South after June 1st, 1861. Thus, covers with a United States stamp from any of the seceded states after May 31,1861, are very rare. But many old 1857 series stamps were found in Southern post offices after the Civil War and they became a source of unused stamps for modern stamp collectors

A New Printing Contract

Toppan, Carpenter & Company's contract expired on June 10, 1861. The Postmaster General Blair asked for bids for a new printing contract on March 27. Among the printers who submitted bids was a new firm, the National Bank Note Company of New York City. National pursued the contract aggressively, and on May 10th won, with the low bid of 12 cents per thousand stamps. The distribution of the new stamps was to have begun August 1st, but did not take place until the 15th of that month.

Premieres Gravures

The National Bank Note Company submitted to the Post Office Department, samples of the new series of stamps in the form of complete sheets, which were gummed and perforated. The denominations were 1, 3, 5, 10, 12, 24, 30, and 90 cents, the same denominations as the 1857 series. These samples for a long time was considered and cataloged as stamps. This accounts for the gap in the Scott's catalog numbers at this point. However, these submitted "stamps" were really essays. Today, they are called the premieres gravures, First Designs, or the August Issue.

The company prepared the original designs while not under the supervision of the United States government. So changes were added to the premieres gravures so the issued stamps were under the supervision of the United States government. Thus, the designs were modified on the 1, 3, 5, 10, 12, and 90-cent essays before they were released. Because of unexpected demand for the 10-cent issue, the original premiere gravure was pressed into service. So there are two 10-cent types. While the original 24 and 30-cent designs were used for the issued 1861 stamps, different colors were used compared with the submitted samples. This makes these samples, trial color proofs.

To summarize, the 1, 3, 5, 12 and 90-cent premieres gravures were never sold as postage stamps. They were just essays, sample stamps. Though listed in the catalogs as real stamps at one time, today they are listed as essays. The 24 and 30-cent premieres gravures are trial color proofs, having the same design but a different color as the actual stamps. Only, the 10-cent premiere gravure had a life as a real postage stamp.

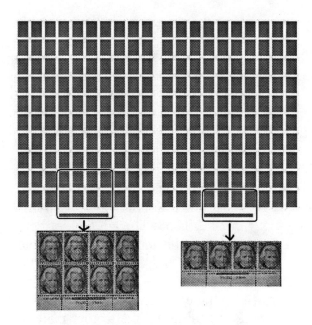

Figure 4-1. 1861 Series Plate Layout, Margin Imprint, Strips, and Blocks. The 1861 series stamps were printed from plates containing 200 stamps. The completed sheets were divided into two panes of 10 by 10 stamps.. The marginal marking was found underneath only the lower part of the pane. To show the markings, collectors save strips of four stamps and blocks of 8 stamps.

The stamps were printed on plates containing 200 stamps. The sheets are divided vertically into two panes of 10 by 10 stamps, left and right. The marginal markings on the plate are: ENGRAVED BY THE NATIONAL BANK NOTE COMPANY CITY OF NEW YORK on one line, with No. X Plate, underneath (X is the plate number). These marginal markings are found only on the bottom of the sheet. Groupings of stamps, with the attached selvage showing the margin markings, are collected as strips of 4 and blocks of 8 stamps.

The date of delivery of the first stamps of this series (1, 5, 10, 12, 24, 30, and 90 cent) was August 16th 1861.On August 17th 1861,

Baltimore, Maryland became the first post office to place this new issue on sale.

These stamps are perforated 12. The paper varies greatly, from nearly transparent to very thick.

Postal Act of 1863

President Lincoln's postmaster general, Montgomery Blair, was a remarkable administrator. He improved American postal service in spite of the ongoing Civil War. His efforts toward postal reform led to the congressional act of March 3, 1863. The act took effect July 1st of that year. First, the law repealed the ten-cent postage rate for over 3,000 miles charge, mostly used to and from California. For the first time, there was a single postal rate for the entire country.

The act divided mail into three classes. First class was letter mail, second class, publications, and third class, all other mail. Third class mail included books and parcels up to four pounds with the rate being the bargain of two cents per four ounces. This rate was in effect until 1872.

The act empowered Blair to establish a free urban letter carrier service. Before this act took effect, most mail was dropped off and picked up at the post office. There was a separate carrier system, which had its own fees. The act increased the cost from one to two cents for drop letters, but delivery, available in 49 cities, was now included. A new 2-cent issue was created to pay for this new rate, the famous "Black Jack" Andrew Jackson stamp. Thus, the act eliminated the carrier system and started free urban delivery.

The fee for drop letters was dropped back to one cent for letters picked up at the post office, on May 1, 1865 with the carrier drop letters still costing two cents.

The registry fee was raised to 20 cents. Registration now provided the sender with a return receipt, for the first time. There still was no insurance for losses. Cash, not stamps, still usually paid the fee. It was not until 1867 that prepayment with stamps was required. The registry fee later was reduced to 15 cents on January 1, 1869.

The postage on ship letters, letters carried by private ships, was changed from an extra 2-cents to double the regular postage rate.

```
┌─────────────────────────────────────────────────────────┐
│              Summary of the Postal Act of 1863           │
│                                                           │
│   •  Uniform first-class postage rate, regardless of      │
│      distance, per ½ ounce-3 cents                        │
│   •  Mail divided into three classes. First class         │
│      (letter mail)                                        │
│      Second class (publications)                          │
│      Third class (all other mail, including books and     │
│      parcels up to four pounds), per four ounces-2 cents. │
│   •  Established free urban letter carrier service,       │
│      eliminated carrier system.                           │
│   •  Drop letters, including free delivery in 49 cities-2 │
│      cents. (Drop letters, not requiring delivery         │
│      reduced to one cent, on May 1, 1865.)                │
│   •  Registry fee-20 cents. (Prepayment with stamps,      │
│      required in 1867. The fee reduced to 15 cents on     │
│      January 1, 1869)                                     │
│   •  Ship letters (letters carried by private ships)-     │
│      double the regular postage rate.                     │
└─────────────────────────────────────────────────────────┘
```

Mourning Stamp

In 1866, one year after the assassination of Lincoln, a 15-cent stamp was issued in his honor. It was the last denomination to be issued of this series. It covered the cost of sending a letter to France or Prussia. Also, the stamp, starting in 1869, paid the new 15-cent registration fee. This stamp started the trend of honoring presidents who died in office with a postage stamp.

Postcards

In 1861, John Charlton copyrighted the concept of printed postcards. He sold the right to Lipman, who printed the first postcards. They mostly were used for business advertisements. The postcard rate was one cent for any card sent up to 1,500 miles.

ONE-CENT FRANKLIN STAMP OF 1861

1861 One-Cent Franklin

Stamp Production

Printer:	National Bank Note Co.
Designer:	James Macdonough
Engravers:	Joseph I. Pease (portrait), Cyrus Durand, David M. Cooper (frame and lettering)
Format:	Sheets of 200, cut vertically into 2 panes of 100
Plate Numbers:	9, 10, 22, 25, 27
Date of Issue:	Aug.16, 1861
Earliest Known Use:	Aug. 17, 1861
Uses:	Circulars and drop letters up to July 1, 1863 and after May 1, 1865. Carrier fee (up to 1863). Postcard rate up to 1,500 miles.
Quantity Issued:	138,000,000

Stamp Feature

Size:	19.5 x 25 mm (0.7 x 1.0 inches)
Watermark:	None
Grill:	None
Perforations:	12
Colors:	Blue, pale blue, bright blue, dark blue, ultramarine
Varieties:	Double transfer, Dot in U, Printed on both sides, Laid paper.
Errors:	Vertical pair imperforate horizontally in between

Collectable Stamp Today
Collectable Cancellation Colors:
Black, blue, red, magenta, green, violet.

Collectable Cancellation Varieties:
1861, 1862, 1863, 1864, 1865, 1866, Free, Paid, Paid All, supplementary mail type A or B, steamship, steam, express company cancellation, red carrier, black carrier, railroad, numerals, Steamboat, precancel for Cumberland Me

Value Unused: $$$$
Value Used: $$$
Surviving Covers: 250,000
Largest Known Multiple: Unused: 100 (complete pane)
Used: 18

The one-cent 1861 stamp features a profile of Benjamin Franklin. It was based on a bust created by Jean Antoine Houdon. The artwork is found today at the Pennsylvania Academy of Fine Arts. As we will continue to see, for over a century, the first United States Postmaster General graces nearly every one-cent regular series issue. An ellipse of lathe work frames the bust, which is facing to the right. The words, U. S. POSTAGE, are above, and ONE CENT are under the portrait. There is a large numeral 1 in each upper corner. In the lower corners of the stamp are the letters, U and S.

The stamp differs from its premiere gravure by an extra dash just under the right tip of the ornament to the right of the left numeral 1.

This stamp has tiny margins and it is difficult to find well centered. Likewise, irregular perforations are common.

Figure 4-2. Difference Between the One-Cent Premiere Gravure and the Issue Stamp. The issued stamp (right) differs from the Premieres Gravure (left) by the addition of a tiny dash in the frame, just under the extreme right tip of the ornament to the right of the left numeral, 1. It is subtle!

Colors

The stamp comes in a several colors: blue, pale blue, bright blue, dark blue, and ultramarine. All are scarce with the exception of the first two. These shades are difficult to distinguish from one another without experience. The blue inks show off the many different colored cancellations.

The one-cent lake and scarlet varieties are color trial proofs, not issued stamps. Both color trial varieties are found perforate and imperforate. The scarlet variety usually is found with a four-line pen cancellation, a mark used at that time to indicate proofs.

Varieties

A common stamp, it is naturally found in several different varieties. One, the dot in the U, is fairly common. The stamp can be found on laid paper, which has ridges from its manufacture. The stamp exists printed on both sides.

Uses and Covers

The earliest known use of the stamp is August 17th 1861. This is one day after the series was issued. The stamp was used to pay the postage for drop letters. It was used to pay the carrier fee until that fee was changed in 1863. Strips of one-cent stamps paid higher postage rates. Since it was a common stamp, there are a quarter million surviving covers. A great variety of cancellations exist. Since this was the Civil War era, there are many patriotic, soldier, and prisoners' covers.

Figure 4-3. Example of a One-Cent Stamp on Cover. Here is an example of a one-cent Franklin stamp being used to pay the drop letter rate for an item mailed locally in Hartford, Connecticut.

Multiples

The largest unused multiple is one complete pane of 100 stamps. However, it recently may have been broken up. Other complete panes also are rumored to exist. The largest used multiple is a block of 18 stamps, off cover; block of 12, on cover.

Errors

This stamp is found in as a vertical pair, imperforate horizontally in between. This error is very rare.

TWO-CENT JACKSON STAMP OF 1863

1863 Two-Cent "Black Jack" Jackson

Stamp Production

Printer: National Bank Note Co.
Designer: James Macdonough
Engravers: Joseph P. Ourdan (portrait), William D. Nichols (frame and lettering)
Format: Sheets of 200, cut vertically into 2 panes of 100
Plate Numbers: 28, 29, 30, 31, 50, 51, 53
Date of Issue: July 1, 1863
Earliest Known Use: July 1, 1863
Uses: Drop-letter rate from July 1, 1863 until May 1, 1865. Drop letter rate with carrier service after July 1, 1863. Circular rate after July 1, 1863.
Quantity Issued: 256,566,000

Stamp Features

Size: 20.5 x 24.5 mm (0.8 x 1.0 inches)
Watermark: None
Grill: None
Perforations: 12
Colors: Black, gray black, intense black.
Varieties: Printed both sides, Double transfer, Atherton shift, Preston shift, Metzger shift, Triple transfer, Short transfer, Cracked plate, Laid paper

Collectable Stamp Today
Collectable Cancellation Colors:
Black, blue, brown, red, orange red, magenta, ultramarine, orange, green.

Collectable Cancellation Varieties:

	1863, 1864, 1865, Paid, Paid All, Way, numeral, railroad, Steam, steamship, Steamboat, express company cancellation, Ship Letter, black carrier, blue carrier, supplementary mail A or B, Short Paid, territorial, China, precancel from Jefferson Ohio
Value Unused:	$$$$
Value Used:	$$$
Surviving Covers:	500,000
Largest Known Multiple:	Unused: 100? (complete pane) or 49
	Used: 12

The 2-cent stamp was not part of the original 1861 series. It was issued July 1,1863, because the Act of Congress of March 3, 1863. This postal law abolished carriers' fees and increased the rate to two cents for drop letters and circulars. The two cents also paid for local delivery if available. This stamp also paid circular rates. The earliest known date of use of this stamp is the first of July in 1863.

The stamp's design is unusual and striking. A portrait of Andrew Jackson takes up most of the stamp, not just the middle. It was the first time the seventh president appeared on a postage stamp. The portrait of Jackson is based on a miniature of him by John Wood Dodge. "Black Jack" is the nickname given for the stamp, combining the figure and the color of the stamp. It is one of the most popular of all United States stamps for collectors. M. F. Cole wrote a classic book about the stamp, "The Black Jacks of 1863-67." H. P. Atherton formed one of the largest collections of it and is considered the expert of Black Jacks.

Printing and Plating

The stamp is infamous for its poor centering. This has created high demand by stamp collectors for well-centered copies. There is little variation in shades of black. Like the rest of the paper used in the series, it varies from thin to thick. The gum varies too, from brownish to white.

Varieties

With many stamps and plates, numerous varieties are found. Double transfers are common and impressive. Several of them even are named. The Atherton shift is a double transfer of the top left corner and the word, POSTAGE. The Preston shift is a double transfer of the right side of the stamp. And the Metzger shift is a double transfer of all the corners of the frame and the hair and the chin. Another double transfer is called the 3-dot variety. This stamp is known with a triple transfer. There is a short transfer, resulting from the failure of the transfer roll to be fully rocked into the plate. The stamp is known printed on both sides and on laid paper.

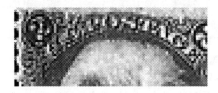

Figure 4-4. The Atherton Shift. One of the most impressive doubles shifts found on United States stamps is the Atherton shift, found on some "Black Jack" two-cent Jackson stamps of 1863. It is a very obvious double transfer of the top left corner and the word, POSTAGE.

Figure 4-5. Preston Shift. A Preston Shift is a large double transfer of a "Black Jack" stamp. It involves the right third of the design. It is most obvious in the scrollwork at the upper right of this stamp.

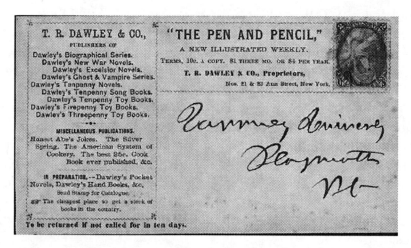

Figure 4-6. Example of a Two-Cent "Black Jack" On Cover. This shows a common use of the 2-cent 1863 stamp. It is used on an advertisement circular sent to Plymouth, Vermont.

Uses and Covers

A widely used and today, a widely collected stamp, there are half a million surviving covers. There is great fun in collecting cancellations: fancy, colored, carriers, paid, and precancel. It is found on Civil War patriotic, military, and prisoner's covers.

The stamp is found, on cover, with only a half used to pay one cent of postage. The diagonal, vertical, and horizontal half all can be found used as such.

Multiples

A complete unused pane of 100 of this stamp did exist. It is not known if it is still intact, today. A block of 49 unused stamps definitely is known to exist. The largest used multiple is block of 12 Black Jack stamps.

THREE-CENT WASHINGTON STAMPS OF 1861

This stamp paid the regular postage rate during the Civil War era. Because of Postmaster General Blair's efforts and the demand created by the war, there was a huge increase in the quantity of mail. As a result, 1.75 billion three-cent stamps were printed. Despite the huge number of stamps printed, there are not many stamp and plate varieties that one might expect.

The stamps are grouped by ink color: rose and pink. The scarlet and lake varieties are trial proofs, not issued stamps. Used copies of these trial color proofs have four horizontal black pen strokes, marks made to indicate they are just samples. The stamp was printed from 25 plates.

The three-cent stamp features a profile of Washington. It is based on a Houdon bust. This continued a mostly unbroken, hundred-year tradition where the first president is found on the stamp that paid the first-class postal rate. He is looking to the left, with his portrait surrounded by lathe work. At the bottom are the words, THREE CENTS, the ends of the printing curling upward. At the top are the words, U.S. POSTAGE, with the ends of the line bending downward. The numeral, 3, is in both upper corners, the letters, U and S in the bottom corners.

The issued stamp is distinguished from its premiere gravure by added balls found at the ends of the corner ornaments.

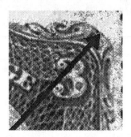 

Figure 4-7. Differences Between the Three-Cent Premiers Gravures and Issued Stamps. The issued stamp (right) has a small ball ornament on the corners that are lacking on the premiere gravure (left).

Cancellations and Covers

Over a million three-cent covers survive until the present day. This makes for an enormous postal history. Collecting Civil War letters and covers attracts history buffs as well as stamp collectors. The letters to and from soldiers are as fascinating history as they provided interesting covers. Patriotic covers, of which there are over 10,000 designs, most of which were franked with the 1861 three-cent stamp are a cover collector's paradise.

Figure 4-8. Example of an 1861 Series Three-Cent Stamp on Cover. Used to pay the basic postage rate, three-cent covers are very common. Here is an example of a three-cent Washington stamp on a letter sent from Vincennes, Indiana to Danville Kentucky.

A fascinating use of the stamp is from Alaska. One rare, always in demand item, is a Pony Express cover, with this stamp.

The light color of the stamp shows off the postmarks. There are many fancy postmarks on these stamps when local postmasters used their vivid imaginations.

Figure 4-9. Example of a Fancy Civil War Cover. Shown is an example of an American Civil War patriotic cover.

Figure 4-10. Fancy Cancellation. A huge variety of fancy cancellations were applied to stamps at this time. Here is an example of a cogwheel cancel applied to a three-cent stamp on a close-up of a surviving letter.

1861 Pink Three-Cent Washington

1861 Pink Three-Cent Washington

Stamp Production
Printer: National Bank Note Co.
Designer: James Macdonough
Engravers: Joseph P. Ourdan (portrait), Cyrus Durand, William D. Nichols (frame and lettering)
Format: Sheets of 200, cut vertically into 2 panes of 100
Plate Numbers: 12
Date of Issue: Aug.16, 1861
Earliest Known Use: Aug.17, 1861 (rose pink and rose, first day covers from Baltimore)
Uses: Domestic first-class rate up to ½ ounce
Quantity Issued: 100,000

Stamp Features
Size: 20 x 25 mm (0.8 x 1.0 inches)
Watermark: None
Grill: None
Perforations: 12
Colors: Pink, Rose pink, pigeon blood
Varieties: None

Collectable Stamp Today
Collectable Cancellation Colors:
Black, blue, red, green, orange red, orange
Collectable Cancellation Varieties:
1861, Paid, Ship, Free, railroad, steamboat, supplement mail type B or C. Paid, Ship

Value Unused:	Pink	$$$$$
	Rose pink	$$$$
	Pigeon blood	$$$$$$
Value Used:	Pink	$$$$
	Rose pink	$$$$
	Pigeon blood	$$$$$
Surviving Covers:	1,000	
Largest Known Multiple:	Unused: 12 (plate block)	
	Used: 4	

The pink varieties of three-cent stamps are relatively scarce. They were printed only from the single plate 12. The pink color has no shade of brown, rose, or red in it. The pink stamps have lots of ink, but a less sharp appearance than the other 3-cent stamps of this series.

Stamp collectors and catalogs subdivide the pink three-cent stamps. The rose pink variety is the most common. It does not have the bluish shade that is associated with the true pink. The very rare shade of pigeon blood is a rich color, deeper than the pink. It is a very scarce stamp, particularly unused.

The earliest known use of this stamp was August 17, 1861, one day after the stamp was issued.

1861 Rose Three-Cent Washington

1861 Rose Three-Cent Washington

Stamp Production

Printer:	National Bank Note Co.
Designer:	James Macdonough
Engravers:	Joseph P. Ourdan (portrait), Cyrus Durand, William D. Nichols (frame and lettering)
Format:	Sheets of 200, cut vertically into 2 panes of 100
Plate Numbers:	11, 12, 13, 14, 19, 20, 21, 23, 24, 32, 33, 34, 35, 36, 37, 42, 43, 44, 45, 46, 47,48, 49, 52
Date of Issue:	Aug.16, 1861
Earliest Known Use:	Aug. 19,1861
Uses:	Domestic first class rate up to ½ ounce
Quantity Issued:	1,782,000,000

Stamp Features

Size:	20 x 25 mm (0.8 x 1.0 inches)

Watermark:	None
Grill:	None
Perforations:	12
Colors:	Rose, bright rose, dull red, rose red, brown red, pale brown red, dull brown red, deep pinkish rose
Varieties:	Printed on both sides, Double impression, Double transfer, Cracked plate, Laid paper
Errors:	Imperforate horizontally (found in pairs)

Collectable Stamp Today
Collectable Cancellation Colors:

Black, blue, ultramarine, brown, red, orange red, violet, magenta, green, olive, orange, yellow

Collectable Cancellation Varieties:

1861, 1862, 1863, 1864, 1865, 1866, 1867, 1868, Paid, Paid All, Mails Suspended, railroad, Way, Free, Collect, Ship, US Ship, Steam, steamship, steamboat, Ship Letter, red carrier, blue carrier, black carrier, numerals, supplementary mail type A B or C, express company cancellation, army field post, packet boat, Registered, Postage Due, Advertised, territorial, St. Thomas, China

Value Unused:	$$$$
Value Used:	$$
Surviving Covers:	1,000,000
Largest Known Multiple:	Unused: 100 (complete pane)
	Used: 12

The rose variety is the other three-cent stamp of the 1861 series. It is, by far, the more common. It was put into service the same time as the pink variety. Shades include: rose, bright rose, dull red, rose red, brown red, pale brown red, bright and dark brown red.

Varieties

Several plate flaws can be seen on some of the 1861 three-cent stamps. A duplication of the upper left corner of the stamp is another variety. The stamp has been found printed on both sides. Also, it exists with a true double impression. The three-cent stamp can be found on laid paper.

Multiples

Several, at least six complete, unused panes of 100 stamps exist for this variety. The largest used multiples include blocks of 12 stamps.

Errors

The stamp exists with a perforation error. It is found in vertical pairs, with the horizontal perforations missing.

FIVE-CENT JEFFERSON STAMPS OF 1861

Like the five-cent stamp of the previous series, this one features Thomas Jefferson. His portrait is surrounded by fancy lathe work. A large numeral, 5, is in each of the upper corners of the stamp. The words, U. S. POSTAGE form the upper curve of the portrait. FIVE CENTS is written below. The letters, U and S, are in the lower corners of the stamp.

The stamp differs from its premiere gravure in that the leaflets project out farther at the corners.

Figure 4-11. Differences Between the Five-Cent Premiere Gravure and Issued Stamp. The Premiere Gravure's (left) leaflet ornaments at the corners do not project as far as on the issued stamp (right).

All of the five-cent stamps were printed from a single plate, number 17. But, because of color changes, there are three five-cent varieties. The first stamps were buff. Next came the red brown of 1862. Finally, in 1863, came the brown issue.

Date Issued	Corner Ornaments	Color
Essay	No Protruding Ornament	Brown
08/19/61	Protruding Ornament	Buff, Brown yellow, Olive yellow
01/02/62	Protruding Ornament	Red brown
02/03/63	Protruding Ornament	Brown, Dark brown, Pale brown, Black brown

1861 Buff Five-Cent Jefferson

1861 Buff Five-Cent Jefferson

Stamp Production
Printer: National Bank Note Co.
Designer: James Macdonough
Engravers: William E. Marshall (portrait), Cyrus Durand, William D. Nichols (frame and lettering)
Format: Sheets of 200, cut vertically into 2 panes of 100
Plate Numbers: 17
Date of Issue: Aug.16, 1861
Earliest Known Use: Aug. 19, 1861
Uses: Usually with other stamps. With 10-cent stamp to France. With 5-cent to India. With 5-cent stamp to Nova Scotia
Quantity Issued: 175,000

Stamp Features
Size: 20.5 x 25.2 mm (0.8 x 1.0 inches)
Watermark: None
Grill: None
Perforations: 12
Colors: Buff, brown yellow, olive yellow
Varieties: None

Collectable Stamp Today
Collectable Cancellation Colors:
Black, red, blue, magenta, green.
Collectable Cancellation Varieties:
1861, 1862, Paid, supplementary mail type A, express company cancellation, numeral, Steamship.

Value Unused: $$$$$$
Value Used: $$$$
Surviving Covers: 500
Largest Known Multiple: Unused: 4 (2x2 block)
                             Used: 6 (strip)

The five-cent stamp of the 1861 series was first printed in buff. Variations of buff included brown yellow and olive yellow. It was first used August 19, 1861.

This stamp is very rare, unused. It is a drab colored stamp. The pale hue is such that cancellations cover the used stamp, very heavily. It has small margins, so well centered stamps are rare. Therefore, it is a difficult stamp to obtain in fine condition.

Figure 4-12. Example of a 1861 Series Five-Cent Stamp On a Cover. Most five-cent stamps at this time were used with other stamps to make us various foreign rates. Here is an example of the 5-cent stamp used with a 10-cent one of the series to pay the 15-cent postage rate to France.

1862 Red Brown Five-Cent Jefferson

1862 Red Brown Five-Cent Jefferson

Stamp Production

Printer:	National Bank Note Co.
Designer:	James Macdonough
Engravers:	William E. Marshall (portrait), Cyrus Durand, William D. Nichols (frame and lettering)
Format:	Sheets of 200, cut vertically into 2 panes of 100
Plate Numbers:	17
Date of Issue:	Dec. 1861?
Earliest Known Use:	Jan. 2, 1862
Uses:	Usually with other stamps. With 10-cent stamp to France. With 5-cent stamp to India. With 5-cent stamp to Nova Scotia
Quantity Issued:	1,000,000

Stamp Features

Size:	20.5 x 25.2 mm (0.8 x 1.0 inches)
Watermark:	None
Grill:	None
Perforations:	12
Colors:	Red brown, dark red brown
Varieties:	Double transfer

Collectable Stamp Today
Collectable Cancellation Colors:
Black, blue, red, magenta.
Collectable Cancellation Varieties:
Paid, town, supplementary mail type A, express company cancellation

Value Unused:	$$$$$
Value Used:	$$$$
Surviving Covers:	2,000
Largest Known Multiple:	Unused: 4 (2x2 block)
	Used: 4 (2x2 block), 6 (strip)

Soon after it was first issued, the dull appearing buff color of the 5-cent stamp was improved by changing it to red brown. The earliest known use of the stamp in this color is January 2, 1862. A variation of the stamp's color is dark red brown.

With its tiny margins, the perforations commonly cut into the stamp's design. Irregular perforations are common. Copies with balanced margins and good perforations clear of the design, therefore, are worth much more the catalog price.

The stamp has a plate variation, a double transfer.

1863 Brown Five-Cent Jefferson

1863 Brown Five-Cent Jefferson

Stamp Production

Printer:	National Bank Note Co.
Designer:	James Macdonough
Engravers:	William E. Marshall (portrait), Cyrus Durand, William D. Nichols (frame and lettering)
Format:	Sheets of 200, cut vertically into 2 panes of 100

Plate Numbers:	17
Date of Issue:	Jan. 1863?
Earliest Known Use:	Feb. 3,1863
Uses:	Usually with other stamps. With 10-cent stamp to France. With 5-cent stamp to India. With 5-cent stamp to Nova Scotia.
Quantity Issued:	6,500,000

Stamp Features

Size:	20.5 x 25.2 mm (0.8 x 1.0 inches)
Watermark:	None
Grill:	None
Perforations:	12
Colors:	Brown, dark brown, pale brown, black brown.
Varieties:	Laid Paper, Double transfer of top frame line, Double transfer of bottom frame line, Double transfer of top and bottom frame lines.

Collectable Stamp Today
Collectable Cancellation Colors:
Black, blue, magenta, red, brown, green
Collectable Cancellation Varieties:
1864, 1865, Paid, Short Paid, town, supplementary mail type A or F, express company cancellation, Steamship, packet boat

Value Unused:	$$$$$
Value Used:	$$$$
Surviving Covers:	10,000
Largest Known Multiple:	Unused: 10 (block)
	Used: 10 (strip), 8 (block)

Type	Center Top	Color	Paper	Date Issued
I	No Outer Curved Line	Dark green, Dark yellow green	Thin	09/17/61
II	Outer Curved Line	Yellow green, Deep yellow green, Green, Dark green, Blue green	Thick	08/20/61

The final and most common shade of the five-cent issue is brown. Like the other five-cent stamps of this series, the margins are small and the perforations cut into the printed area. Variations of the basic color are dark brown, pale brown, and black brown. The black brown shade is the most rare and desirable.

Varieties of this stamp include the use of laid paper. Also, there are double transfers of the top frame line, the bottom frame line, and both top and bottom lines. These double transfers are very common.

TEN-CENT WASHINGTON STAMPS OF 1861

This is the only stamp of the 1861 series that exists in more than one variety, not just as a color difference or a premiere gravure. Though type I was printed second, it is listed first in catalogs, as its plate was prepared first. The earliest use of a type I is September 17, 1861 while Type II was used as early as August 20, 1861. Originally, the type I stamps were a premiere gravure, like the others of the series. The type I design was the one submitted with the bids of the National Bank Note Company The plate bearing type I stamps, plate 4, was put into use, after the type II stamps began to be printed, because of the unexpectedly high demand for 10-cent stamps. Type I stamps were only printed for a short time of the initial high demand. Therefore, only 2% of the ten-cent 1861 stamps are this variety.

The stamp features the head of Washington. Four stars on each side, the words, U. S. POSTAGE above and TEN CENTS below, surround him. There are five more stars at the top of the stamp. The numeral, 10, is in each upper corner, and the letters, U and S, are printed in the two lower corners.

During the first two years of the stamp's life, it paid postage on letters mailed cross-country. Use of this stamp on California mail was common. On July 1, 1863, a single first-class rate of 3 cents per ½ oz. regardless of distance began. This greatly reduced the need for these stamps.

1861 Type I Ten-Cent Washington

1861 Type I Ten-Cent Washington

Stamp Production
Printer: National Bank Note Co.
Designer: James Macdonough
Engravers: William E. Marshall (portrait), William D. Nichols (frame and lettering)

Format:	Sheets of 200, cut vertically into 2 panes of 100
Plate Numbers:	4
Date of Issue:	Sept. 1861
Earliest Known Use:	Sept. 17,1861
Uses:	Transcontinental rate (before 1863). Canada
Quantity Issued:	500,000

Stamp Features

Size:	20.5 x 25.2 mm (0.8 x 1.0 inches)
Watermark:	None
Grill:	None
Perforations:	12
Colors:	Dark green, dark yellow green
Varieties:	Double transfer, Foreign entry of the ninety-cent stamp (94R)

Collectable Stamp Today
Collectable Cancellation Colors:
　　　　　Black, red, blue.
Collectable Cancellation Varieties:
　　　　　Paid, steamship, express company cancellation, supplementary mail type A

Value Unused:	$$$$$
Value Used:	$$$$$
Surviving Covers:	1,000
Largest Known Multiple:	Unused: 4 (2x2 block)
	Used: 4 (2x2 block)

The type I ten-cent variety lacks the added heavy curved line, below and an outer line to all the ornaments above the stars. The paper of the type I stamps is thinner and more transparent than the type II. The stamps were printed in dark green and dark yellow green colors. The stamp is found on Civil War patriotic covers.

1861 Type II Ten-Cent Washington

1861 Type II Ten-Cent Washington

Stamp Production

Printer:	National Bank Note Co.
Designer:	James Macdonough
Engravers:	William E. Marshall (portrait), William D. Nichols (frame and lettering)
Format:	Sheets of 200, cut vertically into 2 panes of 100
Plate Numbers:	15, 26
Date of Issue:	Aug.16, 1861
Earliest Known Use:	Aug. 20, 1861
Uses:	Transcontinental rate (before 1863), Canada
Quantity Issued:	27,300,000

Stamp Features

Size:	20.5 x 25.2 mm (0.8 x 1.0 inches)
Watermark:	None
Grill:	None
Perforations:	12
Colors:	Yellow green, deep yellow green, green, dark green, blue green.
Varieties:	Double transfer, Defective TAG of POSTAGE
Errors:	Vertical pair imperforate horizontally in between

Collectable Stamp Today
Collectable Cancellation Colors:
        Black, blue, red, purple, magenta, brown, green
Collectable Cancellation Varieties:
        1861, 1862, 1863, 1864, 1865, Paid, Collect, Short Paid, P. D. in a circle, Free, numeral, railroad, steamship, Steamboat, supplementary mail type A or D, express company cancellation, red carrier, China, Japan, St. Thomas.
Value Unused: $$$$
Value Used: $$$
Surviving Covers: 10,000
Largest Known Multiple: Unused: 10 (plate block)
        Used: 10

Type II ten-cent stamps were the first used, though the second designed. They were used as early as August 20, 1861. They usually are found on a thicker and more opaque paper. They exist in several shades: green, deep yellow green, yellow green, dark green, and blue green.

Figure 4-13. Differences Between the Type I and Type II Ten-Cent Stamps. The type II ten-cent stamp (right) has an added heavy curved line, below and an outer line to all the ornaments above the stars. This is a very subtle difference!

Double transfers are common. One so-called double transfer is the obvious defective lettering of the TAG of POSTAGE. The defect was caused by metal that had become lodged in a transfer roll. The variety is more prominent on some stamps than others, as the extra metal gradually wore away.

A widely used stamps, there are more than 10,000 surviving covers, including Civil War patriotic covers. These stamps with Japanese cancellations come from the sale of American stamps in Japan for mail being sent from there to the United States.

The largest unused multiple of this variety is a complete plate block of 10 stamps with the marginal imprint from plate 15. The largest used multiple is a pen-canceled block of 10 stamps.

A perforation error exists. There is a vertical pair of used stamps that is imperforate horizontally, in between.

Figure 4-14. Example of a 1861 Ten-Cent Stamp on a Cover. Here is an example of a ten-cent Washington stamp paying for the basic postage rate to Canada. The letter was mailed to Victoria (Note spelling error.) from Detroit. The ten-cent stamp also paid for the transcontinental rate before 1863.

TWELVE-CENT WASHINGTON STAMP OF 1861

1861 Twelve-Cent Washington

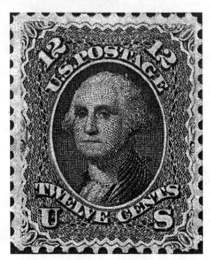

Stamp Production
Printer: National Bank Note Co.
Designer: James Macdonough
Engravers: William E. Marshall (portrait), Cyrus Durand, William D. Nichols (frame)
Format: Sheets of 200, cut vertically into 2 panes of 100
Plate Numbers: 16
Date of Issue: Aug.16, 1861
Earliest Known Use: Aug. 30, 1861
Uses: The 12-cent rate to England. With a 3-cent stamp, the15-cent rate to France.
Quantity Issued: 7,314,000

Stamp Features
Size: 19.5 x 24.5 mm (0.8 x 1.0 inches)
Watermark: None
Grill: None
Perforations: 12
Colors: Black, gray black, intense black.
Varieties: Double transfer of the top frame line, Double transfer of the bottom frame line, Double transfer of top and bottom frame lines.

Collectable Stamp Today
Collectable Cancellation Colors:
Black, blue, red, purple, magenta, green

Collectable Cancellation Varieties:
                        1861, 1862, 1863, 1864, Paid, Registered, supplementary mail type A B or C, express company cancellation, railroad, numeral.
Value Unused: $$$$$
Value Used: $$$$
Surviving Covers: 10,000
Largest Known Multiple: Unused: 6 (block)
                        Used: 10

The twelve-cent stamp of the 1861 series features George Washington. Washington's face is surrounded to the edge of the stamp by a fine geometrical design. The numeral, 12, is in both upper corners. The words, U. S. POSTAGE, are above the portrait, between the numerals. The letters, U and S, are in the lower corners. The words, TWELVE CENTS are just below Washington and they rise at each end, above the U and S. Critics, both then and now, feel this stamp is overly ornate and the Washington head is too small in proportion to the rest of the stamp.

The color of this stamp is black, gray black, or intense black. Because of the dark color, cancellations do not distract from the look of the used stamp. The color does lend itself to easy cleaning and the passing of used stamps as unused, so one should be aware when buying unused copies of it.

All 12-cent stamps of this series were printed from a single plate, number 16. And the stamps are of a single variety. The stamps differ from the essay premiere gravure, in having corner ornaments of ovals and scrolls that serve to square out the stamp.

Figure 4-15. Differences Between the Twelve-Cent Premiere Gravure and Issued Stamp. The stamp differ from the Premieres Gravures (shown to the left), in having corner that square out the stamp.

Double transfers are common varieties. Types include doubling of the top frame line, the bottom frame line, and both frame lines.

The stamp typically was used on foreign mail. It was used by itself on mail to Great Britain and with a 3-cent stamp to pay the postage rate to France.

The largest known unused multiple of 12-cent stamps is a block of six. The largest used multiple is a reconstructed block of 82 stamps.

Figure 4-16. An Example of an 1861 Series Twelve-Cent Stamp On a Cover. This letter shows the most common use of the 1861 series twelve-cent stamp. It is used to pay the postage rate to England.

FIFTEEN-CENT LINCOLN STAMP OF 1866

1866 Fifteen-Cent Lincoln

Stamp Production

Printer:	National Bank Note Co.
Designer:	James Macdonough
Engravers:	James P. Ourdan (portrait), William D. Nichols (frame and lettering)
Format:	Sheets of 200, cut vertically into 2 panes of 100
Plate Numbers:	41
Date of Issue:	Spring 1866
Earliest Known Use:	April 14, 1866
Uses:	New 15-cent registry fee. The 15-cent foreign rate to France and Prussia.
Quantity Issued:	2,139,300

Stamp Features

Size:	19.2 x 24.7 mm (0.8 x 1.0 inches)
Watermark:	None
Grill:	None
Perforations:	12
Colors:	Black, full black.
Varieties:	Double transfer, Cracked plate

Collectable Stamp Today
Collectable Cancellation Colors:
Black, blue, magenta, red, brown, green, purple, lavender, violet, ultramarine, indigo
Collectable Cancellation Varieties:

	Paid, Short Paid, Insufficiently Paid, town, Ship, steamship, supplementary mail type A
Value Unused:	$$$$$
Value Used:	$$$$
Surviving Covers:	7,500-10,000
Largest Known Multiple:	Unused: 20 (block)
	Used: 6 (irregular block)

Not part of the original 1861 stamp series, this stamp was issued in the spring of 1866. It was printed a year after the Abraham Lincoln's assassination to honor him. Issued in black, some collectors consider it a mourning or a commemorative stamp, most grouped it with this series. This denomination paid the new registration fee of 15 cents, the result of in the postal act of Congress of March 3, 1863. It also paid the 15-cent foreign rate on letters sent to France and Prussia.

The stamp features a portrait of Lincoln. On each side of him are fasces. These are bundles of rods bound together, the symbol of authority in ancient Rome. Above the Lincoln portrait are the words, U. S. POSTAGE, on a banner curled at each end, encircling the numerals, 15. Below the portrait are the curved words, FIFTEEN CENTS. The letters, U and S, are in the lower corners, like the rest of the stamps of this series. The paper is thick and the gum ranges from brown to white, in color.

Only one plate, numbered 41, printed all the 15-cent stamps, (including the grilled issues) so there are no major varieties of it. There was little variation in color of this stamp. Being black, it hides cancellations well.

There are 7,500 to 10,000 covers featuring the 15-cent Lincoln stamp. Unfortunately, many covers are the large legal size, used for the registry. This size is not considered desirable from a cover collector's standpoint. (They don't fit into collector's books or boxes well!)

Figure 4-17.   Example of an 1866 Fifteen-Cent Stamp On a Cover. Here is an example of a fifteen-cent Lincoln showing one of its typical uses, paying the postal rate to France.

TWENTY-FOUR-CENT WASHINGTON STAMP OF 1861

The twenty-four cent stamp of the1861 series features George Washington. His portrait is the smallest of the 1861 series. It is surrounded by fine lathe work. On each side, are four small stars. At the top are three more stars, with the numeral, 24, in each corner. In each of the lower corners, there is star, with the letters, U and S found within. The words, U.S. POSTAGE are in the lathe work above Washington, TWENTY FOUR CENTS, below.

Though there is only one design for the 24-cent 1861 stamp, it was printed in a number of colors. They are grouped into major varieties, the violets and the lilacs. All of the twenty-four cent stamps, including the premiere gravure, were made from a single plate, numbered 6. The dark violet 24-cent premiere gravure, in the past thought to be a third major color variation, is now classified as a mere trial color proof.

Figure 4-18. Twenty-Four-Cent Premiere Gravure. The premiere gravure differs from the issued stamp having different colored ink. It is, therefore, officially classified as a trial color proof. Of course, the color difference is impossible to see in this black and white book!

Color	Date Issued	Plates Used
Dark violet	Trial Color Proof	6
Red lilac	1/07/62	6
Brown lilac	2/05/62	6
Steel blue	9/21/61	6
Violet	8/20/61	6
Pale gray violet	9/10/61	6
Lilac	10/29/62	6
Grayish lilac	10/23/62	6
Gray	10/26/62	6
Blackish violet	5/01/63	6

Violet 1861 Twenty-Four-Cent Washington

Violet 1861 Twenty-Four-Cent Washington

Stamp Production

Printer:	National Bank Note Co.
Designer:	James Macdonough
Engravers:	William E. Marshall (portrait), Cyrus Durand, William D. Nichols (frame and lettering)
Format:	Sheets of 200, cut vertically into 2 panes of 100
Plate Numbers:	6
Date of Issue:	Aug. 1861

Earliest Known Use:

Violet:	Aug 20, 1861
Pale gray violet:	Sept. 10, 1861
Steel blue:	Sept. 21, 1861
Red lilac:	Jan. 7, 1862
Brown iliac:	Feb 5, 1862

Uses:	Double letter rate to England
Quantity Issued:	400,000

Stamp Features

Size:	19.5 x 24.0 mm (0.8 x 0.9 inches)
Watermark:	None
Grill:	None
Perforations:	12
Colors:	Violet, pale gray violet, steel blue, red lilac, brown iliac.
Varieties:	Scratch under A of POSTAGE.

Collectable Stamp Today

Collectable Cancellation Colors:

Black, blue, red, magenta, brown, green

Collectable Cancellation Varieties:

1861,1865, Paid, supplementary mail type A or B, express

		company cancellation
Value Unused:	Violet:	$$$$$
	Pale gray violet:	$$$$$
	Steel blue:	$$$$$
	Red lilac:	$$$$$
	Brown iliac:	$$$$$
Value Used:	Violet:	$$$$$
	Pale gray violet:	$$$$$
	Steel blue:	$$$$
	Red lilac:	$$$$
	Brown iliac:	$$$$

Surviving Covers:	500
Largest Known Multiple:	Unused: 6 (block)
	Used: 8 (block)

The first group of stamps are the violets, including violet, steel blue, red lilac, brown lilac, and pale gray violet. The 24-cent violet and pale gray violet were used first. These color varieties are printed on the thin, semi-transparent paper. The color of the ink makes the impressions look blurry. For this reason, the color of the ink was changed, to improve the quality of the impressions. Steel blue is the next color variety, first used on September 21st, 1861. Color changelings of the second major group, the lilac twenty-four cent stamps, are frequently confused as a much more rare, true steel blue. Finally, in 1862, came the more common red iliac and brown lilac color minor varieties.

Most stamps paid the double letter rate to Great Britain. A block of 6 brown lilac stamps is the largest unused multiple, while a block of 8 red lilacs is the largest used multiples.

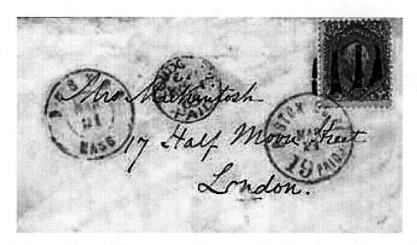

Figure 4-19. Example of an 1861 Series Twenty-Four-Cent Stamp On a Cover.
The most common use of a 24-cent stamp was to pay the double weight postage rate
to England. Here is such an example.   Its stamp is canceled by four black bars. It
was mailed from Boston in 1865 cover to London, England.

Lilac 1862 Twenty-Four-Cent Washington

Lilac 1862 Twenty-Four-Cent Washington

Stamp Production
Printer:	National Bank Note Co.
Designer:	James Macdonough

Engravers:	William E. Marshall (portrait), Cyrus Durand, William D. Nichols (frame and lettering)
Format:	Sheets of 200, cut vertically into 2 panes of 100
Plate Numbers:	6
Date of Issue:	Fall 1862
Earliest Known Use:	Lilac: Oct. 29, 1862
	Grayish lilac: Oct. 23, 1862
	Gray: Oct. 26, 1862
	Blackish violet: May 1, 1863
Uses:	Double letter rate to England
Quantity Issued:	9,620,000

Stamp Features

Size:	19.5 x 24.0 mm (0.8 x 0.9 inches)
Watermark:	None
Grill:	None
Perforations:	12
Colors:	Lilac, grayish lilac, gray, blackish violet
Varieties:	Scratch under A of POSTAGE. Printed on both sides

Collectable Stamp Today
Collectable Cancellation Colors:
Black, blue, red, magenta, green
Collectable Cancellation Varieties:
Paid, numeral, supplementary mail type A, Free

Value Unused:	Lilac:	$$$$$
	Grayish lilac:	$$$$$
	Gray:	$$$$$
	Blackish Violet:	$$$$$$
Value Used:	Lilac:	$$$$
	Grayish lilac:	$$$$
	Gray:	$$$$
	Blackish Violet:	$$$$$
Surviving Covers:	20,000	
Largest Known Multiple:	Unused: 16 (block)	
	Used: 8 (block)	

The second major color variety of the twenty-four cent stamps is the lilacs. The shades vary from lilac to grayish lilac, gray lilac, and gray. The colors get progressively grayer. They probably were not printed in four shades, but over time, the stamps lost the lilac color in which they were printed, creating the minor varieties. The earliest recorded date of use of these shades is October 23, 1862. It is the more common of the two major 24-cent color varieties.

THIRTY-CENT FRANKLIN STAMP OF 1861

1861 Thirty-Cent Franklin

Stamp Production

Printer:	National Bank Note Co.
Designer:	James Macdonough
Engravers:	Joseph I. Pease (portrait), William D. Nichols (lettering and frame)
Format:	Sheets of 200, cut vertically into 2 panes of 100
Plate Numbers:	7
Date of Issue:	Aug. 16, 1861
Earliest Known Use:	Aug. 20,1861
Uses:	Double letter rate to France
Quantity Issued:	3,300,000

Stamp Features

Size:	20.0 x 24.5 mm (0.8 x 1.0 inches)
Watermark:	None
Grill:	None
Perforations:	12
Colors:	Orange, deep orange.
Varieties:	Printed on both sides.

Collectable Stamp Today

Collectable Cancellation Colors:
Black, blue, magenta, brown, red.

Collectable Cancellation Varieties:
1862, 1863, 1864, 1865, Paid, Paid All, railroad, packet boat, Steamship, supplementary mail type A or D, express company cancellation, Japan

Value Unused: $$$$$

Value Used: $$$$
Surviving Covers: 7,500
Largest Known Multiple: Unused: 4
Used: 6 (block)

The 30-cent stamp of this series breaks from a string of George Washington vignettes by featuring Benjamin Franklin. It has his bust, facing to the left. It is enclosed in an oval, surrounded by scrollwork. The words, U. S. POSTAGE, above and THIRTY CENTS below, follow the rim of the oval. The numeral, 30, is in each of the upper corners, and the letters, U and S, are in the lower corners.

Color Used	Paper	Date Issued	Plates
Red orange	Thin	Trial Color Proof	7
Orange	Thick	08/20/61	7

The 30-cent premiere gravure is of the same design as the issued stamp. It is just a different color, red orange, and are found on thin semitransparent paper. The issued stamp is found in just one variety, printed from one plate, in two very close shades: orange and deep orange. These colors cancel poorly, obscuring the stamp design. This makes finding a nice used copy, difficult. It is a hard stamp to find well centered.

A variety of this stamp is one printed on both sides.

The stamp most commonly paid the double letter rate to France and Prussia. The stamp can be rarely found on Civil War patriotic covers.

Figure 4-20. Thirty-Cent Premiere Gravure. The 30-cent Premieres Gravure is of the same exact design as the issued stamp. However, it is a different color, red orange, and are found on thin semitransparent paper.

NINETY-CENT WASHINGTON STAMP OF 1861

1861 Ninety-Cent Washington

Stamp Production
Printer: National Bank Note Co.
Designer: James Macdonough
Engravers: Joseph I. Pease (portrait), William D. Nichols (lettering and frame)

Format: Sheets of 200, cut vertically into 2 panes of 100
Plate Numbers: 18
Date of Issue: Aug. 16, 1861
Earliest Known Use: Nov. 27, 1861
Uses: Overseas, especially China
Quantity Issued: 38,700

Stamp Features
Size: 19.5 x 24.2 mm (0.8 x 1.0 inches)
Watermark: None
Grill: None
Perforations: 12
Colors: Blue, pale blue, dark blue, dull blue.
Varieties: None

Collectable Stamp Today
Collectable Cancellation Colors:
Black, blue, red, green
Collectable Cancellation Varieties:
1865, Paid, Registered, express company cancellation, supplementary mail type A
Value Unused: $$$$$
Value Used: $$$$

Surviving Covers: 62
Largest Known Multiple: Unused: 8 (block)
                            Used: 25 (block on cover)

The 90-cent stamp, like most of this series, was first was issued in August 1861. It features a portrait of George Washington. The portrait is surrounded by the words, U. S. POSTAGE, above and NINETY CENTS, below. The border of the portrait rises to the top of the stamp in a Gothic peak. The numerals, 90, are in the top corners. In the lower corners are the letters U and S. The stamp design is enhanced by its wonderful blue color. The stamp comes in several shades: blue, pale blue, dark blue and dull blue. The issued stamp differs from the premiere gravure essay by the addition of horizontal dashes drawn in the apex of the angle at the top of the stamp.

Figure 4-21. Differences Between the Ninety-Cent Premiere Gravure and Issued Stamp. The actual stamp (right) has horizontal dashes drawn in the apex of the angle at the top of the stamp, unlike the premiere gravure (left).

There are only 62 surviving 90-cent covers, nearly all used overseas. Therefore, it is an expensive stamp on cover. The largest unused multiple is a block of eight stamps. Used, there is a block of 25 stamps on a cover with 2-cent Black Jack.

Essays, Proofs, and Specimens

Essays

Essays, both from the National Bank Note Company of the New York, the printer of the 1861 series of stamps, and from losing companies for the stamp-printing bid, exist today. Companies that produced essays, that is, sample stamps for 1861 printing contract, include Toppan, Carpenter, and Company, which printed the previous stamp series. They produced essays of 1 through 90-cents denomination that are similar in design to their 1851 and 1857 series. The American Bank Note Company made three, five, and twelve-cent essays featuring Washington. Other essays exist from this time, whose printers are unknown. These essays include vignettes of Native Americans, the numeral, two and Liberty heads.

Figure 4-22. Example of a Losing Company's Essay for the 1861 Series. The American Bank Note Company, which bid for but did not win the 1861 stamp production contract, produced various essays featuring George Washington.

Essays from the National Bank Note Company, the winner of the contract, include samples from one through 90 cents. Included in these essays are various incomplete designs and naturally, the premiere gravures.

Proofs

Figure 4-23. Example of an 1861 Series Large Die Proof. This is a beautiful example of a five-cent large die proof.

Die and plate proofs of the stamps of this series exist. They include large die proofs of all the denominations. Small die proofs of all the denominations of the 1861 series from both the Roosevelt album and the Panama-Pacific issue also can be found. Plate proofs can be found both on India paper and cards. Color trial proofs, of the large die type and plate type on India paper also are available. Included in the color trial proofs are the premieres gravures of the 24 (dark violet) and 30 (red orange) cent denominations.

Figure 4-24. Example of a Roosevelt Small Die Proof. Small die proofs of all the denominations of the 1861 series were made for the Roosevelt album. Here is an example of a three-cent of the series.

The Atlanta plate trial color proofs, printed by the American Bank Note Company, are color trial plate proofs of all the reproductions and reissues through the 1875 designs. The 1861 series reissue Atlanta trial color plate proofs come in five colors (black, scarlet, brown, green, and blue). They are printed on thin cardboard.

Figure 4-25. Example of an 1861 Series Plate Proof. Shown is an example of a pair of two one-cent Franklin plate proofs.

Figure 4-26. 1861 Series Specimen Example. Stamps, overprinted with the word, Specimen, are found for all the denominations of the 1861 series. Shown is a one-cent Specimen stamp from this series.

Specimens

Samples of the actual printed stamps, but overprinted with the word, Specimen, are found for all of the denominations of the 1861 series. Some of the later grilled stamps of this series also exist as overprinted Specimen stamps.

Grilled Issues of 1867

At the time of the American Civil War, the United States Post Office Department became obsessed about the reuse of canceled stamps. It is not known if this was really a widespread practice or just governmental paranoia. In reality, canceling stamps with pen and ink rather than the stamp's design caused any recycling of used stamps. The solution, in retrospect, was to use handstamps, rather than the easy to remove pen ink. Several inventions to stop the stamp cleaning were proposed. These unused proposals exist today, as essays. From all of these ideas, the Post Office Department selected the grilling of stamps.

Figure 4-27. Examples of Grill Essays. There were several experimental ideas that were tested to prevent the reuse of stamps. Shown are two such examples. On the left is the music box essay. This stamp was punctured with multiple rows of tiny pins. On the right is the shield essay where an unprinted area of the stamp was embossed with a grill the shape of a shield.

Charles F. Steel invented grilling. The idea was to roll finished stamps with raised or depressed designs to weaken the paper for better absorption of the canceling ink. A pair of rollers pressed the grills into the face of stamps.

The Grilled Issues

Each stamp of the 1861 series was remade with added grill. The regular issues of 1869 and 1871 also were grilled. This section discusses the grilled stamps of 1866, but they really just modified

1861 stamps. Though separated from the preceding issue in discussion, they closely related to them in design. The National Bank Note Company of New York still printed the stamps. The designs, colors, paper, gum and perforations remained the same.

Types of Grills

There are two major types of grills, based on the type of roller that applied them. A female roller was pitted with tiny depressions. The face of the stamp was forced up into the female roller, resulting in a grill with points up, as viewed from the face. One feels the little bumps on the face of the stamp, with the depressions on the gummed side.

The male roller was covered with rows of tiny raised pyramids. When a male roller pressed the face of the stamp, the grill had its points down when viewed from the face of the stamp. One feels the little bumps on the gummed side of the stamp, with the depressions on the face.

William L. Stevenson, between 1913 and 1916, defined the families of grills according to this characteristic, as well as their size. The letter A is assigned to the largest grills, B to the next size, and so on until the letter D. Then the letter Z is placed. After Z, the sequence is continues from E to J. This sequence is also chronological, for the largest grills were made first. The A, B, and C grills are female, while D, Z, E, F, G, H, I, and J, are male.

Identifying Grills

Only half of grilled stamps are easily detected, the rest require some tried and true tests. The easiest test is feeling for the grill by running a fingernail over the face of the stamp. Sometimes, one can see the grill by placing a light under the stamp. Watermark fluid often finds a subtle grill. Finally, there is the carbon test. On a sheet of paper, one makes a square of graphite with a pencil. Then one rubs one's finger over the square and then the back of the stamp. The graphite will reveal the subtle watermark.

Using a ruler and magnifier, one measures the size of the grilled area of the stamp and the number of grills. One also takes note if the grill is a female or male type.

The value of certain grilled stamps led forgers to add grills to non-grilled issues. Fakes can be spotted by unnaturally heavy grills or dull tips of the grill that resemble dots rather than points. For the stamp collector buying expensive grilled stamps, an expert should certify the stamp.

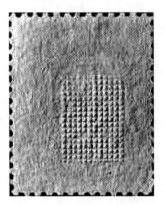

Figure 4-28. Example of a Grill. Grills on stamps are classified by whether the points are down (female) or up (male, as in this case) from the face of the stamp. But remember it is usually easier to detect the grill on the back of the stamp, so one must remember to reverse directions! The second criterion for grills is the size, measured both in number of grill points and actual dimension of grilled area on the stamp. Since this is 12 x 15 grill points, it is a F grill.

Grilled Essays

Essays for the grilled stamps took the form of experimental designs and impressions, including letters, numerals, shields, circles, and stars grilled into the essay. The best-known essay is the 3-cent music box grill essay. It consists of a pattern of vertical rows of pinpricks placed all over the stamp. Printing companies whose essays exist today include: Henry Lowenberg, John M. Sturgeon, Wilbur I. Trafton, the American Bank Note Company, the National Bank Note Company, and the Continental Bank Note Company.

Grill	A	B	C	D	Z	E	F
Type	Female	Female	Female	Male	Male	Male	Male
Size(mm)	All Over	18x15	13x 6	12x14	11x14	11x13	9x13
Direction	Vertical	Vertical	Vertical	Vertical	Horizontal	Vertical	Vertical
Points		22x 28	16-17x 18-21	15x 17-88	13-14x 17-18	14x 15-17	11-12x 15-17
1 c					X	X	X
2 c				X	X	X	X
3 c	X	X	X	X	X	X	X
5 c	X						X
10 c					X	X	X
12 c					X	X	X
15 c					X	X	X
24 c							X
30 c	X						X
90 c							X

Grilled Varieties

There are production varieties that are unique to grilled stamps. They result from either the placement of two grills on one stamp or the misalignment of the grill roller and sheet of stamps.

Double grilled stamps show two applications of the grill roller on one stamp. The second application was an attempt to fix a faint or poorly centered first application of the grill. There are even triple grills, three grills on one stamp.

Split grilled stamps show parts of two or more grills on the same stamp. Improper centering of the sheet with the grill roller causes this. *Quadruple split grill* is a variety of split grill where there is a part of four separate grills in each corner of the stamp. Sometimes, split grills are one of a pair of a double grill.

Inverted grilled stamps had their grills applied upside down. That is, the grill was applied from the back of the stamp rather than the face as was usually done. Some inverted grills are one of a pair of a double grill.

One variety often seen is an ***end roller*** (margin) ***grill***. It comes from a continuous strip of grilling that extends the length of the grill cylinder.

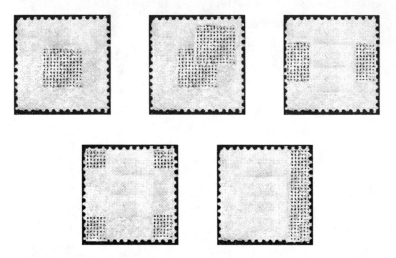

Figure 4-29. Grill Varieties. These stamp varieties occur on grilled stamps as a result of the placement of two or more grills on one stamp or the misalignment of the grill roller on the sheet of stamps. The back of the first stamp shows a normal grill. The second is a double grilled stamps with two applications of the grill roller on one stamp. The third is a split grilled stamps showing parts of two grills on the same stamp because of improper centering of the sheet with the grill roller. The first stamp on the second row has a quadruple split grill, a variety of split grill where there is a part of four separate grills in each corner of the stamp. The last stamp has an end roller or margin grill, the result of a continuous strip of grilling that extends the length of the grill cylinder.

End of Forwarding Fees

Until this time, there was an additional charge for forwarding mail. To forward means mail sent to someone at one address redirected to the same person at a second address because the person moved. After 1867, this fee was eliminated.

A GRILLED STAMPS

This is the all over grill, meaning the grilling covers the entire stamp. It is a female grill. So the points are up and one feels the bumps on the face of the stamp and the depressions on the gummed side. Covering the whole stamp, it is easy to identify. Only the 3, 5, and 30-cent stamps had an added A grill. All are rare stamps, especially the 5 and 30-cent issues. These stamps have ragged perforations, for the grill broke the paper so much, it was difficult to separate them. Because the grills allowed the glue to leak through these stamps, staining them, the stamp paper became yellow.

Three-Cent A Grilled Washington

Three-Cent A Grilled Washington

Stamp Production

Printer:	National Bank Note
Designer:	James Macdonough
Engravers:	Joseph P. Ourdan (portrait), Cyrus Durand, William D. Nichols (frame and lettering)
Format:	Sheets of 200, cut vertically into 2 panes of 100
Plate Numbers:	11, 52
Date of Issue:	Aug. 8, 1867
Earliest Known Use:	Aug. 13, 1867

Uses:	Half-ounce domestic first class rate
Quantity Issued:	50,000

Stamp Features

Size:	20 x 25 mm (0.8 x 1.0 inches)
Watermark:	None
Grill:	A
Perforations:	12
Colors:	Rose.
Varieties:	Printed on both sides.

Collectable Stamp Today
Collectable Cancellation Colors:

Black, blue, ultramarine.

Collectable Cancellation Varieties:

railroad

Value Unused:	$$$$$
Value Used:	$$$$$
Surviving Covers:	75-100
Largest Known Multiple:	Unused: 8 (block)
	Used: 3 (strip), 4? (block)

This was the first United States grilled stamp, first used on August 13, 1867. The three-cent stamp is rose and its color is very uniform. The stamp has one known variety, printed on both sides. The largest unused multiple is an unused block of 8 stamps, used is a strip of three, though a block of four stamps may exist.

Five-Cent A Grilled Jefferson

Five-Cent A Grilled Jefferson

Stamp Production

Printer:	National Bank Note
Designer:	James Macdonough
Engravers:	William E. Marshall (portrait), Cyrus Durand, William D, Nichols (frame and lettering)
Format:	Sheets of 200, cut vertically into 2 panes of 100
Plate Numbers:	17
Date of Issue:	1867
Earliest Known Use:	Unknown
Uses:	Usually with other stamps. With 10-cent stamp to France. With 5-cent stamp to India. With 5-cent stamp to Nova Scotia
Quantity Issued:	2,000

Stamp Features

Size:	20.5 x 25.2 mm (0.8 x 1.0 inches)
Watermark:	None
Grill:	A
Perforations:	12
Colors:	Brown, dark brown
Varieties:	None

Collectable Stamp Today

Collectable Cancellation Colors:	
	None
Collectable Cancellation Varieties:	
	None
Surviving Copies:	8
Value Unused:	No sales
Value Used:	$$$$$$
Surviving Covers:	0
Largest Known Multiple:	Unused: 1
	Used: 1

The 5-cent grilled-all-over (A grill) is an extremely rare stamp with only eight copies (four unused and four used) known. All are either slightly faulty or off-center. There are no existing multiples, unused or used, of this stamp. No covers with this stamp exist, either.

Thirty-Cent A Grilled Franklin

Thirty-Cent A Grilled Franklin

Stamp Production
Printer: National Bank Note
Designer: James Macdonough
Engravers: Joseph I. Pease (portrait), William D. Nichols (frame and lettering)
Format: Sheets of 200, cut vertically into 2 panes of 100
Plate Numbers: 7
Date of Issue: 1867
Earliest Known Use: Unknown
Quantity Issued: 2,000

Stamp Features
Size: 20.0 x 24.5 mm (0.8 x 1.0 inches)
Watermark: None
Grill: A
Perforations: 12
Colors: Orange
Varieties: None

Collectable Stamp Today
Collectable Cancellation Colors:
Black
Collectable Cancellation Varieties:
None
Surviving Copies: 8 (all used)
Value Used: $$$$$
Surviving Covers: 0
Largest Known Multiple: Unused: 0
Used: 1

This is another extreme rare stamp. There are only eight all-over grilled 30-cent stamps still in existence. All are used, off cover, and found as single stamps.

B GRILLED STAMPS

Only one stamp, the 3 cent, can be found with a B grill. This grill was the result of a partial removal of the A grill roller on its way in becoming a C grill. It is female grill, with the points up on the face of the stamp. The grilled area is 18 mm. wide by 15 mm. long, or 22 x 18 rows of points. It is an extremely rare stamp with only four known copies in existence. Once, this variety was considered just an essay, but today, it is classified as an issued stamp.

Three-Cent B Grilled Washington

Three-Cent B Grilled Washington

Stamp Production
Printer: National Bank Note
Designer: James Macdonough
Engravers: Joseph P. Ourdan (portrait), Cyrus Durand, William D. Nichols (frame and lettering)

Format:	Sheets of 200, cut vertically into 2 panes of 100
Plate Numbers:	Unknown
Date of Issue:	1869?
Earliest Known Use:	February 1869
Uses:	Half-ounce domestic first class rate
Quantity Issued:	1,000

Stamp Features

Size:	20 x 25 mm (0.8 x 1.0 inches)
Watermark:	None
Grill:	B
Perforations:	12
Colors:	Rose
Varieties:	None

Collectable Stamp Today
Collectable Cancellation Colors:
None
Collectable Cancellation Varieties:
None

Surviving Copies:	4 (all used)
Value Used:	$$$$$$$
Surviving Covers:	0
Largest Known Multiple:	Unused: 0
	Used: 1

All B grilled stamps are 3-cent denominations. Only four used copies of this variety exist. All came from a single letter, mailed to Germany. Since their discovery, the stamps have been removed from the cover and sold separately.

C GRILLED STAMPS

The C grill measures 13 x 16 mm. or 16-17 x 18-21 points. It is the last female grills used, that is, having points up on the stamp's face. There is just one denomination that has this variety of grill, the three-cent stamp.

Three-Cent C Grilled Washington

Three-Cent C Grilled Washington

Stamp Production
Printer: National Bank Note
Designer: James Macdonough
Engravers: Joseph P. Ourdan (portrait), Cyrus Durand, William D. Nichols (frame and lettering)
Format: Sheets of 200, cut vertically into 2 panes of 100
Plate Numbers: 14
Date of Issue: 1867
Earliest Known Use: Nov. 16,1867
Uses: Half-ounce domestic first class rate
Quantity Issued: 300,000

Stamp Features
Size: 20 x 25 mm (0.8 x 1.0 inches)
Watermark: None
Grill: C
Perforations: 12
Colors: Rose
Varieties: Double grill, Grill with points down.

Collectable Stamp Today
Collectable Cancellation Colors:
                         Black, blue.
Collectable Cancellation Varieties:
                         black town.
Value Unused: $$$$$
Value Used: $$$$$
Surviving Covers: 500-700
Largest Known Multiple: Unused: 4 (2x2 block)
                         Used: 6 (block)

This is the only stamp that comes with the C grill. It is not rare. The stamp is rose, with little color variation seen. The C grill area often has a fainted grill area, next to it, on the left or the right. It represents the incomplete erasure of points on the grill, when the roller was converted from an A or B roller, to the smaller C.

This stamp is known with a double grill, that is, two overlapping grills, on a single stamp. It also exists with the points of the grill downward, the result of the finished sheet fed into the grill roller, upside down.

D GRILLED STAMPS

The D grill is the first of the male grills, with the points down when viewed from the stamp's face. On the back of these stamps one finds rows of tiny colorless pyramids with tips being short vertical ridges. The D grill is relatively large: 12 x 14 mm., or 15 x 17-18 points. It is found on the 2-cent Black Jack, and the 3-cent stamps.

Two-Cent D Grilled "Black Jack" Jackson

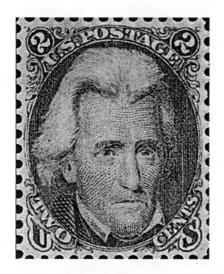

Two-Cent D Grilled "Black Jack" Jackson

Stamp Production

Printer:	National Bank Note
Designer:	James Macdonough
Engravers:	Joseph P, Ourdan (portrait), William D. Nichols (frame and lettering)
Format:	Sheets of 200, cut vertically into 2 panes of 100
Plate Numbers:	Unknown
Issue Date:	1868
Earliest Known Use:	Feb. 15,1868
Uses:	Drop letter fee. Circular rate.
Quantity Issued:	200,000

Stamp Features

Size:	20.5 x 24.5 mm (0.8 x 1.0 inches)
Watermark:	None
Grill:	D

Perforations:	12
Colors:	Black
Varieties:	Double transfer, Split grill

Collectable Stamp Today
Collectable Cancellation Colors:
    Black, red.
Collectable Cancellation Varieties:
    Paid All
Value Unused: $$$$$$
Value Used: $$$$$
Surviving Covers: 50
Largest Known Multiple: Unused: 6 (3x2 imprint block)
    Used: 4 (2x2 block)

This is the first grilled "Black Jack" stamp. It is a rare stamp, unused. The largest unused multiple is an imprint block of six stamps (3x2), used, a block of four.

Three-Cent D Grilled Washington

Three-Cent D Grilled Washington

Stamp Production

Printer:	National Bank Note
Designer:	James Macdonough
Engravers:	Joseph P. Ourdan (portrait), Cyrus Durand, William D. Nichols (frame and lettering)
Format:	Sheets of 200, cut vertically into 2 panes of 100
Plate Numbers:	Unknown
Date of Issue:	1868
Earliest Known Use:	Feb. 2, 1868
Uses:	Half-ounce domestic first class rate
Quantity Issued:	500,000

Stamp Features
Size: 20 x 25 mm (0.8 x 1.0 inches)
Watermark: None
Grill: D
Perforations: 12
Colors: Rose
Varieties: Split grill, Double grill.

Collectable Stamp Today
Collectable Cancellation Colors:
                           Black, blue, green.
Collectable Cancellation Varieties:
                           Paid
Value Unused: $$$$$
Value Used: $$$$$
Surviving Covers: 600
Largest Known Multiple: Unused: 6 (block)
                           Used: 4 (2x2 block)

This three-cent grilled stamp is rose and uniform in color. This stamp can be found with a double grill and also a split grill.

Z GRILLED STAMPS

The Z grilled stamps are the rarest and most valuable of all United States stamps. The dimensions of a Z grill, a male type, are 11 x 14 mm or 13-14 x 17-18 points, almost the same size as the D and E grills. The significant difference is the tips of the grill. Only on the Z grill are the tips, horizontal, rather than vertical. That is, the paper of a Z grill stamp is broken in a horizontal rather than vertical direction. Six denominations (1, 2, 3, 10, 12, and 15 cents) have Z grills. All are uncommon. But the 1,10, and 15-cent Z grilled stamps are among the greatest rarities of all United States stamps.

One-Cent Z Grilled Franklin

One-Cent Z Grilled Franklin

Stamp Production

Printer:	National Bank Note
Designer:	James Macdonough
Engravers:	Joseph I. Pease (portrait), Cyrus Durand, David M. Cooper (frame and lettering)
Format:	Sheets of 200, cut vertically into 2 panes of 100
Plate Numbers:	Unknown
Date of Issue:	1868
Earliest Known Use:	Feb. or Mar. 1868
Uses:	Non-carrier drop rate. Multiples used for other rates.
Quantity Issued:	1,000

Stamp Features

Size:	19.5 x 25 mm (0.7 x 1.0 inches)
Watermark:	None
Grill:	Z
Perforations:	12
Colors:	Blue
Varieties:	None

Collectable Stamp Today
Collectable Cancellation Colors:
None
Collectable Cancellation Varieties:
None

Surviving Copies:	2 (both used)
Value Used:	$$$$$$$$
Surviving Covers:	0
Largest Known Multiple:	Unused: 0
	Used: 1

This is the rarest and most expensive of all United States stamps. There are only two known copies of a one-cent Franklin with a Z grill. Both are used and exist off cover. One is in the New York Public Library collection. The other is in private hands. It sold in 1998 to the Mystic Stamp Company for $935,000. Then in 2005, Bill Gross, of Newport Beach, California, obtained it in a trade with Mystic, giving up of a block of four inverted Jenny stamps to obtain it. This was the biggest stamp trade in history!

Two-Cent Z Grilled "Black Jack" Jackson

Two-Cent Z Grilled "Black Jack" Jackson

Stamp Production

Printer:	National Bank Note
Designer:	James Macdonough
Engravers:	Joseph P, Ourdan (portrait), William D. Nichols (frame and lettering))
Format:	Sheets of 200, cut vertically into 2 panes of 100
Plate Numbers:	Unknown
Date of Issue:	1868
Earliest Known Use:	Jan. 17,1868
Uses:	Drop letter rate with carrier service after July 1, 1863. Circular rate after July 1, 1863.
Quantity Issued:	500,000

Stamp Features

Size:	20.5 x 24.5 mm (0.8 x 1.0 inches)
Watermark:	None
Grill:	Z
Perforations:	12
Colors:	Black
Varieties:	Double transfer, Double grill, Split grill

Collectable Stamp Today
Collectable Cancellation Colors:
Black, blue, red.
Collectable Cancellation Varieties:
black carrier, Paid All

Value Unused:	$$$$$
Value Used:	$$$$$
Surviving Covers:	750-1,000
Largest Known Multiple:	Unused: 5 (strip)
	Used: 4 (2x2 block)

The 2-cent Black Jack is the most common of the Z grilled stamps. These stamps have two known varieties: a double transfer and double grills.

Three-Cent Z Grilled Washington

Three-Cent Z Grilled Washington

Stamp Production

Printer:	National Bank Note
Designer:	James Macdonough
Engravers:	Joseph P. Ourdan (portrait), Cyrus Durand, William D. Nichols (frame and lettering)
Format:	Sheets of 200, cut vertically into 2 panes of 100
Plate Numbers:	Unknown
Date of Issue:	1868
Earliest Known Use:	Feb. 12, 1868
Uses:	Half-ounce domestic first class rate
Quantity Issued:	100,000

Stamp Features

Size:	20 x 25 mm (0.8 x 1.0 inches)
Watermark:	None
Grill:	Z
Perforations:	12
Colors:	Rose
Varieties:	Double grill

Collectable Stamp Today
Collectable Cancellation Colors:
Black, blue, green, red.
Collectable Cancellation Varieties:
Paid

Value Unused:	$$$$$$
Value Used:	$$$$$
Surviving Covers:	50
Largest Known Multiple:	Unused: 9 (3x3 block)
	Used: 7 (strip)

The 3-cent Z grilled stamp is uncommon but not news worthy rare. The largest unused multiple of it is a block of nine stamps, used, a vertical strip of seven stamps.

Ten-Cent Z Grilled Washington

Ten-Cent Z Grilled Washington

Stamp Production

Printer:	National Bank Note
Designer:	James Macdonough
Engravers:	William E. Marshall (portrait), William D. Nichols (frame and lettering)
Format:	Sheets of 200, cut vertically into 2 panes of 100
Plate Numbers:	Unknown
Date of Issue:	1868
Earliest Known Use:	Feb. or Mar. 1868
Uses:	To Canada
Quantity Issued:	2,000

Stamp Features

Size:	20.5 x 25.2 mm (0.8 x 1.0 inches)
Watermark:	None
Grill:	Z
Perforations:	12
Colors:	Green
Varieties:	None

Collectable Stamp Today
Collectable Cancellation Colors:
                            None
Collectable Cancellation Varieties:
                            black town
Surviving Copies: 6 (all used)
Value Used: $$$$$$$
Surviving Covers: 0
Largest Known Multiple: Unused: 0
                            Used: 1

The 10-cent stamp with a Z grill is another great rarity. Only six copies are known to exist, with one found in the New York Public Library collection. All are used, single stamps, off cover.

Twelve-Cent Z Grilled Washington

Twelve-Cent Z Grilled Washington

Stamp Production
Printer: National Bank Note
Designer: James Macdonough
Engravers: William E. Marshall (portrait), Cyrus Durand, William D. Nichols (frame)
Format: Sheets of 200, cut vertically into 2 panes of 100
Plate Numbers: 16
Date of Issue: 1868

Earliest Known Use:	Feb. 15, 1868
Uses:	To pay the single rate to England
Quantity Issued:	100,000

Stamp Features

Size:	19.5 x 24.5 mm (0.8 x 1.0 inches)
Watermark:	None
Grill:	Z
Perforations:	12
Colors:	Black
Varieties:	Double transfer of top frame line

Collectable Stamp Today
Collectable Cancellation Colors:
None
Collectable Cancellation Varieties:
None

Value Unused:	$$$$$$
Value Used:	$$$$$
Surviving Covers:	75-100
Largest Known Multiple:	Unused: 9 (3x3 block)
	Used: 4 (2x2 block)

This is the first 12-cent stamp with a grill. Most stamps have intense black color.

Fifteen-Cent Z Grilled Lincoln

Fifteen-Cent Z Grilled Lincoln

Stamp Production

Printer:	National Bank Note
Designer:	James Macdonough
Engravers:	James P. Ourdan (portrait), William D. Nichols (frame and lettering)
Format:	Sheets of 200, cut vertically into 2 panes of 100
Plate Numbers:	41
Date of Issue:	1868
Earliest Known Use:	Feb. or Mar. 1868
Uses:	Registry fee. The 15-cent foreign rate to France and Prussia.
Quantity Issued:	1,000

Stamp Features

Size:	19.2 x 24.7 mm (0.8 x 1.0 inches)

Watermark:	None
Grill:	Z
Perforations:	12
Colors:	Black
Varieties:	Double transfer of top frame line

Collectable Stamp Today
Collectable Cancellation Colors:
None.
Collectable Cancellation Varieties:
None
Surviving Copies: 2 (all used)
Value Used: $$$$$$$
Surviving Covers: 0
Largest Known Multiple: Unused: 0
Used: 1

This is another great Z grilled rarity. Only two, single, off cover, used stamps still exist. The price of a copy of the stamp when it last sold at an auction in 2003, was $190,000.

E GRILLED STAMPS

These are much more common grilled stamps, especially the 3-cent denomination. It is also found on five other denominations, none that are exceedingly rare. The E is a male grill with vertical tips. The grill size is 14 by 15 to17 points or 11 x 13 mm.

One-Cent E Grilled Franklin

One-Cent E Grilled Franklin

Stamp Production
Printer:	National Bank Note
Designer:	James Macdonough
Engravers:	Joseph I. Pease (portrait), Cyrus Durand, David M. Cooper (frame and lettering)
Format:	Sheets of 200, cut vertically into 2 panes of 100
Plate Numbers:	Unknown
Date of Issue:	1868
Earliest Known Use:	Mar. 9, 1868
Uses:	Non-carrier drop rate. Multiples used for other rates.
Quantity Issued:	3,000,000

Stamp Features
Size:	19.5 x 25 mm (0.7 x 1.0 inches)
Watermark:	None
Grill:	E
Perforations:	12
Colors:	Blue, dull blue

Varieties: Double grill, Split grill

Collectable Stamp Today
Collectable Cancellation Colors:
Black, blue, red, green.
Collectable Cancellation Varieties:
Paid, steamboat, red carrier.
Value Unused: $$$$$
Value Used: $$$$
Surviving Covers: 3,000
Largest Known Multiple: Unused: 50 (block)
Used: 18 (block)

This stamp, though common, is difficult stamp to find in excellent condition. A half sheet block of 50 unused stamps with the top imprint is known to exist. Used, a block of 18 stamps is the largest existing multiple.

Two-Cent E Grilled "Black Jack" Jackson

Two-Cent E Grilled "Black Jack" Jackson

Stamp Production
Printer: National Bank Note
Designer: James Macdonough

Engravers:	Joseph P, Ourdan (portrait), William D. Nichols (frame and lettering))
Format:	Sheets of 200, cut vertically into 2 panes of 100
Plate Numbers:	29
Date of Issue:	1868
Earliest Known Use:	Mar. 7,1868
Uses:	Drop letter fee. Circular rate.
Quantity Issued:	25,000,000

Stamp Features

Size:	20.5 x 24.5 mm (0.8 x 1.0 inches)
Watermark:	None
Grill:	E
Perforations:	12
Colors:	Black, intense black, gray black
Varieties:	Double transfer, Double grill, Triple grill, Split grill, Double grill with one split, Grill with points up

Collectable Stamp Today
Collectable Cancellation Colors:

Black, blue, purple, brown, red, green.

Collectable Cancellation Varieties:

Paid, steamship, black carrier, Paid All, Short Paid, Japan.

Value Unused:	$$$$$
Value Used:	$$$$
Surviving Covers:	10,000
Largest Known Multiple:	Unused: 6 (block)
	Used: 8 (strip)

This is a common stamp. Thousands of covers with an E grilled "Black Jack" exist. But, as is true of any Black Jack stamp, it is hard to find well centered. The stamp was used bisected (diagonal and vertical) to pay a one-cent postage fee and can be found that way on covers, today. Several grill varieties can be found, including grills with the points up, split grill, double grill, and even a triple grill.

Three Cent E Grilled Washington

Three Cent E Grilled Washington

Stamp Production

Printer:	National Bank Note
Designer:	James Macdonough
Engravers:	Joseph P. Ourdan (portrait), Cyrus Durand, William D. Nichols (frame and lettering)

Format: Sheets of 200, cut vertically into 2 panes of 100
Plate Numbers: 36, 55
Date of Issue: 1868
Earliest Known Use: Feb. 12, 1868
Uses: Half-ounce domestic first class rate
Quantity Issued: 80,000,000

Stamp Features
Size: 20 x 25 mm (0.8 x 1.0 inches)
Watermark: None
Grill: E
Perforations: 12
Colors: Rose, pale rose, rose red, lake red.
Varieties: Double grill, Triple grill, Split grill, Thin paper.

Collectable Stamp Today
Collectable Cancellation Colors:
Black, blue, red, ultramarine, green.
Collectable Cancellation Varieties:
Paid, Way, numeral, steamboat, railroad, express company cancellation.
Value Unused: $$$$
Value Used: $$$
Surviving Covers: 25,000
Largest Known Multiple: Unused: 100 (complete pane)
Used: 8 (block)

This is the second most common of all of the grilled stamps of 1867 series. It often is found on a very thin paper, an experiment to get better grills out out of the roller onto the stamp. A complete, unused left pane of 100 stamps from plate 36 still can be found. The largest used multiple is a block of eight stamps.

Ten-Cent E Grilled Washington

Ten-Cent E Grilled Washington

Stamp Production
Printer: National Bank Note
Designer: James Macdonough
Engravers: William E. Marshall (portrait), William D. Nichols (frame and lettering)
Format: Sheets of 200, cut vertically into 2 panes of 100
Plate Numbers: 15
Date of Issue: 1868
Earliest Known Use: Feb. 21,1868
Uses: To Canada
Quantity Issued: 1,500,000

Stamp Features
Size: 20.5 x 25.2 mm (0.8 x 1.0 inches)
Watermark: None
Grill: E
Perforations: 12
Colors: Green, dark green, blue green
Varieties: Double grill, Split grill, Double transfer, Thin paper.

Collectable Stamp Today
Collectable Cancellation Colors:
                          Black, blue, red.
Collectable Cancellation Varieties:
                          Paid, steamship, Japan.

Surviving Copies:	6 (all used)
Value Unused:	$$$$$
Value Used:	$$$$
Surviving Covers:	3,000
Largest Known Multiple:	Unused: 18 (block)
	Used: 4 (2x2 block)

Like the 3-cent, the 10-cent E-grilled stamp is found on thin paper, as a variety. It is another very difficult stamp to find well centered.

Twelve-Cent E Grilled Washington

Twelve-Cent E Grilled Washington

Stamp Production

Printer:	National Bank Note
Designer:	James Macdonough
Engravers:	William E. Marshall (portrait), Cyrus Durand, William D. Nichols (frame)
Format:	Sheets of 200, cut vertically into 2 panes of 100
Plate Numbers:	16
Date of Issue:	1868
Earliest Known Use:	March 3, 1868

Uses:	To pay the single rate to England
Quantity Issued:	1,000,000
Stamp Features	
Size:	19.5 x 24.5 mm (0.8 x 1.0 inches)
Watermark:	None
Grill:	E
Perforations:	12
Colors:	Black, gray black, intense black.
Varieties:	Double transfer of top frame line, Double transfer of bottom frame line, Double transfer of top and bottom frame line, Double grill, Split grill.

Collectable Stamp Today	
Collectable Cancellation Colors:	
	Black, blue, red, purple, green.
Collectable Cancellation Varieties:	
	Paid, railroad.
Value Unused:	$$$$$
Value Used:	$$$$
Surviving Covers:	2,500
Largest Known Multiple:	Unused: 6 (3x2 block)
	Used: 4 (2x2 block)

Fine well-centered copies of this stamp are easier to find than any other denominations with an E grill.

Fifteen Cent E Grilled Lincoln

Fifteen Cent E Grilled Lincoln

Stamp Production

Printer:	National Bank Note
Designer:	James Macdonough
Engravers:	James P. Ourdan (portrait), William D. Nichols (frame and lettering)
Format:	Sheets of 200, cut vertically into 2 panes of 100
Plate Numbers:	41
Date of Issue:	1868
Earliest Known Use:	May 2, 1868
Uses:	Overseas rate to France or Prussia
Quantity Issued:	500,000

Stamp Features

Size:	19.2 x 24.7 mm (0.8 x 1.0 inches)
Watermark:	None
Grill:	E
Perforations:	12
Color:	Black, gray black.
Varieties:	Double grill, Split grill.

Collectable Stamp Today
Collectable Cancellation Colors:
Black, blue, red, magenta
Collectable Cancellation Varieties:
Paid, supplementary mail type A.

Value Unused:	$$$$$
Value Used:	$$$$
Surviving Covers:	1,750
Largest Known Multiple:	Unused: 4 (2x2 block)
	Used: 4 (2x2 block)

This is the highest denomination E grilled stamp.. Both unused and used, the largest surviving multiples are blocks of four stamps.

F GRILL STAMPS

This is the most common of the grills used on the 1866 series of stamps. It also was the last size grill used on this series of stamps. It is the only grill type that can be found on all the stamp denominations. The grill is a male type, the smallest size found in this series of stamps. It measures 9 x 13 mm., or 11-12 x 15-17 points. A thin paper was used for many F grill stamps, to better take the grills.

One Cent F Grilled Franklin

One Cent F Grilled Franklin

Stamp Production
Printer: National Bank Note
Designer: James Macdonough
Engravers: Joseph I. Pease (portrait), Cyrus Durand, David M. Cooper (frame and lettering)
Format: Sheets of 200, cut vertically into 2 panes of 100
Plate Numbers: 10, 22, 27
Date of Issue: 1868
Earliest Known Use: Aug. 11,1868
Uses: Non-carrier drop rate. As multiples for other rates.
Quantity Issued: 7,000,000

Stamp Features
Size: 19.5 x 25 mm (0.7 x 1.0 inches)
Watermark: None

Grill: F
Perforations: 12
Colors: Blue, pale blue, dark blue.
Varieties: Double transfer, Double grill, Split gill, Thin paper

Collectable Stamp Today
Collectable Cancellation Colors:
Black, blue, red, green
Collectable Cancellation Varieties:
Paid, red carrier, Paid All.
Value Unused: $$$$$
Value Used: $$$$
Surviving Covers: 7,000
Largest Known Multiple: Unused: 6 (margin block)
Used: 12 (block)

Figure 4-30. Example of a Cover with a One-Cent Franklin Stamp with an F Grill. This stamp paid the drop rate for the letter mailed in Olton, Illinois.

This is the most common one-cent grilled stamp of this series. It is found on thin as well as regular paper. Though a common stamp, it is usually found poorly centered. The largest unused multiple is a margin block of six stamps with part of the marginal imprint from plate 27. The largest used multiple is a block of 12, found on a cover.

Two-Cent F Grilled "Black Jack" Jackson

Two-Cent F Grilled "Black Jack" Jackson

Stamp Production
Printer: National Bank Note
Designer: James Macdonough
Engravers: Joseph P, Ourdan (portrait), William D. Nichols (frame and lettering))
Format: Sheets of 200, cut vertically into 2 panes of 100
Plate Numbers: 28, 30, 50, 51, 53
Date of Issue: 1868
Earliest Known Use: Mar. 27, 1868
Uses: Drop letter fee. Circular rate.
Quantity Issued: 50,000,000

Stamp Features
Size: 20.5 x 24.5 mm (0.8 x 1.0 inches)
Watermark: None
Grill: F
Perforations: 12
Colors: Black, gray black
Varieties: Double transfer, Double grill, Split grill, Double grill one split, Double grill one quadruple split, Thin paper

Collectable Stamp Today
Collectable Cancellation Colors:
Black, blue, red, green
Collectable Cancellation Varieties:
Paid, Paid All, black carrier, red carrier, Japan.
Value Unused: $$$$

Value Used: $$$
Surviving Covers: 20,000
Largest Known Multiple: Unused: 100 (complete pane)
Used: 15 (block)

Though a very common stamp, there is very little color variation, just like its ungrilled cousin. One can find bisects, with half a stamp used for one-cent of postage, on cover. A complete unused pane of 100 stamps from plate 30 still exists. Used, the largest multiple is a block of 15 stamps.

Three-Cent F Grilled Washington

Three-Cent F Grilled Washington

Stamp Production
Printer: National Bank Note
Designer: James Macdonough
Engravers: Joseph P. Ourdan (portrait), Cyrus Durand, William D. Nichols (frame and lettering)
Format: Sheets of 200, cut vertically into 2 panes of 100
Plate Numbers: 11, 32, 34, 35
Date of Issue: 1868
Earliest Known Use: Mar. 21, 1868
Uses: Half-ounce domestic first class rate

Quantity Issued: 225,000,000

Stamp Features
Size: 20 x 25 mm (0.8 x 1.0 inches)
Watermark: None
Grill: F
Perforations: 12
Colors: Red, rose red, rose.
Varieties: Double transfer, Printed on both sides, Double grill, Double grill one with the points up, Double grill one with the points quadruple split, Triple grill, Marginal grill, Split grill, Quadruple split grill, Grill with points up, Thin paper, Printed on both sides
Errors: Vertical pair with no horizontal perforations in between

Collectable Stamp Today
Collectable Cancellation Colors:
                          Black, blue, ultramarine, red, violet, green.
Collectable Cancellation Varieties:
                          1867, 1868, 1869, Paid, Paid All, Free, numerals, railroad, steamboat, packet boat, express company cancellation.
Value Unused: $$$$
Value Used: $$
Surviving Covers: 200,000
Largest Known Multiple: Unused: 100 (complete pane)
                          Used: 22

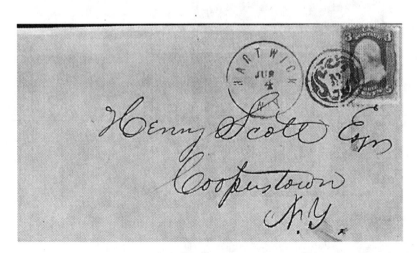

Figure 4-31. Example of a Cover with a Three-Cent Washington Stamp with an F Grill. This stamp, which paid the basic first-class postage rate of the time, three cents, shows its grill very well, even on cover. Notice the very fancy cancellation mark.

The three-cent F grilled stamp is the most common of all issued of the 1867 series. The stamp exists with every grill variety: a double grill, triple grill, marginal grill, split grill, quadruple split grill, and a grill with points up, instead of down. A common stamp, it is found on 200,000 surviving covers. It can even be found as a complete unused pane of 100 stamps.

The stamp exists with a perforation error. There is a vertical pair of the stamps with no horizontal perforations in between.

Five-Cent F Grilled Jefferson

Five-Cent F Grilled Jefferson

Stamp Production

Printer:	National Bank Note
Designer:	James Macdonough
Engravers:	William E. Marshall (portrait), Cyrus Durand, William D, Nichols (frame and lettering)
Format:	Sheets of 200, cut vertically into 2 panes of 100
Plate Numbers:	17
Date of Issue:	1868
Earliest Known Use:	Aug. 19, 1868
Quantity Issued:	680,000
Uses:	Usually with other stamps. With 10-cent stamp to France. With 5-cent stamp to India. With 5-cent stamp to Nova Scotia

Stamp Features
Size: 20.5 x 25.2 mm (0.8 x 1.0 inches)
Watermark: None
Grill: F
Perforations: 12
Colors: Brown, black brown, dark brown
Varieties: Double transfer of top frame line, Double transfer of bottom frame line, Double grill, Split grill, Thin paper

Collectable Stamp Today
Collectable Cancellation Colors:
Black, blue, magenta, violet, red, green.
Collectable Cancellation Varieties:
Paid, Free, Steamship.
Value Unused: $$$$$
Value Used: $$$$
Surviving Covers: 750-1,000
Largest Known Multiple: Unused: 10 (block)
Used: 4 (2x2 block)

The 5-cent F grilled stamp is found with brown, black brown, and dark brown inks. The black brown is a little more rare than the other shades. Unused, the largest multiple are two blocks of 10 stamps, one that has its full gum intact.

Ten-Cent F Grilled Washington

Ten-Cent F Grilled Washington

Stamp Production

Printer:	National Bank Note
Designer:	James Macdonough
Engravers:	William E. Marshall (portrait), William D. Nichols (frame and lettering)
Format:	Sheets of 200, cut vertically into 2 panes of 100
Plate Numbers:	15, 26
Date of Issue:	1868
Earliest Known Use:	May 28, 1868
Uses:	To Canada
Quantity Issued:	3,800,000

Stamp Features

Size:	20.5 x 25.2 mm (0.8 x 1.0 inches)
Watermark:	None
Grill:	F
Perforations:	12
Colors:	Yellow green, green, dark green, blue green.
Varieties:	Double transfer, Double grill, Split grill, Quadruple split grill, Thin paper

Collectable Stamp Today
Collectable Cancellation Colors:
Black, blue, red, magenta, green.
Collectable Cancellation Varieties:
Paid, Free, steamship, supplementary mail type A, China, Japan.

Value Unused:	$$$$$
Value Used:	$$$$
Surviving Covers:	5,000-7,500
Largest Known Multiple:	Unused: 15 (block)
	Used: 6 (block)

Although the 1861 issue had two types of the ten-cent stamp, only type II (not the premiere gravure) was issued with a grill.

Twelve-Cent F Grilled Washington

Twelve-Cent F Grilled Washington

Stamp Production

Printer:	National Bank Note
Designer:	James Macdonough
Engravers:	William E. Marshall (portrait), Cyrus Durand, William D. Nichols (frame)

Format:	Sheets of 200, cut vertically into 2 panes of 100
Plate Numbers:	16
Date of Issue:	1868
Earliest Known Use:	May 27, 1868
Uses:	To pay the single rate to England
Quantity Issued:	2,600,000

Stamp Features

Size:	19.5 x 24.5 mm (0.8 x 1.0 inches)
Watermark:	None
Grill:	F
Perforations:	12
Colors:	Black, gray black
Varieties:	Double transfer of top frame line, Double transfer of bottom frame line, Double transfer of top and bottom frame lines, Double grill, Triple grill, Split grill, Marginal grill, Thin paper

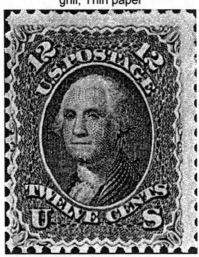

Collectable Stamp Today
Collectable Cancellation Colors:
    Black, blue, red, magenta, brown, green, purple
Collectable Cancellation Varieties:
    Paid, Insufficiently Prepaid, Paid All, supplementary mail type A

Value Unused:	$$$$$
Value Used:	$$$$
Surviving Covers:	7,500
Largest Known Multiple:	Unused: 8 (4x2 block)
	Used: 6 (3x2 block)

This denomination comes better centered than the other stamps of this series. A common stamp, it was used on a lot of overseas mail.

Fifteen-Cent F Grilled Lincoln

Fifteen-Cent F Grilled Lincoln

Stamp Production
Printer: National Bank Note
Designer: James Macdonough
Engravers: James P. Ourdan (portrait), William D. Nichols (frame and
                                  lettering)
Format: Sheets of 200, cut vertically into 2 panes of 100
Plate Numbers: 41
Date of Issue: 1868
Earliest Known Use: May 4, 1868
Uses: Overseas rate to France or Prussia. New registration fee
                                  after Jan 1, 1869
Quantity Issued: 2,000,000

Stamp Features
Size: 19.2 x 24.7 mm (0.8 x 1.0 inches)
Watermark: None
Grill: F
Perforations: 12
Colors: Black, gray black
Varieties: Double transfer of upper right corner, Double grill, Split
                                  grill, Quadruple split grill, Thin paper.

Collectable Stamp Today
Collectable Cancellation Colors:
                                  Black, blue, magenta, red, orange red, green, orange,
                                  purple

Collectable Cancellation Varieties:

Paid, supplementary mail type A, Insufficiently Prepaid, Insufficiently Paid, Japan.

Value Unused:	$$$$$
Value Used:	$$$$
Surviving Covers:	5,000
Largest Known Multiple:	Unused: 20 (10x2 block)
	Used: 4 (2x2 block)

More 15-cent Lincoln stamps can be found with the F grill than without a grill. This is because the 15-cent stamp was issued just before stamps started to receive grills. Also, there was greater demand for the grilled stamp when the registration fee was raised to 15 cents in 1869.

This is the highest denomination of this series that is printed on the very thin paper of the stamps. There were no printings of the higher values on such paper because enough of the high value stamps were already available when the thin paper started to be used.

Figure 4-32. Example of a Fifteen-Cent F Grill Lincoln Stamp on a Cover. This stamp really shows off its grill. It paid the then fifteen-cent postage rate to Germany.

Twenty-Four-Cent F Grilled Washington

Twenty-Four-Cent F Grilled Washington

Stamp Production
Printer: National Bank Note Co.
Designer: James Macdonough
Engravers: William E. Marshall (portrait), Cyrus Durand, William D. Nichols (frame and lettering)
Format: Sheets of 200, cut vertically into 2 panes of 100
Plate Numbers: 6
Date of Issue: 1868?
Earliest Known Use: Jan. 5, 1869
Uses: Double letter rate to England
Quantity Issued: 200,000

Stamp Features
Size: 19.5 x 24.0 mm (0.8 x 0.9 inches)
Watermark: None
Grill: F
Perforations: 12
Colors: Gray lilac, gray
Varieties: Double grill, Split grill, Scratch under A of POSTAGE.

Collectable Stamp Today
Collectable Cancellation Colors:
Black, blue, red.
Collectable Cancellation Varieties:
Paid.
Value Unused: $$$$$
Value Used: $$$$
Surviving Covers: 40

Largest Known Multiple: Unused: 15 (5x3 block)
                                                    Used: 9 (3x3 block)

    This issue is almost always found poorly centered. Also, because of the stamp's light ink color, most cancellations ruin the appearance of a used stamp.

Thirty-Cent F Grilled Franklin

Thirty-Cent F Grilled Franklin

Stamp Production

Printer:	National Bank Note
Designer:	James Macdonough
Engravers:	Joseph I. Pease (portrait), William D. Nichols (lettering and frame)
Format:	Sheets of 200, cut vertically into 2 panes of 100
Plate Numbers:	7
Date of Issue:	1868
Earliest Known Use:	Nov. 10, 1868
Uses:	Double letter rate to France
Quantity Issued:	280,000

Stamp Features

Size:	20.0 x 24.5 mm (0.8 x 1.0 inches)
Watermark:	None
Grill:	F
Perforations:	12

Colors: Orange, deep orange
Varieties: Double grill, Split grill, Double grill one split. .

Collectable Stamp Today
Collectable Cancellation Colors:
                           Black, blue, red, magenta
Collectable Cancellation Varieties:
                           Paid, supplementary mail type A, Japan.
Value Unused: $$$$$
Value Used: $$$$
Surviving Covers: 40
Largest Known Multiple: Unused: 6 (2x3 block)
                           Used: 6 (block)

Most cancellations cover this stamp because it is printed in light colors. Only 40 covers remain with this high denomination stamp.

Ninety-Cent F Grilled Washington

Ninety-Cent F Grilled Washington

Stamp Production
Printer: National Bank Note Co.
Designer: James Macdonough
Engravers: Joseph I. Pease (portrait), William D. Nichols (lettering and frame)
Format: Sheets of 200, cut vertically into 2 panes of 100
Plate Numbers: 18
Date of Issue: 1869?

Earliest Known Use:	May 8, 1869
Uses:	Overseas, especially Japan
Quantity Issued:	30,000

Stamp Features

Size:	19.5 x 24.2 mm (0.8 x 1.0 inches)
Watermark:	None
Grill:	F
Perforations:	12
Colors:	Blue, dark blue
Varieties:	Double grill, Split grill

Collectable Stamp Today
Collectable Cancellation Colors:
    Black, blue, red
Collectable Cancellation Varieties:
    Paid, Japan

Value Unused:	$$$$$$
Value Used:	$$$$$
Surviving Covers:	2
Largest Known Multiple:	Unused: 4 (2x2 block)
	Used: 4 (2x2 block)

The highest denomination grilled stamp is the rare ninety-cent F grilled issue. There are only two covers with the stamp. One is a large piece from 1871, with a Bank Note stamp on it also. A smaller cover dates from April 26, 1869. Both unused and used, the largest multiples are block of four stamps.

1875 Reissued Stamps of the 1861-66 Series

Like the two previous series of stamps, the stamps of the 1861 through 1867 series were remade in preparation for the American Centennial. In the case of the 1861-66 issues, the special printings for the Philadelphia Centennial Exposition are called reissues because the original stamps were still valid for postage use. These reissues also were good (and still are!) for postage.

Like the original stamps, the National Bank Note Company printed the 1875 reissues. And like the original stamps, the reissues were perforated 12. The reissues were not grilled, so in a sense, they are more closely related to the 1861 stamp series than the 1867 series.

The 1, 2, 5, 10 and 12 cent reissues were printed from new plates of 100 stamps each. For the rest of the series, old plates simply were reused.

The reissues can be distinguished from the original stamps by their brighter colors and sharper appearance. The reissues also have very white paper with crackled gum, as compared with yellowish paper and smooth gum of the original stamps.

1875 One-Cent Franklin Reissue

Stamp Production
Printer: National Bank Note Company
Designer: James Macdonough
Engravers: Joseph I. Pease (portrait), Cyrus Durand, David M. Cooper (frame and lettering)
Format: Sheets of 100
Plate Numbers: New unnumbered plate
Date of Issue: 1875
Uses: Souvenir. Valid for postal use.
Quantity Issued: 3,195

Stamp Features
Size: 19.5 x 25 mm (0.7 x 1.0 inches)
Watermark: None
Grill: None
Perforations: 12
Colors: Blue
Varieties: None

Collectable Stamp Today
Value Unused: $$$$
Value Used: $$$$$

1875 Two-Cent Jackson Reissue

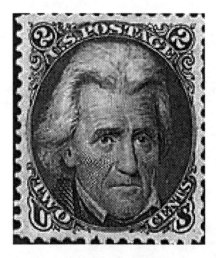

Stamp Production
Printer: National Bank Note Company
Designer: James Macdonough

Engravers:	Joseph P. Ourdan (portrait), William D. Nichols (frame and lettering)
Format:	Sheets of 100
Plate Numbers:	New unnumbered plate
Date of Issue:	1875
Uses:	Souvenir. Valid for postal use.
Quantity Issued:	979

Stamp Features

Size:	20.5 x 24.5 mm (0.8 x 1.0 inches)
Watermark:	None
Grill:	None
Perforations:	12
Colors:	Black
Varieties:	None

Collectable Stamp Today

Value Unused:	$$$$$
Value Used:	$$$$$

1875 Three-Cent Washington Reissue

Stamp Production

Printer:	National Bank Note Company
Designer:	James Macdonough
Engravers:	Joseph P. Ourdan (portrait), Cyrus Durand, William D. Nichols (frame and lettering)
Format:	2 panes of 100
Plate Numbers:	Original plate
Date of Issue:	1875

Uses:	Souvenir. Valid for postal use.
Quantity Issued:	465

Stamp Features

Size:	20 x 25 mm (0.8 x 1.0 inches)
Watermark:	None
Grill:	None
Perforations:	12
Colors:	Brown red
Varieties:	None

Collectable Stamp Today

Value Unused:	$$$$$
Value Used:	$$$$$

1875 Five-Cent Jefferson Reissue

Stamp Production

Printer:	National Bank Note Company
Designer:	James Macdonough
Engravers:	William E. Marshall (portrait), Cyrus Durand, William D. Nichols (frame and lettering)
Format:	Sheet of 100
Plate Numbers:	New unnumbered plate
Date of Issue:	1875
Uses:	Souvenir. Valid for postal use.
Quantity Issued:	672

Stamp Features

Size:	20.5 x 25.2 mm (0.8 x 1.0 inches)
Watermark:	None
Grill:	None
Perforations:	12
Colors:	Brown
Varieties:	None

Collectable Stamp Today

Value Unused:	$$$$$
Value Used:	$$$$$

1875 Ten-Cent Washington Reissue

Stamp Production

Printer:	National Bank Note Company
Designer:	James Macdonough
Engravers:	William E. Marshall (portrait), William D. Nichols (frame and lettering)
Format:	Sheet of 100
Plate Numbers:	New unnumbered plate
Date of Issue:	1875
Uses:	Souvenir. Valid for postal use.
Quantity Issued:	451

Stamp Features

Size:	20.5 x 25.2 mm (0.8 x 1.0 inches)
Watermark:	None
Grill:	None
Perforations:	12
Colors:	Green

Varieties: None
Collectable Stamp Today
Value Unused: $$$$$
Value Used: $$$$$$

1875 Twelve-Cent Washington Reissue

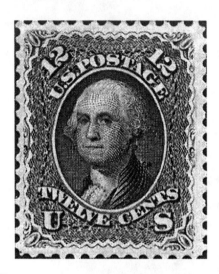

Stamp Production
Printer: National Bank Note Company
Designer: James Macdonough
Engravers: William E. Marshall (portrait), Cyrus Durand, William D. Nichols (frame)
Format: Sheet of 100
Plate Numbers: New unnumbered plate
Date of Issue: 1875
Uses: Souvenir. Valid for postal use.
Quantity Issued: 389

Stamp Features
Size: 20.5 x 25.2 mm (0.8 x 1.0 inches)
Watermark: None
Grill: None
Perforations: 12
Colors: Black
Varieties: None

Collectable Stamp Today
Value Unused: $$$$$
Value Used: $$$$$

1875 Fifteen-Cent Lincoln Reissue

Stamp Production
Printer:	National Bank Note Company
Designer:	James Macdonough
Engravers:	James P. Ourdan (portrait), William D. Nichols (frame and lettering)
Format:	2 panes of 100
Plate Numbers:	Original plate 41
Date of Issue:	1875
Uses:	Souvenir. Valid for postal use.
Quantity Issued:	397

Stamp Features
Size:	19.2 x 24.7 mm (0.8 x 1.0 inches)
Watermark:	None
Grill:	None
Perforations:	12
Colors:	Black
Varieties:	None

Collectable Stamp Today
Value Unused:	$$$$$
Value Used:	$$$$$

1875 Twenty-Four-Cent Washington Reissue

Stamp Production
Printer: National Bank Note Company
Designer: James Macdonough
Engravers: William E. Marshall (portrait), Cyrus Durand, William D. Nichols (frame and lettering)
Format: 2 panes of 100
Plate Numbers: Original plate 6
Date of Issue: 1875
Uses: Souvenir. Valid for postal use.
Quantity Issued: 346

Stamp Features
Size: 19.5 x 24.0 mm (0.8 x 0.9 inches)
Watermark: None
Grill: None
Perforations: 12
Colors: Deep violet
Varieties: None

Collectable Stamp Today
Value Unused: $$$$$
Value Used: $$$$$

1875 Thirty-Cent Franklin Reissue

Stamp Production

Printer:	National Bank Note Company
Designer:	James Macdonough
Engravers:	Joseph I. Pease (portrait), William D. Nichols (lettering and frame)
Format:	2 panes of 100
Plate Numbers:	Original plate 7
Date of Issue:	1875
Uses:	Souvenir. Valid for postal use.
Quantity Issued:	346

Stamp Features

Size:	20.0 x 24.5 mm (0.8 x 1.0 inches)
Watermark:	None
Grill:	None
Perforations:	12
Colors:	Brownish orange
Varieties:	None

Collectable Stamp Today

Value Unused:	$$$$$
Value Used:	$$$$$$

1875 Ninety-Cent Washington Reissue

Stamp Production

Printer:	National Bank Note Company
Designer:	James Macdonough

Engravers:	Joseph I. Pease (portrait), William D. Nichols (lettering and frame)
Format:	2 panes of 100
Plate Numbers:	Original plate 18
Date of Issue:	1875
Uses:	Souvenir. Valid for postal use.
Quantity Issued:	317

Stamp Features

Size:	19.5 x 24.2 mm (0.8 x 1.0 inches)
Watermark:	None
Grill:	None
Perforations:	12
Colors:	Blue
Varieties:	None

Collectable Stamp Today

Value Unused:	$$$$$
Value Used:	$$$$$$

Stamps of the Confederacy

After the Southern States seceded from the Union, they formed the Confederate States of America on February 8,1861. Postal service was vital in building a new country. For postmaster general, President Jefferson Davis picked John H. Reagan, a Texas lawyer. Reagan had the impossible task of creating a postal service throughout a large country at war.

Reagan's first directed the local postmasters of the new Confederate States to continue their usual work, use United States stamps and give all payments to the United States Government. This was to give the Confederacy time to create its own postal system. But running low on United States stamps, six local postmasters issued 3-cent provisional stamps for the rate then in effect. Thus mail was sent throughout the Confederacy using Union stamps. And the proceeds were given to the United States!

Figure 4-33. Example of a Confederate Cover With a United States Stamp.
Before the CSA issued stamps, the United States stamps in stock were used and the proceeds sent to the government in Washington DC. Here is one such example. This letter was mailed from Montgomery, Alabama on March 11, 1861 and sent to Southwick, Massachusetts. It is franked with a 3-cent stamp from the1857 series of stamps.

On May 13, 1861, Reagan issued a proclamation assuming Confederate control of postal service on the first day of June of that year. He set the postage rates at five cents per half ounce for letters going less than 500 miles, ten cents for greater distances, twenty cents for letters crossing the Mississippi River, and two cents for drop letters. But runaway inflation in the Confederate economy led to a doubling of the basic letter rate to ten cents within one year.

CONFEDERATE PROVISIONAL STAMPS

So on June 1, 1861, the Confederate postal service was on its own, independent of the United States system. But yet there were no Confederate postage stamps. So the individual local postmasters between June 1, 1861, when the use of United States stamps stopped being used in the Confederacy, and October 16, 1861, when the first Confederate Government stamps were available, had to improvise.

Figure 4-34. Example of a Confederate Local Provisional Stamp. Here is one of the many examples of a confederate local provisional stamp used before the general issue stamps became available. This one is from Mobile, Alabama.

Some local postmasters collected postage in cash and marked the amount paid with either pen or handstamp markings. Many local postmasters prepared their own provisional stamps for local use, just like the earlier postmasters' provisional issues of the 1840's. Today, there is a huge variety of Confederacy provisional postal stamps to collect.

Key Dates in Confederate Postal History	
February 8, 1861	The Confederate States of America are formed.
Spring, 1861	The Confederacy uses United States stamps and six local postmaster provisional stamps for postage. Proceeds go to the United Stated Post Office Department.
May 13, 1861	CSA Postmaster Reagan has the Confederacy assume control of the postal system within its borders.
June 1, 1861	CSA now has an independent postal system. Use of USA stamps is now on illegal. A wide variety of local postmaster provisional issues are created to fill the void of needed postage.
October 16, 1861	The First Confederate general issue stamps are available.
June 1, 1862	Due to runaway inflation, postage rates are increased. The basic first-class is doubled form five to ten-cents.
April, 1865	Fall of the Confederacy and end of the CSA postal system.

Figure 4-35. Photograph of the Confederate Postmaster General John H. Reagan

HOYER & LUDWIG LITHOGRAPHS ISSUES

Because most of the American printing industry was located in the North, the first Confederate stamp contract was made with a London company, Thomas De La Rue. However, there were delays in the production and shipment of this issue. This included the capture of the first stamp shipment by the Union blockade. This delay led to domestically printed stamps as the first Confederate stamp issue. So the Richmond firm of Hoyer and Ludwig made postage stamps while the De La Rue issue was being prepared in England. They issued three stamps, in October 1861. These issues are poor quality lithographs.

Hoyer & Ludwig Two-Cent Jackson

Hoyer & Ludwig Two-Cent Jackson

Stamp Production

Printer:	Hoyer and Ludwig of Richmond Virginia
Format:	Lithography with two panes of 100 stamps each
Date of Issue:	March 1862
Earliest Known Use:	March 21, 1862
Uses:	Drop rate. Circular rate.

Stamp Features

Watermark:	None
Perforation:	Imperforate
Colors:	Green, light green, dark green, bright yellow green.
Varieties:	Acid flaw

Collectable Stamp Today
Collectable Cancellation Varieties:
          blue town, red town, Arkansas town, Texas town, blue gridiron, Paid, express company cancellation, railroad, pen
Value Unused: $$$$
Value Used: $$$$

The two-cent green stamp was issued in early 1862. It featured a portrait of Andrew Jackson in an oval frame with scrollwork around it. The words, CONFEDERATE STATES, are printed around the top of the frame. It paid the Confederate drop letter and the circular rates.

Hoyer & Ludwig Five-Cent Davis

Green Hoyer & Ludwig Five-Cent Davis

Stamp Production
Printer: Hoyer and Ludwig of Richmond Virginia
Format: Lithography with two panes of 100 stamps each
Date of Issue: Fall 1861
Earliest Known Use: Oct 16, 1861
Uses: Basic postage rate less than 500 miles.

Stamp Features
Watermark: None
Perforation: Imperforate
Colors: Green, light green, dark green, bright green, dull green, olive green.

Varieties: Rouletted, Misplaced transfer, Spur in upper left scroll, Acid flaw, Flaw on at of States, While curl at back of head, Imprint

Collectable Stamp Today
Collectable Cancellation Varieties:
blue town, red town, green town, Arkansas town, Florida town, Texas town, Kentucky town, blue gridiron, red gridiron, blue concentric, star, flower, numeral, Paid, Steamboat, express company cancellation, railroad, pen, 1861

Value Unused: $$$$
Value Used: $$$$

Blue Hoyer & Ludwig Five-Cent Davis

Stamp Production
Printer: Hoyer and Ludwig of Richmond Virginia
Format: Lithography with two panes of 100 stamps each
Date of Issue: Early 1862
Earliest Known Use: Feb. 26, 1862
Uses: Basic postage rate less than 500 miles.

Stamp Features
Watermark: None
Perforation: Imperforate
Colors: Blue, light milky blue, dark blue.
Varieties: Misplaced transfer, Spur in upper left scroll, Thin hard paper, Tops of C and E of cents joined by flaw, Flying bird above lower left corner ornament

Collectable Stamp Today
Collectable Cancellation Varieties:

blue town, red town, Arkansas town, Florida town, Texas town, straight line town, blue gridiron, red gridiron, star, flowers, numeral, Paid, Steamboat, express company cancellation, railroad, pen, Way

Value Unused: $$$$
Value Used: $$$$

Figure 4-36. Example of Confederate Stamps on a Cover. Shown are two CSA stamps on a typical cover of the times. The stamp are Hoyer and Ludwig green five-cent Davis and Hoyer and Ludwig blue ten-cent Jefferson (Scott 2).

The five-cent Hoyer and Ludwig stamp features a portrait of President Jefferson Davis in an oval frame. The words, CONFEDERATE STATES OF AMERICA, are inside the frame over Davis's head. At the top of the stamp is the word, POSTAGE, and at the bottom, the words, FIVE CENTS. The first stamp color was green. It paid the basic postage rate. It comes in a variety of hues, stone varieties, cancellations, and covers. In early 1862, the stamp's ink color was changed to blue.

Ten-Cent Jefferson

Blue Ten-Cent Jefferson

Stamp Production
Printer:	Hoyer and Ludwig of Richmond Virginia
Format:	Lithography with two panes of 100 stamps each
Date of Issue:	Fall 1861
Earliest Known Use:	Nov. 8, 1861
Uses:	Basic postage rate over 500 miles.

Stamp Features
Watermark:	None
Perforation:	Imperforate
Colors:	Blue, light blue, dark blue, indigo, greenish blue.
Varieties:	Malformed O of POSTAGE, Malformed T of TEN, G and E of POSTAGE joined, Circular flaw upper left star, Rouletted

Collectable Stamp Today
Collectable Cancellation Varieties:

blue town, red town, green town, violet town, Arkansas town, Florida town, Texas town, Kentucky town, straight line town, blue gridiron, red gridiron, blue concentric, numeral, Paid, star, flower, express company cancellation, railroad, pen, 1861, 1862

Value Unused:	$$$$
Value Used:	$$$$

Rose Ten-Cent Jefferson

Stamp Production

Printer:	Hoyer and Ludwig of Richmond Virginia
Format:	Lithography with two panes of 100 stamps each
Date of Issue:	Early 1862
Earliest Known Use:	March 10, 1862
Uses:	Basic postage rate over 500 miles.

Stamp Features

Watermark:	None
Perforation:	Imperforate
Colors:	Rose, dull rose, brown rose, deep rose, carmine rose, carmine.
Varieties:	Malformed T of TEN, G and E of POSTAGE joined, Circular flaw upper left star, Third spiked ornament at right, Scratched stone, Imprint.

Collectable Stamp Today

Collectable Cancellation Varieties:	blue town, red town, green town, Arkansas town, Texas town, straight line town, blue gridiron, red gridiron, blue concentric, black concentric, numeral, Paid, express company cancellation, railroad, pen, 1862
Value Unused:	$$$$
Value Used:	$$$$

The highest denomination 1861 Hoyer and Ludwig lithographed stamp features a Thomas Jefferson portrait in a bordered oval frame. The words, CONFEDERATE STATES OF AMERICA, are found in the frame's border. The words, POSTAGE, are at the top of the stamp, and TEN CENTS, at the bottom. The numeral, 10, is found in each of the stamp's four corners. In early 1862, the stamp's color was changed from blue to rose. This stamp paid the basic postage rate for letters traveling more than 500 miles.

Another printer, the J. T. Paterson Company, later produced the ten-cent stamps. These were issued in mid-1862. There are only very subtle differences from the Hoyer and Ludwig printing.

DE LA RUE STAMPS

The first De La Rue stamps arrived from London in April 1862. The plate, which had also been shipped from England, was transferred to the Richmond printing firm of Archer and Daly for local printings. These are typographic engraved stamps.

Five-Cent Davis

De La Rue Five-Cent Davis

Stamp Production
Printer: De La Rue and Company of London
Format: Typography with four panes of 100 stamps each
Date of Issue: April 1862
Earliest Known Use: Apr. 16, 1862
Uses: Basic postage rate less than 500 miles. After July 1, 1862 pair paid basic postage rate

Stamp Features
Watermark: None
Perforation: Imperforate

Colors: Light blue

Collectable Stamp Today
Collectable Cancellation Varieties:

blue town, red town, green town, Arkansas town, Texas town, straight line town, blue gridiron, red gridiron, blue concentric, Paid, express company cancellation, railroad, pen.

Value Unused: $$$
Value Used: $$$

Archer & Daly Five-Cent Davis

Stamp Production
Printer: Archer and Daly of Richmond
Format: Typography with four panes of 100 stamps each
Date of Issue: Aug. 1862
Earliest Known Use: Aug. 15, 1862
Uses: Pair paid basic postage rate

Stamp Features
Watermark: None
Perforation: Imperforate
Colors: Blue, deep blue
Varieties: Printed on both sides, White tie, Thin paper, Thick paper

Collectable Stamp Today
Collectable Cancellation Varieties:

blue town, red town, brown town, violet town, green town, Arkansas town, Texas town, Florida town, straight line town, blue gridiron, red gridiron, blue concentric, Paid, express company cancellation, railroad, pen.

Value Unused: $$$
Value Used: $$$

Figure 4-37. Example of a Confederate Patriotic Cover. Like the North, the Confederate States had a wide variety of patriotic decorative stamp covers.

Only the five-cent De La Rue stamps made it to the Confederacy. They, and the locally printed stamps made from the same plate, feature a portrait of Jefferson Davis in a circular frame within a square. There is a star in each comer. The words, CONFEDERATE STATES, are at the top, and FIVE CENTS, at the bottom of the stamp. It was printed with blue ink. Archer and Daly of Richmond Virginia printed the locally made stamps. The Archer stamps are coarser, duller, and blurred, and thus easily distinguished from the English made stamps.

Only two months after the stamps from De La Rue were put into service, the Confederacy basic letter rate was raised to ten cents. Since the ten-cent value of the lithographed issue was in short supply, most people used two of these five-cent typography stamps to pay for the then ten-cent basic postage rate.

One-Cent Calhoun

One-Cent Calhoun

Stamp Production
Printer:	De La Rue and Company of London
Format:	Typography
Date Issued:	1862
Uses:	Never used

Stamp Features
Watermark:	None
Perforation:	Imperforate
Colors:	Orange, deep orange

Collectable Stamp Today
Value Unused:	$$$$

A one-cent was printed in 1862 by De La Rue of London, but was never formally issued because there was never a need for such a low rate. The orange typographic stamp features a portrait of John C. Calhoun in a circular frame ornamented in the same manner as the five-cent De La Rue issue of 1862.

ARCHER AND DALY STAMPS

The Archer and Daly firm made the next Confederate stamps. They produced their own engraved postage stamp issues: a two-cent stamp for drop letters and circulars, a ten-cent for the standard letter rate, and a twenty-cent stamp to cover double rate letters. The trans-Mississippi rate of forty cents required two 20-cent stamps.

Two-Cent Archer & Daly Jackson

Two-Cent Archer & Daly Jackson

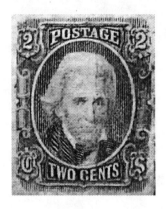

Stamp Production
Printer:	Archer and Daly of Richmond
Format:	Intaglio with two panes of 100 stamps each
Date of Issue:	Apr. 1863
Earliest Known Use:	Apr. 21, 1863
Uses:	Drop letter rate

Stamp Features
Watermark:	None
Perforation:	Imperforate
Colors:	Brown red, pale red
Varieties:	Double transfer

Collectable Stamp Today
Collectable Cancellation Varieties:

blue town, red town, army of Tennessee, blue gridiron, black numeral, railroad.

Value Unused: $$$
Value Used: $$$$

The intaglio two-cent stamps features Andrew Jackson in an oval frame surrounded with scrollwork. The word, POSTAGE, appears in a solid label at the top of the stamp, and TWO CENTS is at the bottom. This is the only Confederate postage stamp, which does not have the Confederate States or CSA in the design. The initials C and S appear in small shields in the lower corners. The color of the stamp is reddish brown.

Archer & Daly Ten-Cent Davis

Archer & Daly Ten-Cent Davis "TEN CENTS"

Stamp Production
Printer: Archer and Daly of Richmond
Format: Intaglio with two panes of 100 stamps each
Date of Issue: Apr. 1863
Earliest Known Use: Apr. 23, 1863
Uses: Basic postal rate

Stamp Features
Watermark: None
Perforation: Imperforate
Colors: Blue, milky blue, gray blue.
Varieties: Double transfer, Damaged plate, Curved lines outside the label at the top and bottom are broken

Collectable Stamp Today
Collectable Cancellation Varieties:

        blue town, red town, green town, violet town, straight line town, 1863, black gridiron, blue gridiron, railroad, circle of wedges, pen

Value Unused: $$$$
Value Used: $$$$

Archer & Daly Ten-Cent Davis "Rectangular Frame"

Stamp Production
Printer: Archer and Daly of Richmond
Format: Intaglio with one pane of 100 stamps
Date of Issue: Apr. 1863
Earliest Known Use: Apr. 19, 1863
Uses: Basic postal rate

Stamp Features
Watermark: None
Perforation: Imperforate
Colors: Blue, milky blue, greenish blue, dark blue.
Varieties: Double transfer

Collectable Stamp Today
Collectable Cancellation Varieties:

        blue town, red town, straight line town, 1863, blue gridiron, pen

Value Unused: $$$$$
Value Used: $$$$$

Archer & Daly Ten-Cent Davis "No Rectangular Frame"

Stamp Production
Printer: Archer and Daly of Richmond, Keatings and Ball of
                          Columbia, SC
Format: Intaglio with two panes of 100 stamps each
Date of Issue: 1863
Earliest Known Use: Apr. 21, 1863
Uses: Basic postal rate

Stamp Features
Watermark: None
Perforation: Imperforate, rouletted, or perforated 12 ½
Colors: Blue, milky blue, dark blue, greenish blue, green.
Varieties: Double transfer, Rouletted, Perforated 12 ½

Collectable Stamp Today
Collectable Cancellation Varieties:
                          blue town, red town, orange town, brown town, green
                          town, violet town, Texas town, Arkansas town, Florida
                          town, straight line town, army of Tennessee, Free, 1863,
                          blue gridiron, black concentric circles, star, crossroads,
                          Paid, railroad, steamboat, pen
Value Unused: $$
Value Used: $$$$

Archer & Daly Ten-Cent Davis "Wavy Frame"

Stamp Production

Printer:	Archer and Daly of Richmond, Keatings and Ball of Columbia, SC
Format:	Intaglio with two panes of 100 stamps each
Date of Issue:	1863
Earliest Known Use:	May 1, 1863
Uses:	Basic postal rate

Stamp Features

Watermark:	None
Perforation:	Imperforate, rouletted, or perforated 12 ½
Colors:	Blue, milky blue, light blue, greenish blue, dark blue, green.
Varieties:	Double transfer, Rouletted, Perforated 12 ½

Collectable Stamp Today
Collectable Cancellation Varieties:

blue town, red town, brown town, green town, violet town, Texas town, Arkansas town, Florida town, straight line town, army of Tennessee, 1863, blue gridiron, black concentric circles, railroad, pen

Value Unused:	$$$
Value Used:	$$$

This stamp has a portrait of Jefferson Davis inside an oval surrounded with scrollwork. The words, POSTAGE is in a solid label at the top, and THE CONFEDERATE STATES OF AMERICA split into two labels to the right and left of the portrait.

Archer and Daly printed four types of these intaglio ten-cent stamps. The first type was printed with the words, TEN CENTS, at the bottom. This inscription then was changed to 10 CENTS, produced in three major varieties. The first has a rectangular frame outside each of the stamp designs. The second does not have frame lines. And the third is slightly modified with scrollwork and a wavy frame line, close to the design. The color for all the 10-cent Davis stamps is blue but in a wide variety of shades.

Archer & Daly Twenty-Cent Washington

Archer & Daly Twenty-Cent Washington

Stamp Production

Printer:	Archer and Daly of Richmond
Format:	Intaglio with two panes of 100 stamps each
Date of Issue:	June 1863
Earliest Known Use:	June 1, 1863
Uses:	Double-weight letters. Two paid the trans-Mississippi rate

Stamp Features

Watermark:	None
Perforation:	Imperforate, rouletted,
Colors:	Green, yellow green, dark green.
Varieties:	Double transfer, Rouletted, 20 on forehead

Collectable Stamp Today
Collectable Cancellation Varieties:

	blue town, red town, violet town, Texas town, Arkansas town, Tennessee town, railroad
Value Unused:	$$$
Value Used:	$$$$

This stamp has a portrait of George Washington in an oval frame with scrollwork arch above and looped ribbons below. The numeral,

20, appears at top center, flanked by the words, THE CONFEDERATE STATES OF AMERICA. The ribbon at the bottom is inscribed with the words, POSTAGE TWENTY CENTS. The color of the stamp is green. The stamp was used as confederate currency for small change.

Keating and Ball Reissues

The ten-cent stamps of the last two types were reprinted from the same plates by Keating and Ball of Columbia, South Carolina. The Keating and Ball stamps can be recognizable by their poor quality printing and darker blue color.

DECLINE OF THE CONFEDERATE POSTAL SYSTEM

The confederate postal system, from the start, struggled with the multiple problems of having to start from anew during a war with a poor transportation system, manpower storages, and runaway inflation. The most serious disruption occurred in 1863 with the capture of Vicksburg on the Mississippi River. Union forces then controlled the entire Mississippi. This cut off regular east-west mail service for the Confederacy. To get mail across the Mississippi, Postmaster General Reagan contracted blockade-runners who would dodge troops to cross with the mail. Service was twice a week; with the charge was forty cents per half ounce of mail.

The South, by 1864, had shortages of all materials, including postal items. Stamps were in short supply. Some postmasters went back to handstamping the letters or using provisional stamps again.

5 | The Pictorial Stamps of 1869

This United States regular stamp issue, though in service for only about a year, is this country's most fascinating. The series was so criticized when it was released, it had to be replaced. But today, the pictorial stamps of the 1869 stamp series are voted our most handsome regular series stamps. They were revolutionary for their time. They include the first United States pictorials, scenes not just portraits. They include the first American bicolor stamps. The stamps were odd-sized, tiny and square. Finally, they included unusual designs and subjects.

A New Printing Contract

Figure 5-1. Postmaster General Alexander W. Randall. Alexander Randall was Postmaster General at the time of the 1869 issue. Born in New York, he spent most of his life in Wisconsin where he studied and practiced law. He was governor of Wisconsin, had a military carrier, was United States minister to the Papal States, and first assistant postmaster general. President Andrew Johnson appointed him postmaster general in July 1866.

In June 1868, Postmaster General Alexander Randall asked printers for bids for the new series of stamps. Four submitted bids: American Bank Note Company, Butler and Carpenter of Philadelphia, George T. Jones, and the current printer, the National Bank Note Company. Essays from one of the losing bidders, George T. Jones, exist today. They feature vignettes of U. S. Grant and the U. S. Treasury Department seal. National won the contract, and went on to print stamps for ten more years. This is despite Butler and Carpenter submitting the lowest bid. Butler and Carpenter fought this decision, but a congressional committee investigated the matter and found in favor of National. The contract was signed December 12, 1868. It was for four years, starting February 1, 1869. National Bank Note Company held the patent on grilling. This won them the contract despite being outbid by Butler because the Post Office Department was convinced that grills were needed to prevent stamp reuse.

The Grills

The only type of grill found on this issue is the G type. It is 9 x 9 mm square or 12 x 12 rows of points. They are male grills with points down, when viewed from the face of the stamp. In general, the grills are faint. Very few copies show a strong grill impression. Many show only a few points. It was becoming apparent that grills were not serving their role in preventing stamp reuse.

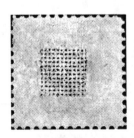

Figure 5-2. G Grill. This is the grill found on the 1869 series stamps. It measures 9 by 9 mm, square or 12 by 12 rows of points. They are male grills, that is the points are down when viewed from the face of the stamp.

A rare and valuable variety of the stamps of this issue is the no grill type. Because, the grills can be very faint, in order to qualify as ungrilled, it must be an unused stamp and have its original gum. The 1, 2, 3, 15 (type I), 24, 30, and 90 denominations exist without grills. Causes of these varieties include: multiple sheet grilling where sheets in the center of the bundle did not get grilled, off center grilling where rows of stamps failed to be grilled, or defective points on the grilling machine.

The grill varieties (split, double, marginal, etc.) are common in this series.

Original	Proposed Design	Issued	Actual Design
1 Cent	Franklin	1 Cent	Franklin
2 Cent	Postal Rider	2 Cent	Postal Rider
3 Cent	Locomotive	3 Cent	Locomotive
5 Cent	Washington	6 Cent	Washington
10 Cent	Lincoln	10 Cent	Eagle and Shield
15 Cent	Landing of Columbus	10 Cent	Landing of Columbus
12 Cent	Ocean Steamer	12 Cent	Ocean Steamer
24 Cent	Decl.. of Independence	24 Cent	Decl. of Independence
30 Cent	Surrender of Burgoyne	30 Cent	Flag, Eagle, and Shield
90 Cent	Washington	90 Cent	Lincoln

Originally, the new stamps were to be issued on February 1, 1869. The first submitted dies were: 1-cent Franklin, 2-cent post rider, 3-cent locomotive, 5-cent Washington, 10-cent Lincoln, 12-cent ocean steamer, 15-cent the landing of Columbus, 24-cent signing of the Declaration of Independence, 30-cent surrender of Burgoyne, and 90-cent Washington. Every one of these designs was rejected or altered before the stamps were printed. Because the 5-cent denomination was not needed, it was eliminated and a 6-cent stamp for double weight letters added. Lincoln was moved from the 10 to the 90-cent stamp and replaced with a shield and eagle design, To save the eyesight of postal clerks, the size of all of the numerals on the issued stamps were increased.

An Unpopular Series

Today, the 1869 series is one of the most popular of all the United States issues among collectors. But, when the stamps appeared they were ridiculed. They were lampooned in the newspapers. Part of this negative attitude was because they were approved during the previous unpopular Andrew Johnson administration. So many protests were received that by October1869, the Post Office Department asked that the remaining supplies of this issue be returned and soon a new issue was printed. Because of the short duration of this series, this means they are relatively rare stamps, today.

New Plate Layout

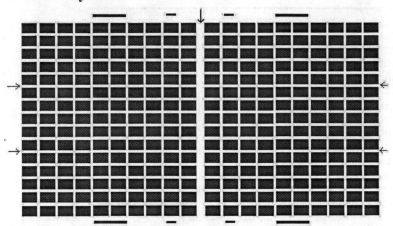

Figure 5-3. Plate Layout of the Lower Denomination Stamps of the 1869 Series.
The one to twelve-cent stamps of the 1869 series were printed from plates of 300
stamps. The sheet was divided into two panes, left and right, of 150 stamps each.
Each pane consists of fifteen rows of 10 stamps per row.

Because of the individual stamps' small size, the panes of the
denominations 12-cent and below contain 150 stamps. The plate
arrangement were sheets of 300, cut vertically into two panes of 150,
left and right. Therefore, one finds 15 stamps per pane (30 per sheet)
with a straight edge on the left or right side.

Vertical arrows were etched into the plate on the top and bottom
margins to guide cutting the sheet into two panes. The plate had two
sets of horizontal arrows, though they weren't used for cutting. They
are at the right side of the right pane and at the left side of the left pane
between the fifth and sixth and the tenth and eleventh horizontal rows.

Figure 5-4. Plate Block. The marginal markings consist of the imprint name, the plate number, and position arrows. The imprint name is found at the top and bottom of each pane spanning the fifth and sixth column. The plate number is found above and below the ninth column of the left pane and the second column of the right pane.

A block with four stamps with the attached selvage showing the arrow centered on one edge is called a margin block with arrow.

One can see printing varieties called position copies. Position copies are capture stamps. They are off-center as to take in marginal markings such these imprints, plate numbers, and parts of the arrows.

Figure 5-5. Arrow Block. Arrows are found in the margins at the top and bottom between the two panes. They served as a guide to cut the sheet into panes. Arrows also are found between the fifth and sixth and the tenth and eleventh rows to the left of the left pane and to the right of the right pane, though no cutting was done here. One can collect an arrow block of four stamps with the attached arrow selvage.

The 15-cent and higher denomination stamps were made in single panes of just 100 stamps. These series stamps were printed on a hard, white, woven paper. All stamps are perforated 12.

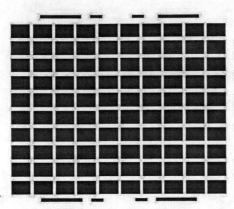

Figure 5-6. Plate Layout of the Higher Denomination Stamps of the 1869 Series. The 15-cent and higher denomination stamps of this series were printed from plates that had one pane that contained just 100 stamps. There are two imprints, one for each of the two inks used on these bicolor stamps.

The Infamous Inverts

Included in this series are three famous errors, the inverts. The inverts are found on the 15 (type II), 24, and 30-cent stamps. They occurred because the bicolor stamps of the series were printed by passing a sheet of stamps twice through a press, once for each color. Though called inverted center this is technically wrong. Since the centers were printed first, it was the frames that were printed upside down and the true source of the error!

The Issued Stamps

ONE-CENT FRANKLIN

1869 One-Cent Franklin

Stamp Production
Printer:	National Bank Note Co.
Designer:	E. Pitcher
Engravers:	Joseph I. Pease (portrait), William D. Nichols (frame), J.C. Kenworthy (lettering)
Format:	Sheets of 300, cut vertically into panes of 150
Plate Numbers:	1, 2
Date of Issue:	Mar. 19, 1869
Earliest Known Use:	Apr.1, 1869
Uses:	Circulars. Drop rate without carrier service. Used as multiples or with other stamps.
Quantity Issued:	12,020,550

Stamp Features
Size:	20.2 x 20.2 mm (0.8 x 0.8 inches)
Watermark:	None
Grill:	G
Perforation:	12
Colors:	Buff, brown orange, dark brown orange.
Varieties:	Double transfer, Double grill, Split grill, Without grill with original gum, Double grill one split quadruple, Double grill one split, Cracked plate, Paper folds, Scratched Plate

Collectable Stamp Today
Collectable Cancellation Colors:
Black, blue, ultramarine, magenta, purple, red, green.

Collectable Cancellation Varieties:

> Paid, numeral, steamship, black town, blue town, red town, black carrier, blue carrier, Japan.

Value Unused: $$$$
Value Used: $$$$
Surviving Covers: 2,000
Largest Known Multiple: Unused: 48 (block)
Used: 12 (block)

The one-cent stamp of the 1869 series is so much different than previous and later stamp designs. It still features the ever present Franklin but in a circle! The triangular corners of it are blank. This left-facing bust of Benjamin Franklin was based on a sculpture by Frenchman, Jean-Antoine Houdon. It was criticized, at that time of printing, as having an appearance of a fireman!

The stamp is rarely well centered. This stamp was printed from just two plates, 1 and 2. The stamp was issued March 19, 1869.

Colors

The stamp is found in buff, brown orange, and dark brown orange, pale brown orange, and ocher. Since the yellow dye pigment oxidizes easily, it is hard to know what are real differences in dye color versus what are chemical changelings. All the color varieties are of equal value. The stamp's pale color added to the poor centering makes it hard to find good canceled copies today.

Varieties

This stamp has several grill varieties. The most rare is "the no grill." This rare variety can only be proven if the stamp has its original gum. Another rare grill variety is two grills, one split quadruple with a segment striking each corner of the stamp. This is the result of two passes through the grilling machine, one pass on and one pass off center. The stamp can be found with a double grill, and a split grill.

There are the usual plate varieties, including cracked plates, paper folds, double transfers and scratched plate copies.

Use and Covers

This stamp paid the drop (local) letter without carrier service rate. Strips and multiples paid higher rates. About two thousand covers with this stamp are still in existence. The greatest 1869 cover, and one of the greatest of all United States covers is franked with three 1869 one-cent stamps. It is canceled with three running birds. The cover was from Waterbury, Connecticut, a source of many such fancy cancels. Poster worker and part-time cork whittler, John W. Hill, made these fancy cancels. This marking was made near Thanksgiving, meaning the bird is probably a turkey, running for his life. However today, it is called the "Running Chicken Cover."

Multiples

The largest unused multiple of the one-cent Franklin is a block of 48 stamps, showing the left margin arrow. Used, there is a block of 12 stamps.

TWO-CENT POST RIDER

1869 Two-Cent Post Rider

Stamp Production
Printer: National Bank Note Co.

Designer:	James Macdonough
Engravers:	Christian Rost (vignette), George W. Thurber (frame and lettering)
Format:	Sheets of 300, cut vertically into panes of 150
Plate Numbers:	3, 4, 5, 6, 27, 28
Date of Issue:	Mar. 19, 1869
Earliest Known Use:	Mar. 20, 1869
Uses:	Local rate with carrier. Unsealed circulars
Quantity Issued:	72,109,050

Stamp Features

Size:	20.2 x 20.0 mm (0.8 x 0.8 inches)
Watermark:	None
Grill:	G
Perforation:	12
Colors:	Brown, pale brown, dark brown, yellow brown.
Varieties:	Double grill, Split grill, Quadruple split grill, Marginal grill, Double transfer, Without grill with original gum, Plate crack, Double impression, Printed on both sides.

Collectable Stamp Today
Collectable Cancellation Colors:

Black, blue, red, orange, orange red, magenta, purple, ultramarine, green, brown

Collectable Cancellation Varieties:

Paid, Paid All, steamship, blue town, black town, Japan, China, steamship, blue carrier, black carrier, precancelled Jefferson Ohio

Value Unused:	$$$$
Value Used:	$$$
Surviving Covers:	5,000-25,000
Largest Known Multiple:	Unused: 120 (10x12 block)
	Used: 10 (2x5 block)

This stamp features a post rider. It shows a figure of a horse and rider with the horse's legs outstretched. It was based on a crayon and wash drawing by W.E. Hadden. Like the rest of the series, the design received poor reviews when issued. One newspaper said the stamp represented John Wilkes Booth's death ride. It was criticized because the horse's legs appear to be leaping rather than galloping.

Like so many 19th century stamps, the design is poorly centered in relationship to the perforations. According to the stamp expert Brookman, only one copy in a thousand is well centered. The poor centering is the result of sloppy work when the finished sheets were placed through the perforating machine.

Varieties

Varieties include grill changes: double grill and split grill (horizontal or vertical). There are many plate varieties: plate crack, double transfer, double impression, arrow single, straddle pane single, plate number capture single (from plates 3, 4, 5, 6, 27, and 28) and a unique stamp printed on both sides.

Uses and Covers

The earliest known use of this stamp is March 20, 1869, the earliest of any 1869 series stamp. Used for drop rate with carrier service, the two-cent post rider stamp is common on cover, only a little less common than the three-cent stamp of this series. The stamp was used as a bisect, although such covers are rare.

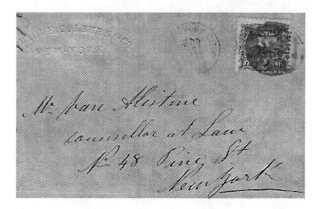

Figure 5-7. Example of Two-Cent Stamp on a Cover. Here is a cover showing the most common use of the two-cent postal rider stamp of the 1869 series. It paid the two-cent local rate with carrier service, in this case, New York City.

Multiples

Collectible multiples of the post rider stamp includes pairs, margin blocks of four stamps with arrow selvage attached, and plate blocks of 10 from the top or bottom of the plate with the imprint and plate number on the marginal selvage. The largest unused multiple is a block of 120 stamps (10 x 12), with the marginal imprint and plate number 3.

THREE-CENT LOCOMOTIVE

1869 Three-Cent Locomotive

Stamp Production

Printer:	National Bank Note Co.
Designer:	James Macdonough
Engravers:	Christian Rost (vignette), George W. Thurber (frame and lettering)
Format:	Sheets of 300, cut vertically into panes of 150
Plate Numbers:	7, 8, 9, 10, 11,12, 25, 26, 29, 30
Date of Issue:	Mar. 19, 1869
Earliest Known Use:	Mar. 27,1869
Uses:	Single-rate first class domestic letter
Quantity Issued:	335,534,850

Stamp Features

Size:	20.5 x 20.0 mm (0.8 x 0.8 inches)
Watermark:	None
Grill:	G
Perforation:	12
Colors:	Ultramarine, pale ultramarine, dark ultramarine, blue, violet blue
Varieties:	Double transfer, Double grill, Triple grill, Split grill, Quadruple split grill, Marginal grill, Sextuple grill, Grill with points up, Printed on both sides, Without grill and with original gum, Cracked plate.

Collectable Stamp Today
Collectable Cancellation Colors:

> Black, blue, ultramarine, magenta, purple, violet, red, orange red, brown, green, orange, yellow.

Collectable Cancellation Varieties:

> black town, blue town, red town, Paid, Paid All, Steamboat, Steamship, U.S. Ship, numerals, ship, railroad, packet boat, black carrier, blue carrier, express company cancellation, Way, Free, Alaska, Japan.

Value Unused:	$$$$
Value Used:	$$$
Surviving Covers:	175,000
Largest Known Multiple:	Unused: 150 (full panes)
	Used: 13

Figure 5-8. Source of the Three-Cent Stamp Design. The origin of the locomotive design of the three-cent 1869 series stamp is a National Bank Note Company design, "The Crossing," showing a locomotive crossing a stream on a stone bridge. It also was used on bank notes printed by the company.

The three-cent stamp of 1869 features a locomotive moving toward the right. It is surrounded by Victorian ornamental scrollwork. The stamp comes in the colors: ultramarine, pale ultramarine, dark ultramarine, blue, and violet blue. The origin of the locomotive design is a National Bank Note Company design, "The Crossing," showing a locomotive crossing a stream on a stone bridge.

When this stamp was released in 1869, the public complained about just about everything on the stamp, including its color, lettering and design. The domestic letter rate stamp traditionally had George

Washington as its vignette. Therefore, it was viewed as unpatriotic not to have him on this stamp. It was ridiculed by statement that the stamp represented how Congressmen make money. But the real reason for the locomotive was to show the fast mail service of the time. It also celebrated the completion of the transcontinental railroad that year. In a sense, this was the first United States commemorative stamp.

Varieties

The most common stamp of the 1869 series, it has the most varieties. The grill varieties include split grill (both horizontally and vertically), quarter grill, quadruple split grill, double grill, double grill with one split horizontally, grill with the points up instead of down, and a unique copy with sextuple grill. Of course, there is the rare unused 3-cent stamp lacking any grill.

Printing varieties include: scored plate, re-entry, double transfer, double impression, printed on both sides, preprinting paper crease, and stamps with an added triangle over the O of POSTAGE.

Covers

The most common denomination of this series, it survives on 175,000 covers. Most paid the three-cent first-class domestic mail rate. Very rare are bisects of the stamps on cover. One can have a vertical one-third trisect used as a 1-cent stamp or a vertical two-thirds used as a 2-cent stamp on cover. Stever found the stamp on cover sent to 34 different foreign countries.

Figure 5-9. Example of a Three-Cent 1869 Stamp on a Cover. The most common stamp found on cover from the 1869 series is the three-cent locomotive as it paid the basic first-class postage rate of the time. Here is such a letter sent from Oweno to Geneva, New York.

Multiples

Several full panes of 150 stamps (10x15) with the complete selvage exist. The largest used multiple of the 1869 three-cent stamp is an irregular block of 13 stamps.

SIX-CENT WASHINGTON

1869 Six-Cent Washington

Stamp Production

Printer:	National Bank Note Co.
Designer:	E. Pitcher
Engravers:	William E. Marshall (vignette), J.C. Kenworthy (letters), William D. Nichols (frame)
Format:	Sheets of 300, cut vertically into panes of 150
Plate Numbers:	13,14
Date of Issue:	Mar. 19, 1869
Earliest Known Use:	Apr. 26, 1869
Uses:	Double weight domestic letter rate. Six-cent rate to Canada. Six-cent rate to Great Britain (starting 1870).
Quantity Issued:	4,293,100

Stamp Features
Size: 20.5 x 20.0 mm (0.8 x 0.8 inches)
Watermark: None
Grill: G
Perforation: 12
Colors: Ultramarine, pale ultramarine
Varieties: Double grill, Split grill, Quadruple split grill, Double transfer.

Collectable Stamp Today
Collectable Cancellation Colors:
                           Black, blue, brown, magenta, purple, red, green.
Collectable Cancellation Varieties:
                           Paid, Paid All, black town, Short Paid, Insufficiently Paid, steamship, railroad, Japan
Value Unused: $$$$$
Value Used: $$$$
Surviving Covers: 1,350
Largest Known Multiple: Unused: 14 (4x4 block)
                           Used: 4

This is the only stamp of the series that features George Washington ever-present on American stamps. The three-quarter-face design was taken from a Gilbert Stuart portrait of Washington, painted from his life at Germantown, Pennsylvania. The head of Washington is within a circle lined with pearls. It has a square frame, tessellated at the corners. The 6-cent portrait of Washington stamp was the only one of this series to escape public criticism

Of all the 1869 stamps, the 6-cent Washington is the most difficult stamp to find well centered, which is saying a lot!

Figure 5-10. "Six"-Cent Essay. The essays for the six-cent stamp are of 5-cent denomination. In the essays, the numerals, 5, are in both bottom corners on each side of the wording, FIVE CENTS. On the issued stamps, in this place are the words, SIX CENTS, with the numeral, 6, divides this lettering.

The 6-cent Washington was proposed as a 5-cent issue. In fact, all the essays for the six-cent stamp are of 5-cent denomination. The previous series always had such a denomination, but it never saw widespread use. In April 1868, the postage rate to Canada was reduced from 10 to 6 cents, creating its need. Plus, the six-cent stamp paid the double letter weight first-class (one half to one ounce) rate. In 1870, the postage rate to Great Britain was reduced to six cents, finding another use for this stamp.

Colors

Ultramarine was picked as the color for the stamp. This was the same color as the three-cent, to save money on printing by using one ink. This wasn't a smart idea as it confused the clerks of the time who sorted the mail. There is little variation in the color of this stamp, as it is found only in ultramarine and pale ultramarine. Cancellations obliterate the light color of the design, making a find of a good used stamp, a rare one.

Varieties

There are four grill varieties: split grill, double grill, quadruple split grill and double transfer.

Figure 5-11. Example of an 1869 Six-Cent Stamp on a Cover. This cover shows the use of a 1869 six-cent stamp paying the postage rate to Canada, in this case from Cleveland, Ohio to Hamilton, Ontario.

Uses and Covers

Most covers were sent to Great Britain or Canada, paying their foreign rates. The stamp can be found sent to 31 foreign countries. Some covers show the stamp paying the double weight domestic rate. The most rare, in fact, a unique use is a vertical half stamp used to pay the basic 3-cent rate from Mechanicsville, New York, to Vermont.

Multiples

The largest unused multiples of a six-cent Washington are two blocks of 16 stamps (4x4). The largest used multiple is a block of four.

TEN-CENT EAGLE AND SHIELD

1869 Ten-Cent Eagle and Shield

Stamp Production

Printer:	National Bank Note Co.
Designer:	Douglas S. Ronaldson
Engravers:	Douglas S. Ronaldson
Format:	Sheets of 300, cut vertically into panes of 150
Plate Numbers:	15,16
Date of Issue:	Mar. 19, 1869
Earliest Known Use:	Apr. 1, 1869
Uses:	Foreign rate to Germany
Quantity Issued:	2,713,800

Stamp Features

Size:	20.0 x 19.7 mm (0.8 x 0.8 inches)
Watermark:	None
Grill:	G
Perforation:	12
Colors:	Yellow, yellowish orange.
Varieties:	Split grill, Double grill, Marginal grill.

Collectable Stamp Today
Collectable Cancellation Colors:
Black, blue, magenta, purple, red, ultramarine, green.
Collectable Cancellation Varieties:
Paid, Paid All, Insufficiently Paid, black town, steamship, railroad, supplementary mail type A, express company cancellation, China, Hawaii, Japan, St. Thomas.

Value Unused:	$$$$$
Value Used:	$$$$
Surviving Covers:	1,500
Largest Known Multiple:	Unused: 15 (3x5 block)
	Used: 6 (strip)

This stamp features a shield and eagle theme. This was the first United Stamps stamp to depict the eagle, the symbol of the country. It was the country's first yellow stamp, too. The eagle and shield represented the country's spirit of newfound patriotism. This symbol was mailed overseas, to show this patriotism to the rest of the world. The stamp is very similar to the 24-cent stamp of the series, except the higher denomination stamp has flags and is bicolor.

Colors

The color of the stamp is uniform, yellow or yellowish orange. However, the pale color detracts from the otherwise beautiful stamp. Critics of the time thought the stamp would be beautiful if the color were any other than yellow. Today's collectors dislike how the pale color is wiped out by any cancellation mark the stamp may have.

Varieties

Grill varieties can be found on the ten-cent shield and eagle stamp, including a horizontal split grill, vertical split grill, double grill, end-roller (margin) grill and quadruple split grill.

Figure 5-12. Ten-Cent Essay. Originally, the 10-cent stamp was to feature Lincoln, framed by bundles of rods tied with ribbons. Eventually, Lincoln claimed the 90-cent stamp of this series.

Uses and Covers

The issue was used mainly on foreign mail to Asia, the Caribbean and Germany. It is also found on single rate letters to Austria, Brazil Alaska, Mexico, Nicaragua, and Panama. Less than 5 percent of the covers were for domestic use.

Figure 5-13. Example of an 1869 Ten-Cent Stamp on a Cover. This cover shows the most common use of the ten-cent 1869 stamp, paying the postage to Germany, in this case from Baltimore to Breman.

Multiples

The largest unused multiple of the ten-cent stamp is a mint imprint block of 15 stamps (3x5). The largest used multiple is a horizontal strip of six stamps with New York steamship cancels.

TWELVE-CENT ADRIATIC

1869 Twelve-Cent Adriatic

Stamp Production
Printer: National Bank Note Co.
Designer: James Macdonough

Engravers:	James Smillie (vignette), George W. Thurber (frame and lettering)
Format:	Sheets of 300, cut vertically into panes of 150
Plate Numbers:	17, 18
Date of Issue:	Mar. 19. 1869
Earliest Known Use:	Apr. 1, 1869
Uses:	Single rate to Great Britain (until January 1, 1870), Double weight and supplementary mail to Great Britain (after January 1, 1870)
Quantity Issued:	3,012,700

Stamp Features

Size:	20.2 x 20.0 mm (0.8 x 0.8 inches)
Watermark:	None
Grill:	G
Perforation:	12
Colors:	Green, deep green, bluish green, yellowish green.
Varieties:	Double grill, Split grill, Marginal grill, Double grill one quadruple split.

Collectable Stamp Today
Collectable Cancellation Colors:
Black, blue, magenta, purple, brown, red, green.
Collectable Cancellation Varieties:
Paid, Paid All, Too Late, black town, red town, numeral, Insufficiently Paid, Japan

Value Unused:	$$$$$
Value Used:	$$$$
Surviving Covers:	1,000
Largest Known Multiple:	Unused: 17 (block)
	Used: 37

Stamp collectors rank this stamp the best design of the 1869 series and one of the most beautiful of all United States stamps. It shows the famous Collins Line steamer, S. S. Adriatic. The ship was the finest of the wooden paddle liners of its time. When launched in 1857, the Adriatic was the largest and fastest steamship in the world. The ship was the subject of numerous illustrations, including a famous one by Currier & Ives. The Adriatic first appeared on a bank note created by the National Bank Note Company for the Citizens Bank of Louisiana. The use of this design made sense as the stamp mostly was used on letters crossing the seas to Great Britain. And it celebrates the fast mail transportation provided by ocean steamer.

Figure 5-14. Basis of the Twelve-Cent Stamp Design. The vignette of the twelve-cent 1869 stamp shows the famous Collins Line steamer, S. S. Adriatic, built in 1856.

Centering is better compared with other 1869 stamps so excellent specimens are available.

Colors

The stamp is a shade of green complementing its marine theme. It may be found in four shades: green, deep green, bluish green and yellowish green. The official post office name for the color was milori green.

Varieties

The 12-cent stamp of the 1869 series is found with three grill varieties: double grill, split grill and end roller grill. Other varieties include copies printed from a cracked and a scratched plate.

Uses and Covers

Most stamps were used to the British Isles. Before January 1, 1870, the basic postage rate to Great Britain was 12 cents, so this stamp paid that rate. After that date, the rate was reduced to 6 cents. Then, the stamp was used on double weight letters or supplementary mail to Great Britain. Supplementary mail was a special service that for double the usual postage rate, there was special service ensuring the letter reached soon departing ships.

Covers can be found going to 26 different foreign countries.

Figure 5-15. Example of an 1869 Twelve-Cent Stamp on a Cover. This cover shows the most common use of the twelve-cent 1869 stamp, paying the postage to England, in this case to Liverpool from New York.

Multiples

The largest unused multiple is an original gummed block of 12 stamps. Used, the largest multiple is an irregular block of 37.

FIFTEEN-CENT LANDING OF COLUMBUS

Type I 1869 Fifteen-Cent Landing of Columbus

Stamp Production

Printer:	National Bank Note Co.
Designer:	E. Pitcher
Engravers:	James Smillie (vignette), J.C. Kenworthy (lettering), Douglas S. Ronaldson (frame)
Format:	Sheets of 300, cut vertically into panes of 150
Plate Numbers:	19 (one each for frame and vignette)
Date of Issue:	Mar. 19. 1869
Earliest Known Use:	Mar. 31, 1869
Uses:	Letter rate to France (1869)
Quantity Issued:	120,000

Stamp Features

Size:	21.7 x 21.7 mm (0.9 x 0.9 inches)
Watermark:	None
Grill:	G
Perforation:	12
Colors:	Red brown and blue, dark red brown and blue, pale red brown and blue.
Varieties:	Double grill, Split grill, Without grill and with original gum, Double transfer.

Collectable Stamp Today
Collectable Cancellation Colors:
Black, blue, red, brown.
Collectable Cancellation Varieties:
Paid, Paid All, Insufficiently Paid, black town, blue town, steamship.
Value Unused: $$$$
Value Used: $$$
Surviving Covers: 150-175
Largest Known Multiple: Unused: 9 (3x3 block)
Used: 5 (strip) 4 (2x2 block)

Type II 1869 Fifteen-Cent Landing of Columbus

Stamp Production
Printer: National Bank Note Co.
Designer: E. Pitcher
Engravers: James Smillie (vignette), J.C. Kenworthy (lettering), Douglas S. Ronaldson (frame)
Format: Sheets of 300, cut vertically into panes of 150
Plate Numbers: 23 (one each for frame and vignette)
Date of Issue: May 1869
Earliest Known Use: Apr. 5, 1869
Uses: Letter rate to France and Germany (1869). Domestic registry fee
Quantity Issued: 1,376,700

Stamp Features
Size: 21.7 x 21.7 mm (0.9 x 0.9 inches)
Watermark: None
Grill: G
Perforation: 12
Colors: Brown and blue, dark brown and blue.
Varieties: Double transfer, Double grill, Split grill.

Errors: Inverted center

Collectable Stamp Today
Collectable Cancellation Colors:
                    Black, blue, purple, magenta, red, brown, green.
Collectable Cancellation Varieties:
                    Paid, Paid All, black town, blue town, red town, Steamship, numeral, supplementary mail type A or F, Japan.
Value Unused: $$$$$
Value Used: $$$$
Surviving Covers: 500-600
Largest Known Multiple: Unused: 20 (block)
                    Used: 9 (3x3 block)

Figure 5-16. Basis of the Fifteen-Cent Stamp. The 15-cent 1869 stamp is based on John Vanderlyn's 1839 painting "The Landing of Columbus."

The 15-cent 1869 stamp features the Landing of Columbus. The central design of the stamp was taken from an 1839 painting. The scene appeared on bank notes of the time. It is extremely detailed, showing off the engraver's fine skills. The 15-cent denomination is the first of four bicolor stamps of 1869.

The plate is arranged into a single pane sheet of 100. The top of the sheet has the plate number and the imprint of the National Bank Note Company in the frame color, red brown. The same marginal markings appear on the bottom in dark blue, the color of the vignette. Two separate plates, one for the vignette and one for the frame were needed to print these bicolor stamps. Printing of bicolor stamps was done by feeding the sheets twice through the presses. The first pass printed the central portrait. The second pass printed the frame design.

Plate 19 was the designated number both for the frame and the vignette plates of type I stamps. Type II stamps were printed from a single frame plate, 23, and a single vignette plate, also numbered 23.

Figure 5-17. Type of Fifteen-Cent Stamps. The first fifteen-cent stamp, Type I (top), has a single red-brown line surrounding the blue vignette. To hide poor alignment, a second band of three lines was added around the vignette on the later type II (middle). Therefore, a type I is called unframed, a type II, framed. Type III (bottom) is the name of the design of the 1875 reissue. It resembles the type I, with the single heavy line framing the vignette. The presence or absence of the triangle under the STA of POSTAGE is the easiest way to tell the types apart.

Types

This is the only stamp of the series printed in two types. The second appeared a month and a half after the first. It was changed to hide the frequent poor alignment of the frames with the centers.

On a type I frame, a single red-brown line surrounds the blue vignette. To hide poor alignment, a second band of three red-brown lines was added to the frame by re-engraving surrounding the vignette on the later type II. Therefore, a type II is called framed, a type I, unframed. Re-engraving is when either the master die (in this case) or a plate itself is tempered (softened) and recut.

To see the most obvious difference between the two types, one looks at the white area below the middle letters STA in POSTAGE. On type I, it is a blank. On Type II, there is a small diamond.

A type I stamp is four times as valuable a type II, today.

Colors

Type I stamps were printed in red brown, dark red brown or pale red brown and blue. Type II stamps are brown or dark brown and blue. Experts can tell the types apart by vignette color alone!

Varieties

The type I varieties include stamps with a split grill, and the very rare double grill (found in a used condition only) and without grill types. Copies exist showing double transfers and preprinting paper folds.

Type II varieties include preprinting paper fold, double transfers, plate crack, plate scratch and misalign center. Grill varieties include split grill and the rare double grill.

Uses and Covers

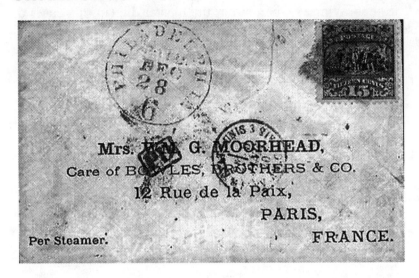

Figure 5-18. Example of an 1869 Fifteen-Cent Stamp on a Cover. This cover shows the most common use of the fifteen-cent 1869 stamp, paying the postage to France, in this case to Paris from Philadelphia.

The stamp paid postage on single weight letters to France, Germany, Italy and Switzerland. It also paid the registration fee. That fee was 15 cents from January 1, 1869 through December 31, 1873. For the more rare type I fifteen-cent stamp, it is estimated there are 150 to 175 surviving covers. For the later type II, there are 500 to 600 surviving covers.

Multiples

The largest unused multiple of the type I is an original gum block of nine stamps. Used, it is a horizontal strip of 5 stamps and a block of 4. For type II stamps, the largest unused multiple is a block of 20 stamps, used, a block of 9.

Errors-The Center Inverts

Figure 5-19. Fifteen-Cent Inverted Center Stamp Error. Shown is a beautiful used example of this spectacular error.

The most famous aspect of this stamp is its printing error, the inverted center. It is really an inverted frame since the vignette was printed first. The 15 (type II, only), 24, and 30-cent stamps all were inverted. The inverts were an embarrassment to The Post Office Department, who already faced public anger over the stamp designs. This is the reason more than 30 years would pass before there would be another bicolor issue, the 1901 Pan-American issue. They were not the world's first invert error. That distinction belongs to the Western Australia Inverted Swan printed in 1854.

Today, three unused and 84 used, but no multiples or covers exist of the estimated 500 printed. In the unused form, the inverts are among the rarest stamps in the world of stamp collecting. As a used stamp, it is the most common of the three invert stamps of this series.

The inversion error of this stamp is very subtle, easily missed on quick examination, why so many stamps wound up canceled.

Three used copies of the invert error show not only inverted frame but also traces of a double vignette, a double variety!

1992 World Columbian Stamp Expo Stamp

Figure 5-20. World Columbian Expo Stamp. A portion of the 15-cent 1869 series, Landing of Columbus stamp is reproduced on this 1992 United States commemorative stamp. The stamp promoted the World Columbian Stamp Expo stamp show, held in Chicago.

Part of this 15-cent stamp is enlarged and reproduced on the 1992 United States commemorative stamp, to promote the World Columbian Stamp Expo '92 stamp show, held in Chicago. This is another example of a "stamp on a stamp."

TWENTY-FOUR-CENT DECLARATION OF INDEPENDENCE

1869 Twenty-Four-Cent Declaration of Independence

Stamp Production
Printer: National Bank Note Co.
Designer: E. Pitcher
Engravers: James Smillie (vignette), Douglas S. Ronaldson (frame), J.C. Kenworthy (lettering)

Format:	Sheets of 300, cut vertically into panes of 150
Plate Numbers:	20 (frame), 20, 24 (vignette)
Date of Issue:	Mar.19, 1869
Earliest Known Use:	Apr.7, 1869
Uses:	Foreign rates. Heavy domestic mail
Quantity Issued:	248,925

Stamp Features

Size:	22 x 22 mm (0.9 x 0.9 inches)
Watermark:	None
Grill:	G
Perforation:	12
Colors:	Green or bluish green and violet.
Varieties:	Double grill, Split grill, Without grill and with original gum.
Errors:	Inverted center

Collectable Stamp Today
Collectable Cancellation Colors:
Black, red, blue.
Collectable Cancellation Varieties:
black town, red town, Paid All, Steamship, supplementary mail type A, China.

Value Unused:	$$$$$
Value Used:	$$$$
Surviving Covers:	76
Largest Known Multiple:	Unused: 9 (3x3 block)
	Used: 4 (2x2 block)

This stamp is one of the finest examples of the engraving for intaglio printing. The stamp is modeled after a painting by Trumbull, the "Signing of the Declaration of Independence." The original hangs in the Yale Art Gallery. On the tiny stamp, all 42 men who were present at the historic event are engraved. Many of figures are so well engraved; they can be recognized under magnification including Thomas Jefferson, Benjamin Franklin and John Adams.

Figure 5-21. Origin of the Twenty-Four-Cent Design. The stamp was based on this Trumbull's painting, the "Signing of the Declaration of Independence," which today is found in the Yale Art Gallery.

When the stamp was issued, it was criticized for failing to identify the scene depicted on it. Editorials of the time stated that foreigners would they were just staring as the group of stately looking Quakers, wonder whether they were enjoying a peep of Congress, or gazing into the President's House. The only clue as to it being Declaration of Independence is the numerals, 1776, below the vignette. Since a common use of the stamp was to Britain, the lack of a label may have been intentional!

The stamp was printed from one frame plate, number 20 and from two possible vignette plates, 20 and 24. The plate numbers and imprints at the top are the frame color and at the bottom is the vignette color. The stamp, a bicolor, was printed green or bluish green and violet.

Varieties

There are three grill varieties: split grill, double grill and the very rare without grill.

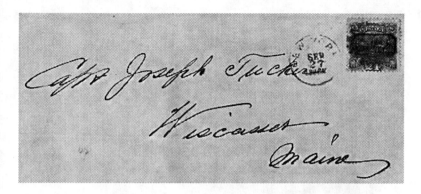

Figure 5-22. Example of an 1869 Twenty-Four-Cent Stamp on a Cover. The twenty-four cent stamp of the 1869 served both domestic and foreign uses. It is used to pay the postage on a multiple weight domestic letter.

Uses and Covers

The use of the stamp was for heavy domestic letters or odd foreign rates. For example, twenty-four cents paid the double-letter rate to the Britain until 1870. Two out of three stamps were on covers sent abroad. The domestic covers are usually legal or government uses, often registered. This issue is rarely found on covers, with only 76 examples today.

Multiples

The largest remaining unused multiple of the stamp is a block of nine. Used, it is a block of four stamps. There also is a block of 4 used stamps with the invert error.

Errors-The Center Inverts

Figure 5-23. Twenty-Four-Cent Inverted Center Stamp.

The most famous variety of the stamp is, of course, the invert. It is estimated about five sheets of the invert error stamps were printed. There exists a single remarkable used block of four, 84 used singles, and 4 unused singles showing the error. Included are two used pairs and single on cover. It is the second scarcest of the 1869 invert errors.

The used invert block of four stamps was found in Liverpool, England, between 1885 and 1895. It was sent to the Britain to pay a multiple of the then twelve-cent rate.

THIRTY-CENT FLAG EAGLE AND SHIELD

1869 Thirty-Cent Eagle and Shield

Stamp Production

Printer:	National Bank Note Co.
Designer:	James Macdonough
Engravers:	Luigi (Louis) Delnoce (vignette), Douglas S. Ronaldson (flags and lettering)
Format:	Sheets of 300, cut vertically into panes of 150
Plate Numbers:	21 (frame), 21 (vignette)
Date of Issue:	Mar.19, 1869
Earliest Known Use:	May 22, 1869
Uses:	Double letter rate to France
Quantity Issued:	304,650

Stamp Features

Size:	22 x 22.2 mm (0.9 x 0.9 inches)
Watermark:	None
Grill:	G
Perforation:	12
Colors:	Blue and carmine, pale blue and carmine, blue and dark carmine.
Varieties:	Double grill, Split grill, Without grill and with original gum.
Errors:	Inverted center

Collectable Stamp Today
Collectable Cancellation Colors:
Black, red, blue, brown, purple, green.
Collectable Cancellation Varieties:
Paid, Paid All, black town, steamship, Steam, supplementary mail type A, China, Japan.

Value Unused:	$$$$$
Value Used:	$$$$
Surviving Covers:	58

Largest Known Multiple: Unused: 15 (5x3 block)
Used: 12 (block)

This is a patriotic theme stamp, the first United States one that is red, white, and blue. The stamp was printed in blue and carmine, pale blue and carmine, and blue and dark carmine, on white paper, the colors of the American flag. The darker ink shades make the best appearance. It has the major symbols of the United States: the draped flags, a shield, and an eagle. It is a beautiful stamp, and for the time, very unusual. Apart from the flags, and two colors, the design is like to the ten-cent 1869 stamp. Its only design fault is its poor lettering. However, contemporaries criticized it as being the "meanest looking stamp seen" and a "bunch of rags hung out of a junk shop."

Figure 5-24. Thirty-Cent Essay. The essay for the 30-cent stamp of the 1869 series featured Trumbull's "The Surrender of Burgoyne."

Figure 5-25. 1994 One-Dollar Surrender of Burgoyne Stamp. The Surrender of Burgoyne was a critical turning point of the American Revolution. The original design for the 1869 thirty-cent stamp was changed because portraying a British surrender on a U.S. stamp would have offended that country where many of the 30-cent stamps would have been sent. However, this design finally became a real stamp in 1994, shown here.

Originally, the thirty-cent stamp was going to feature Trumbull's painting, "The Surrender of Burgoyne." This was a critical turning point of the American Revolution. The design was changed because portraying a British surrender on an U.S. stamp would have offended that country. Also, the 24-cent vignette already was taken from a Trumbull painting. So to avoid repetition, a substitute design was created. However, this Burgoyne design finally became a stamp in 1994, a one-dollar issue. There are very few flag, eagle and shield essays, demonstrating it was a last minute decision to model the stamp after the 10-cent design.

More thirty-cent 1869 stamps were printed than either the lower denomination 24 or 15-cent type, making the stamp more readily available today.

Like the other bicolor stamps of 1869, on the plates, the imprint at the top is the frame color and at the bottom is the vignette color.

Varieties

This stamp is another of this series known without a grill, proven on stamps with their original gum. Other grilling varieties are examples with double grill or split grill.

Uses and Covers

It is a rare stamp to find on cover, with only 58 still around. Its main use was for foreign mail, especially the double weight rate to France. It also was used on heavy domestic letters.

Figure 5-26. Example of an 1869 Series Thirty-Cent Stamp on a Cover. The thirty-cent stamp of the 1869 was used mainly on foreign covers. Here it is being used to pay the double weight postage rate to France, its most common use.

Multiples

The largest unused multiple is an unused block of 15 thirty-cent stamps (5x3), without grills, and with the bottom imprint and plate number. Otherwise, the largest unused block is of six stamps, a 3x2 block. The largest known used multiple is a block of 12 stamps.

Errors-The Center Inverts

Figure 5-27. Thirty-Cent Invert. This is the highest denomination of the 1869 series that is found with inverted center.

This is the highest denomination of the 1869 series that is found with inverted center printing error. The 30-cent inverts are the least rare of the three 1869 invert errors, unused, with seven known copies. However, it is the least common, used, with 37 known copies. There are no multiples or covers with the error known.

NINETY-CENT LINCOLN

1869 Ninety-Cent Lincoln

Stamp Production
Printer: National Bank Note Co.
Designer: E. Pitcher
Engravers: Joseph P. Ourdan (portrait), Douglas S. Ronaldson (frame), J.C. Kenworthy (lettering)
Format: Sheets of 300, cut vertically into panes of 150
Plate Numbers: 22 (frame), 22 (vignette)
Date of Issue: Mar.19, 1869
Earliest Known Use: May 10, 1869
Uses: High rate foreign. Packages
Quantity Issued: 55,500

Stamp Features
Size: 21.7 x 22.0 mm (0.9 x 0.9 inches)
Watermark: None
Grill: G
Perforation: 12
Colors: Carmine or carmine rose and black.
Varieties: Split grill, Without grill and with original gum, Short transfer, Shift in lower-left, Dot in the O of POSTAGE, Dot in collar, Dash in G, Dot in the 0 of 90, Cracked plate.

Collectable Stamp Today
Collectable Cancellation Colors:
                          Black, blue, red, ultramarine, brown, orange red.
Collectable Cancellation Varieties:
                          Paid, Paid All, black town, red town, magenta town, N Y steamship
Value Unused: $$$$$$
Value Used: $$$$$
Surviving Covers: 1

Largest Known Multiple: Unused: 6 (block)
Used: 7 (strip) 6 (block)

The series ends with a spectacular portrait of Lincoln within an ornate frame. The stamp is a longtime popular (and expensive stamp) among classic United States stamp collectors. But at the time of its issue, it was criticized as looking as if Lincoln was in prison!

The first idea for the 90-cent 1869 stamp was a portrait of George Washington, similar to one found on the 90-cent stamp of the 1861 series. However, the 90-cent stamp wound up featuring Lincoln, modified from the 10-cent essay of the series.

Figure 5-28. Ninety-Cent Essay.
The essays for the 90-cent 1869 stamp featured a portrait of George Washington instead of Lincoln found on the issued stamp.

Only slightly more than 55,000 stamps were issued, but fewer than 25.000 copies were sold. The Post Office upon the return of the unsold remainders destroyed the rest.

The margin markings have the plate number and National Bank Note Company imprint at top, in the carmine-rose frame color and at bottom in the black vignette color.

Virtually all the 90-cent stamps have poor centering, in relationship to the perforations.

Colors

The frame, letters and numerals are either carmine or carmine rose. The Lincoln vignette is a consistent black.

Varieties

The stamp is found with a split grill and is known without a grill (with the original gum to prove it). Other printing varieties include a short transfer at left, a shift in lower-left part of the stamp, a dot in the O of POSTAGE, a dot in collar, a dash in G, a dot in the 0 of 90 and cracked plate. There are no 90-cent inverted center stamps.

Uses and Covers

This high denomination stamp paid for certain overseas postage and for domestic packages.

There is only one surviving covers with a 1869 ninety-cent stamp. It is called the "Ice House Cover" because of the address of where the letter was sent. It is franked with the stamp and 10 and 12-cent Bank Note stamps from the next series of stamp and it was canceled Aug. 3, 1873. The three stamps paid the four times the 28-cent British mail rate to Calcutta, India via Brindisi. The cover was stolen in 1960's. It suddenly reappeared in excellent condition, early in 2006.

Multiples

The largest unused multiple of the 1869 series ninety-cent stamp is two blocks of six stamps. Used, there is a vertical strip of seven stamps, a block of six, and a rejoined block of eight.

1989 World Stamp Expo Issues

Figure 5-29. Reproduction of the 1869 Series Ninety-Cent Lincoln Stamp. Reproduction of the 1869 series ninety-cent Lincoln is found advertising the 1989 World Stamp Expo. A picture of the stamp with a star cancellation is show. It is an example of a "stamp on a stamp."

Reproductions of this beautiful stamp are found on two other United States issues. A picture of the 90-cent Lincoln 1869 series stamp, with a star cancellation is found on the 1989 United States commemorative issue. This stamp advertised the 1989 World Stamp Expo, an international stamp show sponsored by the United States Postal Service. It is a "stamp on stamp."

There is a 1989 souvenir sheet also commemorating the 1989 World Stamp Expo. The sheet has four different color version reproductions of the stamp. The colors include the issued version and three trial color proofs. The souvenir sheet reproductions are larger than the issued stamp.

Figure 5-30. World Stamp Expo '89 Souvenir Sheet. A 1989 United States souvenir sheet has four different color version reproductions of the 1869 ninety-cent stamp. The colors include the issued version and three trial color proofs.

The Reissues

1875 One-Cent Franklin Reissue

Stamp Production

Printer:	National Bank Note Co.
Designer:	E. Pitcher
Engravers:	Joseph I. Pease (portrait), William D. Nichols (frame), J.C. Kenworthy (lettering)
Format:	1 pane of 150
Plate Numbers:	33 (new plate)
Date of Issue:	1875
Earliest Known Use:	Dec. 9, 1877
Uses:	Souvenir. Valid for postal use.
Quantity Issued:	10,000

Stamp Features

Size:	20.2 x 20.2 mm (0.8 x 0.8 inches)
Watermark:	None
Grill:	None
Perforation:	12
Colors:	Buff
Varieties:	None

Collectable Stamp Today

Value Unused:	$$$$
Value Used:	$$$$

1875 Two-Cent Post Rider Reissue

Stamp Production

Printer:	National Bank Note Co.
Designer:	James Macdonough
Engravers:	Christian Rost (vignette), George W. Thurber (frame and lettering)
Format:	Sheets of 300, cut vertically into panes of 150
Plate Numbers:	Original plate
Date of Issue:	1875
Earliest Known Use:	Mar. 20, 1880
Uses:	Souvenir. Valid for postal use.
Quantity Issued:	4,755

Stamp Features

Size:	20.2 x 20.0 mm (0.8 x 0.8 inches)
Watermark:	None
Grill:	None
Perforation:	12
Colors:	Brown
Varieties:	None

Collectable Stamp Today

Value Unused:	$$$$
Value Used:	$$$$

1875 Three-Cent Locomotive Reissue

Stamp Production
Printer: National Bank Note Co.
Designer: James Macdonough
Engravers: Christian Rost (vignette), George W. Thurber (frame and lettering)
Format: Sheets of 300, cut vertically into panes of 150
Plate Numbers: Original plate
Date of Issue: 1875
Earliest Known Use: Unknown
Uses: Souvenir. Valid for postal use.
Quantity Issued: 1,406

Stamp Features
Size: 20.5 x 20.0 mm (0.8 x 0.8 inches)
Watermark: None
Grill: None
Perforation: 12
Colors: Blue
Varieties: Specimen overprint

Collectable Stamp Today
Value Unused: $$$$$
Value Used: $$$$$$

1875 Six-Cent Washington Reissue

Stamp Production

Printer:	National Bank Note Co.
Designer:	E. Pitcher
Engravers:	William E. Marshall (vignette), J.C. Kenworthy (letters), William D. Nichols (frame)
Format:	Sheets of 300, cut vertically into panes of 150
Plate Numbers:	Original plate
Date of Issue:	1875
Earliest Known Use:	Unknown
Uses:	Souvenir. Valid for postal use.
Quantity Issued:	2,226

Stamp Features

Size:	20.5 x 20.0 mm (0.8 x 0.8 inches)
Watermark:	None
Grill:	None
Perforation:	12
Colors:	Blue
Varieties:	None

Collectable Stamp Today

Value Unused:	$$$$$
Value Used:	$$$$$

1875 Ten-Cent Flag and Shield Reissue

Stamp Production
Printer:	National Bank Note Co.
Designer:	Douglas S. Ronaldson
Engravers:	Douglas S. Ronaldson
Format:	Sheets of 300, cut vertically into panes of 150
Plate Numbers:	Original plate
Date of Issue:	1875
Earliest Known Use:	Nov. 11, 1880
Uses:	Souvenir. Valid for postal use.
Quantity Issued:	1,947

Stamp Features
Size:	20.0 x 19.7 mm (0.8 x 0.8 inches)
Watermark:	None
Grill:	None
Perforation:	12
Colors:	Yellow
Varieties:	None

Collectable Stamp Today
Value Unused:	$$$$$
Value Used:	$$$$$

1875 Twelve-Cent Adriatic Reissue

Stamp Production
Printer: National Bank Note Co.
Designer: James Macdonough
Engravers: James Smillie (vignette), George W. Thurber (frame and
                           lettering)
Format: Sheets of 300, cut vertically into panes of 150
Plate Numbers: Original plate
Date of Issue: 1875
Earliest Known Use: Mar. 20, 1880
Uses: Souvenir. Valid for postal use.
Quantity Issued: 1,584

Stamp Features
Size: 20.2 x 20.0 mm (0.8 x 0.8 inches)
Watermark: None
Grill: None
Perforation: 12
Colors: Green
Varieties: None

Collectable Stamp Today
Value Unused: $$$$$
Value Used: $$$$$

1875 Type III Fifteen-Cent Landing of Columbus Reissue

Stamp Production

Printer:	National Bank Note Co.
Designer:	E. Pitcher
Engravers:	James Smillie (vignette), J.C. Kenworthy (lettering), Douglas S. Ronaldson (frame)
Format:	1 pane of 100
Plate Numbers:	New plates
Date of Issue:	1875
Earliest Known Use:	Mar. 20, 1880
Uses:	Souvenir. Valid for postal use.
Quantity Issued:	1,981

Stamp Features

Size:	21.7 x 21.7 mm (0.9 x 0.9 inches)
Watermark:	None
Grill:	None
Perforation:	12
Colors:	Brown and blue
Varieties:	None
Errors:	Imperforate horizontally

Collectable Stamp Today

Value Unused:	$$$$$
Value Used:	$$$$$

1875 Twenty-Four-Cent Declaration of Independence Reissue

Stamp Production
Printer:	National Bank Note Co.
Designer:	E. Pitcher
Engravers:	James Smillie (vignette), Douglas S. Ronaldson (frame), J.C. Kenworthy (lettering)
Format:	1 pane of 100
Plate Numbers:	New plates
Date of Issue:	1875
Earliest Known Use:	Mar. 27, 1880
Uses:	Souvenir. Valid for postal use.
Quantity Issued:	2,091

Stamp Features
Size:	22 x 22 mm (0.9 x 0.9 inches)
Watermark:	None
Grill:	None
Perforation:	12
Colors:	Green and violet
Varieties:	None

Collectable Stamp Today
Value Unused:	$$$$$
Value Used:	$$$$$

1875 Thirty-Cent Eagle and Shield Reissue

Stamp Production
Printer:	National Bank Note Co.
Designer:	James Macdonough
Engravers:	Luigi (Louis) Delnoce (vignette), Douglas S. Ronaldson (flags and lettering)
Format:	1 pane of 100
Plate Numbers:	New plates
Date of Issue:	1875
Earliest Known Use:	None
Uses:	Souvenir. Valid for postal use.
Quantity Issued:	1,535

Stamp Features
Size:	22 x 22.2 mm (0.9 x 0.9 inches)
Watermark:	None
Grill:	None
Perforation:	12
Colors:	Ultramarine and carmine
Varieties:	None

Collectable Stamp Today
Value Unused:	$$$$$
Value Used:	$$$$$

1875 Ninety-Cent Lincoln Reissue

Stamp Production
Printer: National Bank Note Co.
Designer: E. Pitcher
Engravers: Joseph P. Ourdan (portrait), Douglas S. Ronaldson (frame), J.C. Kenworthy (lettering)
Format: 1 pane of 100
Plate Numbers: New plates
Date of Issue: 1875
Earliest Known Use: None
Uses: Souvenir. Valid for postal use.
Quantity Issued: 1,356

Stamp Features
Size: 21.7 x 22.0 mm (0.9 x 0.9 inches)
Watermark: None
Grill: None
Perforation: 12
Colors: Carmine and black
Varieties: None

Collectable Stamp Today
Value Unused: $$$$$
Value Used: $$$$$

All of the denominations of the 1869 series were reissued in 1875, for the Philadelphia Centennial Exposition of 1876. The National Bank Note Company, the original manufacturers of the series, did the printing. They were perforated 12 on ungrilled, hard white paper with white crackle gum. Since they were valid for postage, being reissues, they are found used, usually on philatelic covers of the time. However, both used reissued stamps and their covers are very rare.

All the stamps are of the original design, except for the 15-cent stamp. Type III is the name of the design of the 1875 reissue. Type III is a new frame. It resembles the type I, with the single heavy line framing the vignette. The distinguishing feature is the absence of shading lines surrounding the vignette. A new plate was made for the one-cent stamp, number 33, consisting of 150 subjects.

This 15-cent stamp can be found with an error. There are unused singles that are imperforate horizontally.

The reissued 3-cent stamp is known with a Specimen overprint.

1880 American Bank Note One-Cent Franklin Reissue

Stamp Production

Printer:	American Bank Note Company
Designer:	E. Pitcher
Engravers:	Joseph I. Pease (portrait), William D. Nichols (frame), J.C. Kenworthy (lettering)
Format:	1 pane of 150
Plate Numbers:	33
Date of Issue:	1880
Earliest Known Use:	Oct. 5, 1880
Uses:	Souvenir. Valid for postal use.
Quantity Issued:	23,252

Stamp Features

Size:	20.2 x 20.2 mm (0.8 x 0.8 inches)
Watermark:	None

Grill:	None
Perforation:	12
Colors:	Buff (with gum), Brown orange (without gum)
Varieties:	None

Collectable Stamp Today
Value Unused:	$$$$
Value Used:	$$$$

There was an additional one-cent stamp reprint made by the American Bank Note Company in 1880 on soft porous paper, without grills. They were printed in two shades. The buff shade had gum, while the brown orange had none. These reissues, too, were produced from the new plate 33.

Distinguishing Features

How does one tell the original stamps apart from the reissues? The originals were printed on hard wove paper, with whitish, yellow gum, which shows minute cracking, and are grilled. The National reissue of 1875 was printed without a grill or gum. They were printed on hard paper similar to the regular series. The lone one-cent American reissue of 1880 is found on soft porous paper and without a grill.

Essays, Proofs, and Specimens

ESSAYS

As described earlier, essays exist for all the denominations of this series since the designs of the stamps were changed at the last minute.

In general, the essays featured designs with smaller numerals. There also were some changes in the denomination set-up.

The essay for the one-cent Franklin is more ornate than the issued stamp. The numeral of the essay was enlarged and the design around the numeral was changed from an oval to a panel in the final design. These essays are found gummed and grilled. They are in several colors, both perforated and imperforate.

The two-cent post rider essays resembled the issued stamp. The only difference is in the numeral that is smaller and higher on the essay. The essays exist on India paper and regular stamp paper. Some essays are perforated, gummed and grilled.

Figure 5-31. Two-Cent Essay. The two-cent post rider essay resembles the issued stamp. The only difference is in the numeral is smaller and higher on the essay.

The three-cent locomotive essays of this stamp show a smaller numeral, but otherwise are like the issued stamp.

As the six-cent stamp originally was to be a five-cent denomination, so are the essays. On the essay, the numerals, 5, are in both bottom corners around the words, FIVE CENTS.

When the National Bank Note Company submitted a design for the 10-cent stamp, it was a picture of Lincoln, framed by bundles of rods tied with ribbons. This design was rejected and the portrait of Lincoln was used on the 90-cent value because officials wanted the Lincoln portrait on the highest value, which was to be bicolor and thus more distinguished.

The second series of ten-cent essays featured the signing of the Declaration of Independence, after the famous Trumbull painting of it. That design ultimately was used on the 24-cent stamp, so it, too, could be bicolor. Finally, there are essays showing the actually used eagle and shield design. These are progressive die essays, showing the steps in the production of engraving the die.

As the steamship was originally planned for the 12-cent denomination, the essays are similar to the actual stamp except for smaller numerals. Twelve-cent essays can be found with letterpress printing. The National Bank Note Company was experimenting with this form of typography, as well as lithography.

The type I fifteen-cent essays were made in the summer of 1868. They were prepared in one color and featured smaller numerals, typical of all the series essays. After the single colors essays were made, National Bank Note decided to print the four high values in two colors, to help them win the printing contract. Type II fifteen-cent essays are very rare.

Twenty-four-cent essays exist with the complete Declaration of Independence design, but with small numerals instead, in one color. There are essays of the frame only, showing the actually used large numerals type. Other essays just show the vignette of the finished stamp.

The original essays for the 30-cent stamp show a reproduction of Trumbull's painting, "The Surrender of Burgoyne." As described above, a last minute decision was the change to the flag, eagle, and shield design. Therefore, there are very few flag, eagle and shield type essays, like the issued stamp.

The original essays prepared for the 90-cent 1869 stamp had a portrait of George Washington. These essays included types with both small and large numerals.

Safety Paper Essays

The safety paper essays are unique to the 1869 series. They were part of the ongoing effort to produce stamps that were difficult to reuse. They were printed on thin wove paper, underprinted with various engraved safety paper designs in another color. About 100 safety paper essay items have been recorded.

Figure 5-32. Example of a Safety Paper Essay. The safety paper essays were an experiment to produce stamps that were difficult to reuse. They were essays on thin paper, underprinted with engraved safety paper designs in another color.

PROOFS

Large Die Proofs

There are the usual nineteenth century groups of proofs for the 1869 series. The large die proofs are called such because of the large piece of paper on which they are printed, India paper, and then backed by cardboard. The large die proof measures 40mm by 50mm, the original die block size. It shows an imprint and sometimes letters and numbers of identification.   A few are even autographed by the engraver.

The large die proofs for the 15, 24, and 90-cent denominations are hybrids. This is because the stamps are bicolor. Hybrids are plate proofs cut close to the design and mounted on cardboard the size of the die, to resemble large die proofs. On the back of the card is a welt the size of the stamp design, caused by the extra piece of India paper being pressed into the card.

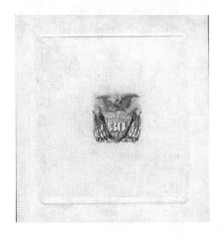

Figure 5-33. Example of a Hybrid Large Die Proof. The large die proofs for the higher denominations of the 1869 series are hybrids. Hybrids are plate proofs cut close to the design and mounted on cardboard the size of the die, to resemble large die proofs. Here is the 30-cent example.

The 15-cent large die proof are of two varieties: type II, like one of the two original 1869 stamps and type III, like the design of the 1875 reissue.

Small Die Proofs

The small die proofs come in two types, made in the 20th century by the Bureau of Engraving and Printing, which had inherited the original dies of the 1869 series, when they took over the stamp printing business.

In 1904, 85 sets were prepared for presentation albums given out during the Theodore Roosevelt administration, the Roosevelt small die proofs. The die proofs are close to the original colors of the stamps. Printing was done with aniline inks on white wove paper. They are mounted on gray surface cardboard with glue.

In 1915, the Bureau of Engraving and Printing printed more small die proofs, using the original die, the Panama-Pacific small die proofs. They can be distinguished from the Roosevelt small die proofs by having smaller margins (2.5 to 3mm) and are printed on a different soft, yellowish wove paper type of paper.

Like the 15-cent large die proofs, the small die proofs are of two varieties: type II and type III.

Plate Proofs

Figure 5-34. Plate Proof Example. The American Bank Note Company made the 1869 series plate proofs on cardboard in five printings from 1879 to 1893. Here is a block of four 12-cent plate proofs.

These are printed from the same plate that the stamps were printed. The first set of plate proofs were on India paper, were made by the National Bank Note Company just before the actual stamps, in about the same colors as the issued stamps. Like the 15-cent die proofs, the India small die proofs are of two varieties: type II and type III.

The plate proofs on cardboard were created in five printings between 1879 and 1893 by the American Bank Note Company, which by then had taken over the National Bank Note Company. These printings were provided as favors to inside collectors. Like the 15-cent die proofs, the cardboard plate proofs are of two varieties: type II and type III. These cardboard plate proofs also reproduce the famous invert errors of the 1869 series: the 15, 24, 30, and 90-cent denominations.

For today's collectors, these plate proofs are less expensive, more handsome, and more available than unused copies of the actual 1869 issued stamps.

Figure 5-35. Example of an Inverted Plate Proof. Some of the cardboard plate proofs were made to reproduce the famous invert errors of the 1869 series. Shown are a pair of 15-cent inverts.

Trial Color Proofs

For all the denominations of the 1869 series, there are various large die trial color proofs. The 1, 2, 3, 12 and 24-cent trial color proofs come only in black. The 6-cent proofs are deep dull blue and black. The 10-cent proofs come in several colors: black, dull dark violet, deep green, dull dark orange, dull rose, copper red, chocolate, and dark Prussian blue. The 15-cent color trial proofs are dull dark violet, deep blue, dull red brown, black, and dark blue gray. The bicolor 30-cent large die color proofs come in eleven color combinations. The 90-cent bicolor proofs are either brown and deep green or green and black.

Figure 5-36. The Atlanta Plate Proofs. This is a group of plate trial color proofs created by The American Bank Note Company for the 1881 International Cotton Exhibition held in Atlanta, Georgia. Here are examples of four different combinations for the 90-cent denomination. (Of course the different colors don't show up in black and white photos!)

The Atlanta set is another group of plate trial color proofs that were created. The American Bank Note Company printed plate proofs of all the reissues (not the original stamps) in five different colors for the 1881 International Cotton Exhibition held in Atlanta, Georgia. These were printed on thin cardboard.

SPECIMENS

Specimen overprints of the 1869 series were samples of new issues that were distributed to postal officials as examples of them. The 1, 2, 6, 10, 12, 15, 24, 30, and 90-cent specimen stamps are overprinted with a black specimen lettering that is 12 mm long. The 3, 6, and 10 (reissue) cent specimen stamps also are overprinted with a blue specimen lettering that is 15 mm long. There are additional 1 and 2-cent specimen stamps have this same font but with black ink.

Figure 5-37. Specimen Stamps. Specimen overprints of the 1869 series were sample stamps that are distributed to foreign postal officials as examples for them.)

6

The Bank Note Series

The postage stamps issued from 1870 through 1890 are called the Bank Notes because they were printed by private bank note engraving firms. Before and after, however, such companies also printed United States postage stamps. From 1847 to 1894, firms that printed stock and bond papers, bank certificates, bid for contracts to produce all the United States postage stamps. So the term "Bank Note" just for this series is misleading.

These stamps replaced those issued in 1869. The public disliked these stamps. They didn't like their small size, exotic subjects and designs, poor printing quality and inferior gum. This ground swell of popular opinion led to their very quick replacement.

Though the beginning stamp collector is confused by their subtle differences, the experienced collector appreciates their beauty. They represent a vast improvement in stamp design and production. They are praised for their classical appearance, three-dimensional feel, ornate frames, and bright colors.

A Huge Variety of Stamps

Fifty-nine stamps issued from April 1870 to November 21, 1888 make up the Bank Note issues. There were 11 original designs, supplemented with five more for a total of 16. There were lots of subtle production changes to each design. In addition to the 59, there are 29 more stamps in the form of the souvenir reissues of 1875, 1880, 1882, and 1883.

	1 cent Franklin	2 cent Jackson	2 cent Washington	3 cent Washington	4 cent Jackson	5 cent Taylor	5 cent Garfield
Portrait							
National							
Grilled	*	*		*			
Ungrilled	*	*		*			
Continental							
Secret Mark	*	*		*			
Color Change							
No Secret Mark						*	
New Color		*					
American							
No Secret Mark							
Soft Paper	*	*	*	*		*	
Re-Engraved	*			*			
New Design	*				*		*
New Color			*	*	*		*
Special Printings							
Continental	*	* *		*		*	
American	*	* *	*	*	*	*	*

	6 cent Lincoln	7 cent Stanton	10 cent Jefferson	12 cent Clay	15 cent Webster	24 cent Scott	30 cent Hamilton	90 cent Perry
Portrait								
National								
Grilled	*	*	*	*	*	*	*	*
Ungrilled	*	*	*	*	*	*	*	*
Continental								
Secret Mark	*	*	*	*	*	*		
Color Change Only							*	*
No Secret Mark								
New Color								
American								
Soft Paper, No Secret Mark			*					
Soft Paper Change	*		*		*		*	*
Re-Engraved	*		*					
New Design								
New Color							*	*
Special Printings								
Continental	*	*	*	*	*	*	*	*
American	*	*	*	*	*	*	*	*

404

The Printers

The National Bank Note Company had the stamp printing contract since 1861 and kept it so it printed the first group of Bank Note stamps from 1870 to early 1873.

The Postmaster General in December 1872, advertised for bids for the postage stamp printing contract from May 1, 1873 until April 30, 1877. The Continental Bank Note Company won that contract. The company printed the stamps on the top floor of The Equitable Life Insurance Company building on Broadway and Cedar Streets in New York City. Rather than starting out with new dies, Continental used the old National Bank Note Company printing dies and plates. Continental held the printing contract until the consolidation of bank note manufacturers. This is the second group of the Bank Note stamps.

In 1877, while Continental was printing postage stamps, Congress passed a law requiring the Bureau of Engraving do the printing of all securities. The law left the large printing companies, National, Continental and American with little business. So the three firms merged into one company, the American Bank Note Company. And American assumed the stamp contract held by Continental on February 4, 1879. The old stamp dies and plates, used by Continental, were taken over and then used by American. The stamps made from Feb. 4, 1879 to 1890, the end of the period, were printed by American. This is the third and last group of Bank Note stamps.

Basic Stamp Proprieties

All Bank Note stamps were printed from plates of 200 subjects divided in a vertical direction, into two panes of 100, left and right. They are all perforated 12. The date of issue of all the stamps except the 4, 5, 7, and the 24-cent, is April 12, 1870.

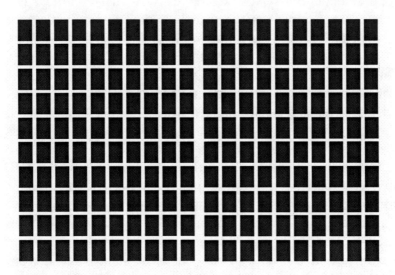

Figure 6-1. Bank Note Series Plate Layout. The Bank Note stamps were printed by all three printers from plates of 200 subjects divided vertically into two panes of 100, left and right.

Plate Layout and Marginal Markings

For all the Bank Note stamps, there are four sets of marginal markings per plate (or two per sheet). The markings for both panes are in the top and bottom margins. There are white lettering on a colored background, the color of the stamps.

Figure 6-2 Early National Marginal Markings. For the early National series plates, the imprint consist of the words, NATIONAL BANK NOTE Co. NEW YORK on one line.

For National, the marginal markings are the words, NATIONAL BANK NOTE Co. NEW YORK (one line) on the early plates and ENGRAVED & PRINTED BY THE NATIONAL BANK NOTE CO. NEW YORK (two lines) on the later plates. The plate numbers, preceded by No., follow the company imprint in left positions, and come before it in the right positions. An imprint strip is 5 stamps with the attached selvage's marginal markings, an imprint block is 10 stamps (5x2).

Figure 6-3. Late National Marginal Markings. On later National stamp plates, one finds ENGRAVED & PRINTED BY THE NATIONAL BANK NOTE CO. NEW YORK on two lines as the imprint.

For Continental stamps, the imprint is on two lines. The markings are wider than the National is. Therefore, an imprint strip needs 6 or 7 stamps. The imprint has the words, PRINTED BY THE CONTINENTAL BANK NOTE CO. NEW YORK and the plate number. Like National's, the plate numbers follow the imprint on the two left plate positions, and precede it in the two right positions. The initial plate (2-193) numerals are etched numerals, while numerals 1 and 219-310 are huge engraved script numerals. Since the National plates were used for the 30 and 90-cent stamps, they have National plate markings.

The first American Bank Note Company plates are leftovers from Continental. Later plates have a one line imprint, AMERICAN BANK NOTE COMPANY. Plate numbers follow the imprint on two left positions; precede it on the two right positions. An imprint strip consists of 6 stamps with the marginal markings on the selvage, and an imprint block, 12 stamps.

Starting in 1885, letters were added to the top positions of plates used on the steam-powered presses. The letters are found between the imprint box and the plate number.

Figure 6-4. Continental Marginal Markings. For stamps printed by the Continental, the imprint is on two lines. The markings are wider than the National, so a plate block has 12 or 14 stamps. The imprint contains the words, PRINTED BY THE CONTINENTAL BANK NOTE CO. NEW YORK. The initial plate numerals are etched numerals, while for the later plates, there are engraved script numerals.

Figure 6-5. American Marginal Markings. The plates used by the American Bank Note Company have a one line imprint, AMERICAN BANK NOTE COMPANY. A plate block has 12 stamps.

Figure 6-6. American Steam Plate Marginal Markings. Starting in 1885, letters were added to the American plates used on the steam-powered presses, inserted between the imprint and the plate number.

Grills

Grilling of stamps, which started in 1867, still was part of stamp printing at the start of the Bank Note period. Since stamp grills did little to prevent the removal of canceling ink, they soon were abandoned. Calvet M. Hahn thinks all National stamps had the attempt to be grilled. The absence of a grill on a National stamp is poor quality control, rather than the stoppage of the technique. Proof is grilled and ungrilled stamps were printed from same plates at the same time.

Two types of grills were used on some of these National Bank series. These are the H grill, measuring 10 x 12 mm and the I grill, measuring 8 x 10 mm. These are the smallest of all United States grills. As they were made with worn rollers, they usually show only a few points. At this time, several, instead of a single sheet of stamps were passed through the grilling machine at the same time. This practice caused wide, heavy grills on the top sheets and narrower, lighter grills, or no grills at all, to appear on the bottom sheets.

The stamp catalogs lump together the H and I grills under single listings. They are products of the male roller that produced a pattern with points down, when viewed from the face of the stamp. Though National Bank Note printers produced grilled and ungrilled stamps, at the same time, they are listed as separate issues.

The Continental Bank Note Company placed an experimental male grill, the J grill (7 x 9 mm.), on some of its stamps. Authorities consider these as essays, not issued stamps.

Hard versus Soft

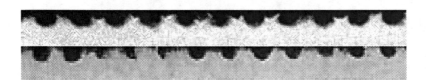

Figure 6-7. Close Up of Hard Versus Soft Stamp Paper.

	Hard Paper (top)	Soft Paper (bottom)
Feel	Bond paper	Newspaper
Color	White	Yellow
Edges	Sharp	Ragged
Opacity	Translucent	Opaque
Snap	Sharp	Dull

One must be able to separate hard and soft stamp papers to understand the Bank Note series. It often is the only way to tell apart the printings of the manufacturers.

Hard paper is crisp like bond paper. It is very white. It feels strong. Soft paper is coarse and has a cheap feel like newspaper. It has a yellow tint to it. The edges of the stamp are ragged not clean. Hard paper is translucent, soft paper, opaque.

There are simple tests to distinguish the type of paper. One is the snap test. One flicks one's finger against the stamp. It produces a sharp clean, metallic sound if the paper is hard, a dull floppy sound results if the paper is soft.

The second test is the comparison test. Since the issues of 1861 were printed on hard paper, a copy of one can be used as a standard. Likewise, the small bank note stamps are printed on soft paper, this is the second paper standard.

Secret Marks

Small design differences, barely seen by the unaided eye, account for many of the differences of the Bank Note stamps. As a general rule, they appear after the National Bank Note stopped printing stamps. There are seven of them found in obscure places on the 1873 Continental and 1879 American stamps.

John Luff, the expert of this series, felt that the secret marks were added to the stamp dies by the Continental Company as a way of identifying their stamps from the earlier National Bank Note Company stamps. Evidence this is the case is the large die proofs signed "Secret Marks put on by Chas. Skinner" and he was a Continental engraver.

There are several exceptions to the rule that secret marks appear with the introduction of the Continental Note stamps. The ten-cent denomination has two types of the American Note stamps. One has the secret mark and one does not. As we shall see, there are several theories as to the cause of the missing secret mark.

There is a great debate as to whether the 15-cent secret mark truly is such or just plate wear.

For the twenty-four cent stamp, there is no secret mark. Continental did print this denomination, but their work cannot be distinguished from National. Both printers used the same unaltered plates. The only proven 24-cent Continental stamp is one on ribbed paper, used by that printer, but not National.

The 30-cent Hamilton Continental hard paper stamp of 1873 also has no secret mark. However, it can be distinguished by its gray or greenish black color versus the plain black of a National stamp.

Likewise, the 90-cent 1873 hard paper Continental has no secret mark. It, too, is distinguished by its rose carmine color with its yellow tint.

Re-engraved and Reissue Stamps

American Bank Note Company decided that certain plates they were using were not making good impressions. The changes are either simple retouching of the die or making a completely new die. In 1881-82, the 1, 3, 6, and 10-cent denomination designs were altered. This group of bank note stamps is called the re-engravings.

In 1887-88, some stamps were completed redesigned with new dies, called the reissues.

Paper Variations

There are several variations of paper that are found as minor varieties of the Bank Note stamps.

Ribbed paper, found on the Continental stamps, is the most common. The ribs are parallel ridges, 40 to the inch that run horizontally or vertically across the stamp. They are the result of the rib shape of the screen that made the paper. Since most ribbed paper stamps come in strong colors, it is easy to see.

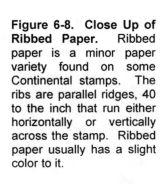

Figure 6-8. Close Up of Ribbed Paper. Ribbed paper is a minor paper variety found on some Continental stamps. The ribs are parallel ridges, 40 to the inch that run either horizontally or vertically across the stamp. Ribbed paper usually has a slight color to it.

Techniques to prevent the reuse of stamps were tried during this time. A method tried on some Continental stamps was the cogwheel punch. A circle of eight punches shaped like the letter U was punched into the stamp. If someone tried to remove a stamp from an envelope, the stamp would tear apart in pieces.

The American Bank Note Company used a Douglas Patent device. It is similar to the cogwheel punch. It was made up of eight small round holes arranged in a circle punched into the upper layer of double paper. This supposedly weakens the paper to absorb more cancellation ink.

Figure 6-9. Douglas Patent Stamp Example. The American Bank Note Company used a Douglas Patent device on some of its stamps. The circle punch consisted of eight small round holes punched into the upper layer of double paper and arranged in a circle. This was to weaken the paper to improve the absorption of canceling ink.

Another was double paper. It consisted of two layers of paper, a thin upper and a thick lower. If someone tried to erase the cancellation, the stamp would tear apart.

Figure 6-10. Double Paper Stamp. Such stamp paper had two layers, the top one, thin and the bottom one, thick. One can see the double paper at the edges of this stamp. Any attempt to erase the cancellation would tear apart the stamp.

Some Bank Note stamps were printed on chemical paper. They have an oily appearance, due to chemicals in the paper used to prevent cancellation removal.

Some stamps of this series have paper with silk fibers.

Fancy Cancellations

This was a time of fancy cancellations on stamps and letters. Numeral cancellations were widely used for the first time. Today, numeral cancellations increase the value of the stamp when they are located in the center of the stamp. They are called a "sock on the nose." The numerals can be found inside circles, bull's-eyes or grids.

Bank Note Denominations

The typical Bank Note stamp is found first on a National hard paper, both with and without a grill. Then, it is made on a Continental hard paper, with an added secret mark. Next comes the American soft paper stamp, still with a secret mark. Finally comes any re-engraved or re-issued stamp by American. Not every denomination follows this pattern completely.

The 1-cent Franklin stamp was used to pay postage on circulars and printed publications, and for drop (local) letters posted at offices having no carrier service. The stamp follows the typical Bank Note progression of stamps. In addition, the 1-cent stamp was re-engraving by American in 1881. And a completely new design was made in 1887 when the ornamentation was removed from the upper corners of the stamp.

The 2-cent Jackson stamps first were used for drop letters mailed at carrier offices for local delivery. In 1875, the 2-cent Continental stamp's color was changed to vermilion from brown to prevent confusion between it and 10-cent Continental. The 2-cent stamp's use increased vastly on Oct 1, 1883 when the regular letter rate became 2 cents. A change in design followed this postal rate reduction. The new design featured Washington in a simple frame. Finally, the color of the new 2-cent Washington stamp was changed to green in 1887.

From the before the beginning of the Bank Note series to Sept. 30, 1883, the basic first-class letter rate was three cents. Therefore, the three-cent Washington denomination is the most commonly used stamp of the period. After the postage reduction, it saw little use. To avoid confusion with the new 2-cent green Washington, the color of the 3-cent was changed from green to orange, at the same time.

Originally, there were no 4-cent Bank Note stamps. Later, they were issued to pay double the reduced basic 2-cent first-class rates. The 4-cent Jackson stamps first appeared on Oct. 1, 1883 in a bluish green color. Their color was changed to carmine, due to the decision to print the two-cent stamps in green.

The Universal Postal Union set a rate of five cents for letters going abroad, effective July 1, 1875. The Bank Note series, at that time, did not have a 5-cent denomination, so one was added to the series. The stamp first had a portrait of General Zachary Taylor. In 1882, just months after President Garfield's assassination, the Taylor stamp was replaced by a 5-cent stamp featuring him. Originally, the Garfield stamp was brown. The stamp's color was changed to indigo in 1888.

The 6-cent stamp features a profile of Lincoln. They originally paid double the basic three-cent postage rate. After the rate reduction of Sept. 30, 1883, there was little use for them, except for some foreign rates. In 1882, the 6-cent stamp was re-engraved by American.

The 7-cent Stanton stamp was not issued until 1875. It paid postage on letters to the German States carried by direct steamers. The stamp was temporarily stranded when this rate was reduced by a penny. On Oct. 1, 1871, the stamp had a second life. The old 10-cent rate for mail sent to this area by Prussian Closed Mail, via England, was reduced to seven cents. This denomination was eliminated from the Bank Notes series after five-years' service, due to the five-cent Universal Postal Union international rate. The end of this denomination's service at this point means there are no 7-cent soft paper American stamps or re-engravings.

The 10-cent Jefferson stamp was used commonly on registered mail from 1875 onward. The ten-cent stamps were also used on international mail. As mentioned previously, it is the only Continental stamp found both with and without a secret mark. The stamp later was re-engraved, giving the stamp a new appearance.

The 12-cent Clay stamps paid for a mixed variety of domestic and foreign uses. Its Continental secret mark is the most obvious one of the series. There are no American 12-cent stamps.

The 15-cent stamp paid the registration fee, until it was lowered in 1875. The Continental secret mark of this stamp is controversial, so much so it probably doesn't exist!

There is no secret mark on the 24-cent stamp. Both National and Continental used the same plates. No 24-cent stamp was issued after June 30, 1885 indicating that its usefulness was confined to high rate foreign postage in the pre-UPU days. Therefore, there are no soft paper American stamps of this denomination.

The 30-cent stamp features Alexander Hamilton. The Continental Note Company stamp is distinguished by color, gray or greenish black versus black of National. It was discovered recently there is a secret mark found on the some American stamps. The last 30-cent stamp appeared in 1888. It is the American issue in a new color, orange brown.

The 90-cent Perry stamps were used on large, multiple rate, first-class packets. The 1873 Continental has no secret mark. It is distinguished by color from the preceding National. In 1888, the American Bank Note Company changed the color of the stamp, dramatically to purple.

One-Cent Franklin Bank Note Stamps

1870	National	Hard paper	Grill	No secret mark
1870	National	Hard paper	No grill	No secret mark
1873	Continental	Hard paper	No grill	Secret mark
1879	American	Soft paper	No grill	Secret mark
1881	American Re-engraved	Soft paper	No grill	Secret mark
1887	American	Soft paper	No grill	New design

Keeping with tradition, the one-cent Bank Note issue again featured the first United States Postmaster General, Benjamin Franklin. It features a Rubrecht bust of him, looking to the left. The background of the stamp is a rectangle. Inside the rectangle is scrollwork and foliated ornaments that fill the space to the vignette. On the upper curve of the vignette is a banner with the words, U. S. POSTAGE. ONE and CENT are on a curve below, separated by the numeral, 1.

1985 AMERIPEX Issue

A 1985 United States commemorative stamp features the upper left corner of a one-cent Franklin Bank Note stamp. This 22-cent issue advertised the 1986 AMERIPEX international stamp show in Chicago, Illinois. This is a further example of a "stamp on a stamp."

Figure 6-10. AMERIPEX Commemorative Stamp. The 1985 United States commemorative stamp shows part of the one-cent Franklin Bank Note stamp. This 22-cent issue advertised the 1986 AMERIPEX international stamp show held in Chicago, Illinois.

NATIONAL GRILLED ONE-CENT FRANKLIN

National Grilled One-Cent Franklin

Stamp Production

Printer:	National Bank Note Company
Designer:	Butler Packard
Engravers:	Joseph I. Pease (portrait), Anthony W. Cunningham (frame and lettering)
Format:	Sheets of 200, cut vertically into 2 panes of 100
Plate Numbers:	16, 17, 50, 51, 52, 53
Date of Issue:	Apr., 1870
Earliest Known Use:	Apr. 9, 1870
Uses:	Circular rate. Publication rate. Drop mail without carrier service
Quantity Issued:	23,000,000

Stamp Features

Size:	20 x 25 mm. (0.8 x 1.0 inches)
Watermark:	None
Grill:	H or I
Paper:	Hard
Perforations:	12
Secret Mark:	None
Colors:	Ultramarine, pale ultramarine, dark ultramarine.
Varieties:	Double grill, Split grill, Quadruple split grill, Marginal grill, Double transfers

Collectable Stamp Today
Collectable Cancellation Colors:
Black, blue, red, green.

Collectable Cancellation Varieties:
Paid, town, Paid All, Steamship.
Value Unused: $$$$$
Value Used: $$$$
Surviving Covers: 6,000-8,000
Largest Known Multiple: Unused: 4 (2x2 block)
Used: 3 (strip)

The National Bank Note Company printed the first one-cent Bank Note stamps. Both National stamps do not have the secret mark. Therefore, the ball to the left of the numeral, 1, is clear. The stamp is printed on hard paper, as are all National stamps.

This issue has a grill. Note the grilled Bank Notes were printed from the same plates, and at the same time, as some of the ungrilled stamps. The grills, mostly, are faint and incomplete. The H grills especially are hard to detect.

NATIONAL WITHOUT GRILL ONE-CENT FRANKLIN

National Without Grill One-Cent Franklin

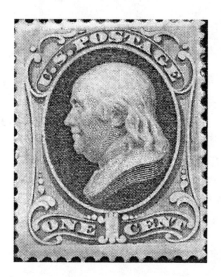

Stamp Production
Printer: National Bank Note Company
Designer: Butler Packard

Engravers:	Joseph I. Pease (portrait), Anthony W. Cunningham (frame and lettering)
Format:	Sheets of 200, cut vertically into 2 panes of 100
Plate Numbers:	16, 17, 50, 51, 52, 53
Date of Issue:	Apr. 1870
Earliest Known Use:	May 7,1870
Uses:	Circular rate. Publication rate. Drop mail without carrier service
Quantity Issued:	120,000,000

Stamp Features

Size:	20 x 25 mm. (0.8 x 1.0 inches)
Watermark:	None
Grill:	None
Paper:	Hard
Perforations:	12
Secret Mark:	None
Colors:	Ultramarine, pale ultramarine, dark ultramarine, gray blue.
Varieties:	Double transfer, Worn plate.

Collectable Stamp Today
Collectable Cancellation Colors:
Black, blue, ultramarine, magenta, purple, brown, red, green.
Collectable Cancellation Varieties:
Paid, Paid All, Steamship, railroad, numeral.

Value Unused:	$$$$
Value Used:	$$$
Surviving Covers:	40,000
Largest Known Multiple:	Unused: 14 (block with marginal imprint)
	Used: 42 (block)

These stamps are identical to the above grilled stamp except for the grills. National printed them on hard paper. In fact, there were printed from the same plates as the grilled stamps, at the same time. By this time, it was realized grills were not needed, as they did little to prevent stamp reuse. So most stamps were being made without them. The ungrilled one-cent National stamps are much more common than ones with grills.

Figure 6-11. Example of a One-Cent Bank Note Stamp on a Cover. Here is a National ungrilled Franklin one-cent stamp paying the circular rate for a Masonic cover. It was mailed in Elizabeth, New Jersey. Note the fancy four-leaf clover cancellation on it!

CONTINENTAL ONE-CENT FRANKLIN

Continental One-Cent Franklin

Stamp Production

Printer:	Continental Bank Note Company
Designer:	Butler Packard
Engravers:	Joseph I. Pease (portrait), Anthony W. Cunningham (frame and lettering), Charles Skinner (secret mark)
Format:	Sheets of 200, cut vertically into 2 panes of 100
Plate Numbers:	12, 13, 16, 26, 125, 126, 127, 128, 142, 143, 144, 146, 147, 156, 157, 58, 159, 160, 181, 182, 229, 230, 294, 296, 298, 299, 300, 301, 307, 308.
Date of Issue:	July 1873
Earliest Known Use:	Aug. 22, 1873
Uses:	Circular rate. Publication rate. Drop mail without carrier service
Quantity Issued:	448,290,000

Stamp Features

Size:	20 x 25 mm. (0.8 x 1.0 inches)
Watermark:	None
Grill:	None
Paper:	Hard
Perforations:	12
Secret Mark:	Present
Colors:	Ultramarine, pale ultramarine, dark ultramarine, gray blue, blue.
Varieties:	Double transfer, Cracked plate, Paper cut with cogwheel punch, Double paper, Ribbed paper, Paper with silk fibers.
Errors:	Imperforate (as a pair)

Collectable Stamp Today
Collectable Cancellation Colors:
Black, blue, purple, magenta, ultramarine, red, orange, orange red, brown, green.

Collectable Cancellation Varieties:
Paid All, Paid, railroad, Free, black carrier, numeral, precancelled G from Glastonbury, Conn., precancelled star from Glen Allen, Va, Alaska, Japan..

Value Unused:	$$$$
Value Used:	$$
Surviving Covers:	25,000
Largest Known Multiple:	Unused: 30 (block)
	Used: 27 (block)

Figure 6-12. Block of One-Cent Bank Note Stamps. This is a very fine block of four unused National ungrilled Franklin one-cent stamps.

When Continental took over the printing of the one-cent Bank Note stamp, it added a secret mark to distinguish its product from the previous National stamp. This is a small dash inside the small ball to the left of the numeral 1. This dash often so subtle requiring a magnifying glass to see it. If even a trace of color is present inside the ball, the stamp is a Continental. Like the National one-cent stamp, it is printed on hard paper.

The stamp is found on various experimental papers: paper cut with a cogwheel punch, double paper, ribbed paper, and paper with silk fibers.

The stamp has a unique perforation error. It can be found, as an imperforate pair in a used condition.

Figure 6-13. One-Cent Bank Note Secret Mark. For the one-cent stamp, Continental added a small dash inside the smll ball just to the left of the numeral 1 (right close up), not seen on the National (left).

AMERICAN ONE-CENT FRANKLIN

American One-Cent Franklin

Stamp Production
Printer: American Bank Note Company
Designer: Butler Packard
Engravers: Joseph I. Pease (portrait), Anthony W. Cunningham (frame and lettering), Charles Skinner (secret mark)
Format: Sheets of 200, cut vertically into 2 panes of 100
Plate Numbers: 301 (old Continental), and 319, 320, 327, 328, 336, 337, 344, 353, 354, 355, 356.
Date of Issue: Feb 4., 1879
Earliest Known Use: Jan. 3, 1879

Uses:	Circular rate. Publication rate. Drop mail without carrier service
Quantity Issued:	591,756,900

Stamp Features

Size:	20 x 25 mm. (0.8 x 1.0 inches)
Watermark:	None
Grill:	None
Paper:	Soft
Perforations:	12
Secret Mark:	Present
Colors:	Dark ultramarine, blue, gray blue.
Varieties:	Double transfer

Collectable Stamp Today

Collectable Cancellation Colors:	
	Black, blue, purple, magenta, red, green.
Collectable Cancellation Varieties:	
	Paid, Ship, numeral, railroad, supplementary mail type F, black carrier, blue carrier, China, printed star precancellation of Glen Allen, Va., printed G precancellation of Glastonbury, Conn.
Value Unused:	$$$$
Value Used:	$$
Surviving Covers:	15,000
Largest Known Multiple:	Unused: 18 (block)
	Used: 10 (block)

These stamps were printed from one of the Continental plates, number 301, and from new plates made with Continental transfer rolls after American Bank Note Company took over the company. This stamp, therefore, has the Continental secret mark. It is identical to it except that it is printed on soft American rather than on hard paper.

AMERICAN RE-ENGRAVED ONE-CENT FRANKLIN

American Re-Engraved One-Cent Franklin

Stamp Production

Printer:	American Bank Note Company
Designer:	Butler Packard
Engravers:	Joseph I. Pease (portrait), Anthony W. Cunningham (frame and lettering), Charles Skinner (secret mark), Douglas S. Ronaldson (new frame and lettering)
Format:	Sheets of 200, cut vertically into 2 panes of 100

Plate Numbers:	301 (old Continental), and 319, 320, 327, 328, 336, 337, 344, 353, 354, 355, 356.
Date of Issue:	Aug 1881
Earliest Known Use:	Nov. 2, 1881
Uses:	Circular rate. Publication rate. Drop mail without carrier service
Quantity Issued:	2,202,470,800

Stamp Features

Size:	20 x 25 mm. (0.8 x 1.0 inches)
Watermark:	None
Grill:	None
Paper:	Soft
Perforations:	12
Secret Mark:	Present
Colors:	Gray blue, ultramarine, dull blue, slate blue.
Varieties:	Double transfer, Punched with Douglas Patent process.

Collectable Stamp Today
Collectable Cancellation Colors:
Black, blue, purple, red, magenta, green, orange, orange red.

Collectable Cancellation Varieties:
Paid, Paid All, numeral, supplementary mail type F, railroad, precancelled star of Glen Allen, Va., China.

Value Unused:	$$$
Value Used:	$
Surviving Covers:	25,000
Largest Known Multiple:	Unused: 100 (complete pane)
	Used: 8 (block)

In August 1881, the American one-cent stamp was re-engraved. The vertical lines outside of the portrait in the top part of the stamp were deepened so they appear as a solid background. The area around the portrait was darkened. This resulted in a solid appearance to the stamp, with the design appearing more flat than raised. Proof that a stamp is re-engraved is found by looking in the ornaments at the top corners of the stamp. In the ball of these ornaments, there is a curve of color that is not found on the stamps of the National, Continental or original American issues.

Figure 6-14. Features of the Re-Engraved One-Cent Bank Note Stamp. The best proof that a stamp is a re-engraved one is found in the ornament at the top corner of the stamp (right close up). In the ball of this ornament, there is a curve of color that is not found on the other one-cent stamps.

Some of one-cent re-engraved stamps have the Douglas Patent paper. This is two-layered paper that is punched with eight small holes in a circle. This is similar to the earlier Flecher Cogwheel. It was designed for the same purpose, to prevent stamp re-use.

Another technologic advance first seen with this stamp is using a steam press for printing. The plates used for the steam production of this stamp were lettered before the plate numbers (C497-501, D502-506, I527-531). Note they are grouped in sets of five plates.

AMERICAN RE-ISSUE ONE CENT FRANKLIN

American Reissue One Cent Franklin

Stamp Production

Printer:	American Bank Note Company
Designer:	Thomas F. Morris
Engravers:	Alfred Jones (portrait), George H. Seymour (frame and lettering)
Format:	Sheets of 200, cut vertically into 2 panes of 100
Plate Numbers:	R573-77, S578-82, T583-87, FF644-48, GG649-53, II664-68, PP694-98, UU719-23 (all plates on steam press)
Date of Issue:	June 11, 1887
Earliest Known Use:	July 15, 1887
Uses:	Circular rate. Publication rate. Drop mail
Quantity Issued:	1,578,043,800

Stamp Features

Size:	20 x 25 mm. (0.8 x 1.0 inches)
Watermark:	None
Grill:	None
Paper:	Soft
Perforations:	12
Secret Mark:	None
Colors:	Ultramarine, bright ultramarine.
Varieties:	Double transfer

Collectable Stamp Today
Collectable Cancellation Colors:
Black, purple, magenta, blue, red.
Collectable Cancellation Varieties:
numeral, railroad, supplementary mail type F, China.

Value Unused: $$$$
Value Used: $$
Surviving Covers: 50,000-80,000
Largest Known Multiple: Unused: 100 (complete pane)
Used: 24

On June 11, 1887, the American Bank Note Company issued a new design for the one-cent stamp. The old die was in poor condition, prompting the decision. The new stamp is very much like its predecessors and therefore it is included in the Bank Note series. The biggest difference is the missing ornaments in the upper corners of the stamp.

Two-Cent Jackson and Washington Bank Note Stamps

1870 Jackson No secret mark	National	Hard paper	Grilled	
1870 Jackson No secret mark	National	Hard paper	No grill	
1873 Jackson Secret mark Brown	Continental	Hard paper	No grill	
1875 Jackson Secret mark Vermilion	Continental	Hard paper	No grill	
1879 Jackson Secret mark Vermilion	American	Soft paper	No grill	
1883 Washington Brown	American	Soft paper	No grill	
1887 Washington Green	American	Soft paper	No grill	

The two-cent Bank Note issue is a confusing group of stamps. There are two different designs, several print colors, plus the usual Bank Note hodgepodge of paper and secret marks. The reason for most of the confusion was the rate reduction for first-class mail from three-cents to two-cents, halfway through this period.

The first set of two-cent Bank Note stamps feature Andrew Jackson. This continued the tradition, starting in 1863 when the "Black Jack" stamp was introduced, of having the seventh president on the two-cent stamp. The stamp has an oval vignette with a profile bust of Jackson. It is modeled after Hiram Powers' statue. The oval sits on a shield, which in turn is on a lined rectangle. On the shield, above Jackson, are the words, U. S. POSTAGE. Across the bottom of the shield are the words, TWO CENTS, divided in the middle by the numeral, 2.

NATIONAL GRILLED TWO-CENT JACKSON

National Grilled Two-Cent Jackson

Stamp Production

Printer:	National Bank Note Company
Designer:	Butler Packard
Engravers:	Luigi (Louis) Delnoce (portrait), Douglas S. Ronaldson (frame and lettering)
Format:	Sheets of 200, cut vertically into 2 panes of 100
Plate Numbers:	12, 13, 14, 15, 28, 30, 34, 35, 45, 46, 47
Date of Issue:	Apr. 1870
Earliest Known Use:	July 14, 1870
Uses:	Drop mail with carrier service
Quantity Issued:	40,000,000

Stamp Features

Size:	20 x 25 mm. (0.8 x 1.0 inches)
Watermark:	None
Grill:	H or I
Paper:	Hard
Perforations:	12
Secret Mark:	None
Colors:	Red brown, pale red brown, dark red brown.
Varieties:	Double grill, Split grill, Double grill one split, Quadruple split grill, Marginal grill, Grill with points up.

Collectable Stamp Today
Collectable Cancellation Colors:
Black, blue, red, brown, green.
Collectable Cancellation Varieties:
Paid, Paid All, town, numeral, China.

Value Unused:	$$$$$
Value Used:	$$$
Surviving Covers:	10,000-15,000
Largest Known Multiple:	Unused: 24 (6x4 block)
	Used: 6 (3x2 block)

The first two-cent Bank Note stamp printed was National's hard paper version. It was printed both with and without a grill, at the same time. Naturally, National stamps don't have a secret mark. The secret mark area is the scroll above the letters, U. S. On the original National stamp, there is no diagonal line, unlike the secret mark of the Continental where there is one. The difference, however, is very subtle.

The best test for a National two-cent stamp is color. The earlier National stamps are red brown whereas the later Continentals are brown or dark brown.

The stamp was used for local mail with delivery, a common service. The stamp, like the earlier two-cent cents, was used bisected as a one-cent stamp. A diagonal and a vertical half are found on cover.

NATIONAL UNGRILLED TWO-CENT JACKSON

National Ungrilled Two-Cent Jackson

Stamp Production

Printer:	National Bank Note Company
Designer:	Butler Packard
Engravers:	Luigi (Louis) Delnoce (portrait), Douglas S. Ronaldson (frame and lettering)
Format:	Sheets of 200, cut vertically into 2 panes of 100
Plate Numbers:	12, 13, 14, 15, 28, 30, 34, 35, 45, 46, 47
Date of Issue:	Apr. 1870
Earliest Known Use:	May 7, 1870
Uses:	Drop mail with carrier service
Quantity Issued:	212,000,000

Stamp Features

Size:	20 x 25 mm. (0.8 x 1.0 inches)
Watermark:	None
Grill:	None
Paper:	Hard
Perforations:	12
Secret Mark:	None

Colors: Red brown, pale red brown, dark red brown, orange brown.

Varieties: Double impression, Double transfer.

Collectable Stamp Today
Collectable Cancellation Colors:
Black, blue, purple, red, green, brown.
Collectable Cancellation Varieties:
Paid, Paid All, numeral, Steamship, black carrier, China, Curacao, Japan.

Value Unused: $$$$
Value Used: $$
Surviving Covers: 7,500
Largest Known Multiple: Unused: 23 (block)
Used: 23

This stamp is identical to the above-described National two-cent stamp, except that it is missing the grill. It lacks the secret mark, is printed in the same shades, and is found on hard paper. That is because the stamp was printed from the same plates at the same time as the grilled issues. The ungrilled stamp is five times more common than its grilled counterpart.

The stamp exists with an excellent example of a double print variety.

Sought after covers are those that a half of the stamp is used for one-cent postage. Such halves are vertical, diagonal, or horizontal.

CONTINENTAL BROWN TWO-CENT JACKSON

Continental Brown Two-Cent Jackson

Stamp Production

Printer:	Continental Bank Note Company
Designer:	Butler Packard
Engravers:	Luigi (Louis) Delnoce (portrait), Douglas S. Ronaldson (frame and lettering), Charles Skinner (secret mark)
Format:	Sheets of 200, cut vertically into 2 panes of 100
Plate Numbers:	2, 3, 4, 6, 161, 162, 163, 164, 165, 166, 167, 168, 169, 234, 241, 242.
Date of Issue:	July 1873
Earliest Known Use:	July 12, 1873
Uses:	Drop mail with carrier service. Private postcard rate.
Quantity Issued:	140,905,800

Stamp Features

Size:	20 x 25 mm. (0.8 x 1.0 inches)
Watermark:	None
Grill:	None
Paper:	Hard
Perforations:	12
Secret Mark:	Present
Colors:	Brown, dark brown, dark reddish brown, yellowish brown.
Varieties:	Double impression, Double transfer, Cracked plate, Double paper, Ribbed paper.

Collectable Stamp Today
Collectable Cancellation Colors:

> Black, blue, magenta, purple, red, orange, orange red, green.

Collectable Cancellation Varieties:

> Paid, Insufficiently Paid, Paid All, P.D. in circle, town, numeral, black carrier, Steamship, supplementary mail type F, China, Japan, printed star precancellation of Glen Allen, Va..

Value Unused:	$$$$
Value Used:	$$$
Surviving Covers:	10,000
Largest Known Multiple:	Unused: 90 (block)
	Used: 20 (block)

Continental first printed this stamp in July 1873. The stamp's color was brown. The shade is different from that of the two-cent National Bank Note stamps, making ink color the best differentiation between the stamps. Like the National stamps, the Continental stamps are printed on hard paper. The stamp is found on Continental's experimental double and ribbed papers. The stamp can be found with a grill, called the Continental Grill, but most authorities believe such stamps are just essays.

The Continental secret mark is very subtle. Under the scroll, to the left and above the letters, U. S., there is a small diagonal line not found on National stamps. Or to put it another way, the ball of the scroll is joined to the frame of the banner of U. S. POSTAGE.

Figure 6-15. Two-Cent Bank Note Secret Mark. The added Continental secret mark on the two-cent issue is a subtle! The scroll ball is joined to the frame of U. S. POSTAGE (right diagram). It is not joined on the National two-cent stamps (left).

The stamp exists with a striking double impression.

The stamp is known bisected with the vertical half used as one-cent postage.

On May 1st, 1873, the United States Post Office Department started printing their own postcards. The cost to send these cards was one cent. However, the cost of privately printed postcards became two cents, meaning this and the remaining two-cent Bank Note stamps were used to pay this postage rate.

CONTINENTAL VERMILION TWO-CENT JACKSON

Continental Vermilion Two-Cent Jackson

Stamp Production

Printer:	Continental Bank Note Company
Designer:	Butler Packard
Engravers:	Luigi (Louis) Delnoce (portrait), Douglas S. Ronaldson (frame and lettering), Charles Skinner (secret mark)
Format:	Sheets of 200, cut vertically into 2 panes of 100
Plate Numbers:	161, 162, 163, 164, 165, 166, 167, 168, 169, 234, 241, 242.
Date of Issue:	June 21, 1875
Earliest Known Use:	July 15,1875
Uses:	Drop mail with carrier service. Private postcard rate.
Quantity Issued:	112,191,250

Stamp Features
Size:	20 x 25 mm. (0.8 x 1.0 inches)
Watermark:	None
Grill:	None
Paper:	Hard
Perforations:	12
Secret Mark:	Present
Colors:	Vermilion
Varieties:	Double paper, Paper with silk fibers, Ribbed paper, Double transfer.

Collectable Stamp Today
Collectable Cancellation Colors:
Black, blue, purple, magenta, red.
Collectable Cancellation Varieties:
Paid, Steamship, supplementary mail type F, black carrier, railroad.
Value Unused:	$$$$
Value Used:	$$$
Surviving Covers:	10,000
Largest Known Multiple:	Unused: 27 (block)
	Used: 8 (block)

On June 21, 1875 the color of the two-cent Continental was changed to vermilion. There was confusion between the colors of the 2-cent and the 10-cent Continentals, both of which were brown. The vermilion color was available since the 7-cent vermilion stamp had been withdrawn. This color of the stamp makes cancellations show strongly.

The stamp exists on Continental experimental papers: double paper, paper with silk fibers, and ribbed paper. This 2-cent stamp can be found with a Continental Grill, and imperforate. They are viewed as proofs and essays, not issued stamps.

Figure 6-16. Two-Cent Jackson Cover. Shown is an example of the two-cent vermilion Jackson stamp paying the local with carrier service rate, in the case, for a business letter mailed and locally delivered in Boston.

The stamp is known bisected with a horizontal half of the stamp being used as one cent of postage on cover.

The largest known unused multiple is a block of 27 that includes the marginal plate number and imprint. The largest known used multiple is a block of eight stamps on cover.

AMERICAN TWO-CENT JACKSON

American Two-Cent Jackson

Stamp Production

Printer:	American Bank Note Company
Designer:	Butler Packard
Engravers:	Luigi (Louis) Delnoce (portrait), Douglas S. Ronaldson (frame and lettering), Charles Skinner (secret mark)
Format:	Sheets of 200, cut vertically into 2 panes of 100
Plate Numbers:	296, 297 (Continental), 338, 339, 391, 392, 393, 394, 412, 413.
Date of Issue:	Feb. 4, 1879
Earliest Known Use:	Aug. 19, 1878
Uses:	Drop mail with carrier service. Private postcard rate.
Quantity Issued:	547,073,700

Stamp Features

Size:	20 x 25 mm. (0.8 x 1.0 inches)
Watermark:	None
Grill:	None
Paper:	Soft
Perforations:	12
Secret Mark:	Present
Colors:	Vermilion, orange vermilion.
Varieties:	Double impression, Double transfer.

Collectable Stamp Today
Collectable Cancellation Colors:
Black, blue, purple, magenta, red, green.

Collectable Cancellation Varieties:
Paid, Paid All, Ship, numeral, railroad, supplementary mail type F, printed star precancellation of Glen Allen, Va. in black or red, China.

Value Unused: $$$$
Value Used: $$
Surviving Covers: 20,000
Largest Known Multiple: Unused: 100 (complete pane)
Used: 12 (block)

American Bank Note Company started to print this stamp after it took over Continental. It was printed from two of the Continental plates and then new plates made from Continental transfer rolls and dies. Therefore, these stamps have the secret mark. The difference is the soft American paper. The ink is a lighter shade, also.

A commonly used stamp, it is found today on more than 20,000 covers. The stamp is known used, bisected as a one-cent of postage on cover.

AMERICAN BROWN TWO-CENT WASHINGTON

American Brown Two-Cent Washington

Stamp Production
Printer: American Bank Note Company
Designer: Thomas F. Morris
Engravers: Alfred Jones (portrait), Douglas S. Ronaldson (frame and lettering)
Format: Sheets of 200, cut vertically into 2 panes of 100
Plate Numbers: 430, 431, 432, 433, 434, 435, 436, 437, 438, 439, 440, 441, 442, 443, 444, 445, 446, 447, 448, 449, 450, 451, 452, 453, 454, 455, 458, 459, 460, 461, 462, 463, 466, 467, 468, 469, 470, 471, 472, 473, 474, 476, 477, 478, 479, A483-487, B490-494, E507-511, F512-616, G517-521, H522-526, J532-536, N553-557, O558-562, P563-567, F512-516, G517-521, H522-526, 553.
Date of Issue: Oct. 1, 1883
Earliest Known Use: Oct. 1, 1883 (First day cover)

Uses: First class domestic mail for first one half ounce. Private postcard rate.

Quantity Issued: 4,490,699,200

Stamp Features

Size: 20 x 25 mm. (0.8 x 1.0 inches)
Watermark: None
Grill: None
Paper: Soft
Perforations: 12
Secret Mark: None
Colors: Red brown, dark red brown, orange brown.
Varieties: Double transfer, Imperforate.

Collectable Stamp Today
Collectable Cancellation Colors:
                       Black, purple, magenta, blue, violet, brown, red, green.
Collectable Cancellation Varieties:
                       Paid, railroad, express company cancellation, supplementary mail type F, Ship, Steamboat, numeral, China.
Value Unused: $$$
Value Used: $
Surviving Covers: 500,000-750,000
Largest Known Multiple: Unused: 100 (complete pane)
                       Used: 8 (block)

This stamp was created because of the Postal Act of Congress of March 3, 1883. This act lowered the first class rate from three-cents to two-cents per half-ounce on October 1, 1883. Therefore, the two-cent stamp was redesigned, featuring Washington. It became the most commonly used stamp. In fact, it is one of the most common of all 19th century United States stamps.

The two-cent Washington features a shield. On the shield is an oval with a profile bust of George Washington, looking to the left. Above the oval, surrounding the head are the words, UNITED STATES POSTAGE. Underneath the tablet are the words, TWO CENTS. The numeral, 2, separates the words TWO and CENTS.

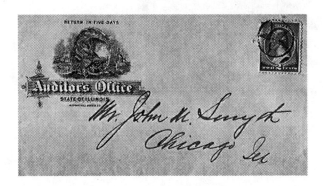

Figure 6-17. Example of a Brown Two-Cent Washington Stamp on a Cover. Here is an example of a two-cent Bank Note Washington stamp paying the first-class postage rate. The letter was sent from Springfield to Chicago. Note the fancy star cancellation.

Most of these stamps were printed on the steam printing press. The plate numbers that have a letter preceding it designate such plates used on the steam printing press. They come in groups of five plates.

Double transfers and other plate variations are common on this stamp.

It is a favorite among fancy cancellation collectors, especially since there are 500,000 to 750,000 surviving covers. This item is known in imperforate unused pairs.

AMERICAN GREEN TWO-CENT WASHINGTON

American Green Two-Cent Washington

Stamp Production

Printer:	American Bank Note Company
Designer:	Thomas F. Morris
Engravers:	Alfred Jones (portrait), Douglas S. Ronaldson (frame and lettering)
Format:	Sheets of 200, cut vertically into 2 panes of 100
Plate Numbers:	N553-557, 0558-562, Q568-572, U588-592 V593-597 W598-602, X603-607, Y608-613, AA619-623, BB624-628, CC629-633, DD634-638, EE639-643, HH654-658, II659-663, KK669-673, LL674-678, MM679-683, NN684-688, OO689-693, QQ699-703, RR704-708, SS709-713, TT714-718.
Date of Issue:	Sept. 10, 1887
Earliest Known Use:	Sept. 20, 1887
Uses:	First-class domestic mail for first one-half ounce. Private postcard rate.
Quantity Issued:	4,542,239,300

Stamp Features

Size:	20 x 25 mm. (0.8 x 1.0 inches)
Watermark:	None
Grill:	None
Paper:	Soft
Perforations:	12
Secret Mark:	None
Colors:	Green, bright green, dark green.
Varieties:	Double transfer, Printed on both sides, Imperforate.

Collectable Stamp Today
Collectable Cancellation Colors:
        Black, purple, magenta, blue, red, green.
Collectable Cancellation Varieties:
        Paid, railroad, numeral, Steam, Steamboat,
        supplementary mail type F, China, Japan.
Value Unused: $$$
Value Used: $
Surviving Covers: 500,000
Largest Known Multiple: Unused: 50 (block)
        Used: 20 (block)

In the fall of 1887, the color of the two-cent stamp was changed to green. The green color reflected that the 2-cent stamp now paid for the basic first-class postage rate. All of the 2-cent green Washington stamps were printed on steam presses. Therefore, the plates were made and used in sets of five, as demonstrated by the initial letter before the plate number.

The stamp can be found printed on both sides. A few copies of the stamp are known imperforate, both in used and unused states.

This stamp is very common, made by the billions. With a half million surviving covers, it is a favorite among cancellation and cover collectors. Rare diagonal bisects of this stamp for one-cent frankage exist on cover.

The largest unused multiple of the stamp is a block of 50, used a block of 20 stamps.

Three-Cent Bank Note Stamps

1870	National	Hard paper	Grilled	No secret mark
1870	National	Hard paper	No grill	No secret mark
1873	Continental	Hard paper	No grill	Secret mark
1879	American	Soft paper	No grill	Secret mark
1881	American Re-Engraved	Soft paper Green	No grill	Secret mark
1887	American Re-Engraved	Soft paper Vermilion	No grill	Secret mark

The most widely used stamp of the first half of the Bank Note era was the three-cent Washington. Until the postage rate for first-class mail was lowered from three to two-cents on October 1, 1883, it was by far, the most commonly used United States postage stamp. The stamp featured George Washington. This restarted the tradition, broken only briefly by the pictorial series of 1869, of having the first president on the denomination that paid the first-class postage rate.

Most of the stamp is taken up by a shield, which sits on a faint lined background. On the shield is an oval that features a bust of Washington, modeled after Houdon's statue of him. Above the oval following its curve are the words, U. S. POSTAGE. Under the portrait, on a flowing ribbon, are the words, THREE CENTS, separated in the middle, by the numeral, 3.

NATIONAL GRILLED THREE-CENT WASHINGTON

National Grilled Three-Cent Washington

Stamp Production
Printer: National Bank Note Company
Designer: Butler Packard
Engravers: Joseph P. Ourdan (portrait), Douglas S. Ronaldson (frame and lettering)
Format: Sheets of 200, cut vertically into 2 panes of 100

Plate Numbers:	1, 2, 3, 4, 5, 6, 7, 8, 9, 10, 11, 25, 29, 31, 32, 36, 37, 38, 39, 40, 41, 42, 43, 44, 54, 55
Date of Issue:	Mar. 1870
Earliest Known Use:	Mar. 24, 1870
Uses:	First-class domestic mail up to one half ounce
Quantity Issued:	172,000,000

Stamp Features

Size:	20 x 25 mm. (0.8 x 1.0 inches)
Watermark:	None
Grill:	H or I
Paper:	Hard
Perforations:	12
Secret Mark:	None
Colors:	Green, pale green, yellow green, deep green.
Varieties:	Double transfer, Cracked plate, Double grill, Split grill, Quadruple split grill, Marginal grill.

Collectable Stamp Today

Collectable Cancellation Colors:	Black, blue, purple, magenta, red, orange, orange red, brown, green.
Collectable Cancellation Varieties:	Paid, railroad, Steamship, Paid All, numeral, Free.
Value Unused:	$$$$
Value Used:	$$$
Surviving Covers:	25,000
Largest Known Multiple:	Unused: 32 (block)
	Used: 10

Like most of the Bank Note issues, the National Bank Note Company first made the three-cent Washington stamps. Such stamps were printed both with and without grills, at the same time, from the same plates. This stamp is the most common grilled Bank Note issue.

The distinctive feature of the three-cent National is the missing secret mark. The lower left ribbon is not shaded as it is in the Continental and American stamps. The National stamps are printed only on hard paper. Also, the National three-cent stamps have a lighter shade of green ink than the stamps of the other companies.

A copy of this stamp is found printed on both sides. It exists with all the usual grilled varieties. This stamp, both in its grilled and ungrilled types can be found imperforate, though such issues are essays. There is even an unused imperforate block of 20 stamps, but it, too, is considered an essay.

NATIONAL UNGRILLED THREE-CENT WASHINGTON

National Ungrilled Three-Cent Washington

Stamp Production
Printer:	National Bank Note Company
Designer:	Butler Packard
Engravers:	Joseph P. Ourdan (portrait), Douglas S. Ronaldson (frame and lettering)
Format:	Sheets of 200, cut vertically into 2 panes of 100
Plate Numbers:	1, 2, 3, 4, 5, 6, 7, 8, 9, 10, 11, 25, 29, 31, 32, 36, 37, 38, 39, 40, 41, 42, 43, 44, 54, 55.
Date of Issue:	Mar. 1870
Earliest Known Use:	Mar. 1, 1870
Uses:	First-class domestic mail up to one half ounce
Quantity Issued:	1,033,000,000

Stamp Features
Size:	20 x 25 mm. (0.8 x 1.0 inches)
Watermark:	None
Grill:	None
Paper:	Hard
Perforations:	12
Secret Mark:	None
Colors:	Green, pale green, dark green, yellow green.
Varieties:	Printed on both sides, Double impression, Double transfer, Short transfer at bottom, Cracked plate, Worn plate.

Collectable Stamp Today
Collectable Cancellation Colors:
> Black, blue, purple, magenta, brown, red, ultramarine, green.

Collectable Cancellation Varieties:
> Paid, Paid All, numeral, Free, railroad, express company cancellation, Steamboat, Steamship, ship, Japan.

Value Unused: $$$$
Value Used: $$
Surviving Covers: 225,000
Largest Known Multiple: Unused: 14 (block)
> Used: 20 (block)

This stamp is an identical stamp to the three-cent National grilled issue, except for missing the grill. Used for the basic first-class postage, it is a common stamp. In fact, over a billion were printed. It is several times more common than its grilled counterpart.

Like the three-cent grilled National, it exists in an unissued imperforate state. In fact, a block of ten imperforate stamps (5x2), with the bottom imprint and plate number 11 can be found. These are classified as essays, not issued stamps.

The stamp has a double impression variety that is the most striking of the Bank Note series. A copy of this stamp is known printed on both sides. Also, the stamp is found with a very obvious and fairly common, short transfer at bottom.

CONTINENTAL THREE-CENT WASHINGTON

Continental Three-Cent Washington

Stamp Production

Printer:	Continental Bank Note Company
Designer:	Butler Packard
Engravers:	Joseph P. Ourdan (portrait), Douglas S. Ronaldson (frame and lettering), Charles Skinner (secret mark)
Format:	Sheets of 200, cut vertically into 2 panes of 100
Plate Numbers:	1, 5, 7, 8, 9, 10, 11, 14, 15, 17, 19, 20, 129, 130, 131, 132, 133, 135, 136 138,139,148,149, 150, 151, 152,153,154, 155,170,171, 172, 173,174,175, 176, 177, 178, 179, 180, 183, 184, 185, 186, 187, 188, 189, 190, 191, 192, 193, 219, 220. ;21, 222, 223, 224, 225, 226, 227, 228, 231, 232, 235, 236. 237, 238, 239, 240, 250, 251, 262, 253, 254, 255, 256, 258, 259, 260, 261, 262, 263, 264, 265, 266, 267, 268, 269, 270, 271, 272, 273, 274, 275, 276, 277, 278, 279, 280, 281, 282, 283, 286, 287, 288, 289, 290, 291, 292, 293, 309, 310.
Date of Issue:	July 1873
Earliest Known Use:	July 17, 1873
Uses:	First-class domestic mail up to one half ounce
Quantity Issued:	2,661,293,500

Stamp Features

Size:	20 x 25 mm. (0.8 x 1.0 inches)
Watermark:	None
Grill:	None
Paper:	Hard
Perforations:	12
Secret Mark:	Present

Colors:	Green, bluish green, yellow green, dark yellow green, dark green, olive green.
Varieties:	Double impression, Printed on both sides, Cracked plate, Double transfer, Short transfer at bottom, Double paper, Paper cut with cogwheel punch, Ribbed paper, Paper with silk fibers, Grilled.
Errors:	Horizontal pair imperforate vertically in between, Horizontal pair imperforate vertically

Collectable Stamp Today
Collectable Cancellation Colors:
Black, blue, magenta, purple, ultramarine, red, orange, orange red, green.
Collectable Cancellation Varieties:
Paid. Paid All, Free, numeral, town, railroad, R. P. O., P. D. in circle, Steamboat, Steamship, supplementary mail type D or F, express company cancellation, black carrier, red carrier, China, Alaska, Japan.

Value Unused:	$$$$
Value Used:	$
Surviving Covers:	500,000
Largest Known Multiple:	Unused: 25 (block)
	Used: 36 (block)

The three-cent Continental stamp differs from the earlier issued National stamps by the added secret mark. It is the shading of the ribbon, to the left of the bottom of the numeral, 3.

Figure 6-18. Three-Cent Bank Note Secret Mark. The National three-cent stamp (left) does not have a secret mark. The lower left ribbon is not shaded. It is shaded as a secret mark on the Continental and American stamps (right).

There are several interesting varieties of the three-cent Continental. This includes paper variations: double paper, paper cut with the cogwheel punch, ribbed paper, and paper with silk fibers. With so many stamps printed, it is not surprising to found the stamp with plate varieties including double impressions, cracked plate, double transfers, and short transfers. The stamp can be found grilled, which are just essays. The stamp exists as an imperforate with and without grills, also essays.

The stamp also can be found with imperforate errors. The stamp is known as a horizontal pair, imperforate in between (where the missing perforation is just between the stamps of the pair), and as a horizontal pair, imperforate vertically (where every vertical perforation is missing).

Cancellation collectors have a field day with the vast variety seen with this issue. This is because the stamp is found on more than half million covers, today.

Figure 6-19. Example of a Three-Cent Bank Note Stamp on a Cover. Here is an example of a three-cent Continental Bank Note stamp on a letter. The stamp paid the basic first-class postage rate of three cents. The letter was mailed from Chicago to Philadelphia.

AMERICAN THREE-CENT WASHINGTON

American Three-Cent Washington

Stamp Production
Printer:	American Bank Note Company
Designer:	Butler Packard
Engravers:	Joseph P. Ourdan (portrait), Douglas S. Ronaldson (frame and lettering), Charles Skinner (secret mark)

Format:	Sheets of 200, cut vertically into 2 panes of 100
Plate Numbers:	292, 309, 310 (Continental), 311, 312, 321, 322, 323, 324, 329, 330, 334, 335, 340, 341, 341A, 342, 343, 345, 346, 347, 348, 349, 350, 350A, 351, 352, 357, 368.
Date of Issue:	1878
Earliest Known Use:	July 2, 1878
Uses:	First-class domestic mail up to one half ounce
Quantity Issued:	1,270,843,200

Stamp Features

Size:	20 x 25 mm. (0.8 x 1.0 inches)
Watermark:	None
Grill:	None
Paper:	Soft
Perforations:	12
Secret Mark:	Present
Colors:	Green, light green, dark green.
Varieties:	Double transfer, Short transfer, Double impression.

Collectable Stamp Today
Collectable Cancellation Colors:
Black, blue, magenta, purple, brown, violet, red, green.
Collectable Cancellation Varieties:
Paid, Free, numeral, railroad, Steamboat, supplementary mail type F, printed star precancel of Glen Allen, Va., China, Alaska.

Value Unused:	$$$$
Value Used:	$
Surviving Covers:	1,000,000
Largest Known Multiple:	Unused: 100 (complete pane)
	Used: 31 (block)

The difference between this stamp and the Continental 3-cent stamp is in the paper. The American printings use soft paper versus the hard of the Continental stamps. The stamps were printed from three plates originally used by Continental, and new plates made by American. The stamp is found imperforate, in pairs, but these are essays.

Because of its common use on first-class mail, it can be found on more than a million covers, today.

Figure 6-20. Example of a Plate Block of the Three-Cent Bank Note Stamp. Shown is a large block of fourteen stamps of the three-cent Continental Bank Note stamp with the top selvage showing the imprint and plate number.

AMERICAN THREE-CENT WASHINGTON RE-ENGRAVED GREEN

American Re-Engraved Green Three-Cent Washington

Stamp Production
Printer: American Bank Note Company
Designer: Butler Packard
Engravers: Joseph P. Ourdan (portrait), George K. Seymour (new frame)
Format: Sheets of 200, cut vertically into 2 panes of 100
Plate Numbers: 365, 366, 367, 368, 369, 370, 371, 372, 373, 374, 375, 376, 381, 382, 383, 384, 385, 386, 395, 396, 397, 398, 408, 409, 410, 411, 414, 415, 416, 417, 418, 419, 420, 421.
Date of Issue: July 16, 1881
Earliest Known Use: Aug. 7, 1881

Uses:	First-class domestic mail up to one half ounce. Make up various rates after reduction in first-class domestic mail to two cents.
Quantity Issued:	1,482,380,900

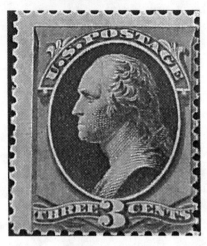

Stamp Features

Size:	20 x 25 mm. (0.8 x 1.0 inches)
Watermark:	None
Grill:	None
Paper:	Soft
Perforations:	12
Secret Mark:	Present
Colors:	Blue green, green, yellow green.
Varieties:	Double transfer, Cracked plate, Double impression, Punched by Douglas Patent process.

Collectable Stamp Today
Collectable Cancellation Colors:
Black, purple, magenta, blue, brown, red.
Collectable Cancellation Varieties:
Paid, Paid All, numeral, Ship, supplementary mail type F, railroad, printed star precancel of Glen Allen, Va.

Value Unused:	$$$
Value Used:	$
Surviving Covers:	500,000
Largest Known Multiple:	Unused: 100 (complete pane)
	Used: 49 (block)

The re-engraved three-cent stamps were printed from new plates, produced from new transfer rolls, in turn, made from a re-engraved die. The stamp resembles the old American stamp but with some obvious differences. While the vignette is unchanged, the framing is new. The shading line, which surrounds the oval of the portrait of Washington, is much narrower on the re-engraving. Vertical lines were added and deepened inside the oval. It now appears as a solid color. An identifying mark is a straight dash under the ribbon, immediately under the letters, TS of CENTS.

Figure 6-21. Differences of the American Re-Engraved Three-Cent Washington Stamp. Close-ups of a original (left) and re-engraved (right) three-cent Washington Bank Note stamps are shown. The shading line, which surrounds the oval of the portrait of Washington, is narrower on the re-engraved stamp compared with the original (top arrows). Vertical lines were added during the re-engraving which results that the design that appears as a solid color (bottom arrows).

There is an unusual cracked plate variety of this stamp. Two roughly parallel, broken into short sections cracks extend from the TA of POSTAGE to the right of the numeral, 3.

The Douglas Patent punch was used on a small lot of these stamps from plate 367.

The stamp's main reason for existence ended on September 30, 1883, when the basic first-class postage rate for the first one half ounce was reduced from three to two cents. The stamp then was just used to make up other odd postage rates.

AMERICAN THREE-CENT WASHINGTON RE-ENGRAVED VERMILION

American Re-Engraved Vermilion Three-Cent Washington

Stamp Production
Printer: American Bank Note Company
Designer: Butler Packard

Engravers:	Joseph P. Ourdan (portrait), George K. Seymour (new frame)
Format:	Sheets of 200, cut vertically into 2 panes of 100
Plate Numbers:	421
Date of Issue:	Sept. 1887
Earliest Known Use:	Sept. 23, 1887
Uses:	Makeup stamp for unusual or odd rates
Quantity Issued:	20,167,800

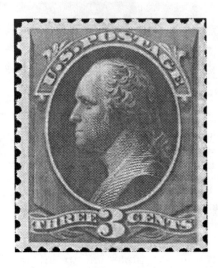

Stamp Features

Size:	20 x 25 mm. (0.8 x 1.0 inches)
Watermark:	None
Grill:	None
Paper:	Soft
Perforations:	12
Secret Mark:	Present
Colors:	Vermilion
Varieties:	None

Collectable Stamp Today
Collectable Cancellation Colors:
Black, purple, magenta, blue, green.
Collectable Cancellation Varieties:
supplementary mail type F, railroad.

Value Unused:	$$$$
Value Used:	$$$$
Surviving Covers:	3,000
Largest Known Multiple:	Unused: 100 (complete pane)
	Used: 8 (block)

In the fall of 1887, the color of the re-engraved American three-cent Washington stamp was changed to vermilion from green. This was so not to confuse the stamp with the new two-cent green Washington stamp, used to pay the basic firs-class rate. The combination of this new color and the design make it one of the most beautiful United States classic stamps.

The stamp was printed from a single plate, number 421, one of the plates used for the green American three-cent stamps.

Singles of this stamp on cover are very rare as the first class rate, now, was two cents. Unlike the other three-cent Bank Note stamps, this one saw limited use to make up odd postage rates.

Four Cent Bank Note Stamps

1883	American	Soft paper	No grill	Blue green
1883	American	Soft paper	No grill	Carmine

This denomination was not an original part of the Bank Note series. In fact, it was a latecomer. It was first issued October 1, 1883, when the basic first-class postage rate was reduced from three to two cents per half-ounce. It was created to pay double weight letter postage.

The stamp features Andrew Jackson, whose portrait had been removed from the two-cent stamp. The stamp has a rectangle, covering most of the stamp. Inside it is an oval vignette with a profile bust of Andrew Jackson looking to the left. The words, UNITED STATES POSTAGE, in small white capital letters, follow the upper border of the portrait oval. In the lower corners are large white numerals, 4. Straight across the bottom of the stamp are the words, FOUR CENTS, in white letters.

The American Bank Note Company printed all the four-cent Bank Note stamps. Therefore, they all are on soft paper. Since they were not produced until late in the Bank Note era, no major changes occurred or secret marks added.

BLUE-GREEN AMERICAN FOUR-CENT JACKSON

American Blue-Green Four-Cent Jackson

Stamp Production
Printer: American Bank Note Company
Designer: Thomas F. Morris
Engravers: Alfred Jones (portrait), Douglas S. Ronaldson (frame and lettering)
Format: Sheets of 200, cut vertically into 2 panes of 100
Plate Numbers: 456, 457, L542-546 (steam press).
Date of Issue: Oct. 1, 1883
Earliest Known Use: Oct. 1, 1883 (First day cover)
Uses: Double-weight first-class domestic mail.
Quantity Issued: 76,164,425

Stamp Features
Size: 20 x 25 mm. (0.8 x 1.0 inches)
Watermark: None
Grill: None
Paper: Soft
Perforations: 12
Secret Mark: N/A
Colors: Blue-green, deep blue-green.
Varieties: Double transfer, Cracked plate.

Collectable Stamp Today
Collectable Cancellation Colors:
                  Black, purple, magenta, green, blue.
Collectable Cancellation Varieties:
                  supplementary mail type F, numeral.
Value Unused: $$$$

Value Used: $$$
Surviving Covers: 7,500
Largest Known Multiple: Unused: 66 (block)
Used: 4 (2x2 block)

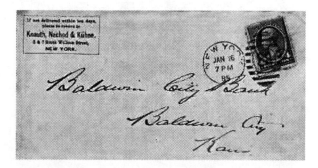

Figure 6-22. Example of a Four-Cent Bank Note Stamp on a Cover. Shown is an example of a blue-green four-cent Jackson Bank Note stamp on a letter. The stamp paid for a double-weight first-class domestic mail, in this case a business letter sent from New York City to Baldwin, Kansas.

When the four-cent Jackson first was issued, it was printed with blue-green ink. A diagonal half of the stamp has been found used on a cover as two-cent postage.

CARMINE AMERICAN FOUR-CENT JACKSON

American Carmine Four-Cent Jackson

Stamp Production

Printer:	American Bank Note Company
Designer:	Thomas F. Morris
Engravers:	Alfred Jones (portrait), Douglas S. Ronaldson (frame and lettering)
Format:	Sheets of 200, cut vertically into 2 panes of 100
Plate Numbers:	L542-546 (steam press)
Date of Issue:	Nov. 1888
Earliest Known Use:	Jan. 18, 1889
Uses:	Double-weight first-class domestic mail.
Quantity Issued:	28,105,850

Stamp Features

Size:	20 x 25 mm. (0.8 x 1.0 inches)
Watermark:	None
Grill:	None
Paper:	Soft
Perforations:	12
Secret Mark:	N/A
Colors:	Carmine, rose carmine, pale rose.
Varieties:	Double transfer.

Collectable Stamp Today
Collectable Cancellation Colors:
Black, blue, red, purple, magenta.
Collectable Cancellation Varieties:
supplementary mail type F

Value Unused:	$$$$
Value Used:	$$$
Surviving Covers:	6,000
Largest Known Multiple:	Unused: 40 (block)
	Used: 8 (block)

Late in 1888, the color of the 4-cent Jackson was changed from blue-green to carmine. The change was needed due to the change in the color of the two-cent stamp to green. This stamp is scarcer than the blue green, but it still is a common stamp. It was printed from the same steam press plates that produced the blue green stamps.

Five-Cent Bank Note Stamps

1875	Taylor	Continental	Hard paper
1879	Taylor	American	Soft paper
1882	Garfield Yellow brown	American	Soft paper
1888	Garfield Blue	American	Soft paper

Like the four-cent denomination, the five-cent Bank Note stamp was not an original part of this series. It was needed to pay the new five-cent postage to the Universal Postal Union countries. Up until that time, mailing letters among countries was complicated by multiple rates based on complex treaties between countries. In August 1862, then Postmaster General Montgomery Blair arranged for sixteen countries to meet in Paris to discuss the problem. Next, representatives from twenty countries met in Berne, Switzerland, and signed a treaty on October 9th, 1874 for uniform postal rates among the members. The countries were Germany, Austria, Hungary, Belgium, Denmark, Egypt, Spain, Greece, Italy, Luxembourg, Norway, Netherlands, Portugal, Romania, Russia, Serbia, Sweden, Switzerland, Turkey and the United States. The Universal Postal Union treaty set a standard postage rate of five-cents for United States letters going to any of these countries. The rate became effective on July 1, 1875. What is amazing is that the five-cent rate remained in effect for 78 years! It wasn't changed to 8 cents until November 1, 1953.

The first five-cent design featured president and Mexican War hero, Zachary Taylor. It was the first time he appeared on a United States postage stamp. The design borrowed the frame of the ten-cent Bank Note stamp and a portrait of Taylor from the tobacco revenue snuff stamp of 1871. The revenue portrait was based on a daguerreotype of him. He is dressed in an open double-breasted military coat and high white collar. The portrait of General Zachary Taylor is the only full face one of the series.

Figure 6-23.
Daguerreotype of Zachary Taylor. This photo of President Zachary ultimately became the basis of the five-cent Taylor bank note stamps.

CONTINENTAL FIVE-CENT TAYLOR

Continental Five-Cent Taylor

Stamp Production

Printer:	Continental Bank Note Company
Designer:	Butler Packard (frame). The designer of the portrait is an unknown person at the Bureau of Engraving and Printing who designed the original tobacco revenue stamp.
Engravers:	S. Ronaldson (frame and lettering)
Format:	Sheets of 200, cut vertically into 2 panes of 100
Plate Numbers:	243, 244, 247, 248, 284, 306.
Date of Issue:	June 1875

Earliest Known Use: July 10, 1875
Uses: Foreign mail rate to Universal Postal Union members
Quantity Issued: 15,290,000

Stamp Features
Size: 20 x 25 mm. (0.8 x 1.0 inches)
Watermark: None
Grill: None
Paper: Hard
Perforations: 12
Secret Mark: N/A
Colors: Blue, dark blue, bright blue, light blue, greenish blue.
Varieties: Cracked plate, Double transfer, Double paper, Ribbed paper, Paper with silk fibers.

Collectable Stamp Today
Collectable Cancellation Colors:
Black, blue, purple, magenta, ultramarine, red, green.
Collectable Cancellation Varieties:
railroad, numeral, supplementary mail type E and F, Steamship, Ship, China, Peru, Japan.
Value Unused: $$$$
Value Used: $$$
Surviving Covers: 7,500
Largest Known Multiple: Unused: 36 (6x6 block)
Used: 14 (block)

Figure 6-23. Example of a Five-Cent Taylor Bank Note Stamp on a Cover. The five-cent bank note stamps paid the new Universal Postal Union overseas rate. Therefore, they usually are found on foreign covers. Here is one such letter, a Continental five-cent Taylor paying the postage from Cincinnati via New York City to Germany. Note the fancy duplex cancellation.

National did not print this denomination stamp. Since Continental first made it, it has no secret mark. But since American later printed it, it is necessary to check the paper to make sure it is of the hard type.

There is a huge cracked plate variety that extends through five stamps.

The Continental grill essay can be found for this issue. The stamp can be found on the various Continental paper varieties include double paper, ribbed paper, and paper with silk fibers.

The stamp is found mostly on foreign covers, especially Europe.

AMERICAN FIVE-CENT TAYLOR

American Five-Cent Taylor

Stamp Production

Printer:	American Bank Note Company
Designer:	Butler Packard (frame). The designer of the portrait is an unknown person at the Bureau of Engraving and Printing who designed the original tobacco revenue stamp.
Engravers:	S. Ronaldson (frame and lettering)
Format:	Sheets of 200, cut vertically into 2 panes of 100
Plate Numbers:	306 (Continental), 325, 326, 379, 380.
Date of Issue:	Feb. 1979
Earliest Known Use:	Jan 16, 1879
Uses:	Foreign mail rate to Universal Postal Union members
Quantity Issued:	42,000,000

Stamp Features
Size:	20 x 25 mm. (0.8 x 1.0 inches)
Watermark:	None
Grill:	None
Paper:	Soft
Perforations:	12
Secret Mark:	N/A
Colors:	Blue, light blue, bright blue, dark blue.
Varieties:	Double transfer.

Collectable Stamp Today
Collectable Cancellation Colors:
Black, blue, purple, magenta, ultramarine, red.
Collectable Cancellation Varieties:
railroad, numeral, supplementary mail type F, Steamship, China, Peru, Panama.

Value Unused:	$$$$
Value Used:	$$$
Surviving Covers:	15,000
Largest Known Multiple:	Unused: 16 (6x6 block)
	Used: 20 (block)

This American soft paper Bank Note stamp is more common than the Continental hard paper stamp. Most stamps were used on the five-cent foreign rate mail to countries belonging to the Universal Postal Union, usually to Europe. The largest unused multiple of the stamp is a block of 16, with the plate number and imprint. Used, it is a block of 20 stamps, 16 stamps on cover.

AMERICAN YELLOW BROWN FIVE-CENT GARFIELD

American Yellow-Brown Five-Cent Garfield

Stamp Production
Printer:	American Bank Note Company
Designer:	Thomas F. Morris
Engravers:	Charles Skinner (portrait), Douglas S. Ronaldson (frame and lettering)
Format:	Sheets of 200, cut vertically into 2 panes of 100
Plate Numbers:	399, 400, 488, 489, K537-541.
Date of Issue:	Apr. 10, 1882
Earliest Known Use:	Feb. 18, 1882
Uses:	Foreign mail rate to Universal Postal Union members
Quantity Issued:	170,894,020

Stamp Features

Size:	20 x 25 mm. (0.8 x 1.0 inches)
Watermark:	None
Grill:	None
Paper:	Soft
Perforations:	12
Secret Mark:	N/A
Colors:	Yellow brown, brown, gray brown.
Varieties:	None

Collectable Stamp Today
Collectable Cancellation Colors:
Black, purple, magenta, blue, red.
Collectable Cancellation Varieties:
Ship, numeral, supplementary mail type F, red express company, China, Japan, Samoa. Puerto Rico.

Value Unused:	$$$$
Value Used:	$$$
Surviving Covers:	17,500
Largest Known Multiple:	Unused: 10 (block)
	Used: 20 (block)

The five-cent Taylor stamp was not popular with the American public. The full-faced portrait of him was too large for the stamp and it did not match the profiles found on the other stamps of the series. So after the assassination of President James A. Garfield, it was decided to honor him on the five-cent stamp. So, a new design was issued in early 1882.

Originally, the stamp was to be black, a symbol of mourning, like the 15-cent stamp issued after the death of Lincoln. However, Garfield's widow suggested that the stamp's color be brown.

The stamp features a background shield, on which is an oval portrait of Garfield. A line of small white beads borders the portrait. The words, U. S. POSTAGE, are at the bottom of the stamp. The words FIVE CENTS are above this line, divided by a large star, which contains the numeral, 5.

Like its preceding five-cent Taylor, the stamp mostly was used for postage to overseas Universal Postal Union members.

AMERICAN INDIGO FIVE-CENT GARFIELD

American Indigo Five-Cent Garfield

Stamp Production

Printer:	American Bank Note Company
Designer:	Thomas F. Morris
Engravers:	Charles Skinner (portrait), Douglas S. Ronaldson (frame and lettering)
Format:	Sheets of 200, cut vertically into 2 panes of 100
Plate Numbers:	K537-541.
Date of Issue:	Feb.18, 1888
Earliest Known Use:	Mar. 15, 1888
Uses:	Foreign mail rate to Universal Postal Union members
Quantity Issued:	58,898,680

Stamp Features

Size:	20 x 25 mm. (0.8 x 1.0 inches)
Watermark:	None
Grill:	None
Paper:	Soft
Perforations:	12
Secret Mark:	N/A
Colors:	Indigo, deep blue.
Varieties:	None

Collectable Stamp Today
Collectable Cancellation Colors:
        Black, purple, magenta, blue.
Collectable Cancellation Varieties:
        supplementary mail type F, China, Japan, Porto Rico, Samoa.

Value Unused:	$$$$
Value Used:	$$$
Surviving Covers:	35,000
Largest Known Multiple:	Unused: 100 (complete pane)
	Used: 10 (block)

On February 18, 1888, the color of the 5-cent Garfield stamp was changed from yellow brown to indigo. It still was printed from the same steam press plates, K537-541 as the old brown stamps. It is the more common color of the two Garfield stamps

This stamp exists on pink paper, found in Portland, Maine in March 1889. The nature of this stamp and its paper has been much debated over the years. Most likely, it is a freak stamp, rather than error or experimental variety.

It is estimated the stamp today can be found on 30,000 to 40,000 covers. The largest unused multiple of the stamp is a complete pane of 100 stamps, used, a block of 10.

Six Cent Bank Note Stamps

1870	National No secret mark	Hard paper	Grilled
1870	National No secret mark	Hard paper	No grill
1873	Continental Secret mark	Hard paper	No grill
1879	American Secret mark	Soft paper	No grill
1882	American Secret mark	Soft paper Re-engraved	No grill

Stamp collectors, especially those with an artistic bent, call the six-cent stamp the best design of the Bank Note series. It features a profile bust of gaunt Abraham Lincoln, looking to the left. The design is from a sculpture by Thomas D. Jones made in 1863-1864. The stamp's bust demonstrates the three-dimensional feel of the Bank Note series. The bust sits inside an oval, itself on a shield. The words, U.S. POSTAGE, are at the top of the design. The words, SIX CENTS, are the bottom, split by the numeral, 6.

This denomination paid the double the basic first-class rate of three cents. After the rate reduction of Sept. 30, 1883 to two cents, there was little use for this issue, except for some odd foreign rates.

Figure 6-24. Basis of the Six-Cent Bank Note Stamp. The design of the six-cent bank note stamp features Lincoln. It is based on a bust by Thomas D. Jones.

NATIONAL GRILLED SIX-CENT LINCOLN

National Grilled Six-Cent Lincoln

Stamp Production

Printer:	National Bank Note Company
Designer:	Butler Packard
Engravers:	Joseph P. Ourdan (portrait), Douglas S. Ronaldson (frame and lettering)
Format:	Sheets of 200, cut vertically into 2 panes of 100
Plate Numbers:	26, 27
Date of Issue:	Apr. 1870
Earliest Known Use:	Apr.11, I870
Uses:	Double-rate first-class domestic mail, Single rate to Great Britain, Germany, after June 1870
Quantity Issued:	1,562,000

Stamp Features

Size:	20 x 25 mm. (0.8 x 1.0 inches)
Watermark:	None
Grill:	H or I
Paper:	Hard
Perforations:	12
Secret Mark:	None
Colors:	Carmine, pale carmine, carmine rose.
Varieties:	Double grill, Split grill, Quadruple split grill, Marginal grill.

Collectable Stamp Today
Collectable Cancellation Colors:
Black, blue, red.

Collectable Cancellation Varieties:
                            Paid.
Value Unused: $$$$$
Value Used: $$$$
Surviving Covers: 9,000
Largest Known Multiple: Unused: 4 (2x2 block)
                            Used: 6 (block)

The National six-cent stamp follows the pattern of being made on hard paper and not having a secret mark. The later Continental secret mark, missing on these stamps, is a strengthening of the first four vertical lines in the lower part of the left ribbon.

The color of the National stamp is deep carmine. This is another way to distinguish the issue from the dull pink six-cent Continental stamp.

The grilled stamps were made at the same time from the same plates as the non-grilled stamps. Most stamps have just a few male points, not complete and heavy grills. The stamp can be found in several grill varieties: double grill, split grill, quadruple split grill, and a marginal grill.

The stamp's main use was for double-rate (half to one ounce) first-class domestic mail. It also paid for single rate mail, overseas to Great Britain and Germany, after June 1870.

NATIONAL UNGRILLED SIX-CENT LINCOLN

National Ungrilled Six-Cent Lincoln

Stamp Production

Printer:	National Bank Note Company
Designer:	Butler Packard
Engravers:	Joseph P. Ourdan (portrait), Douglas S. Ronaldson (frame and lettering)
Format:	Sheets of 200, cut vertically into 2 panes of 100
Plate Numbers:	26, 27
Date of Issue:	Mar. 1870
Earliest Known Use:	Mar. 28,1870
Uses:	Double-rate first-class domestic mail, Single rate to Great Britain, Germany, after June 1870
Quantity Issued:	25,837,000

Stamp Features

Size:	20 x 25 mm. (0.8 x 1.0 inches)
Watermark:	None
Grill:	None
Paper:	Hard
Perforations:	12
Secret Mark:	None
Colors:	Carmine, dark carmine, rose, brown carmine, violet carmine.
Varieties:	Double transfer, Double impression, Double paper

Collectable Stamp Today
Collectable Cancellation Colors:

Black, blue, purple, violet, brown, red, brown, claret, orange red, orange, ultramarine, green.

Collectable Cancellation Varieties:
Paid, Steamship, Paid All, numeral, supplementary mail type A or D, China, Japan.
Value Unused: $$$$$
Value Used: $$$
Surviving Covers: 12,000-15,000
Largest Known Multiple: Unused: 6 (block)
Used: 18 (block)

Figure 6-25. Example of a Six-Cent Bank Note Stamp on a Cover. This stamp, a National six-cent Lincoln without a grill, paid the overseas postage rate to England. This letter was sent from New Jersey to London. It has postal markings from New Jersey, New York City, and London, showing its route of travel.

This stamp is just like the previous issue, with the same hard paper, same missing secret mark, and printed from the same printing plates. The only difference is the absent grill.

The stamp is known with a fine double impression of a portion of the stamp, as well as a double transfer.

This stamp found domestic use on double weight letters and was used on single weight letters to Canada, Great Britain, Prussia, and the German and Austrian states. A vertical half of the stamp has been found on cover used as three cents postage.

CONTINENTAL SIX-CENT LINCOLN

Continental Six-Cent Lincoln

Stamp Production

Printer:	Continental Bank Note Company
Designer:	Butler Packard
Engravers:	Joseph P. Ourdan (portrait), Douglas S. Ronaldson (frame and lettering), Charles Skinner (secret mark)
Format:	Sheets of 200, cut vertically into 2 panes of 100
Plate Numbers:	18, 21, 304, 305.
Date of Issue:	1873
Earliest Known Use:	June 8, 1873
Uses:	Double-rate first-class domestic mail, Single rate to Great Britain, Germany until July 1, 1875
Quantity Issued:	38,311,500

Stamp Features

Size:	20 x 25 mm. (0.8 x 1.0 inches)
Watermark:	None
Grill:	None
Paper:	Hard
Perforations:	12
Secret Mark:	Present
Colors:	Dull pink, brown rose.
Varieties:	Double paper, Ribbed paper, Paper with silk fibers.

Collectable Stamp Today
Collectable Cancellation Colors:
Black, blue, indigo, magenta, purple, violet, orange red, ultramarine, red, green.

Collectable Cancellation Varieties:
numeral, Paid, Paid All, supplementary mail type D, E, or F, railroad, R. P. O., China, Japan.
Value Unused: $$$$
Value Used: $$$
Surviving Covers: 12,000-15,000
Largest Known Multiple: Unused: 50 (block)
Used: 12 (block)

The secret mark, which distinguishes the 6-cent Continental from the earlier National printings, is a strengthening (darkening) of the first four vertical lines of the left side of the lower part of the left ribbon. This secret mark is very obvious. The Continental stamps can be identified by color, too. They are a dull pink instead of the National carmine.

The stamp is found with the Continental Grill, considered just an experimental essay. The stamp is found on the various Continental paper varieties: double paper, ribbed paper, and paper with silk fibers.

The stamp paid the double-rate domestic postage rate. It also paid for postage to Great Britain and Germany before July 1, 1875, when the five-cent Universal Postage Union rate took effect. This stamp is known bisected and used as 3-cents frankage on cover.

 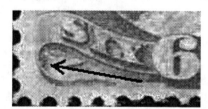

Figure 6-26. Six-Cent Secret Mark. The secret mark of the 6-cent Bank Note stamps is a darkening of the first four vertical lines of the left side of the lower part of the left ribbon. A close up of the National stamp is on the left, the Continental on the right.

AMERICAN SIX-CENT LINCOLN

American Six-Cent Lincoln

Stamp Production

Printer:	American Bank Note Company
Designer:	Butler Packard
Engravers:	Joseph P. Ourdan (portrait), Douglas S. Ronaldson (frame and lettering), Charles Skinner (secret mark)
Format:	Sheets of 200, cut vertically into 2 panes of 100
Plate Numbers:	304 (?), 305 Continental.
Date Issued:	1879
Earliest Known Use:	July 1, 1879
Uses:	Double-rate first-class domestic mail, Single rate mail to Australia and New Zealand
Quantity Issued:	20,738,150

Stamp Features

Size:	20 x 25 mm. (0.8 x 1.0 inches)
Watermark:	None
Grill:	None
Paper:	Soft
Perforations:	12
Secret Mark:	Present
Colors:	Pink, dull pink, brown rose.
Varieties:	None

Collectable Stamp Today
Collectable Cancellation Colors:
                       Black, blue, purple, ultramarine, magenta, red.
Collectable Cancellation Varieties:
                       supplementary mail type F, railroad, numeral, China.
Value Unused: $$$$$
Value Used: $$$
Surviving Covers: 10,000
Largest Known Multiple: Unused: 6 (block)
                       Used: 6 (block)

The stamp is identical to the Continental except that the paper is soft. In fact, it was printed from Continental plates. Continental plates numbered 305 and probably 304 were used. No American six-cent plates were produced. The stamp, therefore, shows the secret mark of the Continental. The light ink and the soft paper that absorbs the canceling ink ruins the appearance of many used six-cent American stamps.

AMERICAN SIX-CENT LINCOLN RE-ENGRAVED

Re-Engraved American Six-Cent Lincoln

Stamp Production
Printer: American Bank Note Company
Designer: Butler Packard

Engravers:	Joseph P. Ourdan (portrait), George H. Seymour (new frame)
Format:	Sheets of 200, cut vertically into 2 panes of 100
Plate Numbers:	426, 427.
Date of Issue:	June 1, 1882
Earliest Known Use:	June 1, 1882 (first day cover)
Uses:	Double-rate first-class domestic mail until Sept. 30, 1883
Quantity Issued:	11,689,400

Stamp Features

Size:	20 x 25 mm. (0.8 x 1.0 inches)
Watermark:	None
Grill:	None
Paper:	Soft
Perforations:	12
Secret Mark:	Present
Colors:	Rose, dull rose, deep brown red.
Varieties:	Double transfer

Collectable Stamp Today
Collectable Cancellation Colors:
Black, magenta, purple, blue, red.
Collectable Cancellation Varieties:
supplementary mail type F

Value Unused:	$$$$
Value Used:	$$$
Surviving Covers:	2,000
Largest Known Multiple:	Unused: 25 (6x4 block)
	Used: 6 (block)

The six-cent American stamp was re-engraved June 1882. A new die was made from the original transfer roll. The frame around the portrait was erased and a new frame was engraved. From this new die, a new transfer roll was made. It was used to make the two new original American plates. On the original stamps, there are four vertical lines from the left side of the shield to the edge of the stamp. On the re-engraved stamps, there are just three lines in the same place.

The stamp lost its main use, paying the double-rate domestic postage rate, after September 30, 1883 because after that date, the domestic postage rate was reduced to two-cents. Therefore, this stamp is less common than the original six-cent American stamp.

Seven-Cent Bank Note Stamps

1870	National	Hard paper	Grilled
	No secret mark		
1870	National	Hard paper	No grill
	No secret mark		
1873	Continental	Hard paper	No grill
	Secret mark		

This first United States seven-cent stamp was issued March 6, 1871, a year after the start of the Bank Note series. It was used to pay postage to Germany, Prussia, and Austria. The mail was sent directly to Germany via the Hamburg-American Line or North German Lloyd ships. That rate of seven cents took effect on July 1, 1870. When this rate for direct mail to Germany was reduced to six cents in 1871, this stamp lost its purpose, but just temporarily. On October 1, 1871, the rate for Germany and Austria for letters sent by Prussian closed mail via England was reduced from ten cents to seven cents. Most seven-cent Bank Note stamps seen today were used for this latter purpose. On January 1, 1872, the postage rate to Denmark was seven cents. In 1873, the seven-cent rate applied to Hungary and Luxembourg, too. When the Universal Postal Union five-cent rate became effective on July 1, 1875, this stamp again lost its purpose and soon was discontinued. Therefore, the 7-cent issues end with the Continental stamp.

The design of the stamp is a large rectangle with balls in the four corners. On the rectangle, there is an oval containing the profile bust of Lincoln's Secretary of War, Edwin M. Stanton. Above the figure are words, U. S. POSTAGE, while below are words SEVEN CENTS, in white, separated in the middle by the numeral, 7.

Figure 6-27. Edwin Stanton.
Stanton was Abraham Lincoln's Secretary of War and is the subject of the seven-cent Bank Note stamps.

Edwin Stanton (1814–69) was Abraham Lincoln's Secretary of War. He was one of the leading political radicals of his administration. After Lincoln's death, Stanton remained in the new President Andrew Johnson's cabinet. Serious differences over Reconstruction policy led Johnson to demand his resignation. When he refused to resign, Stanton barricaded himself in his office. The radicals in Congress, who supported him, initiated impeachment proceedings against Johnson as a result. He died shortly after President Grant appointed him to the Supreme Court.

NATIONAL GRILLED SEVEN-CENT STANTON

National Grilled Seven-Cent Stanton

Stamp Production
Printer: National Bank Note Company
Designer: Butler Packard
Engravers: Joseph P. Ourdan (portrait), Douglas S. Ronaldson (frame and lettering)
:   Sheets of 200, cut vertically into 2 panes of 100
Plate Numbers: 33
Date of Issue: Feb. 1871
Earliest Known Use: Feb. 12, 1871
Uses: Foreign-mail rates to Germany, Prussia, and Austria
Quantity Issued: 800,000

Stamp Features
Size:	20 x 25 mm. (0.8 x 1.0 inches)
Watermark:	None
Grill:	H or I
Paper:	Hard
Perforations:	12
Secret Mark:	None
Colors:	Vermilion, deep vermilion.
Varieties:	Split grill, Double grill, Quadruple split grill, Marginal grill.

Collectable Stamp Today
Collectable Cancellation Colors:
Black, blue, purple, red, green.
Collectable Cancellation Varieties:
Paid
Value Unused:	$$$$$
Value Used:	$$$$
Surviving Covers:	3,000
Largest Known Multiple:	Unused: 6 (block)
	Used: 4 (2x2 block)

All seven-cent Bank Note stamps are on hard paper, as American never printed them. The difference between the National and the Continental stamps is the Continental's secret mark, small semi-circles drawn around the ends of the lines that outline the ornament in the lower right corner of the stamp. The lack of a secret mark indicates a National stamp.

These stamps have an H or I grill. The grills are usually faint and incomplete. The grilled stamps were printed from the same plate, at the same time as the ungrilled National seven-cent stamp. The stamp has the typical grill varieties: split grill, double grill, quadruple split grill, and marginal grill.

Most surviving covers were sent to Germany.

NATIONAL UNGRILLED SEVEN-CENT STANTON

National Ungrilled Seven-Cent Stanton

Stamp Production

Printer:	National Bank Note Company
Designer:	Butler Packard
Engravers:	Joseph P. Ourdan (portrait), Douglas S. Ronaldson (frame and lettering)
Format:	Sheets of 200, cut vertically into 2 panes of 100
Plate Numbers:	33
Date of Issue:	Mar. 1871
Earliest Known Use:	May 11,1871
Uses:	Foreign-mail rate to Germany, Prussia, and Austria
Quantity Issued:	2,070,000

Stamp Features

Size:	20 x 25 mm. (0.8 x 1.0 inches)
Watermark:	None
Grill:	None

Paper:	Hard
Perforations:	12
Secret Mark:	None
Colors:	Vermilion, deep vermilion.
Varieties:	Cracked plate, Double transfer.

Collectable Stamp Today
Collectable Cancellation Colors:
　　　　　　Black, blue, purple, ultramarine, red, green.
Collectable Cancellation Varieties:
　　　　　　Japan.

Value Unused:	$$$$
Value Used:	$$$
Surviving Covers:	10,000
Largest Known Multiple:	Unused: 10 (block)
	Used: 5 (strip)

Like the other National Bank Note stamps, this ungrilled variety is more common than the grilled stamp. The stamp mostly was used on mail to Germany.

CONTINENTAL SEVEN-CENT STANTON

Continental Seven-Cent Stanton

Stamp Production
Printer:	Continental Bank Note Company
Designer:	Butler Packard

Engravers:	Joseph P. Ourdan (portrait), Douglas S. Ronaldson (frame and lettering), Charles Skinner (secret mark)
Format:	Sheets of 200, cut vertically into 2 panes of 100
Plate Numbers:	22
Date of Issue:	1873
Earliest Known Use:	Sept. 10, 1873
Uses:	Foreign-mail rate to Germany, Prussia, and Austria
Quantity Issued:	2,500,000

Stamp Features

Size:	20 x 25 mm. (0.8 x 1.0 inches)
Watermark:	None
Grill:	None
Paper:	Hard
Perforations:	12
Secret Mark:	Present
Colors:	Orange vermilion, vermilion.
Varieties:	Double transfer of SEVEN CENTS (1R), Double transfer in lower left corner, Ribbed paper, Double paper, Paper with silk fibers.

Collectable Stamp Today
Collectable Cancellation Colors:
Black, blue, red, purple, brown.
Collectable Cancellation Varieties:
Paid

Value Unused:	$$$$$
Value Used:	$$$
Surviving Covers:	4,000
Largest Known Multiple:	Unused: 20 (plate block)
	Used: 4 (block)

The secret mark on the seven-cent Continental is easy to see. It is two small semi-circles drawn at the ends of the lines that outline the ornament at the lower right corner of the stamp.

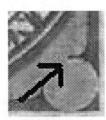 

Figure 6-28. The Secret Mark of the Seven-Cent Bank Note Stamp. The secret mark (on the close on the right) is the extra marks at the base of the ornament on the lower right corner of the stamp.

The stamp exists on the usual Continental paper varieties: ribbed paper, and paper with silk fibers. The Continental essay grill can be found for this 7-cent denomination.

Though more Continental 7-cent stamps were made, they are scarcer on cover than is the National. The largest unused multiple of the Continental 7-cent is a plate number and imprint block of twenty stamps.

With the introduction of the Universal Postal Union five-cent rate, this issue became obsolete. Many of the Continental stamps were destroyed. And no American (soft paper) seven-cent stamps ever were printed.

Ten-Cent Jefferson Bank Note Stamps

1870	National No secret mark	Hard paper	Grilled
1870	National No secret mark	Hard paper	No grill
1873	Continental Secret mark	Hard paper	No grill
1879	American No secret mark	Soft paper	No grill
1879	American Secret mark	Soft paper	No grill
1882	American No secret mark	Soft paper	No grill Re-engraved

The 10-cent Bank Note stamps feature Thomas Jefferson. The stamps' production spanned the entire Bank Note period. It started with the National (both grilled and ungrilled) continued through Continental (both with and without a secret mark) and ended with the American (both original and re-engraved varieties).

The ten-cent stamps originally were used on odd rate international mail, especially to the Caribbean. The stamps saw much use on registered mail from 1875 onward, when that rate was changed to ten-cents. At the same time, the stamp began paying the double the Universal Postal Union rate of five cents.

The design of the ten-cent bank note stamp consists of an oval on a large faint shield atop a dark rectangle. The oval contains a bust of Thomas Jefferson, looking to the left. It is based on a plaster model of him made by Hiram Powers. Above the oval are the words, U. S. POSTAGE. Below are the words, TEN CENTS, separated in the middle by the numeral, 10.

Figure 6-29. Jefferson Model. The ten-cent Bank Note stamp features Thomas Jefferson. The bust was modeled after this plaster figure of him created by Hiram Powers between 1860 and 1862.

NATIONAL GRILLED TEN-CENT JEFFERSON

National Grilled Ten-Cent Jefferson

Stamp Production

Printer:	National Bank Note Company
Designer:	Butler Packard
Engravers:	Luigi (Louis) Delnoce (portrait), Douglas S. Ronaldson (frame and lettering)
Format:	Sheets of 200, cut vertically into 2 panes of 100
Plate Numbers:	18, 19, 48, 49 (all uncertain)
Date of Issue:	Apr. 1870
Earliest Known Use:	May 6, 1870
Uses:	Foreign rates, especially Caribbean.
Quantity Issued:	479,000

Stamp Features

Size:	20 x 25 mm. (0.8 x 1.0 inches)
Watermark:	None
Grill:	H
Paper:	Hard
Perforations:	12
Secret Mark:	None
Colors:	Brown, yellow brown, dark brown.
Varieties:	Double grill, Split grill, Marginal grill.

Collectable Stamp Today

Collectable Cancellation Colors:	
	Black, blue, red.
Collectable Cancellation Varieties:	
	Steamship, Honolulu Paid All
Value Unused:	$$$$$
Value Used:	$$$$
Surviving Covers:	8,000
Largest Known Multiple:	Unused: 6 (block)
	Used: 6 (block)

The distinguishing characteristics of the National stamp from the other ten-cent Bank Note stamps are its hard paper and the lack of a secret mark. The ten-cent secret mark is a crescent inside the ball that extends from the lower portion of the right side of the label that contains the words, U. S. POSTAGE. Since there is an American ten-cent issue without a secret mark, the paper type also must be checked.

The grilled National 10-cent stamp is less common than its ungrilled counterpart. Only the H size grill can be found on the ten-cent stamp. The stamp exists in several grill varieties: double grill, split grill and marginal grill.

This is relatively uncommon stamp on cover, because the stamp, then, had limited use on odd foreign postage rates.

NATIONAL UNGRILLED TEN-CENT JEFFERSON

National Ungrilled Ten-Cent Jefferson

Stamp Production
Printer: National Bank Note Company
Designer: Butler Packard
Engravers: Luigi (Louis) Delnoce (portrait), Douglas S. Ronaldson (frame and lettering)
Format: Sheets of 200, cut vertically into 2 panes of 100
Plate Numbers: 18, 19, 48, 49.
Date of Issue: Apr. 1870
Earliest Known Use: May 14, 1870
Uses: Foreign rates, especially Caribbean.
Quantity Issued: 10,166,500

Stamp Features
Size: 20 x 25 mm. (0.8 x 1.0 inches)
Watermark: None
Grill: None
Paper: Hard
Perforations: 12
Secret Mark: None
Colors: Brown, dark brown, yellow brown.
Varieties: Double transfer

Collectable Stamp Today
Collectable Cancellation Colors:
Black, blue, purple, magenta, ultramarine, red, orange red, green, orange, brown.

Collectable Cancellation Varieties:
Paid All, Steamship, supplementary mail type A or D, China, Japan, St. Thomas.
Value Unused: $$$$$
Value Used: $$$
Surviving Covers: 20,000
Largest Known Multiple: Unused: 10 (block)
Used: 4 (2x2 block)

The stamp is identical to the ungrilled National ten-cent variety, except, of course, for the grill. Like the other denominations of the series, both stamps were made from the same printing plates at the same time. It is much more common than its grilled counterpart. The stamp must, of course, be on hard paper for there is an American printing of this stamp that is identical to it, except for the soft paper.

There are 15,000 to 25,000 covers with the stamp, most sent to foreign destinations.

The largest unused multiple of the stamp is a block of 10, used, a block of four stamps.

CONTINENTAL TEN-CENT JEFFERSON

Continental Ten-Cent Jefferson

Stamp Production

Printer:	Continental Bank Note Company
Designer:	Butler Packard
Engravers:	Luigi (Louis) Delnoce (portrait), Douglas S. Ronaldson (frame and lettering), Charles Skinner (secret mark)
Format:	Sheets of 200, cut vertically into 2 panes of 100
Plate Numbers:	23, 25, 302, 303
Date of Issue:	June or July 1873
Earliest Known Use:	Aug. 2, 1873
Uses:	Foreign rates. Registry fee after July 1, 1875. Double five cent Universal Postal Union rate after July 1, 1875
Quantity Issued:	21,471,000

Stamp Features

Size:	20 x 25 mm. (0.8 x 1.0 inches)
Watermark:	None
Grill:	None
Paper:	Hard
Perforations:	12
Secret Mark:	Present
Colors:	Brown, dark brown, yellow brown.
Varieties:	Double transfer, Double paper, Ribbed paper, Paper with silk fibers.
Errors:	Horizontal pair vertical imperforate in between

Collectable Stamp Today
Collectable Cancellation Colors:
Black, blue, purple, red, magenta, orange, orange red, brown, green.
Collectable Cancellation Varieties:
Paid, P. D. in a circle, town, Steamship, supplemental mail type E or F, Alaska, China, Japan.

Value Unused:	$$$$$
Value Used:	$$$
Surviving Covers:	20,000
Largest Known Multiple:	Unused: 16 (block)
	Used: 8 (block)

Figure 6-30. Ten-Cent Bank Note Secret Mark. The secret mark for the ten-cent Bank Note stamp is one of the more obvious. It is the addition of a comma in the ball that is under the E of POSTAGE, at the right side of the stamp (right close up).

This stamp was first used during the summer of 1873. It differs from the National printing by its added secret mark. This is a small semi-circle in the small ball that is directly under the E of POSTAGE, at the top right of the stamp.

The stamp can be found on the Continental paper varieties: double paper, ribbed paper, and paper with silk fibers. The Continental grill essay also is found on the 10-cent denomination.

After July 1, 1875, the stamp paid the new ten-cent registry fee. The registry fee remained that rate until it was lowered to eight cents on January 1, 1893. It also paid the double five-cent Universal Postal Union rate, also effective July 1, 1875.

The stamp exists with a missing perforation error. There are two horizontal pairs that are missing the vertical perforations in between.

AMERICAN TEN-CENT JEFFERSON, NO SECRET MARK

American Ten-Cent Jefferson Without a Secret Mark

Stamp Production
Printer: American Bank Note Company
Designer: Butler Packard
Engravers: Luigi (Louis) Delnoce (portrait), Douglas S. Ronaldson (frame and lettering).

Format:	Sheets of 200, cut vertically into 2 panes of 100
Plate Numbers:	302, 303 (Continental); 377, 378
Date of Issue:	1879
Earliest Known Use:	Sept. 5, 1879
Uses:	Double five-cent Universal Postal Union rate. Registry fee.
Quantity Issued:	11,000,000

Stamp Features

Size:	20 x 25 mm. (0.8 x 1.0 inches)
Watermark:	None
Grill:	None
Paper:	Soft
Perforations:	12
Secret Mark:	None
Colors:	Brown, yellow brown.
Varieties:	Double transfer, Double paper.

Collectable Stamp Today

Collectable Cancellation Colors:
Black, blue, red, magenta.

Collectable Cancellation Varieties:
Paid, supplementary mail type F, China.

Value Unused:	$$$$$
Value Used:	$$$
Surviving Covers:	10,000
Largest Known Multiple:	Unused: 12 (block)
	Used: 5 (strip)

There are two varieties of the American ten-cent stamp, one with and one without the Continental secret mark. One variety, like the National stamp, does not have the added arc in the ball, under the E of POSTAGE. The second variety, like the Continental, does.

The Continental plates 302 and 303 made all of the American stamps with the secret mark on soft paper. They also made some of those American issues, missing the secret mark. In fact, there are pairs and blocks of the ten-cent American, with some stamps with and some without the secret mark. The secret mark may have worn off with use from certain positions of these plates. Another possibility is that the secret mark area of the plate could have filled with debris or ink on a few positions. Or as a third possibility, the printing plate might have warped and the uneven surface did not print the secret mark.

The variety without the secret mark comes not only from the old Continental plates 302 and 303 but also the new American plates 377 and 378. Since the American-made plates 377 and 378 produced stamps, all lacking the secret mark, the fine curved line of the secret mark must have broken away from the transfer roll, before the new American plates were made.

The stamp can be found on 8,000 to 12,000 surviving covers.

The largest unused multiple is a block of four, containing stamps both with and without a secret mark, and 12, with all stamps missing the secret mark.

AMERICAN TEN-CENT JEFFERSON, SECRET MARK

American Ten-Cent Jefferson With a Secret Mark

Stamp Production

Printer:	American Bank Note Company
Designer:	Butler Packard
Engravers:	Luigi (Louis) Delnoce (portrait), Douglas S. Ronaldson (frame and lettering), Charles Skinner (secret mark).
Format:	Sheets of 200, cut vertically into 2 panes of 100
Plate Numbers:	302, 303 (Continental)
Date Issued:	1878
Earliest Known Use:	Oct. 5, 1878
Uses:	Double five-cent Universal Postal Union rate. Registry fee.
Quantity Issued:	11,000,000

Stamp Features

Size:	20 x 25 mm. (0.8 x 1.0 inches)
Watermark:	None
Grill:	None
Paper:	Soft
Perforations:	12
Secret Mark:	Present
Colors:	Brown, yellow brown, black brown.
Varieties:	Double transfer, Cracked plate

Collectable Stamp Today
Collectable Cancellation Colors:
Black, blue, ultramarine, purple, magenta, red, green.
Collectable Cancellation Varieties:
Paid, supplementary mail type F, numeral, printed star precancellation of Glen Allen, Virginia.

Value Unused:	$$$$$
Value Used:	$$$
Surviving Covers:	7,000
Largest Known Multiple:	Unused: 6 (block)
	Used: 12 (block)

The American ten-cent stamp with the secret mark is twice as common as those stamps without the mark. The stamps with the secret mark are found from earlier dates, adding evidence that the missing secret mark was the result of wear and tear to the plate.

AMERICAN TEN-CENT JEFFERSON, RE-ENGRAVED

Re-Engraved American Ten-Cent Jefferson

Stamp Production
Printer: American Bank Note Company
Designer: Butler Packard
Engravers: Luigi (Louis) Delnoce (portrait), Edward F. Bourke (new frame)
Format: Sheets of 200, cut vertically into 2 panes of 100
Plate Numbers: 403, 403A, 404, 404A, 480, 481, M547-551 (steam press).
Date of Issue: 1879
Earliest Known Use: Sept. 5, 1879
Uses: Double five-cent Universal Postal Union rate. Registry fee.
Quantity Issued: 11,000,000

Stamp Features
Size: 20 x 25 mm. (0.8 x 1.0 inches)
Watermark: None
Grill: None
Paper: Soft
Perforations: 12
Secret Mark: None
Colors: Brown, yellow brown, orange brown, purple brown, olive brown, black brown.
Varieties: Double impression.

Collectable Stamp Today
Collectable Cancellation Colors:
Black, purple, magenta, blue, red, green.

Collectable Cancellation Varieties:
numeral, Paid, supplementary mail type F, express company cancellation, China, Japan, Samoa.

Value Unused: $$$$
Value Used: $$
Surviving Covers: 15,000
Largest Known Multiple: Unused: 100 (complete pane)
Used: 10 (block)

Figure 6-31. Example of a Ten-Cent Bank Note Stamp on a Cover. This letter was sent from Hartford, Connecticut to New York City. It has 2-cent Bank Note stamp that paid the first-class postage rate. It also has a 10-cent re-engraved Bank Note stamp that paid the registry fee as noted by the markings on the lower left corner of the cover and the handwritten markings to the left of the stamps.

Figure 6-32. Close Up of a Ten-Cent Re-Engraved Bank Note Stamp. The easiest way to tell if a ten-cent bank note stamp is re-engraved is to count the number of lines between the left edge of the portrait and the edge of the shield. There are four lines between on the re-engraving, as shown here instead of five on the original stamp. Note some lines in Jefferson's portrait were added and others were strengthened.

The ten-cent American bank note stamp was re-engraved, April 1882. Using an old National transfer roll, which had no secret mark, a new die was made. The original frame was erased and remade, resulting in this new die. Also, the background of the stamp was deepened. The portrait was retouched, lines were added and some were strengthened, especially in the hair above Jefferson's forehead.

The best test for this stamp from the rest is the number of lines between the left edge of the portrait and the edge of the shield. There are four lines between on the re-engraving, instead of five on the original stamp. Also, the words, U. S. POSTAGE, touch the shield at the left instead of there being a small space in between.

Twelve Cent Clay Bank Note Stamps

1872	National No secret mark	Hard paper	Grilled
1870	National No secret mark	Hard paper	No grill
1874	Continental Secret mark	Hard paper	No grill

The 12-cent Bank Note stamp features Henry Clay. The stamps paid for a variety of odd and multiple rate foreign uses. It also paid for the quadruple domestic first class rate (from one and a half to 2 ounces), of the basic postal rate of three cents. Only National and Continental made twelve-cent stamps. Since the stamp saw limited use, no twelve-cent American Bank Note stamps were printed.

The design of the twelve-cent features a lined rectangular frame, with beveled edges. On this panel there is an oval with a profile bust of Henry Clay by Joel T. Hart. Above the oval are the words, in white capitals. U. S. POSTAGE. Below the oval are the words, TWELVE CENTS, separated in the middle by the numeral, 12.

Henry Clay (1777-1852), was one of the greatest American statesmen. He was secretary of state under John Quincy Adams and unsuccessful candidate for the presidency in 1824, 1832, and 1844. He was one of the most influential political leaders in American history. His genius in the art of compromise three times resolved political conflicts that threatened to tear the nation apart in the years before the Civil War. That won him the title, "The Great Pacificator."

NATIONAL GRILLED TWELVE CENT CLAY

National Grilled Twelve-Cent Clay

Stamp Production
Printer: National Bank Note Company
Designer: Butler Packard
Engravers: Luigi (Louis) Delnoce (portrait), Douglas S. Ronaldson (frame and lettering)
Format: Sheets of 200, cut vertically into 2 panes of 100
Plate Numbers: 24
Date of Issue: April 1870
Earliest Known Use: June 17, 1870
Uses: Foreign rates. Multiple (quadruple) domestic rate.
Quantity Issued: 66,000

Stamp Features
Size: 20 x 25 mm. (0.8 x 1.0 inches)
Watermark: None
Grill: H
Paper: Hard
Perforations: 12
Secret Mark: None
Colors: Dull violet
Varieties: Split grill, Marginal grill.

Collectable Stamp Today
Collectable Cancellation Colors:
Black, blue, red.
Collectable Cancellation Varieties:
Paid All
Value Unused: $$$$$$
Value Used: $$$$$
Surviving Covers: 10
Largest Known Multiple: Unused: 4 (2x2 block)
Used: 2 (strip)

All twelve-cent National stamps are uncommon. The version with a grill is extra scarce. The grill almost always is faint and consists of only a few grill points. The stamp collector should beware of the many fake copies with phony grills on the market. The stamp can be found with the grill varieties: split grill and marginal grill.

The distinguishing feature between the National and Continental stamps is the shape of the round ball at the lower portion of the 2 of the numeral, 12. This ball is round on the National stamp, while on the Continental, this area has the crescent-shaped secret mark.

NATIONAL UNGRILLED TWELVE-CENT CLAY

National Ungrilled Twelve-Cent Clay

Stamp Production

Printer:	National Bank Note Company
Designer:	Butler Packard
Engravers:	Luigi (Louis) Delnoce (portrait), Douglas S. Ronaldson (frame and lettering)
Format:	Sheets of 200, cut vertically into 2 panes of 100
Plate Numbers:	24
Date of Issue:	1870
Earliest Known Use:	July 9, 1870
Uses:	Foreign rates. Multiple (quadruple) domestic rate.
Quantity Issued:	3,263,845

Stamp Features

Size:	20 x 25 mm. (0.8 x 1.0 inches)
Watermark:	None
Grill:	None
Paper:	Hard
Perforations:	12
Secret Mark:	None
Colors:	Dull violet, violet, dark violet.
Varieties:	Colored dot in top center of oval frame. .

Collectable Stamp Today

Collectable Cancellation Colors:

Black, blue, magenta, red, orange, green.

Collectable Cancellation Varieties:

town, Supplementary Mail Type A or D, Paid All, Steamship, Japan.

Value Unused:	$$$$$
Value Used:	$$$$
Surviving Covers:	800
Largest Known Multiple:	Unused: 12 (block)
	Used: 5 (strip)

The ungrilled issue is the more common version of the twelve-cent National Bank Note Company stamp. Except for missing the grill, it is identical to the grilled stamp. Sounding like a broken CD, it was printed from the same plate as it, at the same time.

Figure 6-33. Example of a Twelve-Cent Bank Note Stamp on a Cover. The twelve-cent Bank Note stamp paid for a variety of odd overseas foreign rates. Shown is a letter sent to Turkey from Massachusetts, franked with a twelve-cent National ungrilled stamp.

CONTINENTAL TWELVE-CENT CLAY

Continental Twelve-Cent Clay

Stamp Production
Printer: Continental Bank Note Company
Designer: Butler Packard
Engravers: Luigi (Louis) Delnoce (portrait), Douglas S. Ronaldson
                           (frame and lettering), Charles Skinner (secret mark)
Format: Sheets of 200, cut vertically into 2 panes of 100
Plate Numbers: 24, 137.
Date of Issue: 1874
Earliest Known Use: Jan. 3, 1874
Uses: Foreign rates. Multiple (quadruple) domestic rate.
Quantity Issued: 2,915,000

Stamp Features
Size: 20 x 25 mm. (0.8 x 1.0 inches)
Watermark: None
Grill: None
Paper: Hard
Perforations: 12
Secret Mark: Present
Colors: Blackish violet.
Varieties: Ribbed paper.

Collectable Stamp Today
Collectable Cancellation Colors:
                           Black, blue, ultramarine, brown, red.
Collectable Cancellation Varieties:
                           town, Supplementary Mail Type D, Japan.
Value Unused: $$$$$

Value Used: $$$$
Surviving Covers: 2,500
Largest Known Multiple: Unused: 6 (block)
                        Used: 4 (2x2 block)

Figure 6-34. Twelve-Cent Secret Mark. The twelve-cent secret is found in the end of the balls that forms part of the numeral, 2. They are crescent shaped (right) rather than round (left).

The Continental secret mark of this stamp is the easiest of all to see. It is found in the end of the ball of the numeral, 2. It is crescent-shaped rather than round. The Continental 12-cent stamp is beautiful stamp. It is darker, compared with the National, making the tiny details of the stamp stand out.

The stamp, like all the Continental Bank Note stamps, is on hard paper. It can be found on the Continental ribbed paper variety and with the Continental essay grill.

Fifteen Cent Webster Bank Note Stamps

1870	National No secret mark	Hard paper	Grilled
1870	National No secret mark	Hard paper	No grill
1873	Continental Secret mark	Hard paper	No grill
1879	American Secret mark	Soft paper	No grill

Controversy and confusion follow the fifteen-cent Bank Note stamp. The denomination paid the 15-cent registration fee, until it was lowered to 10-cents in 1875. It also paid for a variety of odd overseas postage rates.

Figure 6-35. Daniel Webster. The design of the fifteen-cent Bank Note stamps features a bust of Webster by S. V. Clevenge.

The design followed the general design of the rest of the Bank Note series. The stamp features the American statesman, Daniel Webster. A bust of Webster, by S. V. Clevenge, looking to the left, sits on an oval. There are triangles, in of the each four corners of the stamp. The words, U. S. POSTAGE, follow the arc at the top of the portrait oval, while the words, FIFTEEN CENTS, are below Webster. The numeral, 15, is at the bottom center of the stamp, splitting the words, FIFTEEN CENTS.

Daniel Webster, (1782-1852) was a statesman, lawyer, and orator. He was a strong advocate for American nationalism. Webster's views helped to preserve the Union in the years before the Civil War.

The basic problem of the fifteen-cent Bank Note denomination is how to tell apart from each other the two hard paper stamps, the National and the Continental. The ink shades are partially helpful, differing between the two companies. The lighter shade and more yellow stamps usually are Continentals. But to a non-expert eye, they look very much alike.

What about the usual distinguishing feature between the National and Continental stamps, the secret mark? It suppose to be is the addition of V-shaped lines of color in the lower part of the upper left triangle of the stamp. It is quite a subtle difference and not found on all fifteen-cent Continental and American stamps.

The famous 19th century stamp expert, Brookman, believed the dark area was not truly a secret mark. He felt that the heavy line at the bottom of the upper left triangle was just the result of plate wear. Excessive plate use wore off the edges of the triangle's lines leading to more ink at the bottom of the triangle.

There are other wearing differences between the National and the Continental. The National plate printed stamps with many fine lines on the four corner triangles and at the two ends of the band that contains the words, U.S. POSTAGE. The more worn plate used by the time Continental and American produced stamps whose lines are indistinct or incomplete.

NATIONAL GRILLED FIFTEEN CENT WEBSTER

National Grilled Fifteen-Cent Webster

Stamp Production
Printer: National Bank Note Company
Designer: Butler Packard
Engravers: Luigi (Louis) Delnoce (portrait), Douglas S. Ronaldson (frame and lettering)
Format: Sheets of 200, cut vertically into 2 panes of 100
Plate Numbers: 20
Date of Issue: Apr. 1870
Earliest Known Use: June 2, 1870

Uses:	Registry rate (1870-74). Single rate to South Africa.
Quantity Issued:	558,000

Stamp Features

Size:	20 x 25 mm. (0.8 x 1.0 inches)
Watermark:	None
Grill:	H
Paper:	Hard
Perforations:	12
Secret Mark:	None
Colors:	Orange, bright orange, deep orange.
Varieties:	Split grill, Double grill, Quadruple split grill.

Collectable Stamp Today
Collectable Cancellation Colors:

	Black, blue, purple, red, green.
Collectable Cancellation Varieties:	
	None
Value Unused:	$$$$$
Value Used:	$$$$$
Surviving Covers:	500
Largest Known Multiple:	Unused: 4 (2x2 block)
	Used: 4 (2x2 block)

These fifteen-cent National stamps don't have either the so-called secret mark or the plate wear area in the lower part of the upper left triangle. But this test is not perfect. The printing on the National is sharper than on the Continental, as they were made from new plates.

Like all National stamps, it is found on hard paper. And like other grilled National stamps, it is much less common than its ungrilled counterpart. This stamp exists in the typical grilled varieties of a split grill, double grill, and quadruple split grill. It was used mainly to pay the registry fee.

NATIONAL UNGRILLED FIFTEEN-CENT WEBSTER

National Ungrilled Fifteen-Cent Webster

Stamp Production

Printer:	National Bank Note Company
Designer:	Butler Packard
Engravers:	Luigi (Louis) Delnoce (portrait), Douglas S. Ronaldson (frame and lettering)

Format:	Sheets of 200, cut vertically into 2 panes of 100
Plate Numbers:	20
Date of Issue:	1870
Earliest Known Use:	June 24, 1870
Uses:	Registry rate (1870-74). Single rate to South Africa.
Quantity Issued:	5,033,300

Stamp Features

Size:	20 x 25 mm. (0.8 x 1.0 inches)
Watermark:	None
Grill:	None
Paper:	Hard
Perforations:	12
Secret Mark:	None
Colors:	Bright orange, deep orange.
Varieties:	Double impression.

Collectable Stamp Today
Collectable Cancellation Colors:
Black, blue, magenta, ultramarine, red.
Collectable Cancellation Varieties:
Paid, Steamship, supplementary mail type A or F, China.

Value Unused:	$$$$$
Value Used:	$$$$
Surviving Covers:	2,500
Largest Known Multiple:	Unused: 6 (block)
	Used: 6 (block)

This stamp is identical to ungrilled variety except for of course for the grill! It was printed from the same plate at the same time as the grilled version. It is the more common of the two stamps. The stamp mostly was used for the registry rate.

CONTINENTAL FIFTEEN-CENT WEBSTER

Continental Fifteen-Cent Webster

Stamp Production

Printer:	Continental Bank Note Company
Designer:	Butler Packard
Engravers:	Luigi (Louis) Delnoce (portrait), Douglas S. Ronaldson (frame and lettering), Charles Skinner (secret mark)
Format:	Sheets of 200, cut vertically into 2 panes of 100
Plate Numbers:	31
Date of Issue:	1873
Earliest Known Use:	July 22,1873
Uses:	Registry rate (1873-74). Multiple and misc. foreign rates.
Quantity Issued:	3,052,000

Stamp Features

Size:	20 x 25 mm. (0.8 x 1.0 inches)
Watermark:	None
Grill:	None
Paper:	Hard
Perforations:	12
Secret Mark:	Present
Colors:	Yellow orange, pale orange, reddish orange.
Varieties:	Paper with silk fibers, Ribbed paper, Double paper.

Collectable Stamp Today
Collectable Cancellation Colors:
                        Black, blue, purple, red, green, brown.
Collectable Cancellation Varieties:
                        supplementary mail type E or F, Steamship, numeral,
                        China, Porto Rico.
Value Unused: $$$$$
Value Used: $$$$
Surviving Covers: 5,000
Largest Known Multiple: Unused: 14 (block)
                        Used: 6 (block)

The heavy line at the bottom of the upper left triangle defines the Continental 15-cent stamp. Whether this is true secret mark added by a Continental engraver, or the result of plate wear is an open debate. In general, the Continental stamp is less sharp and has less fine lines than its National counterpart. The Continental stamps are a lighter shade, but the difference is subtle. Still the best way to tell a Continental fifteen-cent stamp is that it is less sharp and has less fine lines showing than its National counterpart.

The Continental 15-cent stamp exists in the ribbed paper, double paper and added silk fiber varieties. The stamp can be found with the Continental grill, which is an essay.

It mainly paid for the registry fee.

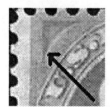 

Figure 6-36. Fifteen-Cent Bank Note Secret Mark??? Classically, the extra heavy line forming a "V" at the bottom of the upper left triangle is the secret mark of the Continental 15-cent Bank Note stamps (right). Whether this is truly a secret mark, added by a Continental engraver, or much more likely, the result of plate wear is open to debate.

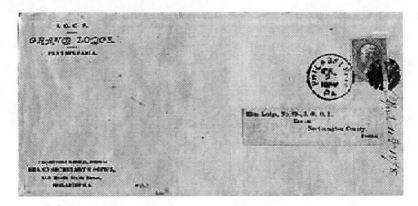

Figure 6-37. Example of a Fifteen-Cent Bank Note Stamp on a Cover. Here is an example of a Continental fifteen-cent Bank Note stamp on cover, paying a multiple (5 times) weight domestic rate.

AMERICAN FIFTEEN-CENT WEBSTER

American Fifteen-Cent Webster

Stamp Production

Printer:	American Bank Note Company
Designer:	Butler Packard
Engravers:	Luigi (Louis) Delnoce (portrait), Douglas S. Ronaldson (frame and lettering), Charles Skinner (secret mark)
Format:	Sheets of 200, cut vertically into 2 panes of 100

Plate Numbers:	31 (Continental).
Date of Issue:	1879
Earliest Known Use:	Jan. 20,1879
Uses:	Multiple and misc. foreign rates.
Quantity Issued:	14,405,240

Stamp Features

Size:	20 x 25 mm. (0.8 x 1.0 inches)
Watermark:	None
Grill:	None
Paper:	Soft
Perforations:	12
Secret Mark:	Present
Colors:	Red orange, orange, yellow orange.
Varieties:	Double transfer.

Collectable Stamp Today
Collectable Cancellation Colors:
Black, blue, purple, magenta, ultramarine, red.
Collectable Cancellation Varieties:
Steamship, supplementary mail type E or F, China, Japan.

Value Unused:	$$$$
Value Used:	$$$
Surviving Covers:	7,500
Largest Known Multiple:	Unused: 100 (complete pane)
	Used: 20 (block)

The soft paper distinguishes the American 15-cent Bank Note stamps from the others. These stamps were printed from plate 31, the same plate made and used by the Continental. However, the American stamps are crisper. In fact, they are closer in appearance to the National stamps. The reason for the paradox is the soft paper better absorbed the ink even though the plate was more worn. The stamp also can be identified by its red-orange shade.

This, by far, is the most common 15-cent Bank Note series stamp, even though the registry rate was now lower.

Twenty-Four-Cent Scott Bank Note Stamps

1870	National	Grilled	
1870	National	No grill	
1873	Continental	No grill	? Difference

The twenty-four-cent Bank Note stamps feature General Winfield Scott. The stamp was used for high foreign postage rates. But the stamp became obsolete when the Universal Postal Union rates took effect for most foreign countries. That is why the stamp was discontinued during its Continental Bank Note printing. Therefore, there are no American (soft paper) twenty-four-cent bank note stamps.

The design of the stamp differs from the lower denominations. It features a left-facing bust of Scott by Coffee in an oval. Above the oval are thirteen stars. The central stars contain the letters of the words, U.S. POSTAGE. Below the bust, are the words, TWENTY FOUR CENTS in two lines. The upper corners of the stamp have the numerals, 24.

Winfield Scott (1786-1866) was a hero of the War of 1812 and Black Hawk War, commander of U.S. forces in the Mexican War, and unsuccessful Whig presidential candidate in 1852. Scott is nicknamed "Old Fuss and Feathers" because of his love of military pomp and protocol. He was the Union's first general-in-chief at the start of the Civil War. He developed the Anaconda Plan, which eventually became the Union strategy for winning the Civil War.

The mystery of the twenty-four cent Bank Note stamps is how to tell a National from a Continental issue. Both are printed on hard paper. There is no secret mark, the usual difference. In fact, Continental used the National plates. Since the ink color varies greatly among individual stamps, identification based on color is not possible. If the stamp has a grill, identification is easy as only National stamps were routinely grilled. If the stamp is ungrilled, as of today, there is no known distinguishing characteristic. Therefore, there is only one known certain Continental twenty-four cent stamp. The Philatelic Foundation certified it since it as such since it was printed on vertically ribbed paper and only Continental used this type of paper.

All the remaining ungrilled twenty-four cent bank note stamps, by default, are classified as National.

Figure 6-38. Winfield Scott. Scott was an American General and military hero and is the subject of the twenty-four cent Bank Note stamps.

NATIONAL GRILLED TWENTY-FOUR-CENT SCOTT

National Grilled Twenty-Four-Cent Scott

Stamp Production
Printer: National Bank Note Company
Designer: Butler Packard
Engravers: Joseph P. Ourdan (portrait), Douglas S. Ronaldson (frame and lettering)
Format: Sheets of 200, cut vertically into 2 panes of 100

Plate Numbers:	21
Date of Issue:	1870
Earliest Known Use:	July 11, 1872
Uses:	Multiple or odd foreign rates.
Quantity Issued:	8,500

Stamp Features

Size:	20 x 25 mm. (0.8 x 1.0 inches)
Watermark:	None
Grill:	H
Paper:	Hard
Perforations:	12
Secret Mark:	None
Colors:	Purple
Varieties:	Double grill, Split grill, Quadruple split grill, marginal grill.

Collectable Stamp Today
Collectable Cancellation Colors:
Black, red, blue, purple.
Collectable Cancellation Varieties:
None

Value Unused:	$$$$$$
Value Used:	$$$$$
Surviving Covers:	3
Largest Known Multiple:	Unused: 1
	Used: 2

The twenty-four cent National grilled stamp is uncommon and therefore expensive to buy today. The great nineteenth century stamp expert, Brookman, estimated that 9 out of 10 copies of this stamp he saw were fakes with added grills. The color of this stamp is almost always changed or faded from the original deep purple ink.

This stamp is known on cover but there are only three total. There are no known unused multiples of the stamps, only singles are known. The largest used multiple is a pair, which also has a double grill.

NATIONAL UNGRILLED TWENTY-FOUR-CENT SCOTT

National Ungrilled Twenty-Four-Cent Scott

Stamp Production

Printer:	National Bank Note Company
Designer:	Butler Packard
Engravers:	Joseph P. Ourdan (portrait), Douglas S. Ronaldson (frame and lettering)
Format:	Sheets of 200, cut vertically into 2 panes of 100
Plate Numbers:	21
Date of Issue:	1870
Earliest Known Use:	Nov. 18, 1870
Uses:	Multiple or odd foreign rates.
Quantity Issued:	1,144,400

Stamp Features

Size:	20 x 25 mm. (0.8 x 1.0 inches)
Watermark:	None
Grill:	None
Paper:	Hard
Perforations:	12
Secret Mark:	None
Colors:	Purple, bright purple.
Varieties:	Double paper.

Collectable Stamp Today
Collectable Cancellation Colors:
Black, red, blue, purple.
Collectable Cancellation Varieties:

	Paid, town, Steamship, supplementary mail type A, D or F.
Value Unused:	$$$$$
Value Used:	$$$$
Surviving Covers:	200
Largest Known Multiple:	Unused: 6 (block)
	Used: 16 (block)

The stamp is much more common than its grilled counterpart. Like the other twenty-four cent bank note stamps, it is a color changeling due to the combination of light, paper, and time exposure. The stamp can be found on double paper.

CONTINENTAL TWENTY-FOUR-CENT SCOTT

Continental Twenty-Four-Cent Scott

Stamp Production

Printer:	Continental Bank Note Company
Designer:	Butler Packard
Engravers:	Joseph P. Ourdan (portrait), Douglas S. Ronaldson (frame and lettering)
Format:	Sheets of 200, cut vertically into 2 panes of 100
Plate Numbers:	National 21
Date of Issue:	Jan.1875
Earliest Known Use:	Unknown

Uses:	Multiple or odd foreign rates, especially India and South America
Quantity Issued:	365,000

Stamp Features

Size:	20 x 25 mm. (0.8 x 1.0 inches)
Watermark:	None
Grill:	None
Paper:	Hard
Perforations:	12
Secret Mark:	None
Colors:	Purple
Varieties:	Ribbed paper

Collectable Stamp Today
Collectable Cancellation Colors:
None.
Collectable Cancellation Varieties:
None.

Value Unused:	None known
Value Used:	$$$$$$$$
Surviving Covers:	0
Largest Known Multiple:	Unused: 0
	Used: 1

The 24-cent Continental is a frustration to the collector of classic United States stamps. On one hand, it is known that 365,000 24-cent Continentals were printed between January 1 and June 30, 1875. On the other hand, there is no distinction between it and the National stamp. The Continentals were printed from the old National Plate 21. The plate was not altered from the National Bank Note Company by the addition of a secret mark. Over the years, experts have tried to classify the twenty-four-cent Continental apart from the National by means of color or paper, without any success. For the longest time, no proven 24-cent Continental stamp was proven to exist. The issue even was nicknamed the "Lost Continental." Finally, in the late 1960's, a Sand Diego stamp collector, Al Magazzu found the first and only copy of the stamp. Therefore, today, the only certain 24-cent Continental is the unique stamp found on vertically ribbed paper. That is because only Continental used such paper, not National.

Thirty-Cent Hamilton Bank Note Stamps

1870	National	Hard paper	Grilled
	No secret mark	Black	
1870	National	Hard paper	No grill
	No secret mark	Black	
1874	Continental	Hard paper	No grill
	No secret mark		Grayish or greenish black
1879	American	Soft paper	No grill
	Secret mark		Full or greenish black
1888	American	Soft paper	No grill
	Secret mark		Orange brown

The thirty-cent Bank Note stamp paid multiples of various domestic and foreign rates. The stamp's design followed the pattern of the rest of the series. In the center of the stamp, inside a dark oval, is a leftward facing bust of Alexander Hamilton. The oval, itself, sits on a background shield. Above the oval are the words, U. S. POSTAGE, while below the portrait oval, on a ribbon are the words, THIRTY CENTS. The numeral, 30, splits the two words, THIRTY CENTS.

Figure 6-39. Alexander Hamilton. A portrait of Hamilton is the subject of the thirty-cent Bank Note stamp.

Alexander Hamilton, the stamp's subject, was born in 1755 in the West Indies. In the Revolutionary War, he distinguished himself by becoming General Washington's personal secretary.. He was a driving force in the ratification of the United States Constitution by co-authoring the Federalists papers, arguments for this document. He became the country's first Secretary of the Treasury in 1789. Hamilton believed in a strong national government and the role of American industrial development. Hamilton was the leader of the Federalist Party, and political enemy of Thomas Jefferson. However, Jefferson owed his election to the presidency to Hamilton, who favored him over Aaron Burr, another long time political foe, when the Federalist-dominated House of Representatives was forced to decide the election of 1800. Aaron Burr's failed presidential bid was followed by his campaign to become governor of New York. When Burr requested his endorsement, Hamilton refused, not trusting Burr. Burr's loss in the governor's race led him to challenge Hamilton in a duel. On July 11, 1804, Burr took his revenge, killing Hamilton.

The thirty-cent Continental was printed from the same plate as the initial National stamp. Therefore, the Continental thirty-cent stamp does not have a secret mark. Unlike the confusion seen with the twenty-four cent stamps, the Continental can be distinguished from the National by color. The National stamp is pure black while the Continental stamp has a gray or green tint to its black ink.

Its soft paper, of course, distinguishes the American stamp. In 1989, Jack Rosenthal discovered the secret mark on some of these stamps. The secret mark is located on the S of CENTS. The upper triangle of the S is broader on the American Bank Note printing than on the National or Continental. The plate with the secret mark, 405, did not go into use until 1882. Therefore, the American 30-cent stamps printed between 1874 and 1882 on the old National plate do not have the added secret mark. Note that is the only case of the Bank Note series where American stamps have a secret mark while the Continental stamps do not.

The last 30-cent stamp appeared in 1888. It is the American issue, from the same plate, in a new color, orange brown. The reason for this striking color change is not known.

NATIONAL GRILLED THIRTY-CENT HAMILTON

National Grilled Thirty-Cent Hamilton

Stamp Production
Printer:	National Bank Note Company
Designer:	Butler Packard
Engravers:	Joseph P. Ourdan (portrait), Douglas S. Ronaldson (frame and lettering)
Format:	Sheets of 200, cut vertically into 2 panes of 100
Plate Numbers:	22
Date of Issue:	Apr. 1870
Earliest Known Use:	Aug. 18, 1870
Uses:	Multiples of foreign rates.
Quantity Issued:	77,000

Stamp Features
Size:	20 x 25 mm. (0.8 x 1.0 inches)
Watermark:	None
Grill:	H
Paper:	Hard
Perforations:	12
Secret Mark:	None
Colors:	Black, full black.
Varieties:	Marginal grill, Double grill

Collectable Stamp Today
Collectable Cancellation Colors:
Black, blue, red.
Collectable Cancellation Varieties:
None.

Value Unused:	$$$$$$
Value Used:	$$$$$
Surviving Covers:	20
Largest Known Multiple:	Unused: 4 (2x2 block)
	Used: 4 (2x2 block)

The thirty-cent grilled National stamp is found on hard paper, with deep black ink, and the H size grill. The grill usually is faint and incomplete. The stamp is found with the double grill and marginal grill varieties. This stamp, being a valuable one, often is forged by adding a fake grill. Because the grilled stamp is known only in black and full black, this is the proof that only stamps in these shades are National printings.

NATIONAL UNGRILLED THIRTY-CENT HAMILTON

National Ungrilled Thirty-Cent Hamilton

Stamp Production

Printer:	National Bank Note Company
Designer:	Butler Packard
Engravers:	Joseph P. Ourdan (portrait), Douglas S. Ronaldson (frame and lettering)
Format:	Sheets of 200, cut vertically into 2 panes of 100

Plate Numbers:	22
Date of Issue:	1870
Earliest Known Use:	July 13, 1870
Uses:	Multiples of foreign rates.
Quantity Issued:	785,843

Stamp Features

Size:	20 x 25 mm. (0.8 x 1.0 inches)
Watermark:	None
Grill:	None
Paper:	Hard
Perforations:	12
Secret Mark:	None
Colors:	Black, full black.
Varieties:	None

Collectable Stamp Today
Collectable Cancellation Colors:
Black, magenta, red, brown, blue.
Collectable Cancellation Varieties:
Steamship, supplementary mail type A.

Value Unused:	$$$$$
Value Used:	$$$$
Surviving Covers:	350
Largest Known Multiple:	Unused: 5 (strip)
	Used: 16 (block)

Like the other ungrilled National Bank Note stamps, the ungrilled thirty-cent stamps are an order of magnitude more common than the grilled issue. Though more common on cover than the grilled thirty-cent National stamps, still, it is only found on less than 350 surviving covers.

CONTINENTAL THIRTY-CENT HAMILTON

Continental Thirty-Cent Hamilton

Stamp Production

Printer:	Continental Bank Note Company
Designer:	Butler Packard
Engravers:	Joseph P. Ourdan (portrait), Douglas S. Ronaldson (frame and lettering)
Format:	Sheets of 200, cut vertically into 2 panes of 100
Plate Numbers:	National 22

Date of Issue:	1874
Earliest Known Use:	Oct. 14, 1874
Uses:	Multiples of foreign rates, especially India and Peru
Quantity Issued:	782,500

Stamp Features

Size:	20 x 25 mm. (0.8 x 1.0 inches)
Watermark:	None
Grill:	None
Paper:	Hard
Perforations:	12
Secret Mark:	None
Colors:	Gray black, greenish black.
Varieties:	Double transfer, Double paper, Ribbed paper, Paper with silk fibers.

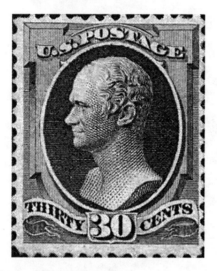

Collectable Stamp Today
Collectable Cancellation Colors:
Black, purple, blue, red, brown, magenta.
Collectable Cancellation Varieties:
town, Steamship, supplementary mail type E or F, Japan.

Value Unused:	$$$$$
Value Used:	$$$$
Largest Known Multiple:	Unused: 6 (plate block)
	Used: 9 (block)

There was no secret mark on the Continental thirty-cent stamp. In fact, they were printed from the same unaltered National plate. This stamp can be distinguished from the National by the ink color. It is gray black or greenish black instead of the black or full black of the

National. The stamp is found with the usual Continental paper varieties including paper with silk fibers, ribbed paper, and double paper. It also exists with the Continental grill essay. The stamp was used on multiple rate overseas letters, especially to India and Peru. The largest unused multiple of the thirty-cent Continental is a complete plate block of six stamps with the selvage. Used, the largest multiple is a block of nine stamps.

AMERICAN THIRTY-CENT BLACK HAMILTON

American Black Thirty-Cent Hamilton

Stamp Production

Printer:	American Bank Note Company
Designer:	Butler Packard
Engravers:	Joseph P. Ourdan (portrait), Douglas S. Ronaldson (frame and lettering)
Format:	Sheets of 200, cut vertically into 2 panes of 100
Plate Numbers:	National 22, American 405
Date of Issue:	1881
Earliest Known Use:	Apr. 5, 1881
Uses:	Multiples of foreign rates, especially India and Peru
Quantity Issued:	4,097,910

Stamp Features

Size:	20 x 25 mm. (0.8 x 1.0 inches)

Watermark:	None
Grill:	None
Paper:	Soft
Perforations:	12
Secret Mark:	May or may not be present
Colors:	Full black, greenish black.
Varieties:	None

Collectable Stamp Today
Collectable Cancellation Colors:
Black, blue, purple, magenta, red.
Collectable Cancellation Varieties:
Steamship, supplementary mail type F, Tahiti, Samoa.

Value Unused:	$$$$$
Value Used:	$$$
Surviving Covers:	2,000
Largest Known Multiple:	Unused: 100 (complete pane)
	Used: 10 (block)

The American 30-cent stamp is easily distinguished from the other 30-cent Bank Note stamps by the soft paper used by that company. It was printed both in a full black and in a greenish black, the first made and the more common.

The American Company used the original National Bank Note Company plate (number 22) that had been passed on to them from Continental. They also made a new plate, American plate 405. As described above, the new plate had a secret mark added to it. The upper triangle of the S of CENTS is broader than in the stamps made from the original plate. Therefore, the earlier American thirty-cent Bank Note stamps do not have the secret mark while the later ones do.

Figure 6-40. Thirty-Cent Bank Note Secret Mark. The secret mark on the thirty-cent Bank Note issue is found on some of the American printed stamps. It is located on the S of CENTS. The triangles of the S is wider and bigger, as seen on the right-sided American stamp versus the Continental on the left.

AMERICAN THIRTY-CENT ORANGE BROWN HAMILTON

American Orange Brown Thirty-Cent Hamilton

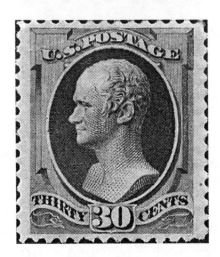

Stamp Production
Printer: American Bank Note Company
Designer: Butler Packard
Engravers: Joseph P. Ourdan (portrait), Douglas S. Ronaldson (frame and lettering)
Format: Sheets of 200, cut vertically into 2 panes of 100
Plate Numbers: 405
Date of Issue: Jan. 1888
Earliest Known Use: Aug. 18, 1888
Uses: Multiples of foreign and domestic rates.
Quantity Issued: 710,720

Stamp Features
Size: 20 x 25 mm. (0.8 x 1.0 inches)
Watermark: None
Grill: None
Paper: Soft
Perforations: 12
Secret Mark: Present
Colors: Orange brown, deep orange brown.
Varieties: None

Collectable Stamp Today
Collectable Cancellation Colors:
    Black, magenta, blue.
Collectable Cancellation Varieties:
    Paid, Paid All, supplementary mail type F.

Value Unused: $$$$
Value Used: $$$$
Surviving Covers: 1,000
Largest Known Multiple: Unused: 100 (complete pane)
                               Used: 15 (block)

In 1888, the color of the 30-cent stamp was changed from black to orange brown. The reason for the color change remains a mystery. The ninety-cent stamp of this series also received a color change at this time. The new color did make the stamp much more striking. Except for the color change, this stamp is identical with the black 30-cent American stamp. It was printed from the same American plate that was used to make the black stamps. So it has the added secret mark.

Ninety-Cent Bank Note Perry Stamps

1870	National Carmine	Hard paper	Grilled	
1870	National Carmine	Hard paper	No grill	
1875	Continental Rose carmine	Hard paper	No	grill
1882	American Carmine	Soft paper	No grill	
1888	American Purple	Soft paper	No grill	

The ninety-cent denomination is the highest of the Bank Note stamps. The stamps paid multiples of many foreign and some odd high-rate domestic postage rates. It features Commodore Oliver Hazard Perry. The design of the stamp has a nautical touch, appropriate to the subject. A bust of Commodore Perry, facing to the left, is in an oval background. Above the oval are the words, U.S. POSTAGE. Below the oval are the words, NINETY CENTS, split in the middle by the numeral, 90. Between the words, U.S. POSTAGE and the oval run a rope. It is attached by a sailor's knot to the ends of the panel that contains the words, NINETY CENTS. In the upper corners of the stamp are stars, while the bottom corners feature anchors.

Commodore Oliver Perry (1785-1819) first fought in the Barbary Wars. He was a hero of the War of 1812. Perry constructed and commanded a fleet of American warships on Lake Erie. When his flagship, Lawrence, was shattered in the Battle of Lake Erie, Perry fired her last effective gun, took his battle flag, and rowed across to another ship, the Niagara, where he fought on to victory. His famous line of the end of the battle was "We have met the enemy and they are ours." The victory gave the United States control of Lake Erie that helped Americans at Ghent to negotiate a treaty favorable to the United States.

Figure 6-41. Commodore Oliver Perry. The American naval hero, Oliver Perry, is the subject of the ninety-cent Bank Note stamps.

There are no secret marks on the ninety-cent Bank Notes. Therefore, the ungrilled National and the Continental stamps must be distinguished by subtle color differences. The National stamp is called carmine but has a bluish tint. The Continental is listed as rose carmine, but has a hint of yellow. This subtle difference makes the 90-cent stamp one of the more difficult denominations to separate into the National and Continental printings. There are two varieties of American ninety cents stamps. The first was carmine, like the stamps of the earlier companies. For the second, the color of the stamp was changed to purple in 1888.

NATIONAL GRILLED NINETY-CENT PERRY

National Grilled Ninety-Cent Perry

Stamp Production

Printer:	National Bank Note Company
Designer:	Butler Packard
Engravers:	Luigi (Louis) Delnoce (portrait), Douglas S. Ronaldson (frame and lettering).
Format:	Sheets of 200, cut vertically into 2 panes of 100
Plate Numbers:	23
Date of Issue:	Apr. 12,1870
Earliest Known Use:	Not found on cover
Uses:	Multiples of foreign rates.
Quantity Issued:	53,300

Stamp Features

Size:	20 x 25 mm. (0.8 x 1.0 inches)
Watermark:	None
Grill:	H
Paper:	Hard
Perforations:	12
Secret Mark:	None
Colors:	Carmine, dark carmine.
Varieties:	Split grill, double grill.

Collectable Stamp Today
Collectable Cancellation Colors:
Black, blue, red.
Collectable Cancellation Varieties:
None

Value Unused:	$$$$$$
Value Used:	$$$$$
Surviving Covers:	0
Largest Known Multiple:	Unused: 4 (block)
	Used: 10 (vertical strip)

Although this is an uncommon stamp, one does not find counterfeit grilled stamps. This is because the ungrilled National stamp also is a valuable stamp. The stamp can be found with the split grill and double grill varieties. There are no known verified covers with the ninety cent grilled National stamp on it.

NATIONAL UNGRILLED NINETY-CENT PERRY

National Ungrilled Ninety-Cent Perry

Stamp Production

Printer:	National Bank Note Company
Designer:	Butler Packard
Engravers:	Luigi (Louis) Delnoce (portrait), Douglas S. Ronaldson (frame and lettering).
Format:	Sheets of 200, cut vertically into 2 panes of 100
Plate Numbers:	23
Date of Issue:	1870
Earliest Known Use:	Sept. 1, 1872

Uses:	Multiples of foreign rates.
Quantity Issued:	160,150

Stamp Features

Size:	20 x 25 mm. (0.8 x 1.0 inches)
Watermark:	None
Grill:	None
Paper:	Hard
Perforations:	12
Secret Mark:	None
Colors:	Carmine, dark carmine.
Varieties:	None

Collectable Stamp Today
Collectable Cancellation Colors:
Black, blue, purple, magenta, green, red.
Collectable Cancellation Varieties:
town, supplementary mail type A or F, Japan.

Value Unused:	$$$$$
Value Used:	$$$$
Surviving Covers:	3
Largest Known Multiple:	Unused: 12 (block)
	Used: 10 (block)

As mentioned in the introduction, there is only a subtle hue difference between the National ungrilled and Continental 90-cent stamps. The National stamp is slightly more blue. Though there is three times as many ungrilled as grilled National stamps, this still is an uncommon stamp.

CONTINENTAL NINETY-CENT PERRY

Continental Ninety-Cent Perry

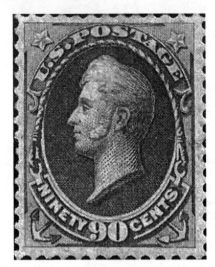

Stamp Production

Printer:	Continental Bank Note Company
Designer:	Butler Packard
Engravers:	Luigi (Louis) Delnoce (portrait), Douglas S. Ronaldson (frame and lettering).
Format:	Sheets of 200, cut vertically into 2 panes of 100
Plate Numbers:	National 23
Date of Issue:	1875
Earliest Known Use:	Jan. 25, 1875
Uses:	Multiples of foreign rates.
Quantity Issued:	197,000

Stamp Features

Size:	20 x 25 mm. (0.8 x 1.0 inches)
Watermark:	None
Grill:	None
Paper:	Hard
Perforations:	12
Secret Mark:	None
Colors:	Rose carmine, pale rose carmine.
Varieties:	None

Collectable Stamp Today:
Collectable Cancellation Colors:
Black, blue, purple, red.
Collectable Cancellation Varieties:
supplementary mail type F.
Value Unused: $$$$$

Value Used: $$$$
Surviving Covers: 20
Largest Known Multiple: Unused: 100 (complete pane)
Used: 12 (3x4 block)

This stamp and all the 90-cent Bank Note stamps were printed from the same National plate. There are known no secret marks. So one must rely on subtle ink color differences to tell the stamps apart. The Continental is slightly more yellow than the National.

This stamp, like all 90-cent stamps, is very rare on cover, with fewer than 20 surviving covers remaining. Most of these are of a large legal size.

AMERICAN CARMINE NINETY-CENT PERRY

American Carmine Ninety-Cent Perry

Stamp Production
Printer: American Bank Note Company
Designer: Butler Packard
Engravers: Luigi (Louis) Delnoce (portrait), Douglas S. Ronaldson (frame and lettering).
Format: Sheets of 200, cut vertically into 2 panes of 100
Plate Numbers: National 23
Date of Issue: 1882

Earliest Known Use:	June 24, 1882
Uses:	Multiples of foreign rates. Parcels.
Quantity Issued:	280,670

Stamp Features

Size:	20 x 25 mm. (0.8 x 1.0 inches)
Watermark:	None
Grill:	None
Paper:	Soft
Perforations:	12
Secret Mark:	None
Colors:	Carmine, rose, carmine rose.
Varieties:	Double paper.

Collectable Stamp Today:
Collectable Cancellation Colors:
Black, blue, purple, red.
Collectable Cancellation Varieties:
supplementary mail type F.

Value Unused:	$$$$$
Value Used:	$$$$
Surviving Covers:	100
Largest Known Multiple:	Unused: 20 (block)
	Used: 20 (block)

American printed their 90-cent stamp from the old National plate 23 they inherited via Continental. It can be identified from the others by its soft paper. Like the rest of this denomination stamps, it is rare on cover, with about 100 remaining.

AMERICAN PURPLE NINETY-CENT PERRY

American Purple Ninety-Cent Perry

Stamp Production

Printer:	American Bank Note Company
Designer:	Butler Packard
Engravers:	Luigi (Louis) Delnoce (portrait), Douglas S. Ronaldson (frame and lettering).
Format:	Sheets of 200, cut vertically into 2 panes of 100
Plate Numbers:	National 23
Date of Issue:	Feb. 1888
Earliest Known Use:	Oct. 10, 1888
Uses:	Multiples of domestic and foreign rates.

Quantity Issued: 103,130
Stamp Features
Size: 20 x 25 mm. (0.8 x 1.0 inches)
Watermark: None
Grill: None
Paper: Soft
Perforations: 12
Secret Mark: None
Colors: Purple, bright purple.
Varieties: None

Collectable Stamp Today:
Collectable Cancellation Colors:
                          Black, blue, purple.
Collectable Cancellation Varieties:
                          supplementary mail type F.
Value Unused: $$$$$
Value Used: $$$$
Surviving Covers: 50
Largest Known Multiple: Unused: 20 (block)
                          Used: 40 (8x5 block)

   The color of the American 90-cent was changed at the about same time as the 30-cent stamp. It is not known why either of the two highest denominations had their ink color change. It was printed from the same plate as all of the 90-cent bank notes, the original National plate 23, so there is no design difference between it and the earlier stamps.

Like the other ninety-cent stamps, it is very rare on cover, with less than 50 remaining. Large blocks of this stamp are not uncommon. The largest unused multiple is a block of 20 stamps, used, a block of 40 (8x5).

Special Printings

Between 1875 and 1884, special printings were made of current designs for sale to stamp collectors. These are neither reprints nor reissues as they were in current use at the time of the printing. Instead, they are called special printings. Very small quantities were sold, less than a thousand of any one type.

It is hard to understand why a special printing was made of stamps that already were in use and could be bought at the local post office!

There are two groups of special printings, based on the company that made them. The first 1875 group is the Continental, the second 1880 is the American.

The post office department did not keep separate records of the number of 1875 and 1880 special printings, but only the total quantity sold:

> 1-cent: 388
> 2-cent brown: 416
> 2-cent vermilion: 917
> 3-cent: 267
> 5-cent: 317
> 6-cent: 185
> 7-cent: 473
> 10-cent: 180
> 12-cent: 282
> 15-cent: 169
> 24-cent: 286
> 30-cent: 179
> 90-cent: 170

CONTINENTAL SPECIAL PRINTINGS

Continental One-Cent Franklin Bank Note Special Printing

Stamp Production
Printer:	Continental Bank Note Company
Designer:	Butler Packard
Engravers:	Joseph I. Pease (portrait), Anthony W. Cunningham (frame and lettering), Charles Skinner (secret mark)
Format:	Sheets of 200, cut vertically into 2 panes of 100
Plate Numbers:	Current Continental plates
Date of Issue:	May 5, 1875.
Uses:	Souvenir. Valid for postal use.
Quantity Issued:	With American 388 total

Stamp Features
Size:	20 x 25 mm. (0.8 x 1.0 inches)
Watermark:	None
Grill:	None
Paper:	Hard
Perforations:	12
Secret Mark:	Present
Colors:	Bright ultramarine
Varieties:	None

Collectable Stamp Today
Value Unused:	$$$$$$

Continental Two-Cent Dark Brown Jackson Bank Note Special Printing

Stamp Production

Printer:	Continental Bank Note Company
Designer:	Butler Packard
Engravers:	Luigi (Louis) Delnoce (portrait), Douglas S. Ronaldson (frame and lettering), Charles Skinner (secret mark)
Format:	Sheets of 200, cut vertically into 2 panes of 100
Plate Numbers:	Current Continental plates
Date of Issue:	May 5, 1875.
Uses:	Souvenir. Valid for postal use.
Quantity Issued:	With American 416 total

Stamp Features

Size:	20 x 25 mm. (0.8 x 1.0 inches)
Watermark:	None
Grill:	None
Paper:	Hard
Perforations:	12
Secret Mark:	Present
Colors:	Dark brown
Varieties:	None

Collectable Stamp Today

Value Unused:	$$$$$

Continental Two-Cent Vermilion Jackson Bank Note Special Printing

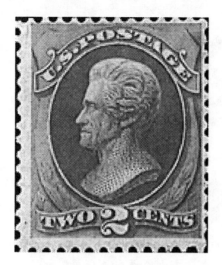

Stamp Production

Printer:	Continental Bank Note Company
Designer:	Butler Packard
Engravers:	Luigi (Louis) Delnoce (portrait), Douglas S. Ronaldson (frame and lettering), Charles Skinner (secret mark)
Format:	Sheets of 200, cut vertically into 2 panes of 100
Plate Numbers:	Current Continental plates
Date of Issue:	1875.
Uses:	Souvenir. Valid for postal use.
Quantity Issued:	With American 917 total

Stamp Features

Size:	20 x 25 mm. (0.8 x 1.0 inches)
Watermark:	None
Grill:	None
Paper:	Hard
Perforations:	12
Secret Mark:	Present
Colors:	Carmine vermilion
Varieties:	None

Collectable Stamp Today
Value Unused: $$$$$$

Continental Three-Cent Washington Bank Note Special Printing

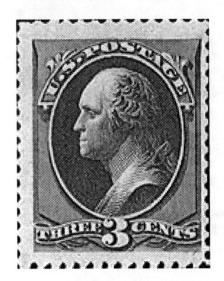

Stamp Production

Printer:	Continental Bank Note Company
Designer:	Butler Packard
Engravers:	Joseph I. Pease (portrait), Anthony W. Cunningham (frame and lettering)
Format:	Sheets of 200, cut vertically into 2 panes of 100
Plate Numbers:	Current Continental plates
Date of Issue:	May 5, 1875.
Uses:	Souvenir. Valid for postal use.
Quantity Issued:	With American 267 total

Stamp Features

Size:	20 x 25 mm. (0.8 x 1.0 inches)
Watermark:	None
Grill:	None
Paper:	Hard
Perforations:	12
Secret Mark:	Present
Colors:	Blue green
Varieties:	None

Collectable Stamp Today

Value Unused:	$$$$$$
Surviving Covers:	1

Continental Five-Cent Taylor Bank Note Special Printing

Stamp Production
Printer:	Continental Bank Note Company
Designer:	Butler Packard
Engravers:	Joseph I. Pease (portrait), Anthony W. Cunningham (frame and lettering)
Format:	Sheets of 200, cut vertically into 2 panes of 100
Plate Numbers:	Current Continental plates
Date of Issue:	1875.
Uses:	Souvenir. Valid for postal use.
Quantity Issued:	With American 317 total

Stamp Features
Size:	20 x 25 mm. (0.8 x 1.0 inches)
Watermark:	None
Grill:	None
Paper:	Hard
Perforations:	12
Secret Mark:	None
Colors:	Bright blue
Varieties:	None

Collectable Stamp Today
Value Unused:	$$$$$$

Continental Six-Cent Lincoln Bank Note Special Printing

Stamp Production

Printer:	Continental Bank Note Company
Designer:	Butler Packard
Engravers:	Joseph I. Pease (portrait), Anthony W. Cunningham (frame and lettering)
Format:	Sheets of 200, cut vertically into 2 panes of 100
Plate Numbers:	Current Continental plates
Date of Issue:	May 5, 1875
Uses:	Souvenir. Valid for postal use.
Quantity Issued:	With American 185 total

Stamp Features

Size:	20 x 25 mm. (0.8 x 1.0 inches)
Watermark:	None
Grill:	None
Paper:	Hard
Perforations:	12
Secret Mark:	Present
Colors:	Dull rose
Varieties:	None

Collectable Stamp Today

Value Unused:	$$$$$$

Continental Seven-Cent Stanton Bank Note Special Printing

Stamp Production

Printer:	Continental Bank Note Company
Designer:	Butler Packard
Engravers:	Joseph I. Pease (portrait), Anthony W. Cunningham (frame and lettering)
Format:	Sheets of 200, cut vertically into 2 panes of 100
Plate Numbers:	Current Continental plates
Date of Issue:	May 5, 1875
Uses:	Souvenir. Valid for postal use.
Quantity Issued:	With American 473 total

Stamp Features

Size:	20 x 25 mm. (0.8 x 1.0 inches)
Watermark:	None
Grill:	None
Paper:	Hard
Perforations:	12
Secret Mark:	None
Colors:	Reddish vermilion
Varieties:	None

Collectable Stamp Today

Value Unused:	$$$$$

Continental Ten-Cent Jefferson Bank Note Special Printing

Stamp Production

Printer:	Continental Bank Note Company
Designer:	Butler Packard
Engravers:	Joseph I. Pease (portrait), Anthony W. Cunningham (frame and lettering)
Format:	Sheets of 200, cut vertically into 2 panes of 100
Plate Numbers:	Current Continental plates
Date of Issue:	May 5, 1875
Uses:	Souvenir. Valid for postal use.
Quantity Issued:	With American 180 total

Stamp Features

Size:	20 x 25 mm. (0.8 x 1.0 inches)
Watermark:	None
Grill:	None
Paper:	Hard
Perforations:	12
Secret Mark:	Present
Colors:	Pale brown
Varieties:	None

Collectable Stamp Today

Value Unused:	$$$$$$

Continental Twelve-Cent Clay Bank Note Special Printing

Stamp Production

Printer:	Continental Bank Note Company
Designer:	Butler Packard
Engravers:	Joseph I. Pease (portrait), Anthony W. Cunningham (frame and lettering)
Format:	Sheets of 200, cut vertically into 2 panes of 100
Plate Numbers:	Current Continental plates
Date of Issue:	May 5, 1875
Uses:	Souvenir. Valid for postal use.
Quantity Issued:	With American 282 total

Stamp Features

Size:	20 x 25 mm. (0.8 x 1.0 inches)
Watermark:	None
Grill:	None
Paper:	Hard
Perforations:	12
Secret Mark:	Present
Colors:	Dark violet
Varieties:	None

Collectable Stamp Today

Value Unused:	$$$$$

Continental Fifteen-Cent Webster Bank Note Special Printing

Stamp Production

Printer:	Continental Bank Note Company
Designer:	Butler Packard
Engravers:	Joseph I. Pease (portrait), Anthony W. Cunningham (frame and lettering)
Format:	Sheets of 200, cut vertically into 2 panes of 100
Plate Numbers:	Current Continental plates
Date of Issue:	May 5, 1875
Uses:	Souvenir. Valid for postal use.
Quantity Issued:	With American 169 total

Stamp Features

Size:	20 x 25 mm. (0.8 x 1.0 inches)
Watermark:	None
Grill:	None
Paper:	Hard
Perforations:	12
Secret Mark:	Present
Colors:	Bright orange
Varieties:	None

Collectable Stamp Today.

Value Unused:	$$$$$$

Continental Twenty-Four-Cent Scott Bank Note Special Printing

Stamp Production
Printer:	Continental Bank Note Company
Designer:	Butler Packard
Engravers:	Joseph I. Pease (portrait), Anthony W. Cunningham (frame and lettering)
Format:	Sheets of 200, cut vertically into 2 panes of 100
Plate Numbers:	Old National plate 21
Date of Issue:	May 5, 1875
Uses:	Souvenir. Valid for postal use.
Quantity Issued:	With American 286 total

Stamp Features
Size:	20 x 25 mm. (0.8 x 1.0 inches)
Watermark:	None
Grill:	None
Paper:	Hard
Perforations:	12
Secret Mark:	None
Colors:	Dull purple
Varieties:	None

Collectable Stamp Today
Value Unused:	$$$$$
Value Used:	$$$$$$

Continental Thirty-Cent Hamilton Bank Note Special Printing

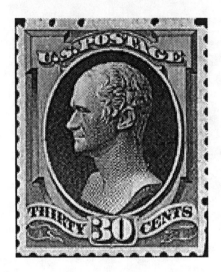

Stamp Production

Printer:	Continental Bank Note Company
Designer:	Butler Packard
Engravers:	Joseph I. Pease (portrait), Anthony W. Cunningham (frame and lettering)
Format:	Sheets of 200, cut vertically into 2 panes of 100
Plate Numbers:	Old National plate 22
Date of Issue:	May 5, 1875
Uses:	Souvenir. Valid for postal use.
Quantity Issued:	With American 179 total

Stamp Features

Size:	20 x 25 mm. (0.8 x 1.0 inches)
Watermark:	None
Grill:	None
Paper:	Hard
Perforations:	12
Secret Mark:	None
Colors:	Greenish black
Varieties:	None

Collectable Stamp Today

Value Unused:	$$$$$$

Continental Ninety-Cent Perry Bank Note Special Printing

Stamp Production
Printer: Continental Bank Note Company
Designer: Butler Packard
Engravers: Joseph I. Pease (portrait), Anthony W. Cunningham (frame and lettering)
Format: Sheets of 200, cut vertically into 2 panes of 100
Plate Numbers: Old National plate 23
Date of Issue: May 5, 1875
Uses: Souvenir. Valid for postal use.
Quantity Issued: With American 170 total

Stamp Features
Size: 20 x 25 mm. (0.8 x 1.0 inches)
Watermark: None
Grill: None
Paper: Hard
Perforations: 12
Secret Mark: None
Colors: Violet carmine
Varieties: None

Collectable Stamp Today
Value Unused: $$$$$$

The Continentals were the first Bank Note special printings made. Their sale began May 5th of 1875. The two-cent vermilion, reflecting the stamp's color change, and the new five-cent Taylor stamp were added to this set later that year. The company made them from the same printing plates then in use. That means Continental printed the 24, 30, and 90-cent stamps from old National plates. Continental plates, reflected by the added secret marks were used for 1 through 15-cent special printing stamps.

They are printed on hard, white, ungummed paper. They are perforated 12, just like the regular issue stamps.

Most 1875 special printing stamps were cut apart with scissors. That means they have clipped perforations. The ink colors are bright and clear giving the stamps a new appearance, reflecting the extra care in their production.

Special printing of the 1873 issue can be distinguished from the regular issue by the extreme whiteness of the paper, their sharp features, and their trimmed perforations.

Only the three-cent special printing is known on a cover and it is unique.

AMERICAN SPECIAL PRINTINGS

American One-Cent Franklin Bank Note Special Printing

Stamp Production

Printer:	American Bank Note Company
Designer:	Butler Packard
Engravers:	Joseph I. Pease (portrait), Anthony W. Cunningham (frame and lettering), Charles Skinner (secret mark)
Format:	Sheets of 200, cut vertically into 2 panes of 100
Plate Numbers:	Current American plates
Date of Issue:	July 16, 1880.
Uses:	Souvenir. Valid for postal use.
Quantity Issued:	With Continental 388 total

Stamp Features

Size:	20 x 25 mm. (0.8 x 1.0 inches)
Watermark:	None
Grill:	None
Paper:	Soft
Perforations:	12
Secret Mark:	Present
Colors:	Dark ultramarine
Varieties:	None

Collectable Stamp Today

Value Unused:	$$$$$

American Two-Cent Black Brown Jackson Bank Note Reissue

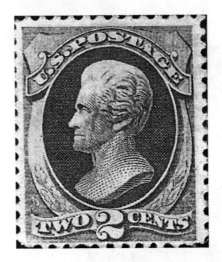

Stamp Production
Printer: American Bank Note Company
Designer: Butler Packard
Engravers: Luigi (Louis) Delnoce (portrait), Douglas S. Ronaldson
                          (frame and lettering), Charles Skinner (secret mark)
Format: Sheets of 200, cut vertically into 2 panes of 100
Plate Numbers: Old Continental plates
Date of Issue: July 16, 1880
Uses: Souvenir. Valid for postal use.
Quantity Issued: With Continental 416 total

Stamp Features
Size: 20 x 25 mm. (0.8 x 1.0 inches)
Watermark: None
Grill: None
Paper: Soft
Perforations: 12
Secret Mark: Present
Colors: Black brown
Varieties: None

Collectable Stamp Today
Value Unused: $$$$$$

American Two-Cent Vermilion Jackson Bank Note Special Printing

Stamp Production
Printer: American Bank Note Company
Designer: Butler Packard
Engravers: Luigi (Louis) Delnoce (portrait), Douglas S. Ronaldson
                       (frame and lettering), Charles Skinner (secret mark)
Format: Sheets of 200, cut vertically into 2 panes of 100
Plate Numbers: Old Continental plates
Date of Issue: July 16, 1880.
Uses: Souvenir. Valid for postal use.
Quantity Issued: With Continental 917 total

Stamp Features
Size: 20 x 25 mm. (0.8 x 1.0 inches)
Watermark: None
Grill: None
Paper: Soft
Perforations: 12
Secret Mark: Present
Colors: Scarlet vermilion.
Varieties: None

Collectable Stamp Today
Value Unused: $$$$$$

American Two-Cent Red Brown Washington Bank Note Special Printing

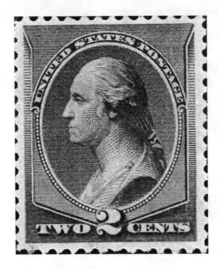

Stamp Production
Printer:	American Bank Note Company
Designer:	Thomas F. Morris
Engravers:	Alfred Jones (portrait), Douglas S. Ronaldson (frame and lettering)
Format:	Sheets of 200, cut vertically into 2 panes of 100
Plate Numbers:	Current American plates
Date of Issue:	Dec. 5, 1883
Uses:	Souvenir. Valid for postal use.
Quantity Issued:	55

Stamp Features
Size:	20 x 25 mm. (0.8 x 1.0 inches)
Watermark:	None
Grill:	None
Paper:	Soft
Perforations:	12
Secret Mark:	None
Colors:	Pale red brown
Varieties:	Horizontal pair, imperforate in between

Collectable Stamp Today
Value Unused:	$$$$

American Three-Cent Washington Bank Note Special Printing

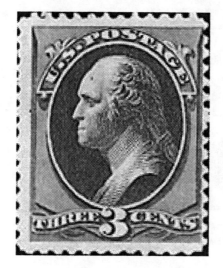

Stamp Production
Printer: American Bank Note Company
Designer: Butler Packard
Engravers: Joseph P. Ourdan (portrait), Douglas S. Ronaldson (frame
                          and lettering), Charles Skinner (secret mark)
Format: Sheets of 200, cut vertically into 2 panes of 100
Plate Numbers: Current American plates
Date of Issue: July 16, 1880
Uses: Souvenir. Valid for postal use.
Quantity Issued: 55

Stamp Features
Size: 20 x 25 mm. (0.8 x 1.0 inches)
Watermark: None
Grill: None
Paper: Soft
Perforations: 12
Secret Mark: Present
Colors: Blue green
Varieties: None

Collectable Stamp Today
Value Unused: $$$$$$

American Four-Cent Jackson Bank Note Special Printing

Stamp Production
Printer:	American Bank Note Company
Designer:	Thomas F. Morris
Engravers:	Alfred Jones (portrait), Douglas S. Ronaldson (frame and lettering)
Format:	Sheets of 200, cut vertically into 2 panes of 100
Plate Numbers:	Current American plates
Date of Issue:	Dec. 5, 1883
Uses:	Souvenir. Valid for postal use.
Quantity Issued:	26

Stamp Features
Size:	20 x 25 mm. (0.8 x 1.0 inches)
Watermark:	None
Grill:	None
Paper:	Soft
Perforations:	12
Secret Mark:	None
Colors:	Deep blue green
Varieties:	None

Collectable Stamp Today
Value Unused:	$$$$$$

American Five-Cent Taylor Bank Note Special Printing

Stamp Production

Printer:	American Bank Note Company
Designer:	Butler Packard (frame). The designer of the portrait is an unknown person at the Bureau of Engraving and Printing who designed the original tobacco revenue stamp.
Engravers:	S. Ronaldson (frame and lettering)
Format:	Sheets of 200, cut vertically into 2 panes of 100
Plate Numbers:	Current American plates
Date of Issue:	July 16, 1880
Uses:	Souvenir. Valid for postal use.
Quantity Issued:	With Continental 317 total

Stamp Features

Size:	20 x 25 mm. (0.8 x 1.0 inches)
Watermark:	None
Grill:	None
Paper:	Soft
Perforations:	12
Secret Mark:	None
Colors:	Deep blue
Varieties:	None

Collectable Stamp Today

Value Unused:	$$$$$$

American Five-Cent Garfield Bank Note Special Printing

Stamp Production

Printer:	American Bank Note Company
Designer:	Thomas F. Morris
Engravers:	Charles Skinner (portrait), Douglas S. Ronaldson (frame and lettering)
Format:	Sheets of 200, cut vertically into 2 panes of 100
Plate Numbers:	Current American plates
Date of Issue:	April 10, 1882
Uses:	Souvenir. Valid for postal use.
Quantity Issued:	2,463

Stamp Features

Size:	20 x 25 mm. (0.8 x 1.0 inches)
Watermark:	None
Grill:	None
Paper:	Soft
Perforations:	12
Secret Mark:	None
Colors:	Gray brown
Varieties:	None

Collectable Stamp Today

Value Unused:	$$$$$$

American Six-Cent Lincoln Bank Note Special Printing

Stamp Production

Printer:	American Bank Note Company
Designer:	Thomas F. Morris
Engravers:	Charles Skinner (portrait), Douglas S. Ronaldson (frame and lettering)
Format:	Sheets of 200, cut vertically into 2 panes of 100
Plate Numbers:	Current American plates
Date of Issue:	July 16, 1880
Uses:	Souvenir. Valid for postal use.
Quantity Issued:	With Continental 185 total

Stamp Features

Size:	20 x 25 mm. (0.8 x 1.0 inches)
Watermark:	None
Grill:	None
Paper:	Soft
Perforations:	12
Secret Mark:	Present
Colors:	Dull rose
Varieties:	None

Collectable Stamp Today

Value Unused:	$$$$$$

American Seven-Cent Stanton Bank Note Reissues

Stamp Production

Printer:	American Bank Note Company
Designer:	Butler Packard
Engravers:	Joseph P. Ourdan (portrait), Douglas S. Ronaldson (frame and lettering), Charles Skinner (secret mark)

Format:	Sheets of 200, cut vertically into 2 panes of 100
Plate Numbers:	Old Continental plates
Date of Issue:	July 16, 1880
Uses:	Souvenir. Valid for postal use.
Quantity Issued:	With Continental 473 total

Stamp Features

Size:	20 x 25 mm. (0.8 x 1.0 inches)
Watermark:	None
Grill:	None
Paper:	Soft
Perforations:	12
Secret Mark:	Present
Colors:	Scarlet vermilion
Varieties:	None

Collectable Stamp Today

Value Unused:	$$$$$

American Ten-Cent Jefferson Bank Note Special Printing

Stamp Production

Printer:	American Bank Note Company
Designer:	Butler Packard
Engravers:	Joseph P. Ourdan (portrait), Douglas S. Ronaldson (frame and lettering), Charles Skinner (secret mark)
Format:	Sheets of 200, cut vertically into 2 panes of 100
Plate Numbers:	Current American plates
Date of Issue:	July 16, 1880
Uses:	Souvenir. Valid for postal use.
Quantity Issued:	With Continental 180 total

Stamp Features

Size:	20 x 25 mm. (0.8 x 1.0 inches)
Watermark:	None
Grill:	None
Paper:	Soft
Perforations:	12
Secret Mark:	None
Colors:	Deep brown
Varieties:	None

Collectable Stamp Today

Value Unused:	$$$$$$

American Twelve-Cent Clay Bank Note Reissues

Stamp Production
Printer:	American Bank Note Company
Designer:	Butler Packard
Engravers:	Luigi (Louis) Delnoce (portrait), Douglas S. Ronaldson (frame and lettering), Charles Skinner (secret mark)
Format:	Sheets of 200, cut vertically into 2 panes of 100
Plate Numbers:	Old Continental plates
Date of Issue:	July 16, 1880
Uses:	Souvenir. Valid for postal use.
Quantity Issued:	With Continental 282 total

Stamp Features
Size:	20 x 25 mm. (0.8 x 1.0 inches)
Watermark:	None
Grill:	None
Paper:	Soft
Perforations:	12
Secret Mark:	None
Colors:	Black violet
Varieties:	None

Collectable Stamp Today
Value Unused:	$$$$$

American Fifteen-Cent Webster Bank Note Special Printing

Stamp Production
Printer: American Bank Note Company
Designer: Butler Packard
Engravers: Luigi (Louis) Delnoce (portrait), Douglas S. Ronaldson
                   (frame and lettering), Charles Skinner (secret mark)
Format: Sheets of 200, cut vertically into 2 panes of 100
Plate Numbers: Current American plates
Date of Issue: July 16, 1880
Uses: Souvenir. Valid for postal use.
Quantity Issued: With Continental 169 total

Stamp Features
Size: 20 x 25 mm. (0.8 x 1.0 inches)
Watermark: None
Grill: None
Paper: Soft
Perforations: 12
Secret Mark: Present
Colors: Deep orange
Varieties: None

Collectable Stamp Today
Value Unused: $$$$$$

American Twenty-Four-Cent Webster Bank Note Reissue

Stamp Production
Printer:	American Bank Note Company
Designer:	Butler Packard
Engravers:	Joseph P. Ourdan (portrait), Douglas S. Ronaldson (frame and lettering)
Format:	Sheets of 200, cut vertically into 2 panes of 100
Plate Numbers:	Old National plates
Date of Issue:	July 16, 1880
Uses:	Souvenir. Valid for postal use.
Quantity Issued:	With Continental 286 total

Stamp Features
Size:	20 x 25 mm. (0.8 x 1.0 inches)
Watermark:	None
Grill:	None
Paper:	Soft
Perforations:	12
Secret Mark:	None
Colors:	Dark purple
Varieties:	None

Collectable Stamp Today
Value Unused:	$$$$$

American Thirty-Cent Hamilton Bank Note Special Printing

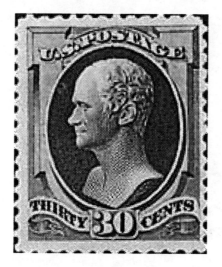

Stamp Production
Printer: American Bank Note Company
Designer: Butler Packard
Engravers: Joseph P. Ourdan (portrait), Douglas S. Ronaldson (frame and lettering)
Format: Sheets of 200, cut vertically into 2 panes of 100
Plate Numbers: Old National plate
Date of Issue: July 16, 1880
Uses: Souvenir. Valid for postal use.
Quantity Issued: With Continental 179 total

Stamp Features
Size: 20 x 25 mm. (0.8 x 1.0 inches)
Watermark: None
Grill: None
Paper: Soft
Perforations: 12
Secret Mark: Present
Colors: Greenish brown
Varieties: None

Collectable Stamp Today
Value Unused: $$$$$$

American Ninety-Cent Perry Bank Note Special Printing

Stamp Production

Printer:	American Bank Note Company
Designer:	Butler Packard
Engravers:	Luigi (Louis) Delnoce (portrait), Douglas S. Ronaldson (frame and lettering).
Format:	Sheets of 200, cut vertically into 2 panes of 100
Plate Numbers:	Old National plate
Date of Issue:	July 16, 1880
Uses:	Souvenir. Valid for postal use.
Quantity Issued:	With Continental 170 total

Stamp Features

Size:	20 x 25 mm. (0.8 x 1.0 inches)
Watermark:	None
Grill:	None
Paper:	Soft
Perforations:	12
Secret Mark:	None
Colors:	Dull carmine
Varieties:	None

Collectable Stamp Today

Value Unused:	$$$$$$

On July 16th, 1880, the American Bank Note Company released its series of special printing stamps. The paper and the perforations are the same as were then in regular use. The stamps were not gummed like the Continental's. The printing is very clear and sharp. All the stamps are very rare. A light brown special printing of the 5-cent Garfield was added in 1882. It exists today as a block of four stamps. On December 5th, 1883, the 2-cent red-brown Washington and 4-cent blue-green Jackson were re-issued. The two-cent is an exception being gummed. It is from a special trial printing by a new steam powered press. Some of these stamps have an imperforate vertical gutter where the sheet was to be cut into panes.

The brown Jackson 2, 7, 12 and 24-cent issues were obsolete by then, not regularly printed by American and are classified as reissues, rather than special printings. The soft porous paper readily distinguishes these four stamps as all the originals were on the hard paper used by the National and Continental companies.

Unlike the 1875 hard paper special printings, the 1880 American special printings were not cut apart with scissors. Therefore, it may be difficult to tell the other values of this set from the regular issue stamps. The only hint is that the colors are deeper, sharper, and richer than the regularly issued stamps. The 10-cent special printing was printed from Continental plate 302 or 303 after plate was re-entered, so it does not have the secret mark.

Essays, Proofs, and Specimens

Essays

There are the Continental essays for the 1870 issue featuring large numerals of value as an unusual central design. Other Continental essays include those that feature a vignette of a stylized version of Columbia. The National essays of 1870 are similar in design to the actual issued stamps that the company eventually did print.

A series of 1877 essays by the Philadelphia Bank Note Company, which did not win the printing contract, come in a range of colors but only two vignette designs. Most feature a bust of Washington and a frame resembling the 3-cent 1851 stamp. One other has a vignette of Lincoln. Most of these essays are lithographed printings. Continental, the eventual winner of the 1877 contract also made a series of essays that featured Franklin, Washington, a vignette of Liberty, and an Indian maiden in a head address, all in 3-cent denominations.

There are American essays for the 1881 including a 1-cent Lincoln, a 10-cent Franklin, and vignette of peace. In 1883 and 1887, American printed essays similar to the actually issued stamps.

Proofs

The proofs for the National ungrilled, Continental, and American stamps are known. Large die proofs, made by the three original bank note companies, can be found for most stamp issues. Continental and

Figure 6-41. Philadelphia Bank Note Company Essay. This is an example of a bank note essay from a company that lost the stamp printing contract. It features a bust of Washington and a frame resembling the three-cent 1851 stamp.

American die proofs of the 24, 30, and 90-cent show secret marks. Since plates were never made from these dies, so there are no plate proofs or issued stamps with the added secret marks.

Figure 6-42. Example of a Bank Note Series Large Die Proof. Large die proofs, were made by the all three Bank Note companies.

The small die proofs, both made for the 1903 Roosevelt album by the Bureau of Engraving and Printing, and the 1915 Panama Pacific Exposition, also exists.

Figure 6-43. Small Die Proofs. For both the 1903 Roosevelt album (left), and the 1915 Panama Pacific Exposition (right), small die Bank Note series proofs exist today.

Plate proofs are found both on India paper and cardboard.

There are a great many trial color die (large and small) and plate proofs but not all values of every group exist.

Figure 6-44. Example of a Pair of Bank Note Plate Proofs.

The Atlanta sets of plate proofs are on thin card in five colors: black, scarlet, brown, green, and blue. The Continental designs of 1873-75 were used for these special items created by the American Bank Note Company in 1881. This was for display at the International Cotton Exposition held in Atlanta, Georgia.

Specimens

Specimen overprints exist for most issues. The ink color and pattern of lettering vary by the Bank Note Company that printed them.

Figure 6-45. Example of a Specimen Stamp. Overprint stamps exist for most issues of the banknote series. The ink and pattern of lettering vary by the Bank Note Company.

7

The Small Bank Note Series

The last nineteenth century regular stamp issue printed by a private a bank note company was the small bank note series. They were in use from 1890 to 1893. They look like the preceding series, but they are smaller. Hence, their name! This size became the standard for regular issue stamps up to this day.

Contract Troubles

As was common, there was a problem in the bidding for the new contract to print this issue. The old contract for the Bank Note stamps expired June 30, 1889. The Post Office Department took bids for stamps of two possible sizes. One size was the same as the Bank Note stamps and a second was for a smaller size. The color of the stamps for the first time was determined by the government specifications of the contract, not by the printer. Two bids were submitted, one by Charles F. Steel of Philadelphia, and the other by the American Bank Note Company of New York, the current stamp printers. Steel placed the lower bid. But American Bank Note Company protested on the grounds that the Steel Company lacked the necessary printing equipment. When Steel failed to show he had the required facilities, his contract was withdrawn. Steel 's failure might have been deliberate, the result of a secret non-competition contract between Steel and American.

The Postmaster General then had a second round of bidding. Between October 1 and December 1, 1889, the American Bank Note Company, printed a temporary supply of stamps, though its contract expired at the end of June. On the second round of bidding, two were submitted, one from the Franklin Bank Note Company and the other from American Bank Note Company. The American Bank Note Company won the contract on October 23. And The Post Office Department decided on the smaller stamp size.

A Simple Series

These stamps are easy for the novice stamp collector. There are no paper, grill, perforation, or watermark varieties. There are eleven denominations: 1, 2, 3, 4, 5, 6, 8, 10, 15, 30, and 90-cents. There are twelve major varieties, because the 2-cent denomination came in two colors, lake and carmine. The one, two, three, six, ten, fifteen, thirty and ninety-cent stamps were placed on sale on February 22, 1890. The four and five cent stamps were issued later, June 2nd of that year. The eight-cent stamp was not an original part of the series. It was issued three years later, March 21st, 1893. Its addition to the starting lineup resulted from the reduction of the registration fee from ten to eight cents.

Postage Rates At the Time of the 1890 Series	
Drop Mail Rate	1 cent
Third Class Rate	1 cent
Postcard Rate (Post Office Card)	1 cent
Postcard Rate (Private Card)	2 cents
First-Class Rate	2 cents/ounce
Foreign Rate (Universal Postal Union members)	5 cents
Registry Fee	10 cents until Jan. 1, 1893 8 cents afterwards

The one and two-cent values were the first ever United States stamps printed from 400 subject size plates. These sheets were divided into four sheets of 100 stamps. The other denominations, as well as some of the 2-cent stamps came from 200 subject plates, divided into 2 panes of 100 stamps each. All stamps are perforated 12.

The 1 and 2-cent stamps were the most widely used, paying for the drop rate and basic first class rate, respectively. Since July 1, 1885, the first class rate paid for up to an ounce of mail, rather than just a half an ounce as in the past. The 5 and 10-cent stamps were used on international mail, to pay the single and double Universal Postal Union rates.

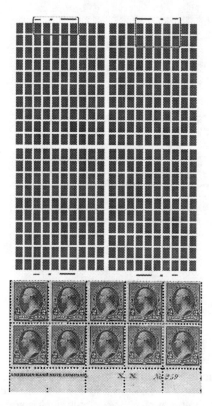

Figure 7-1. Early Steam 400 Subject Small Bank Note Plate Layout and Block Example. The one-cent and some two-cent stamps were printed from 400 subject size plates, divided into four sheets of 100 stamps. The plate imprints are centered on the top and bottom margins of each pane. The plate number is before the imprint in the left margins, and after it in the right margins. On the steam plates letters are in the top and bottom margins between the plate number and imprint on these early 1 and 2 cent plates.

The soft paper and gum are the same as the Bank Note issues made by American.

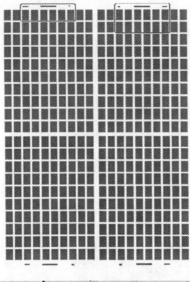

Figure 7-2. Late Steam 400 Subject Small Bank Note Plate Layout and Strip Example. As noted in figure 7-1, the one-cent and some of the two-cent Small Bank Note stamps were printed from 400 subject size plates, which were divided into four sheets of 100 stamps. With the later steam plates, the letters were placed to the outside of the imprint.

Common Designs

The 1890 stamps are of two similar designs. Both designs, all the stamps, have a vignette with a dark background and a narrow white border. Above it, set in a panel curving with the oval, are the words, UNITED STATES POSTAGE, in white capital letters. In two bottom corners is a white numeral of the denomination in an oval surrounded by a fancy scroll. For the lower denominations, up to the eight-cent stamp, below the oval, in a wavy line, are the words, X CENTS, where X is the written word for the denomination. The higher denomination stamps, ten cents and up, set in a panel following the curve, of the border of the vignette are the words of the value of the denomination.

Figure 7-3. Early Steam 200 Subject Small Bank Note Plate Layout and Strip Example. Some of the two-cent and the rest of the higher denomination small bank Note stamps were printed 200 subject plates, divided into 2 sheets of 100 stamps, each. Like the 400 subject plates, the plate imprints are centered on the top and bottom margins of each pane, with the plate number before the imprint in the left upper and lower margins, and after it in the right upper and lower margins. On the early plates, the letters are in the top and bottom margins between the plate number and imprint.

Plate Markings

The plate imprints are found centered, on the top and bottom margins of each pane, two imprints per pane. The words, AMERICAN BANK NOTE COMPANY, are in colored letters with shading to the lower right. The imprint is just the length of the width of two stamps. The plate number, with the word, No., is before the imprint in the left margins, and after it in the right margins.

On the steam printed plates, basically the whole series except the 5, 6, 15, 30, and 90-cent values, letters are used to identify a set of 5 plates used together. The letter is on the top and bottom margins between the plate number and imprint on early 1 and 2 cent plates and all of the higher value plates. For these plates, a strip of 5 stamps will include the imprint and any letter. They were placed outside the imprint on 1 and 2 cent plates of sets A1 -P1. For these plates, a strip of 6 or 7 stamps is needed to include all of the adjacent marginal markings.

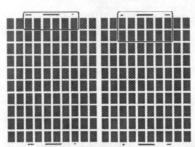

Figure 7-4. Late Steam 200 Subject Small Bank Note Plate Layout. As noted above, some of the two-cent and the rest of the higher denomination small bank Note stamps were printed 200 subject plates, divided into 2 sheets of 100 stamps, each. On the later plates, the steam letters are outside the imprint.

The Imperforates

The small bank note stamps exist imperforate. These proofs are found on regular paper, gummed, and finished except that they are not perforated. They were made at the request of then Postmaster General Wanamaker. He gave them to politic friends, in trade, to acquire rare stamps for the government's National Museum collection. A total of 56 imperforate sets, in pairs or blocks of four were released. Such imperforate proofs are collected in pairs, since cutting the perforations off a regular stamp easily creates a forgery of a single proof.

Figure 7-5. Example of Imperforate Small Bank Note Stamps. Some 1890 stamps are imperforate. They were created as political favors, not issued stamps. Today, they are classified as proofs. They are collected in pairs or blocks of four since cutting the perforations off a single regular stamp would easily create a forgery.

Seapost Mailings

Seapost postal markings are found on transatlantic letters sent between 1891 and World War II. The seapost markings were applied by post offices on ships crossing the ocean. The seapost service sped up letter transit across the Atlantic by having the mail sorted when the ship reached port. It didn't have to be processed at the port post office. There was an extra postal fee for such service. This contrasts with the rest of the mail carried across the ocean that reached the ship in mailbags, postmarked at their point of origin. Such mail was carried in locked bags and processed at the destination point.

ONE-CENT FRANKLIN

One-Cent Small Bank Note Franklin

Stamp Production

Printer:	American Bank Note Company
Designer:	Thomas F. Morris
Engravers:	Edward C. Steimle (portrait), Douglas S. Ronaldson (frame and lettering)
Format:	Sheets of 400, cut into 4 panes of 100
Plate Numbers:	C11-15, G36-40, Q89-93, BB145-149, FF165-169, UU240-244, CI280-284, DI285-289, FI295-299.
Date of Issue:	Feb. 22,1890
Earliest Known Use:	Feb 27,1890
Uses:	Drop mail. Third-class domestic mail.
Quantity Issued:	2,206,093,450

Stamp Features

Size:	19 x 22 mm. (0.7 x 0.9 inches)
Watermark:	None
Perforations:	12
Colors:	Dull blue, blue, deep blue, ultramarine.
Varieties:	Double transfer, Candle flame.

Collectable Stamp Today

Collectable Cancellation Colors:	Black, blue, magenta.
Collectable Cancellation Varieties:	China, Samoa.
Value Unused:	$$$
Value Used:	$
Surviving Covers:	150,000
Largest Known Multiple:	Unused: 100 (complete pane)
	Used: 24 (block)

The one-cent stamp of the 1890 features a profile bust of Benjamin Franklin, after a work by Rubricht. It was issued on February 22,1890. It was printed in several shades: dull blue, blue, deep blue, and ultramarine. These pale colors detract from the appearance of the stamp.

A large number of 400 subject plates printed this issue on steam presses to make billions of stamps.

Varieties-The Candle Flames

The candle flame is a variety of the one-cent stamp of this series. It is a white extension, looking like a flame, on the right foot of the numeral, 1. It can be on one or both of the numerals. They are not constant, stamp-to-stamp. No two are exactly alike. It is printing variety, not a defect or variety of the printing plate. It was caused during the wiping process when too much ink was removed from this portion of the plate from too much pressure on the wiping roller.

Figure 7-6. One-Cent Candle Flame Variety. The candle flames are a printing variety. They are the white flame-like extensions on the right foot of the numeral, 1, on either on one or both (as in this case) of the numerals. They are the result of the wiping process removing too much ink from the plate. Since it is not a plate defect, it is not consistent from stamp to stamp.

LAKE TWO-CENT WASHINGTON

Lake Two-Cent Small Bank Note Washington

Stamp Production
Printer: American Bank Note Company
Designer: Thomas F. Morris
Engravers: Charles Skinner (portrait), Douglas S. Ronaldson (frame and lettering)
Format: Sheets of 400, cut into 4 panes of 100
Plate Numbers: A1, A2, A3, B6, B7, B8, B9, B10, D17, D18, D19, F31, F32, F34, K59, L62, 00214, YY263. The exact plate numbers are unknown but they among the first plates made for this stamp.
Date of Issue: Feb. 22, 1890
Earliest Known Use: Feb. 22, 1890 (first day cover, one known)
Uses: Basic first-class domestic mail. Private postcard rate.
Quantity Issued: 100,000,000

Stamp Features
Size: 19 x 22 mm. (0.7 x 0.9 inches)
Watermark: None
Perforations: 12
Colors: Lake, carmine lake, lake red.
Varieties: Double transfer.

Collectable Stamp Today
Collectable Cancellation Colors:
None
Collectable Cancellation Varieties:
supplementary mail type F.
Value Unused: $$$$

Value Used: $$
Surviving Covers: 40,000
Largest Known Multiple: Unused: 100 (complete pane)
Used: 20 (block)

The two-cent denomination was used for first-class postage. It features a profile bust of George Washington, looking to the left, after a work of Houdon. It was printed in two colors. The first issued stamp was a shade of lake. This ink soon was panned as too flowery in appearance and too gummy in feel. It rubs off on the user's fingers. Soon after it was printed, the color of the stamp was changed. It is the only denomination of the 1890 series with a major variety.

The exact numbered plates that printed the two-cent lake colored stamps are not completely known but they are among the first plates made for this stamp.

CARMINE TWO-CENT WASHINGTON

Lake Two-Cent Small Bank Note Washington

Stamp Production

Printer:	American Bank Note Company
Designer:	Thomas F. Morris
Engravers:	Charles Skinner (portrait), Douglas S. Ronaldson (frame and lettering)
Format:	Sheets of 400, cut into 4 panes of 100, Sheets of 200, cut into 2 panes of 100
Plate Numbers:	A1-5, B6-10, B71, D16-20, F31-35, H41-45, K56-60, L61-65, M66-70, M99, N74-78, O79-83, P84-88, R94-98, S100-104, T105-109, U110-114, V115-119, W120-124, X125-129, Y130-134, Z135-139, AA140-144, CC150-154, DD155-159, EE160-164, GG170-174, HH175-179, II180-184, JJ185-189, kK190-194, LL195-199, NN205-209, OO210-214, PP215-219, QQ220-224, RR226-229, SS230-234, TT235-239, VV245-249, WW250-254, XX255-259, YY260-264, AI270-274, BI275-279, EI290-294, GI300-304, HI305-309, II310-314, JI315-319, KI320-324, LI325-329, MI330-334, N1335-319, OI340-344, PI345-349.
Date of Issue:	May 12, 1890
Earliest Known Use:	Apr. 29,1890
Uses:	Basic first class domestic mail, up to one ounce. Private postcard rate.
Quantity Issued:	6,144,819,500

Stamp Features

Size:	19 x 22 mm. (0.7 x 0.9 inches)
Watermark:	None
Perforations:	12
Colors:	Carmine, dark carmine, rose, carmine rose.

Varieties:	Cap on left 2 (Plates 235, 236, 246, 247, 248), Cap on both 2's (Plates 247 and 248), Double transfer.

Collectable Stamp Today
Collectable Cancellation Colors:
Black, blue, purple.
Collectable Cancellation Varieties:
supplementary mail type F or G, China.

Value Unused:	$$$
Value Used:	$
Surviving Covers:	1,000,000
Largest Known Multiple:	Unused: 100 (complete pane)
	Used: 17 (block)

Postmaster General Wanamaker was forced to change in the color of the two-cent denomination for the reasons noted above. This took place on May 12, 1890, not long after the first colored stamp was issued. The color was changed from lake to carmine. The carmine stamps account for the vast majority of the 1890 two-cent issue.

Figure 7-7. Postmaster General John Wanamaker. The postmaster general at the time of the 1890 stamp series, he made the decision to change the color of the two-cent small bank note stamp. Wanamaker was a famous Philadelphia retailer, businessman, and politician.

Machine cancellations came into common use during the 1890's. Each of the various canceling machine types has their own characteristics. Cover collectors form collections based on the different types.

The 2-cent stamp plates AH, R, W, Y-Z, CC-HH, NN, QQ and SS-TT have 400 stamps, while the rest have 200 subjects.

Plate Varieties

The caps on the 2-cent stamp of this series are the best known United States plate variety. The caps are little white blobs atop the numerals, 2. The plate variety is a result of a transfer roll breakdown that was passed on into the printing plate and then the stamps. There is two cap varieties: a cap on the left 2 (from plates 235, 236, 246, 247, 248) and caps on both 2's (from plates 245, 246). This is a common plate variety. There are even pairs showing the two major cap varieties side by side!

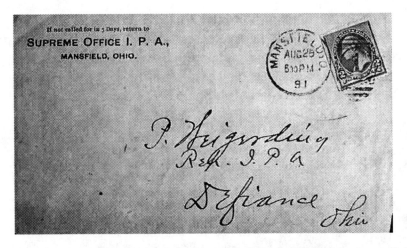

Figure 7-8. Example of a Two-Cent Small Bank Note Stamp on a Cover. Here is an example of the common two-cent Small Bank Note stamp paying the basic first class domestic mail of up to one ounce. In this case, it is on a letter sent from Mansfield to Defiance, Ohio.

Occasionally, a two-cent stamp is found that has a cap on the right 2, only. This is not a plate variety, rather considered an inking variety, like the one-cent candle frame.

Figure 7-9. Caps Variety of the Two-Cent Bank Note Stamps. Caps found on some of the 2-cent stamps of the 1890 series are the best known and most common of all United States plate varieties. The caps are little white extensions on the top of the numerals, 2. They are the result of a transfer roll breakdown. There are two cap varieties: a cap on the left 2 and caps on both 2's (close up shown here).

THREE-CENT JACKSON

Three-Cent Small Bank Note Jackson

Stamp Production

Printer:	American Bank Note Company
Designer:	Thomas F. Morris
Engravers:	Charles Skinner (portrait), Douglas S. Ronaldson (frame and lettering)
Format:	Sheets of 200, cut into 2 panes of 100
Plate Numbers:	21, 22.
Date of Issue:	Feb. 22, 1890
Earliest Known Use:	Feb 28, 1890
Uses:	Makeup for other rates.
Quantity Issued:	46,877,250

Stamp Features

Size:	19 x 22 mm. (0.7 x 0.9 inches)
Watermark:	None
Perforations:	12
Colors:	Purple, bright purple, dark purple.
Varieties:	None

Collectable Stamp Today
Collectable Cancellation Colors:
Black, magenta.
Collectable Cancellation Varieties:
Samoa

Value Unused:	$$$
Value Used:	$$
Surviving Covers:	25,000
Largest Known Multiple:	Unused: 100 (complete pane)
	Used: 10 (block)

The three-cent stamp of this series was issued on February 22, 1890. It features a profile bust of Jackson, looking to the left, after a work by Powers, sitting on an oval.

This stamp and all the higher denominations of the series were printed from 200 subject plates.

This stamp was not widely used, as it did not fill a niche in the postal rate structure. Therefore, it rarely is seen as a single on a cover.

FOUR-CENT LINCOLN

Four-Cent Small Bank Note Lincoln

Stamp Production

Printer:	American Bank Note Company
Designer:	Thomas F. Morris
Engravers:	Alfred Jones (portrait), Douglas S. Ronaldson (frame and lettering)
Format:	Sheets of 200, cut into 2 panes of 100
Plate Numbers:	J51-55, MM200-204
Date of Issue:	June 2, 1890
Earliest Known Use:	July 16, 1890
Uses:	Double weight first-class domestic mail, from one to two ounces.
Quantity Issued:	66,759,475

Stamp Features

Size:	19 x 22 mm. (0.7 x 0.9 inches)
Watermark:	None
Perforations:	12
Colors:	Dark brown, blackish brown.
Varieties:	Double transfer.

Collectable Stamp Today
Collectable Cancellation Colors:
Black, blue, magenta.
Collectable Cancellation Varieties:
China

Value Unused:	$$$
Value Used:	$$
Surviving Covers:	20,000
Largest Known Multiple:	Unused: 100 (complete pane)
	Used: 10 (block)

This stamp was issued a bit later than most of the stamps of the series, not until June 2, 1890. The stamp carries a three-quarters face portrait of Lincoln, looking to the right, after a photograph of him. It is a widely used stamp, since it paid the postage on double weight first-class letters.

FIVE-CENT GRANT

Five-Cent Small Bank Note Grant

Stamp Production
Printer:	American Bank Note Company
Designer:	Thomas F. Morris
Engravers:	Charles Skinner (portrait), Douglas S. Ronaldson (frame and lettering)
Format:	Sheets of 200, cut into 2 panes of 100
Plate Numbers:	I46-50
Date of Issue:	June 2, 1890
Earliest Known Use:	June 14, 1890
Uses:	Basic mail rate to Universal Postal Union foreign destinations
Quantity Issued:	152,236,530

Stamp Features
Size:	19 x 22 mm. (0.7 x 0.9 inches)
Watermark:	None
Perforations:	12
Colors:	Chocolate, yellow brown.
Varieties:	Shading lines of the coat extending into oval, Double transfer.

Collectable Stamp Today
Collectable Cancellation Colors:
Black, blue, magenta.
Collectable Cancellation Varieties:
supplementary mail type F or G, Samoa, China.
Value Unused:	$$$
Value Used:	$$

Surviving Covers: 150,000
Largest Known Multiple: Unused: 100 (complete pane)
Used: 8 (block)

This stamp was issued the same day as the four-cent, June 2, 1890. It is based on a three-quarters face photograph of U. S. Grant, looking to the right.

This is an interesting variety on this stamp. The lines of Grant's coat, on the left side of the stamp, extend into the oval frame surrounding the portrait. This variety is due to the use of an incompletely finished die to make some of the printing plate positions.

SIX-CENT GARFIELD

Six-Cent Small Bank Note Garfield

Stamp Production
Printer: American Bank Note Company
Designer: Thomas F. Morris
Engravers: Charles Skinner (portrait), Douglas S. Ronaldson (frame and lettering)
Format: Sheets of 200, cut into 2 panes of 100
Plate Numbers: 23
Date of Issue: Feb.22, 1890
Earliest Known Use: May 8,1890

| Uses: | Multiple weight (triple) first-class rate. |
| Quantity Issued: | 9,253,400 |

Stamp Features

Size:	19 x 22 mm. (0.7 x 0.9 inches)
Watermark:	None
Perforations:	12
Colors:	Brown red, dark brown red.
Varieties:	None

Collectable Stamp Today
Collectable Cancellation Colors:
Black, blue, magenta.
Collectable Cancellation Varieties:
supplementary mail type F

Value Unused:	$$$
Value Used:	$$$
Surviving Covers:	12,000
Largest Known Multiple:	Unused: 100 (complete pane)
	Used: 12 (plate and number block)

This stamp was issued on February 22, 1890. The design featured a portrait of the recently assassinated president, James Garfield. It is after a photograph of him with a three-quarters face, looking off to the left.

EIGHT-CENT SHERMAN

Eight-Cent Small Bank Note Sherman

Stamp Production

Printer:	American Bank Note Company
Designer:	Thomas F. Morris
Engravers:	Charles Skinner (portrait), Douglas S. Ronaldson (frame and lettering)
Format:	Sheets of 200, cut into 2 panes of 100
Plate Numbers:	ZZ265-269.
Date of Issue:	Mar. 21, 1893
Earliest Known Use:	May 21,1893
Uses:	Registry fee after Jan. 1, 1893
Quantity Issued:	12,087,800

Stamp Features

| Size: | 19 x 22 mm. (0.7 x 0.9 inches) |

Watermark:	None
Perforations:	12
Colors:	Lilac, grayish lilac, magenta.
Varieties:	None

Collectable Stamp Today
Collectable Cancellation Colors:
  Black, blue, magenta.
Collectable Cancellation Varieties:
  None

Value Unused:	$$$
Value Used:	$$$
Surviving Covers:	20,000
Largest Known Multiple:	Unused: 100 (complete pane)
	Used: 5 (block)

This stamp, while part of the 1890 series, was not issued until three years later, on March 21, 1893. It was issued to pay for the new lower rate for registry fees. This fee was reduced from ten cents to eight cents on January 1, 1893. The design of the stamp is based on a full-face photograph of General William T. Sherman.

Figure 7-10. William Sherman. The design of the eight-cent small bank note stamp is based on a photograph of the American Civil War General William T. Sherman.

TEN-CENT WEBSTER

Ten-Cent Small Bank Note Webster

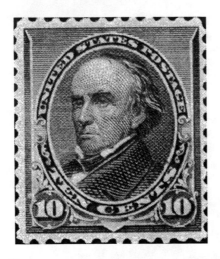

Stamp Production

Printer:	American Bank Note Company
Designer:	Thomas F. Morris
Engravers:	Charles Skinner (portrait), Douglas S. Ronaldson (frame and lettering)
Format:	Sheets of 200, cut into 2 panes of 100
Plate Numbers:	E26-30
Date of Issue:	Feb. 22, 1890
Earliest Known Use:	Mar. 5, 1890
Uses:	Registry rate until Jan. 1, 1893
Quantity Issued:	72,746,160

Stamp Features

Size:	19 x 22 mm. (0.7 x 0.9 inches)
Watermark:	None
Perforations:	12
Colors:	Green, bluish green, dark green.
Varieties:	Double transfer

Collectable Stamp Today
Collectable Cancellation Colors:
Black, magenta.
Collectable Cancellation Varieties:
supplementary mail type F or G, Samoa.

Value Unused:	$$$$
Value Used:	$$
Surviving Covers:	35,000
Largest Known Multiple:	Unused: 100 (complete pane)
	Used: 10 (block)

Like most of the series, this stamp was issued on February 22, 1890. The design is based on a three-quarters face daguerreotype of senator and statesman Daniel Webster. The vignette has him looking off to the left. Several subjects were considered for this denomination. Ten-cent essays include not only Webster, but also John Adams and General Sherman. The stamp was used to pay the ten-cent registry fee until it was reduced to eight cents on January 1, 1893.

FIFTEEN-CENT CLAY

Fifteen-Cent Small Bank Note Clay

Stamp Production
Printer:	American Bank Note Company
Designer:	Thomas F. Morris
Engravers:	Charles Skinner (portrait), Douglas S. Ronaldson (frame and lettering)
Plate Numbers:	22
Date of Issue:	Feb. 22, 1890
Earliest Known Use:	May 27, 1890
Uses:	Multiple rate foreign and domestic postage.
Quantity Issued:	5,548,710

Stamp Features
Size:	19 x 22 mm. (0.7 x 0.9 inches)
Watermark:	None
Perforations:	12
Colors:	Indigo, deep indigo.

Varieties: Double transfer, Triple transfer.

Collectable Stamp Today
Collectable Cancellations:
Black, blue, magenta, purple.
Collectable Cancellation Varieties:
supplementary mail type F, snowshoe
Value Unused: $$$$
Value Used: $$$
Surviving Covers: 3,000
Largest Known Multiple: Unused: 100 (complete pane)
Used: 32 (block)

This stamp was issued on February 22, 1890, like the majority of the stamps of the series. The design was based on a three-quarters face daguerreotype of Henry Clay, looking to the left. Being a high denomination stamp, only one plate was used to print this stamp.

Some stamps are canceled with an oval gridiron in magenta. This cancellation is the snowshoe cancellation, and it is a desirable as a collectable item.

THIRTY-CENT JEFFERSON

Thirty-Cent Small Bank Note Jefferson

Stamp Production

Printer:	American Bank Note Company
Designer:	Thomas F. Morris
Engravers:	Alfred Jones (portrait), Douglas S. Ronaldson (frame and lettering)
Plate Numbers:	24
Date of Issue:	Feb. 22, 1890
Earliest Known Use:	Apr. 14, 1890
Uses:	Multiple rate foreign and domestic postage.
Quantity Issued:	1,504,408

Stamp Features

Size:	19 x 22 mm. (0.7 x 0.9 inches)
Watermark:	None
Perforations:	12
Colors:	Black, gray black, full black.
Varieties:	Double transfer

Collectable Stamp Today

Collectable Cancellation Colors:	
	Black, blue, red.
Collectable Cancellation Varieties:	
	supplementary mail type F
Value Unused:	$$$$
Value Used:	$$$
Surviving Covers:	300
Largest Known Multiple:	Unused: 100 (complete pane)
	Used: 32 (block)

The thirty-cent stamp of the small bank note series was issued on February 22, 1890. The design features a profile of Jefferson, looking to the left. It was based on a work of Ceracchi.

There is an interesting feature to this stamp. The printing of the middle left side of the stamp was lightly transferred from the master die to the transfer roll and then in turn to the printing plate. This results in this area of the stamp appearing like it was rubbed off like with an eraser.

NINETY-CENT PERRY

Ninety-Cent Small Bank Note Perry

Stamp Production

Printer:	American Bank Note Company

Designer:	Thomas P. Morris
Engravers:	Edward C. Steimle (portrait), Douglas S. Ronaldson (frame and lettering)
Plate Numbers:	25
Date of Issue:	Feb. 22, 1890
Earliest Known Use:	Feb. 7, 1892
Uses:	Multiple rate foreign and domestic postage.
Quantity Issued:	219,721

Stamp Features

Size:	19 x 22 mm. (0.7 x 0.9 inches)
Watermark:	None
Perforations:	12
Colors:	Orange, yellow orange, red orange.
Varieties:	Short transfer at the bottom.

Collectable Stamp Today
Collectable Cancellation Colors:
None.
Collectable Cancellation Varieties:
supplementary mail type F or G

Value Unused:	$$$$
Value Used:	$$$$
Surviving Covers:	100
Largest Known Multiple:	Unused: 36 (plate block)
	Used: 25 (block)

This is the highest denomination of the 1890 series. Like the majority of stamps of this series, it issued on February 22, 1890. The design is that of a profile bust of Commodore O. H. Perry, looking to the left, after Wolcott's statue of him.

Because of the stamp's orange color, used stamps have cancellations that obliterate the design. Because it is a rare stamp, there are fewer than 100 surviving covers.

Hundred of mint copies of this stamp were found in the Washington, D. C. Post Office, as late as 1905. It was a source of many of today's collector's existing unused copies.

Essays, Proofs, and Specimens

Essays

Only the American Bank Note Company, the printer of the series, made essays. The essays are similar in design to the finished stamps. They exist for all the denominations of the series. They are either nearly completed designs or just the vignette or frame.

Proofs

Figure 7-11. Large Die Proof of the Small Bank Note Series. These are large die proofs made by American Bank Note Company at the time of the original stamp production.

Proofs of the 1890 small bank note series follow the typical pattern. There are large die proofs of all the denominations, made by American Bank Note Company at the time of the original stamp production. There are two sets of small die proofs, made by the Bureau of Engraving and Printing for the Roosevelt Album in 1903 and the Panama-Pacific Exposition in 1915.

There are plate proofs of all the denominations, both on India paper and card. The plate proofs are both inexpensive to buy today and beautiful to look at.

There are color trial proofs of up to the eight-cent denomination. They may be either die color proofs or plate color proofs, and may be on India paper or card.

Figure 7-12. Small Die Proof of the Small Bank Note Series. There are two small die proofs. One set was made for the Roosevelt Album in 1903 (shown here) and the other for the Panama-Pacific Exposition in 1915.

Specimens

There are sample stamps for all the issues of the series. These stamps are handstamped in dull purple with the plain font printing of the word, Specimen.

8

The Columbian Commemorative Issue of 1893

The Columbian issue of 1893 marked a new era in United States stamps. They are the nation's first commemorative issues. Commemorative stamps differ from regular postal issues as they are made for just a short time. They celebrate a specific theme, such as a country's famous person, place, or historic event. They often are issued in sets. They usually depict detailed scenes making them wonderful stamps for the collector.

The Columbian and future commemorative stamps did not replace but rather supplemented current regular postal stamps. Though they are valid and used for postage, commemorative stamps are made for stamp collectors. Correspondence even of this era shows how postal officials realized that collectors would buy the stamps. And since they were not used for postage, the stamp sales were pure profit for the post office.

However, this first commemorative issue turned out not to be popular with either the public or stamp collectors. Collectors felt exploited. Especially upsetting to them were the dollar values, each of which were a day's wages at the time. Also, 1893 was a depression year, contributing to poor stamp sales.

Many stamp dealers speculated on the high value stamps of the series, hoping to make a profit in the future. But years later, in June 1899, the still unsold Columbian stamps, held in the Washington D. C. city post office were finally withdrawn from sale and burned. The initial glut of unsold stamps was not eased until World War I. But eventually prices went up and continue to rise. Because of the rarity and today's high price of the dollar denominations of this series, the degree of completion of the Columbian series has become a measure of one's American stamp collection. The high value stamps are popular at today's high-end stamp auctions.

The American Bank Note Company, the maker of the then current 1890 small bank note regular series stamps, printed the series. The paper, gum and perforation are the same as the other issues of the American Bank Note Company. They are the last postage stamps printed by a private company for 50 years. That is because in 1894, the Bureau of Printing and Engraving started printing United States stamps.

Figure 8-1. Columbian Exposition. The first United States commemorative stamps were issued for the Columbian Exposition, a world's fair in 1893, held in Chicago, that celebrated the four hundredth anniversary of the discovery of America by Christopher Columbus. Shown is a picture of the fair grounds.

These stamps were issued for the Columbian Exposition, a world's fair of 1893 in Chicago. The expo celebrated the four hundredth anniversary of the discovery of America by Columbus. Actually, the exposition was a year late, as the 400th anniversary was 1892! This was on purpose. To allow for local celebrations of Columbus Day on October 12, 1892, the world's fair was scheduled from May 1st to October 30th, 1893.

The vignettes feature Christopher Columbus and the events of his discovery of America. Because of the complex scenes, a larger stamp size than was used. The size was that of a special delivery stamp, measuring one inch high by 1-11/32 inches, wide.

All the stamps of the series are of a uniform design. The years, 1492 and 1892, are in upper corners. In white shaded capital letters, in a waved line across the top, are the words, "UNITED STATES OF AMERICA." Below this banner, following to the curved frame of the top of the picture under it, is the wording of denomination. These words end on either side of the stamp, with the numeral of the stamp's denomination. Underneath is the vignette, surrounded by a white frame with an arched top. The title of the vignette is at the bottom of the stamp.

The Columbian denominations are basically the same as those of the then current 1890 regular issued series. The exceptions are there were no 90-cent stamps, but there were 50-cent and 1, 2, 3, 4 and 5-dollar stamps.

Plating

The one-cent stamps were printed on sheets of 200. The two-cent stamps were printed on sheets of 200 and 100 stamps. All the other values were printed in sheets of 100 stamps.

The one and some of the two-cent plates are arranged into two panes of 100 stamps, one above the other. Therefore, any straight edges on these stamps are at top or bottom. The 100 stamp sheets produced two panes of 50 stamps each. However, full sheets of 100 stamps (2 panes) of the higher denominational Columbian stamps were made, not cut apart, and still exist today. The marginal markings of the company imprint, plate number, and serial letter appear four times, twice at top and twice at the bottom. On the left side of the plate, the order is the serial letter, then the imprint, American Bank Note Company, then the plate number. On the right side of the plate, it is the plate number, then the company imprint, and finally the serial letter. Plate collectors save imprint strips of 4 stamps and imprint blocks of 8 stamps. The company imprint, alone, appears at each side of the plate.

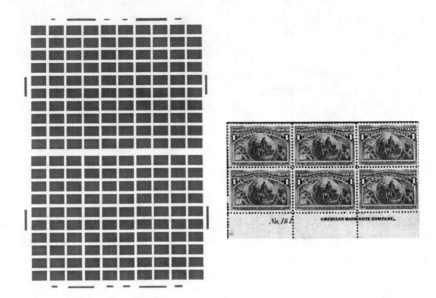

Figure 8-2. 200 Stamp Sheet Colombian Commemorative Stamp Plate. The one-cent and some of the two-cent stamps were printed in sheets of 200. They are arranged into two panes of 100 stamps, one above the other. Shown is the plate layout and an example of a plate block.

The Imperforates

Figure 8-3. The Columbian Imperforates. Some of the Columbian commemorative stamps were made imperforate. They were not a part of the regular issue. Instead, they were gifts given by Postmaster General John Wanamaker to his political friends. They are collected in pairs to prove their imperforate state. Shown is a pair of two-cent imperforate stamps of the series.

The Columbian issue stamps were made imperforate in all denominations. These imperforates were gummed and identical with the issued stamps except naturally for the missing perforations. These imperforate stamps were never regularly issued. They were cut into imperforate pairs that were given to Postmaster General John Wanamaker. He later passed them on as gifts to his political friends.

Covers and Cancellations

All the stamps can be found on cover canceled with the Exposition Station cancellation from the Chicago world's fair site. These covers are of special value and interest today.

The Columbian Exposition stamps were issued January 1, 1893, with the exception of the 8-cent value that was added to the set in March of that year. As January 1st was a Sunday that year, stamp collectors recognize either the 1st or the 2nd as a first-day cover.

Since the series was not available for use for a long time, there are not a wide variety of cancellation types to collect.

Figure 8-4. Exposition Station Cancellation. The Columbian series stamps are found on covers canceled with the Exposition Station cancellation, placed at the Chicago world's fair site. Shown is a close up of the cancellation of a five-cent stamp of the series.

The 1992 Columbian Reissues

Figure 8-5. The 1992 Colombian Reissue. In 1992, the United States Postal Service commemorated the 100th anniversary of the first Colombian commemorative stamps by reissuing them in a set of six souvenir sheets. One of the souvenir sheets is shown above.

In 1992, the United States Postal Service commemorated the 500th anniversary of the Columbus's discovery of America by reissuing the Columbian commemorative stamps of 1893. The 16 stamps were issued in six souvenir sheets. Five sheets contained three stamps each, while the sixth had a single stamp, the $5 value. Each souvenir sheet had an additional illustration related to the subject of one of the stamps on it. The reissues were of all the original denominations, from 1-cent to $5. They were sold in complete sets for the face value of $16.34.

Each stamp was printed from a new plate made from the original 1893 dies. The ink color approximated that of the original. The original dies had been stored at the Bureau of Engraving and Printing. In 1893, the Post Office Department transferred its stamp printing operations to the Bureau of Engraving and Printing. The private printers gave them all their dies, including those of the Columbian series. The dies and original stamps had the year 1892, in the upper right corner. On the reproductions, the date was changed to 1992. Flaws in the original dies were repaired and many technical problems overcome to make these modern reproductions.

ONE-CENT COLUMBUS IN SIGHT OF LAND

One-Cent Columbus in Sight of Land

Stamp Production

Printer:	American Bank Note Company
Designer:	Alfred S. Major
Engravers:	Alfred Jones and Charles Skinner (vignette), Douglas S. Ronaldson (frame and lettering)
Format:	Sheet of 200 stamps divided into 2 panes of 100 stamps
Plate Numbers:	J46-50, K51-55, P65-69, MM149-153, OO159-163, VV194-198.
Date of Issue:	Jan. 2, 1893

Earliest Known Use: Jan. 1, 1893, Jan. 2, 1893 official first day
Uses: Drop letter rate
Quantity Issued: 440,195,550

Stamp Features
Size: 34 x 22 mm. (1.3 x 0.9 inches)
Watermark: None
Perforations: 12
Colors: Deep blue, blue, pale blue.
Varieties: Double transfer, Cracked plate.

Collectable Stamp Today
Collectable Cancellation Colors:
Black, blue, magenta.
Collectable Cancellation Varieties:
China, Philippines
Value Unused: $$$
Value Used: $
Surviving Covers: 60,000
Largest Known Multiple: Unused: 100 (complete pane)
Used: 20 (block)

The one-cent Columbian commemorative features the vignette "Columbus in Sight of Land." It is modeled after the painting by William H. Powell. To the left of this painting, is a Native American woman with her child, and on the right, a chief with headdress of feathers.

There are several double transfers found on this issue. Most are found at the right and left ends of the stamp.

TWO-CENT LANDING OF COLUMBUS

Two-Cent Landing of Columbus

Stamp Production

Printer:	American Bank Note Company
Designer:	Alfred S. Major
Engravers:	Alfred Jones and Charles Skinner (vignette), Douglas S. Ronaldson (frame and lettering)
Format:	Sheets of 200, divided into two panes of 100 and in sheets of 100 divided into two panes of 50
Plate Numbers:	AI-5, C11-15, E21-25, T78-82, V88-92, EE109-13, FF114-18, HH124-28, JJ134-38, KK139-43, LL144-48, NN154-58, PP164-68, QQ169-73, RR174-78, SS179-83, TT184-88, UU189-93 (sheets of 200) F26-30, G31-35, H36-40, 141-45, O60-64, Q70-74, U83-87, X94-98, GG119-23 (sheets of 100)
Date of Issue:	Jan. 2, 1893
Earliest Known Use:	Jan. 1, 1893, Jan. 2, 1893 official first day
Uses:	First-class mail up to one-ounce. Private postcard rate.
Quantity Issued:	1,464,588,750

Stamp Features

Size:	34 x 22 mm. (1.3 x 0.9 inches)
Watermark:	None
Perforations:	12
Colors:	Brown violet, deep brown violet, gray violet.
Varieties:	Double transfer, Triple transfer, Quadruple transfer, Broken hat, Broken frame line, Recut frame lines, Cracked plate.

Collectable Stamp Today

Collectable Cancellation Colors:	Black, blue, red, magenta.

Collectable Cancellation Varieties:
supplementary mail type G, China.
Value Unused: $$$
Value Used: $
Surviving Covers: 200,000
Largest Known Multiple: Unused: 100 (complete pane)
Used: 25 (block)

Figure 8-6. Landing of Columbus. The design for the two-cent Columbian commemorative stamp is based on a painting by Vanderlyn, "Landing of Columbus." Today, it is found in the rotunda of the Capitol building in Washington, DC.

The design on the two-cent Columbian commemorative stamp is the "Landing of Columbus." It is based on a painting by Vanderlyn, found in the rotunda of the Capitol building in Washington, D.C. For trivia buffs, this stamp shows Columbus with a beard whereas the one-cent stamp, which shows Columbus, one day earlier in history, clean-shaven! This is because no one really knows what Columbus looked liked as there are no surviving paintings of him. The Vanderlyn painting is also the basis for the 15-cent stamp of the 1869 regular issue series.

There are many plate varieties, including double, triple, and quadruple transfers. The best-known variety is the "Broken Hat" variety. It is one of the most famous of all United States stamps plate varieties. The famous broken hat is a V-shaped notch in the hat of the third man at Columbus' left. A transfer roll break, used to make the printing plate, is responsible for its existence. It developed gradually as different stamps have different amounts of the break. A relief break, unlike a plate variety, is found on several positions on several different printing plates until the bad transfer roll was discarded. Another variety of this stamp is a broken frame line. The right frame line is broken at the bottom. A flawed transfer roll caused this too. The stamp can be found with recut frame lines. As has been noted throughout this book, recutting is done to improve fading details from a worn-out plate.

Figure 8-7. Broken Hat Variety. A common and famous variety of the two-cent Colombian stamp is the Broken Hat one. It is V-shaped notch found in the hat of the third man to the left of Columbus. It was the result of a transfer roll break, used to create the printing plate.

Like all the Columbian stamps, this stamp exists in an imperforate form. In addition to the imperforate stamps made for Wanamaker, there are two-cent imperforate Columbian stamps picked from the printer's waste.

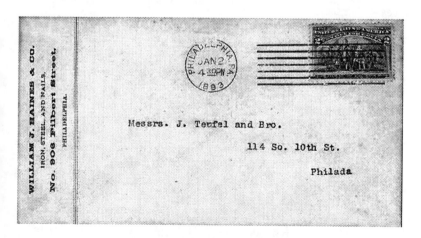

Figure 8-8. Two-Cent Colombian Stamp on Cover. This is an example of a two-cent Colombian commemorative stamp on a first-class business letter.

THREE-CENT FLAGSHIP OF COLUMBUS

Three-Cent Flagship of Columbus

Stamp Production

Printer:	American Bank Note Company
Designer:	Alfred S. Major
Engravers:	Robert Savage (vignette), Douglas S. Ronaldson and George H. Seymour (frame and lettering)
Format:	Sheet of 100 stamps, divided into 2 panes of 50 stamps
Plate Numbers:	L56, L57, R75, R76.
Date of Issue:	Jan. 2, 1893
Earliest Known Use:	Jan. 1, 1893, Jan. 2, 1893 official first day
Uses:	Used with other stamps for various rates.
Quantity Issued:	11,501,250

Stamp Features

Size:	34 x 22 mm. (1.3 x 0.9 inches)
Watermark:	None
Perforations:	12
Colors:	Green, dull green, dark green.
Varieties:	Double transfer

Collectable Stamp Today
Collectable Cancellation Colors:
Black, magenta.
Collectable Cancellation Varieties:
supplementary mail type F or G, China.

Value Unused:	$$$
Value Used:	$$$
Surviving Covers:	20,000
Largest Known Multiple:	Unused: 100 (complete sheet)
	Used: 6 (block)

Figure 8-9. The Ten-Cent Newfoundland Cabot Stamp. Stamp collectors love noting the similarity of designs of the ships on the United States three-cent Colombian Flagship of Columbus and the 10-cent Cabot Newfoundland stamp, shown here.

The three-cent Columbian design is the "Flagship of Columbus." It shows the Santa Maria crossing the ocean. It is based on a Spanish engraving. Interestingly, the 10-cent Cabot stamp issued by Newfoundland uses this same design! The stamp is printed in green, a similar color as the fifteen-cent Columbian stamp.

FOUR-CENT FLEET OF COLUMBUS

Four-Cent Fleet of Columbus

Stamp Production

Printer:	American Bank Note Company
Designer:	Alfred S. Major
Engravers:	Charles Skinner (vignette), Douglas S. Ronaldson and George H. Seymour (frame and lettering)
Format:	Sheet of 100 stamps, divided into 2 panes of 50 stamps
Plate Numbers:	D16-20

Date of Issue:	Jan. 2, 1893
Earliest Known Use:	Jan. 1, 1893, Jan. 2, 1893 official first day
Uses:	Double weight first-class domestic mail
Quantity Issued:	19,181,550

Stamp Features
Size:	34 x 22 mm. (1.3 x 0.9 inches)
Watermark:	None
Perforations:	12
Colors:	Ultramarine, dull ultramarine, deep ultramarine, blue error
Varieties:	Double transfer, Three-leaf variety, Blue error.

Collectable Stamp Today
Collectable Cancellation Colors:
Black, magenta.
Collectable Cancellation Varieties:
supplementary mail type G
Value Unused:	$$$
Value Used:	$$
Surviving Covers:	10,000
Largest Known Multiple:	Unused: 100 (complete sheet)
	Used: 12 (block)

The design of the four-cent stamp of this series, "Fleet of Columbus," is from a Spanish engraving. It features the famous trio, the Nina the Pinta, and the Santa Maria.

The 4-cent Columbian stamp is famous for its blue color error. The color is very different from the normal ultramarine. J. V. Painter of Cleveland found entire sheet of 100 stamps with the error, printed from plate D17.

There is another interesting and famous variety called the three-leaf variety. On the normal stamp, the ornament at the left of the right numeral shows two leaves. On this variety, there are three leaves. This variety is like the one-cent candle flame variety of the 1890 series. It is due too vigorous wiping of the plate during printing, not a defect on the plate itself.

Figure 8-10. The Four-Cent Three-Leaf Variety. On the typical four-cent Colombian stamp, the ornament at the left of the right numeral has two leaves. On this variety, there are three leaves, due too vigorous wiping of the plate during the printing process.

FIVE-CENT COLUMBUS SOLICITING AID OF ISABELLA

Five-Cent Columbus Soliciting Aid of Isabella

Stamp Production

Printer:	American Bank Note Company
Designer:	Alfred S. Major
Engravers:	Charles Skinner (vignette), Douglas S. Ronaldson (frame and lettering)
Format:	Sheet of 100 stamps, divided into 2 panes of 50 stamps
Plate Numbers:	B6-10
Date of Issue:	Jan. 2, 1893
Earliest Known Use:	Jan. 1, 1893, Jan. 2, 1893 official first day
Uses:	Universal Postal Union foreign letter rate
Quantity Issued:	35,248,250

Stamp Features

Size:	34 x 22 mm. (1.3 x 0.9 inches)
Watermark:	None
Perforations:	12
Colors:	Chocolate, dark chocolate, pale brown, yellow brown.
Varieties:	Double transfer

Collectable Stamp Today
Collectable Cancellation Colors:
Black, magenta.
Collectable Cancellation Varieties:
supplementary mail type F, China, Philippines.

Value Unused:	$$$
Value Used:	$$
Surviving Covers:	15,000
Largest Known Multiple:	Unused: 100 (complete sheet)
	Used: 4 (block)

The five-cent Columbian stamp is based on an 1884 painting by the Bohemian artist, Vaczlav Van Brozik, "Seeking Royal Support." The painting now hangs in the Metropolitan Museum of Art in New York City. The stamp is called "Columbus Soliciting Aid of Isabella."

There are more than 15,000 covers with this stamp. Most of these were to overseas destinations as the five cents paid the Universal Postal Union rate of that time.

Figure 8-11. Seeking Royal Support. The five-cent Colombian stamp is based on this 1884 painting by the Bohemian artist, Vaczlav Van Brozik.

Figure 8-12. Example of a Five-Cent Colombian Stamp On a Cover. Shown is an example of the five-cent Colombian stamp paying the basic Universal Postal Union overseas rate, in this case from Cincinnati Ohio to Germany.

SIX-CENT COLUMBUS WELCOMED AT BARCELONA

Six-Cent Columbus Welcomed at Barcelona

Stamp Production
Printer: American Bank Note Company
Designer: Alfred S. Major
Engravers: Robert Savage (vignette), Douglas S. Ronaldson and George H. Seymour (frame and lettering)
Format: Sheet of 100 stamps, divided into 2 panes of 50 stamps
Plate Numbers: Z104
Date of Issue: Jan. 2, 1893
Earliest Known Use: Jan. 2, 1893 (first day cover)
Uses: Triple domestic-letter rate of 2 to 3 ounces
Quantity Issued: 4,707,550

Stamp Features
Size: 34 x 22 mm. (1.3 x 0.9 inches)
Watermark: None
Perforations: 12
Colors: Purple, dull purple, red violet.
Varieties: Double transfer

Collectable Stamp Today
Collectable Cancellation Colors:
Black, magenta.
Collectable Cancellation Varieties:
supplementary mail type F, China.
Value Unused: $$$
Value Used: $$$
Surviving Covers: 8,000
Largest Known Multiple: Unused: 100 (complete sheet)
Used: 12 (block)

The design on the six-cent stamp is "Columbus Welcomed at Barcelona." It is based on a panel on the bronze door of the Capitol in Washington D.C. by Randolph Rogers. On opposite sides of this stamp's scene are statues of King Ferdinand and Balboa.

The stamp's color is purple, a true fugitive ink, changing color with even minimal light exposure.

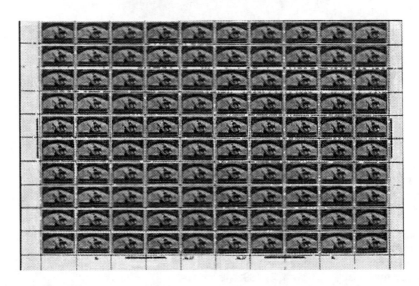

Figure 8-13. Colombian Commemorative 100 Stamp Plate. Some of the two-cent and all of the higher denomination stamps were printed in sheets 100 stamps. These sheets produced two panes of 50 stamps each. However, full sheets of 100 stamps (2 panes) of the higher denominational Colombian stamps were made not cut apart and exist whole today. Shown is such an example, a full sheet of 100 three-cent Columbian stamps.

EIGHT-CENT COLUMBUS RESTORED TO FAVOR

Eight-Cent Columbus Restored to Favor

Stamp Production
Printer: American Bank Note Company
Designer: Alfred S. Major
Engravers: Charles Skinner (vignette), Douglas S. Ronaldson (frame and lettering)
Format: Sheet of 100 stamps, divided into 2 panes of 50 stamps

Plate Numbers: H129-133.
Date of Issue: March 1893
Earliest Known Use: Mar. 18, 1893 (first day cover)
Uses: New 8-cent registry fee
Quantity Issued: 10,656,550

Stamp Features
Size: 34 x 22 mm. (1.3 x 0.9 inches)
Watermark: None
Perforations: 12
Colors: Magenta, light magenta, dark magenta.
Varieties: Double transfer

Collectable Stamp Today
Collectable Cancellation Colors:
                  Black, magenta, purple.
Collectable Cancellation Varieties:
                  China, supplementary mail type F.
Value Unused: $$$
Value Used: $$$
Surviving Covers: 35,000
Largest Known Multiple: Unused: 100 (complete sheet)
                  Used: 21 (block)

     This was the only Columbian stamp not issued on January 2, 1893. Rather, it was issued March of that year. The new stamp was needed for the reduced registered mail fee, from 10 to 8 cents. In fact, it was the very first United States 8-cent stamp, beating out the 8-cent general issue stamp of the 1890 series. Many eight-cent Columbian stamps have a target cancellation then used on registered letters.

     The stamp features the painting by Francisco Jover, "Columbus Restored to Favor." The original painting is found in Spain. After being stripped of his honors because of his actions as a New World governor and forced to return to Spain, Columbus was pardoned by Queen Isabella.

TEN-CENT COLUMBUS PRESENTING NATIVES

Ten-Cent Columbus Presenting Natives

Stamp Production

Printer:	American Bank Note Company
Designer:	Alfred S. Major
Engravers:	Robert Savage (vignette), Douglas S. Ronaldson (frame and lettering)
Format:	Sheet of 100 stamps, divided into 2 panes of 50 stamps
Plate Numbers:	Y99-103
Date of Issue:	Jan. 2, 1893
Earliest Known Use:	Jan. 1, 1893, Jan. 2, 1893 official first day
Uses:	8-cent registry fee and 2-cent single letter rate. Double weight 5-cent Universal Postal Union letter rate.
Quantity Issued:	16,516,950

Stamp Features

Size:	34 x 22 mm. (1.3 x 0.9 inches)
Watermark:	None
Perforations:	12
Colors:	Black brown, dark brown, gray brown
Varieties:	Double transfer, Triple transfer, Irregular lettering

Collectable Stamp Today
Collectable Cancellation Colors:
Black, blue, green, magenta.

Collectable Cancellation Varieties:
Philippines, supplementary mail type F or G.
Value Unused: $$$$
Value Used: $$
Surviving Covers: 35,000
Largest Known Multiple: Unused: 100 (complete sheet)
Used: 20 (block)

Figure 8-14. Return of Columbus and Reception at the Court. The design of the ten-cent Colombian commemorative stamp is based on this painting by Luigi Gregori. This painting is found in the Administration Building of the University of Notre Dame.

The vignette for this ten-cent stamp is based on the painting, "Return of Columbus and Reception at Court," by Luigi Gregori. This painting hangs today in the Administration Building of the University of Notre Dame.

There is a variety of the stamp that is a different lettering of the bottom label. The lettering of Columbus Presenting Natives was when the stamps first were printed, was long, thin, and irregularly aligned. Some of the letters were slanted, particularly the P of Presenting. The printers discovered this irregularity and corrected it on later stamps. Double transfers are common.

FIFTEEN-CENT COLUMBUS ANNOUNCING HIS DISCOVERY

Fifteen-Cent Columbus Announcing His Discovery

Stamp Production
Printer:	American Bank Note Company
Designer:	Alfred S. Major
Engravers:	Charles Skinner (vignette), Douglas S. Ronaldson (frame and lettering)
Format:	Sheet of 100 stamps, divided into 2 panes of 50 stamps
Plate Numbers:	M58
Date of Issue:	Jan. 2, 1893
Earliest Known Use:	Jan. 26, 1893
Uses:	Triple-weight Universal Postal Union letter rate. Make up higher rates.
Quantity Issued:	1,576,950

Stamp Features
Size:	34 x 22 mm. (1.3 x 0.9 inches)
Watermark:	None
Perforations:	12
Colors:	Dark green, green, dull green.
Varieties:	Double transfer

Collectable Stamp Today
Collectable Cancellation Colors:
Black, magenta.
Collectable Cancellation Varieties:
supplementary mail type F, China
Value Unused:	$$$$
Value Used:	$$$
Surviving Covers:	6,000
Largest Known Multiple:	Unused: 100 (complete sheet)
	Used: 8 (block)

Figure 8-15. Columbus Announcing His Discovery. The fifteen-cent Colombian stamp is based on this painting by Baloca, found today in Madrid, Spain.

The fifteen-cent Columbian stamp is "Columbus Announcing His Discovery". It is based upon a painting by R. Baloca, found today in Madrid, Spain. After his return from his first American voyage, Columbus was given a great welcome, at the Spanish royal court, in Barcelona.

THIRTY-CENT COLUMBUS AT LA RABIDA

Thirty-Cent Columbus at La Rabida

Stamp Production

Printer:	American Bank Note Company
Designer:	Alfred S. Major
Engravers:	Alfred Jones (vignette), Douglas S. Ronaldson and George H. Seymour (frame and lettering)
Format:	Sheet of 100 stamps, divided into 2 panes of 50 stamps
Plate Numbers:	N59
Date of Issue:	Jan. 2, 1893
Earliest Known Use:	Jan. 18, 1893
Uses:	Multiple-rate foreign letters. Parcel post, 16 cents per pound up to 4 pounds
Quantity Issued:	617,250

Stamp Features
Size: 34 x 22 mm. (1.3 x 0.9 inches)
Watermark: None
Perforations: 12
Colors: Orange brown, bright orange brown
Varieties: None

Collectable Stamp Today
Collectable Cancellation Colors:
                     None
Collectable Cancellation Varieties:
                     supplementary mail type F or G
Value Unused: $$$$
Value Used: $$$
Surviving Covers: 2,000
Largest Known Multiple: Unused: 100 (complete sheet)
                     Used: 6 (block)

The thirty-cent stamp is Columbus at La Rabida modeled after artwork by R. Easo. Columbus was traveling to France when he paused to stay with friends at the monastery of La Rabida in Spain. Juan Perez, former confessor to Queen Isabella, met him there and this led to an audience before King Ferdinand.

The stamp is orange brown, not a very stable ink. Therefore, today the stamp is a color changeling.

FIFTY-CENT RECALL OF COLUMBUS

Fifty-Cent Recall of Columbus

Stamp Production

Printer:	American Bank Note Company
Designer:	Alfred S. Major
Engravers:	Charles Skinner (vignette), Douglas S. Ronaldson (frame and lettering)
Format:	Sheet of 100 stamps, divided into 2 panes of 50 stamps
Plate Numbers:	S77
Date of Issue:	Jan. 2, 1893
Earliest Known Use:	Feb. 8, 1893
Uses:	Multiple-rate foreign letters. Parcel post, 16 cents per pound up to 4 pounds
Quantity Issued:	243,750

Stamp Features

Size:	34 x 22 mm. (1.3 x 0.9 inches)
Watermark:	None
Perforations:	12
Colors:	Slate blue, dull slate blue
Varieties:	Double transfer, Triple transfer.

Collectable Stamp Today

Collectable Cancellation Colors:	Black, magenta.
Collectable Cancellation Varieties:	supplementary mail type F or G
Value Unused:	$$$$
Value Used:	$$$$
Surviving Covers:	1,500
Largest Known Multiple:	Unused: 100 (complete sheet)
	Used: 6 (block)

The 50-cent Columbian stamp is based on the painting, "Recall of Columbus," by the A. G. Heaton. The painting hangs in the Capitol Building in Washington D.C. Initially, the Spanish royalty turned down Columbus's request for funding his voyage. However, after he had left and traveled only a few miles, a messenger from the Spanish crown caught up with him, and brought him back to the royal court.

Figure 8-16. Recall of Columbus. The fifty-cent Colombian stamp is based upon this painting found in the United States Capitol by the A. G. Heaton.

ONE-DOLLAR ISABELLA PLEDGING HER JEWELS

One-Dollar Isabella Pledging Her Jewels

Stamp Production

Printer:	American Bank Note Company
Designer:	Alfred S. Major
Engravers:	Robert Savage (vignette), Douglas S. Ronaldson and George H. Seymour (frame and lettering)
Format:	Sheet of 100 stamps, divided into 2 panes of 50 stamps
Plate Numbers:	W93
Date of Issue:	Jan. 2, 1893
Earliest Known Use:	Jan. 13, 1893
Uses:	Stamp collectors' covers. Multiple-rate foreign rates
Quantity Issued:	55,050

Stamp Features
Size: 34 x 22 mm. (1.3 x 0.9 inches)
Watermark: None
Perforations: 12
Colors: Salmon, dark salmon.
Varieties: Double transfer

Collectable Stamp Today
Collectable Cancellation Colors:
                      Black, magenta.
Collectable Cancellation Varieties:
                      supplementary mail type F or G
Value Unused: $$$$$
Value Used: $$$$
Surviving Covers: 300
Largest Known Multiple: Unused: 100 (complete sheet)
                      Used: 6 (block)

The vignette of the one-dollar Columbian commemorative is based on the painting by Munoz Degrain, "Isabella Pledging Her Jewels." The original painting is found in the Hall of Legislature in Madrid, Spain. While Queen Isabella offered her jewels to finance Columbus's voyage, this did not become necessary as other funding was found.

The one-dollar stamp was the first dollar value to sell out from the hoard at the Washington D.C. Post Office.

TWO-DOLLAR COLUMBUS IN CHAINS

Two-Dollar Columbus in Chains

Stamp Production
Printer:	American Bank Note Company
Designer:	Alfred S. Major
Engravers:	Charles Skinner (vignette), Douglas S. Ronaldson (frame and lettering)
Format:	Sheet of 100 stamps, divided into 2 panes of 50 stamps
Plate Numbers:	AA105
Date of Issue:	Jan. 2, 1893
Earliest Known Use:	Jan. 2, 1893 (first day cover)
Uses:	Stamp collectors' covers.
Quantity Issued:	45,550

Stamp Features
Size:	34 x 22 mm. (1.3 x 0.9 inches)
Watermark:	None
Perforations:	12
Colors:	Brown red, deep brown red.
Varieties:	None

Collectable Stamp Today
Collectable Cancellation Colors:
Black, magenta.
Collectable Cancellation Varieties:
supplementary mail type G
Value Unused:	$$$$$
Value Used:	$$$$
Surviving Covers:	100
Largest Known Multiple:	Unused: 22 (block)
	Used: 4 (block)

This stamp is based on a painting done in 1841 by K. Leutze of Germantown, Pennsylvania, called "Columbus in Chains". The painting is found, today, in Providence, Rhode Island. When governor of Hispaniola, Columbus was chained by Francisco de Bobadilla, who was sent from Spain to investigate his mistreatment of Native Americans.

Figure 8-17. Columbus in Chains. The two-dollar Colombian commemorative stamp is based on this painting by K. Leutze. The painting is found, today, in Providence, Rhode Island.

This was one of the high denomination Columbian stamps in which there was a great deal of speculation by dealers during the end of the nineteenth century.

THREE-DOLLAR COLUMBUS DESCRIBING THIRD VOYAGE

Three-Dollar Columbus Describing Third Voyage

Stamp Production
Printer:	American Bank Note Company
Designer:	Alfred S. Major
Engravers:	Robert Savage (vignette), Douglas S. Ronaldson (frame and lettering)
Format:	Sheet of 100 stamps, divided into 2 panes of 50 stamps
Plate Numbers:	BB106
Date of Issue:	Jan. 2, 1893
Earliest Known Use:	Mar. 24, 1893
Uses:	Stamp collectors' covers.
Quantity Issued:	27,650

Stamp Features

Size:	34 x 22 mm. (1.3 x 0.9 inches)
Watermark:	None
Perforations:	12
Colors:	Brown red, deep brown red.
Varieties:	None

Collectable Stamp Today
Collectable Cancellation Colors:
    None
Collectable Cancellation Varieties:
    None

Value Unused:	$$$$$
Value Used:	$$$$$
Surviving Covers:	300
Largest Known Multiple:	Unused: 8 (imprint and plate number block)
	Used: 4 (block)

The design of the three-dollar Columbian commemorative is based from the painting, "Columbus Describing Third Voyage," by Francisco Jover.

Luff states 2,937 of this issue were unsold and destroyed in June 1899. Therefore, the real number of stamps issued is 24,713 copies, not the 27,650, which were sent to the postmasters. Like the other dollar value Columbian stamps, there was much early stamp dealer speculation in this issue. The stamp went from being greatly oversold to the valuable stamp it is today. It is hard to believe but it could not be sold even at face value in the early 20th century!

The stamp is found on about 300 covers, today. Late 19th century stamp dealers and collectors created most of them.

Figure 8-18. Columbus Describing His Third Voyage. The design of the three-dollar Colombian commemorative stamp is based on this painting by Francisco Jover.

FOUR-DOLLAR ISABELLA AND COLUMBUS

Four-Dollar Isabella and Columbus

Stamp Production
Printer: American Bank Note Company
Designer: Alfred S. Major
Engravers: Alfred Jones (vignette), George H. Seymour (frame and lettering)
Format: Sheet of 100 stamps, divided into 2 panes of 50 stamps
Plate Numbers: CC107
Date of Issue: Jan. 2, 1893
Earliest Known Use: Mar. 24, 1893
Uses: Stamp collectors' covers.
Quantity Issued: 26,350

Stamp Features
Size: 34 x 22 mm. (1.3 x 0.9 inches)
Watermark: None
Perforations: 12
Colors: Crimson lake, rose carmine, pale aniline rose.
Varieties: None

Collectable Stamp Today
Collectable Cancellation Colors:
                Black, magenta.
Collectable Cancellation Varieties:
                None
Value Unused: $$$$$
Value Used: $$$$$
Surviving Covers: 80
Largest Known Multiple: Unused: 10 (imprint and plate number block)
                              Used: 4 (block)

     The design for four-dollar stamp is two portraits, one each of Queen Isabella and Christopher Columbus. The Columbus was done by Lotto while the Isabella portrait was by an unknown artist.

     The stamp fades easily when exposed to light. Therefore, it is hard to find a stamp with the original rich color.

     Although 26,350 copies were sent to postmasters, 3,357 were destroyed in June 1899, as they were unsold. Therefore, the true issue number is only 22,993. Like the other dollar value Columbian commemorative stamps, it was a speculative issue that has had wild fluctuations in value since it was issued.

     The stamp is found today on about 80 covers, with stamp collectors of the time creating most of them.

FIVE-DOLLAR CHRISTOPHER COLUMBUS

Five-Dollar Christopher Columbus

Stamp Production

Printer:	American Bank Note Company
Designer:	Alfred S. Major
Engravers:	Alfred Jones (vignette), Charles Skinner (side figures) Douglas S. Ronaldson (frame and lettering)
Format:	Sheet of 100 stamps, divided into 2 panes of 50 stamps
Plate Numbers:	DD108
Date of Issue:	Jan. 2, 1893
Earliest Known Use:	Jan. 6, 1893
Uses:	Stamp collectors' covers.
Quantity Issued:	27,350

Stamp Features

Size:	34 x 22 mm. (1.3 x 0.9 inches)
Watermark:	None
Perforations:	12
Colors:	Black, grayish black.
Varieties:	None

Collectable Stamp Today
Collectable Cancellation Colors:
Black, magenta
Collectable Cancellation Varieties:
None

Value Unused:	$$$$$
Value Used:	$$$$$
Surviving Covers:	150
Largest Known Multiple:	Unused: 14 (block)
	Used: 5 (plate number and imprint strip)

The top value of the Columbian commemorative series is the most valuable non-error United States commemorative stamp. The design of the $5 stamp was taken from a medallion of Columbus, struck in Madrid. The design is also the basis for the 50-cent Columbian commemorative half-dollar, also made in 1893, for the Chicago Fair. Olin L. Warner of New York designed the coin based on the Madrid medal. The design is profile of Columbus in a circle. To the right is the figure of America, represented by a Native American woman with a crown of feathers.

There were 27,350 five-dollar stamp originally sent to the postmasters. But the Post Office Department destroyed 5,506 unsold copies in June 1899. This left only 21,844 copies possibly available to today's collectors.

There are approximately 150 stamp covers, today, most originally prepared by stamp collectors.

Figure 8-19. Fifty-Cent Colombian Commemorative Coin. The five-dollar Colombian commemorative stamp's design was based upon a medal of Columbus, struck in Madrid. It also was used for the 50-cent Colombian commemorative half-dollar, shown here. It, like the stamps, was issued for the Chicago Fair.

Essays, Proofs, and Specimens

Essays

Except for a couple of primitive pencil drawings by Lyman H. Bagg, the American Bank Note Company, the printer of the series, made the essays for the Columbian commemorative stamps.

For the proposed one-cent stamp, there are both essays like the completed design and others showing an unadopted vignette of Columbus, looking off to the right. For the two-cent stamp, the essays include ones similar to the completed design, the "Landing of Columbus" and "Columbus Soliciting the Aid of Isabella," used for the five-cent stamp of the series. The three-cent essays all show the "Flagship of Columbus" in various stages of completion. Likewise, the four-cent essays show the "Fleet of Columbus" used for the issued stamp. The five-cent essays feature "Columbus Soliciting the Aid of Isabella," also found as a two-cent essay. The six-cent essays are like the finished design showing "Columbus Welcomed at Barcelona." The eight-cent essays show different design stages of the final stamp, "Columbus Restored to Favor." The ten-cent essays show "Columbus Presenting the Natives," in different states of completion. The fifteen-cent essays feature "Columbus Announcing his Discovery." This essay also exists for a thirty-cent essay. There also are thirty-cent essays with the adopted design, "Columbus at La Rabida." The fifty-cent essays show the adopted design, the "Recall of Columbus." The one-dollar essays show the design phases of the final stamp, "Isabella Pledging Her Jewels." The two and three-dollar essays, likewise, are like the final stamps, "Columbus In Chains" and "Columbus Describing His Third Voyage," respectively. The four-dollar essays show the twin vignettes of Isabella and Columbus used on the issued stamp. The five-dollar essay show both the Columbus medal of the issue stamp and "Columbus in Sight of Land," eventually used for the one-cent stamp.

Proofs

Figure 8-20. Example of a Large Die Proof. Shown is a large die proof of the two-dollar Colombian commemorative stamp, made by the printer at the time of stamp production.

The Columbus commemoratives are found in the nineteenth century variety of proofs. These include large die proofs prepared by the printer at the time of stamp production. There are small die proofs prepared by the Bureau of Engraving and Printing for the Roosevelt Album in 1903 and the Panama-Pacific Exposition in 1915.

Figure 8-21. Complete Set of Colombian Panama-Pacific Small Die Proofs. The Bureau of Engraving and Printing made small die proofs for the Roosevelt Album in 1903 and the Panama-Pacific Exposition in 1915. Shown here are a complete set of Panama-Pacific small die proofs.

The plate proofs are found on India paper and card.

Some of the denominations can be found as trial color die proofs on India paper or card and also trial plate color proofs on India paper.

Specimens

All the Columbian stamps exist as specimen stamps. All values are overprinted with black ink with the word, Specimen, in a simple font. There are 1, 3, 4, 5, 6, and 10-cent and the $3 Specimen stamps with a fancy, 22 mm long Specimen overprinted in magenta. The 2-cent has a black and the 4, and 5-cent stamps, a red Specimen overprint with simple capital letters that are 16 mm. long. Finally, the 2, 3, 4, 6, 10, 15, and 50-cent have red while the 5, 8, and 30 cent have black Specimen overprints that have a manuscript font, 20 mm. in length, placed on an angle.

Figure 8-22. Specimen Stamp. Shown is a four-cent Colombian specimen stamp, which is overprinted with black ink with the word, Specimen, in a small and simple font.

References and Further Reading

Alexander , T. The United States 1847 Issue: A Cover Census, 2001

Brookman, L.G. The 19th Century Postage Stamps of the United States, 1947

Datz, S. R. 2003 Catalogue of Errors on U.S. Postage Stamps, 2003

Datz, S. R. The Buyers Guide. An Analysis of Selected U. S. Postage Stamps, 1992

Graham, R. B. United States Postal History Sampler, 1992

Johnson, K. D. and Cleland W. W. Durland Standard Plate Number Catalog, 2005

Kloetzel, J. L. (editor) Scott 2005 Specialized Catalogue of United States Stamps & Covers, 2005

Landau, E. A. et al, Linn's U.S. Stamp Facts 19th Century, 1999

Lauzon, A. A. The United States Columbian Issue of 1893, 1942

Luff, J. N. The Postage Stamps of the United States, 1902

Micarelli , C.N. The Micarelli Identification Guide to U.S. Stamps, Regular Issues 1847-1934, 2001

Mueller, B. R. United States Postage Stamps. How to Collect, Understand, and Enjoy Them, 1958

Rose, J. Classic United States Imperforate Stamps, 1990

Rose, J. The First Perforated U.S. Issue of 1857, 2005

Rose, J. US Postage Stamps of 1869, 1996

Printed in the United States
141033LV00003B/39/A

9 781598 003871